Learning
from
the Left

Learning
from
the Left

Children's Literature,
the Cold War,
and Radical Politics
in the United States

Julia L. Mickenberg

OXFORD
UNIVERSITY PRESS

2006

OXFORD
UNIVERSITY PRESS

Oxford University Press, Inc., publishes works that further
Oxford University's objective of excellence
in research, scholarship, and education.

Oxford   New York
Auckland   Cape Town   Dar es Salaam   Hong Kong   Karachi
Kuala Lumpur   Madrid   Melbourne   Mexico City   Nairobi
New Delhi   Shanghai   Taipei   Toronto

With offices in
Argentina   Austria   Brazil   Chile   Czech Republic   France   Greece
Guatemala   Hungary   Italy   Japan   Poland   Portugal   Singapore
South Korea   Switzerland   Thailand   Turkey   Ukraine   Vietnam

Published by Oxford University Press, Inc.
198 Madison Avenue, New York, New York 10016

www.oup.com

Oxford is a registered trademark of Oxford University Press

Library of Congress Cataloging-in-Publication Data
Mickenberg, Julia L.
Learning from the left : children's literature, the Cold War, and radical politics
in the United States / Julia L. Mickenberg
    p. cm.
Includes bibliographical references and index.
ISBN-13 978-0-19-515280-7; 978-0-19-515281-4 (pbk.)

1. Children's literature, American—History and criticism.   2. Politics and
literature—United States—History—20th century.   3. Authors, American—
20th century—Political and social views.   4. American literature—20th century—
History and criticism.   5. Right and left (Political science) in literature.   6. Radicalism
in literature.   7. Cold War in literature.   I. Title.
PS228.P6M53 2005
810.9'358'083—dc22   2004065457

Printed in the United States of America

To Fannie and Eddie Mickenberg, my grandparents,
and Lena J. M. Birkholz, my daughter

PREFACE

This is a study of children's literature and the Left in the mid-twentieth century. It is a work of history as well as a work of literary analysis, and its varied scope undoubtedly reflects my interdisciplinary training in American Studies, which encourages scholars to connect seemingly disparate phenomena, events, artifacts, and ways of thinking. In addition to hundreds of children's books, my sources include oral histories; the papers of authors, illustrators, and editors; and the records of institutions ranging from publishing houses to the Child Study Association and the Jefferson School of Social Science. In addition, I have drawn upon government documents, such as the transcripts of legislative hearings and FBI files; radical periodicals; and journals in the fields of education, children's literature, library science, and publishing. To gain a better sense of context, I have looked at advertisements, textbooks, political campaign materials, newspapers, films, trade journals, and popular periodicals from the postwar period; I have listened to children's records; and I have studied childrearing manuals and advice books. But what is foregrounded here are children's books and their authors.

Throughout the process, I have greatly benefited from existing scholarship in a range of fields, and I have also shamelessly solicited the expertise, advice, and good will of an enormous number of people. Listing all the people to whom I owe a debt would be impossible, but more than a few people deserve mention. In many ways, this book represents a collective effort, although I take all of the credit for its weaknesses.

My greatest debt goes to the women and men who shared their personal stories—or information about their family members—with me, in letters, over the telephone, and in long conversations in their own homes, often over homemade meals. These include Hank Abrashkin, Leone Adelson, Irving Adler, Rose Agree, Betty Bacon, Jennifer Charnofsky, Ernest Crichlow, Howard Fast, Stanley Faulkner, Gella Schweid Fishman, Marge Frantz, Joan Goldfrank, Lewis Goldfrank, Barbara Granick, Steve Granick, Tony Hiss, Ed Hoke, Dahlov Ipcar, Nancy Larrick, Meridel Le Sueur, Faith Lindsay, Ann McGovern, Milton Meltzer, Jonathan Moore, Minne Motz, Elsie Nydorf, Lilian Moore Reavin, Herman Schneider, Nina Schneider, Pete Seeger, Miriam Sherman, Jeanne Steig, Dorothy Sterling, Vicky Williams, and Rose Wyler. Mary Elting Folsom, who put me up several times (once along with two cats and my husband, as we were driving across the country) and answered literally dozens of letters, deserves special mention. Several of these individuals have passed away since my research began; I hope this work preserves something of their memory.

For material as well as intellectual support, I am grateful to the University of Minnesota, which provided me with a Harold Leonard Memorial Fellowship, a Lifson, Lifson and Bronzstein Fellowship, and numerous travel and research grants; the Spencer Foundation, which not only gave me a year-long dissertation fellowship but also sponsored several forums at which I was able to share my work with other scholars and benefit especially from the wisdom of people like the fellows director Catherine Lacey; the Smithsonian Institution (for a predoctoral fellowship); the P. E. O. Scholars; the Huntington Library (for a short-term fellowship); Pitzer College (for research and travel funds); and the University of Texas, which has supported me with a Dean's Fellowship, a University Cooperative Subvention Grant, and several research and travel grants. Finally, I would like to thank David Leverenz, Kenneth Kidd, and the English Department faculty at the University of Florida for inviting me to participate in the extremely stimulating American Cultures seminar, which also provided a generous honorarium.

I also owe a great intellectual debt to the many scholars, librarians, and archivists who have offered me advice, information, or encouragement. Elaine Tyler May and Lary May have been wonderful advocates, friends, and mentors, and they deserve special recognition for encouraging me to undertake this project in the first place. Jack Zipes helped put the idea into my head by asking me to write an essay on Meridel Le Sueur for the *Lion and the Unicorn*. Paula Rabinowitz, David Roediger, David Noble, and Riv-Ellen Prell, who were also mentors to me while I was at the University of Minnesota, have all shaped this book in ways they might not even recognize. Charlie McGovern, my advisor during a dissertation fellowship at the Smithsonian, continues to be a supporter and friend. Paula Fass and Daniel Horowitz made extensive comments on the original manuscript and on a second, very different version of it, and their input has improved the work immensely.

Other scholars, whom I have met through research, conferences, speaking engagements, and fellowships or simply through correspondence, have offered useful advice and insights. These include Chris Appy, Molly Arboleda, David Bonner, Paul Buhle, Michael Denning, Spencer Downing, Jim Farrell, Teresa Fernandez-Aceves, Gella Fishman, Richard Flynn, Lisa Rowe Fraustino, Eric Gordon, Elisabeth Hansot, Deborah Harkness, Christine Jenkins, Henry Jenkins, Marti Krow-Lucal, Robbie Lieberman, Stuart McConnell, Margaret Miles, Paul Mishler, Bill Mullen, Phil Nel, Louise Robbins, Franklin Rosemont, Alex Saxton, Neala Schleuning, Diana Selig, Andy Smith, Katharine Capshaw Smith, Barrie Thorne, Roberta Trites, William Tuttle, Lynne Vallone, Alan Wald,

Michael Warner, Steve Watts, Wayne Weigand, and Doug Wixson. Jerry Frakes deserves special mention for traveling with me up to Stanford University to check out the Secular Yiddish Schools Collection and translating materials for me, just because he thought they were cool. My colleagues in the American Studies Department at the University of Texas—Bob Abzug, Janet Davis, Elizabeth Engelhardt, Steve Hoelscher, Nhi Lieu, Jeff Meikle, Mark Smith, and Shirley Thompson—have provided intellectual community and useful feedback. Janice Bradley, Cynthia Frese, Melanie Livingston, Suzanne Colwell, Tiffany Scolnic, and Brian Lemaster all offered invaluable administrative support.

I have visited dozens of libraries and archives in the course of my research, and in every instance the staff graciously took time to guide me toward the right materials. Several librarians and archivists deserve special mention and thanks, however. Peter Filardo and Andrew Lee at the Tamiment Library not only pointed me toward hidden treasures in the library while I was there, but also stayed in touch and continued to assist and encourage me from afar. Karen Nelson Hoyle at the University of Minnesota's Children's Literature Research Collection has been a wonderful guide to the world of children's literature and was patient with my ignorance of the topic when I began the research nearly a decade ago. More recently, John Barneson has gone out of his way on several occasions to get me images of illustrations from manuscripts or books. Dave Klaasen at the University of Minnesota's Social Welfare History Archives has been a great help to me on several occasions, and I also appreciate his enthusiasm for the research. Tracey Baker at the Minnesota Historical Society made a special effort to dig through several boxes of Meridel Le Sueur's papers to help me to avoid a major error in interpretation, and both Richard Oram and Linda Henderson at the Harry Ransom Center also helped me to dodge that bullet. Debbie Miller, Patrick Coleman, and Brian Horrigan, all at the Minnesota History Center, were also helpful to me at different stages of my research. Several curators and librarians at the Smithsonian were especially helpful to me, including Barbara Clarke-Smith, John Fleckner, Jeff Place, Harry Rubenstein, and David Shayt. I also appreciate the assistance of Sanford Berman at the Hennepin County Library, Kris McKusker at University of Colorado Special Collections, and Linda Long in Special Collections at the University of Oregon. The folks at the FBI dealing with Freedom of Information Act materials were also remarkably helpful, even though I have been unable to obtain all of the files I have requested because of delays in processing. Finally, the interlibrary loan office at the University of Texas is amazing.

Several people graciously gave me access to private collections of materials: Stanley Faulkner gave me access to his materials on the Council on Interracial Books for Children; Mary Elting gave me access to papers relating to work by her and her husband, as well as materials on the Authors' Guild and the

Council on Interracial Books for Children; William Abrashkin gave me materials on his father, Raymond Abrashkin, and on Jay Williams; and both Jennifer Charnofsky and Miriam Sherman gave me materials relating to the Children's Book and Music Center. David Bonner also shared material from his extensive research on children's music.

I also appreciate the generosity of people who allowed me to quote or reproduce material without charge. Deep thanks to the Bancroft Library, University of California at Berkeley (for permission to quote League of American Writers material), Jeanne Bendick, Mary Elting, Faith Lindsay, Barbara Granick, Steve Granick, Gene Gropper, Ed Hoke, International Publishers, Heike Martin and the estate of James Daugherty, Harold Ober Associates (for permission to quote Langston Hughes material), Robin Ward Savage, Nina Schneider, Robert Selsam, Jeanne Steig, Ken Tilsen, the University of Oregon Special Collections, and Nanda Ward. Material in chapter 1 originally appeared in my article "Of Funnybones and Steamshovels: Juvenile Publishing, Progressive Education, and the Lyrical Left," *Children's Literature Association Quarterly* 28, no. 3 (Fall 2003): 144–57. Material in chapter 7 originally appeared in my article "Civil Rights, History and the Left: Inventing the Juvenile Black Biography," *MELUS: Multi-Ethnic Literature of the United States* 27, no. 2 (Summer 2002): 65–93. I have also drawn in chapter 7 upon my "Communist in a Coonskin Cap? Meridel Le Sueur's Books for Children and the Reformulation of America's Cold War Frontier Narrative," *Lion and the Unicorn* 21 (1997): 59–85. I'm grateful for permission to use this material.

On the nuts and bolts of writing, the people in my various writing groups in Texas and in Minnesota have been instrumental in shaping the manuscript; thanks to Janet Davis, Carolyn Eastman, Jolie Olcott, Thea Petchler, Andrea Sachs, and Shirley Thompson, as well as to the members of the dissertation group at Elaine and Lary May's house. Joanna Rabiger also read several chapters. My editor at Oxford University Press, Susan Ferber, has been interested in this project from very early in its conception, and she has continued throughout the process to be both a superlative editor and a supportive friend. Stacey Hamilton is a saintly production editor. I feel blessed to have had the opportunity to work with Susan, Stacey, and Oxford University Press in general.

Finally, a number of friends and family members have offered me support in all kinds of ways. Dean and Janet Birkholz, Libby Cowles and Sam Bridgham, Michael Dunn and Shalima Smith, Bill Zachs and Martin Adam, Ruth and Alvin Eller, Risa Mickenberg, and Kimberly Beck all put me up during various research trips. Lotte Feinberg helped me to navigate the world of the Freedom of Information Act and otherwise offered lots of good advice. David Mickenberg spooled through microfilms at the University of Wisconsin for me. My sister, Risa, also read drafts of several chapters and offered great insights.

My mother, Yvette Mickenberg, and father, Ira Mickenberg, have stood by me through just about everything I've ever tried to do in my life, as have my grandparents Eddie and Fannie Mickenberg. Finally, there are no words adequate to thank my daughter, Lena Birkholz, for reminding me that there are things far more important than this book, and my husband, Daniel Birkholz, my best friend, best reader, and true love.

CONTENTS

Learning
from
the Left

Introduction

Children's Literature as a "Wonderful Door"

Tony MacTavish Levy, the protagonist of Howard Fast's *Tony and the Wonderful Door* (1952), is an eleven-year-old boy from a working-class family. He is a hodgepodge of ethnic, racial, national, and religious backgrounds: Scottish, Swedish, Italian, French, German, Haitian, American Indian, Russian, Lithuanian, Polish, and Jewish. But as far as Tony is concerned, his only "national origin" is Brooklyn, where his father was born. Tony grows up in the 1920s, but a "wonderful door" in his backyard allows him to go back in time; it opens not just onto New York's Lower East Side, but also (and just for Tony) opens onto the barnyard where a Dutch boy, Peter Van Doben, lives in 1654.

Peter, and the American Indian children he and Tony befriend, are Tony's guides to old New York, a place that enthralls him. It also inspires him to tell rather wild stories in school, much to the chagrin of his teacher, Miss Clatt, and his parents, who patiently struggle to come to terms with their son's overdeveloped imagination and his disruptive behavior in school. Although Tony's parents consider taking him to see a psychiatrist, they instead turn to their trusted family physician, Doc Forbes. When the eccentric old doctor actually begins to believe Tony's stories, his imagination is granted a certain authority. But as soon as his tales are taken seriously, Tony stops needing the wonderful door, finding life's struggles to be more fulfilling than "the dream world of children."[1]

Yet even after the wonderful door becomes just another door, it remains significant in Tony's life, as all childhood dreams are. The door becomes symbolic of life's many passages into the unknown:

> [S]trangely enough, the wonderful door was not lost. As Tony grew up
> and fought out the struggle to be a doctor, as his good friend had been,
> he discovered that the process of living in a good, full sense, consisted

of confronting many wonderful doors. It took a brave man to open each one, and sometimes when these doors could not be opened by any key or handle, they had to be smashed down, and for that the greatest courage of all was required. For these were doors in walls of ignorance, superstition, fear and injustice. But if one had courage enough to go through these doors, the rewards were as great as those that had come to the child through his first wonderful door. For in all truth, these were doors to more splendid adventures than ever the child had dreamed of.[2]

Tony's childish imagination, which eventually draws in not only Doc Forbes, but also Tony's parents, Miss Clatt, and even a curator at the Museum of Natural History, represents the necessity of standing by one's beliefs and by the truths of one's own experiences. The wonderful door becomes a metaphor for the personal and social struggles that are part of growing up and that are essential to participating fully and conscientiously in an imperfect society that discourages independent thought and nonconformity.

Published independently in 1952 by Howard Fast's own press, the Blue Heron Publishing Company, *Tony and the Wonderful Door* arrived on the scene in the middle of the McCarthy period, when Fast, known for his bestselling historical novels, was having difficulty publishing with mainstream commercial presses because of his open ties to the Communist Party (CP). This story, and the circumstances of its publication, offer some initial clues to why children's literature more generally can serve as *our* door, revealing how and in what particular ways left-wingers like Fast were able to leave a mark on American culture in the twentieth century, even during the era of McCarthyism, blacklisting, and a Cold War, anti-Communist "consensus." The story also begins to suggest why children often emerged as the object of leftists' utopian vision.

The fact that *Tony* was self-published gave Fast greater control over the book's production, but McCarthyism still undoubtedly affected sales. Any would-be censor who knew something about Howard Fast would have fought to keep the book out of children's hands, simply because of its authorship.[3] But even as Fast's books began to disappear from library shelves as a result of local, national, and even international censorship campaigns, "radical sentiments" on a par with those in *Tony* remained in circulation and accessible to children.[4] Indeed, Fast's fame made him an exceptional case: children's books were only very rarely banned from schools or libraries and, for the most part, operated below the radar of red-hunters. In this field, the rare accusation of "pink-tinged pages" was more than drowned out by paeans to "social significance" or, alternately, by the silence that greeted many Left-authored books that neither critics nor red-baiters bothered to look at, despite their popularity with children.

This may partly explain why so many left-wing authors were able to publish children's books in the postwar period and why these books sold well to libraries, schools, and individuals.[5]

The particular logic of the children's book field as it developed alongside, if not together with, the organized Left—on a course closely tied to trends in education—helped to make children's literature a key outlet for leftists in the mid-twentieth century. At the same time, the particular logic of what came to be called "McCarthyism" helped to make children's literature an unlikely target. Why certain cultural workers on the Left began to create books for children; how they were able to publish children's books, especially in an era marked by intense anxiety about radicalism and equally intense anxiety about children; and what they actually wrote, are the subjects of this book. This hidden history of the children's book field provides insights into how and why the turbulent youth rebellions of the 1960s emerged from the seemingly placid 1950s. By maintaining the democratic spirit of the 1930s through the Cold War, children's literature became a kind of bridge between the Old Left and the New Left generations.

Most of this happened by fortuitous circumstance. Some people did turn to children's literature because other avenues were closed to them; Fast himself would claim that "children's books are a freer market" than books for adults.[6] A number of teachers who lost their jobs for political reasons realized they could reach far more children anyway by writing books. Irving Adler, for instance, was dismissed in the early 1950s from his job teaching math and science in the New York City schools. But leaving teaching was ultimately a boon to his career; he published dozens of books in thirty-one countries and nineteen languages, with the total circulation of his books in the United States alone totaling in the millions. He was even invited to talk about his books in the school from which he was fired.[7] Likewise, people out of work thanks to blacklisting or greylisting—including Meridel Le Sueur, Franklin Folsom, Langston Hughes, Anne Terry White, Dorothy Sterling, Louis Hartman, and Priscilla Hiss (the wife of Alger Hiss, who became a copy editor at Golden Books)—ultimately found work in the children's literature field.

But if the political climate and economic necessity sometimes drove authors, artists, and other cultural workers to the children's literature field, more often their motivation was a desire to influence the future through the younger generation. "Some may do it by default," Pete Seeger speculated, acknowledging his own experience playing at summer camps and independent schools and making children's records for Folkways when he was blacklisted. "They say, 'I wish I could sing in concert halls that would pay me thousands of dollars, but since they're not I'll sing for the kids—at least I'll get a few dollars.' But I think many of them are thinking more on the lines of 'If we're going to save this world we've got to reach the kids.'"[8]

Fast certainly had the latter idea in mind when he wrote *Tony and the Wonderful Door*.[9] However, the story offered something to progressive parents as well as to children. For parents, Tony's rebelliousness, independence, and even his ultimate decision to give up the past and move into the future offered hope that children would be carriers for the impulses that adults in the 1950s were forced to repress or disguise. Indeed, Ethel Rosenberg, soon to become a martyr for the Left—and a symbol of the Old Left's utter marginalization and vilification—would ask her lawyer to purchase *Tony* as a holiday gift for her soon-to-be-orphaned sons.[10] Many radicals saw children as the logical outlet for their utopian vision and therefore chose to write for them. This was not a Communist plot to reach the kiddies, however. In reality, leftists often turned to children as their last hope, especially as they became disillusioned with political organizations like the CP.

Fast's 1950s tale of a 1920s boy who can go back in time points to how children's literature can link generations and sustain cultural and political sensibilities. One way we might look at Fast's seemingly timeless story of growing up is to think of Tony as a kind of McCarthy-era poster child for the Popular Front—a moment of radical possibility in the late 1930s and early 1940s when Communists, fellow travelers, and New Deal liberals joined forces against the common enemy of fascism.[11] Tony's working-class, multiethnic origins read like John La Touche's "Ballad for Americans," which has been called the Popular Front "anthem."[12] He is one of "the people," or "everybody who is nobody." And he is fascinated with American history, but not the history he learns in school. He mistrusts his teacher and his textbooks, because what they tell him counters the "truth" of his own experience. While Tony's story is meant to have taken place in 1924 (when Fast himself was Tony's age), it reflects 1950s ideas about children and childrearing, as it draws upon popular notions of psychological and medical expertise. It also contains subtle commentary from a Left perspective on housing conditions (Tony lives in a crowded tenement); the labor movement (Tony's father is active in the union, trying to get higher wages and better working conditions); schooling (very little of value is taught, but, significantly, we are made aware that Tony's teacher is herself exploited and really not to blame for her failures in the classroom); personal commitment (Tony stands by his beliefs); and, subtly, McCarthyism (as Doc Forbes tells Tony's father, "Nothing I like better than talking about doors—especially the kind that open. All too many are kept locked these days").[13] The story's antiauthoritarian strand made it appealing to children, as well as to parents who were dissatisfied with the status quo. Even the message of hope at the end of the book has a kind of subversive ring to it: in "coming of age," Tony becomes less childish, but he retains his childhood idealism, sense of wonder, and commitment to justice.

Unlike *Tony and the Wonderful Door*, most children's books by left-wing writers were published by regular trade presses, and most were widely available—and widely disseminated—not just in bookstores but, even more important, in school and public libraries. The children who read these books were encouraged to trust their own instincts, imaginations, and critical capacities. They were able to find books promoting a sense of social justice and a communitarian ethic; exploring the histories of peoples and groups previously ignored (such as African Americans, women, and the working class); and providing tools for understanding and harnessing science and technology for the good of human beings and the environment. If for no other reason than their authorship (as many of the books by leftists do not seem "political" at all), these books challenged the culture of containment that admonished children—and all Americans—to obey authority, accept the status quo, and embrace the "victory culture" of the United States in the struggle against the "Communist menace" at home and abroad.[14] While school *textbooks* taught children to uphold the values of the Cold War, many of the *trade* books they checked out of the library or bought in bookstores taught them just the opposite.

Children's literature is traditionally understood as a force supporting the dominant, bourgeois status quo. Think of Horatio Alger's *Ragged Dick* stories, which urged children to use pluck and luck to get ahead in life, or Gertrude Crampton's *Tootle*, which sociologist David Riesman called a "modern cautionary tale," for its message that little trains (and, implicitly, little children) must always "stay on the tracks."[15] By reaffirming the existing social order, much of the familiar children's literature of the twentieth century at least implicitly supports the individualistic values of capitalism and the policies of the United States abroad, reifies traditional gender roles, and assumes a white, middle-class norm. Some of it (for example, many early books in Stratemeyer series like the *Bobbsey Twins*) is strikingly racist.[16]

On the other hand, as literary scholar Alison Lurie reminds us, there is a long tradition of "subversive" children's literature, of stories that "appeal to the imaginative, questioning, rebellious child in all of us."[17] Even *Tootle*, which ends with the playful red locomotive finally learning to stay on the tracks, is arguably more about the subversive pleasures of resisting pressures to conform. Certainly this message is vividly expressed in some of the book's pictures by Tibor Gergeley, a Hungarian communist who illustrated some of the most popular Little Golden Books (see figure I.1).[18] As part of a broader reexamination of cultural politics in the mid-twentieth century, *Learning from the Left* asks readers to suspend some of the more traditional assumptions about children's literature and its purposes. Looking at children's literature from a new perspective, we can surmise that postwar American culture was not so contained after all.

Figure I.I. Illustration by Tibor Gergeley from Gertrude Crampton's *Tootle*. Pictures like this one show the pleasures of going *off* the tracks, which might be the more memorable message than "staying on the tracks no matter what." Racine, Wis.: Golden, 1945; copyright renewed 1972 by Random House, Inc. Used by permission of Golden Books, an imprint of Random House Children's Books, a division of Random House, Inc.

New scholarship has begun to reconsider the impact of the Communist or Popular Front Left upon American culture in the mid-twentieth century, beyond the "red decade" of the 1930s. Despite traditional narratives in which youthful idealism was replaced by disenchantment and abnegation after the Second World War, recent work suggests that the reality was far more complex. Many people who moved away from formal affiliations maintained the commitment to social justice that initially radicalized them and that led them to organizations like the CP.[19] Likewise, though the radical cultural expressions of the early 1930s did seem to disappear after the war, the impulses animating those texts were channeled into new media and more subtle forms, from pulp fiction to animation to children's literature.[20]

Among the avenues of cultural production that remained open to left-wingers during the Cold War, children's literature merits special attention. It was, as this book reveals, one of the most significant arenas of leftist influence yet one of the least scrutinized. Indeed, few writers even bothered to use pseudonyms; Franklin Folsom, who liked to use names from the *Mayflower* passenger list, is one exception, but he often used his own name as well. By definition didactic and socializing, children's literature can distill the values of a particular group down to their essence.[21] Moreover, it reaches the nation's most open-minded citizens, often on a massive scale, because of the ready market provided by school libraries. Finally, the sheer number of leftists who worked in the field, writing, illustrating, editing, and disseminating some of the most popular works of twentieth-century children's literature—from Wanda Gág's *Millions of Cats*, Crockett Johnson's *Harold and the Purple Crayon*, and William Steig's *Sylvester and the Magic Pebble* to the more mass-market *Golden Book of Astronomy* by Rose Wyler and Gerald Ames—suggests that children's literature must be taken seriously if we wish to fully understand the Left's impact on twentieth-century American culture.[22]

The very terms *Left* and *leftist* are potentially problematic. My usage of them is deliberately open-ended; however, a more precise definition, as it pertains to the central actors in this study, is probably in order. According to historian John Patrick Diggins, generally speaking, the various "Lefts" of the twentieth century—from the Wobblies, anarchists, and assorted bohemians comprising the Lyrical Left in the early part of the century, to the Communist, progressive, or anti-Stalinist Old Left of the 1930s, to the student radicals comprising the New Left of the 1960s—have "demanded the liquidation of institutionalized power and interest politics, the elimination of social classes, [and] the replacement of competitive life with one of fraternal participation and cooperative fulfillment."[23] Although I look for precedents among the early socialists and Lyrical Leftists in the 1910s and 1920s and conclude with links to the New Left of the 1960s and 1970s, I take as my central focus Old Left products of the "thirties radical upheaval" or, more specifically, the Popular Front "structure of feeling."[24] Communists and former Communists thus have an important role here, but (with the exception of one chapter) this is not a study of Communist children's literature.

Any study of the Left's influence on cultural production in the mid-twentieth century has to take Communism into account. However, the ripple effect produced by the party's organizational apparatus and ideology was more significant than active programmatic efforts, which were minimal, despite strong interest in the issue on the part of a few individuals.[25] As one CP member who devoted her career to children's literature complained of her peers in the party, "anything to do with children was considered by some people to be a woman's issue. We had to fight for literary legitimacy."[26] This lack of literary legitimacy on the Left—and in the literary establishment—was both bane and benefit to leftists in the children's literature field. It devalued their labor but also made that work possible at a time when opportunities were severely limited because of the political climate.

Knowledge and belief systems that grew from CP institutions, culture, and the wider circles of influence around the party *did* affect children's literature, but in an indirect way. As writer Dorothy Sterling put it emphatically, "I learned about Black history from the Left, and then I pursued it myself. No one ever told me what to write." On the other hand, she also suggested, only half-jokingly, that any book by a white writer published before 1965 and sympathetic to African Americans was probably written by a Communist or former Communist,[27] so constricted was the political climate and so fearful were most people of taking risks. In other words, the experience of formal or informal commitment to a political, social, and economic agenda made for a common, if far from unified, consciousness among many politically committed people who valued young readers and the juvenile market. In the end, belief and action counted for more than political affiliation. As writer Rose Wyler put it, "Whether or not people were card-carrying members of the Communist Party was not particularly pertinent. It was a question of how sympathetic they were to leftist ideas."[28] People directly affiliated with the CP were often more militant in their views, were probably more inclined to be activists in terms of pressing for (and against) certain kinds of books, and may have been more inclined to organize on behalf of workers in the field.[29] However, a set of shared understandings and a feeling of cooperation between those of varying political beliefs may have distinguished the children's literature field from many other realms of cultural production, where liberals sought to distance themselves from radicals and where radicals themselves haggled over minute differences.

The core actors in this drama were people who tended to identify publicly as "progressives." These "progressives" were, in the words of writer Vivian Gornick, class-conscious activists "struggling for a better world." They embraced what cultural historian Michael Denning has called the Popular Front "structure of feeling," which included a commitment to challenging fascism, racism, and imperialism; to promoting democracy; and to forging international, working-class solidarity. As some readers probably already gather, *progressive* was often a code word for "Communist," but in most of what follows I will allow the slippage to stand, partly in deference to the privacy of those who do not wish to be identified as such but more in view of the fact that the Communist label, loaded as it is, can cloud more than it reveals.[30]

The individuals discussed in this book were products of a range of experiences and approached politics in a variety of ways. At one extreme were the few for whom the CP played a defining role; at the other end of the spectrum were the greater majority, who, whether or not they actually joined the party, had little interest in political machinations and were drawn to the Popular Front movement because of a desire to end human suffering. It could be argued that most of them were naïve, and many had ties to an organization that was undemocratic and, even more troubling, was closely tied to a totalitarian state. As one recalled in our conversations:

> You know, when I think of the idiotic things we believed about the Soviet Union, and the terrible things that were done that we knew nothing about or refused to believe, I think, you know, I had holes in my head. On the other hand, I think it's given us—and I say us, because I have other friends who feel the same way—a lifelong belief in working for bettering the lives of other people. And that's a different attitude than most people have today I think.[31]

Although most of the people in this book eventually came to recognize and renounce most of their old illusions they continued to believe in the necessity of standing behind their heartfelt convictions.

In the course of interviewing people and reading their published work and private correspondence, I encountered very few people conforming to the stereotype of the dogmatic, closed-minded "Stalinist"—although several remained committed Marxists throughout their adult lives, and at least two, Betty Bacon and Meridel Le Sueur, remained party members until their deaths in the 1990s. But even the most orthodox Marxists tended to share an outlook vis-à-vis children with a broader progressive formation that encompassed well-known and highly influential figures from Dr. Seuss to Dr. Spock.[32] Few, that is, wished to "propagandize" children as that idea is traditionally understood. Instead, they wished to make children autonomous, critical thinkers who questioned authority and believed in social justice.

Author Milton Meltzer, who did not begin writing children's books until the late 1950s (but who is of the same generation and milieu of many other writers treated here), says that "if labels are called for," he'd rather be known as a "progressive" than as a "liberal" or a "radical." At one point in his life, Meltzer considered himself a radical and even thought the Russian Revolution held the key to fulfilling "the promise of life, liberty, and the pursuit of happiness." Seeing the Soviet Union in a very different light did not "deflect me from the goal of trying to make life better, fairer, more equitable, more decent, more honest for everyone," he says. All of Meltzer's writings for children reflect his concern for social justice, a concern undoubtedly influenced by his years as a radical, even though that period ended long before his career as a writer for children began. Meltzer hopes that his work "encourages young readers to protect individual rights and the common good, to seek justice, equality of opportunity for all, to cherish diversity and truth." He writes books that he hopes will "strengthen a sense of community, of the need to work with others to solve problems or accomplish tasks."[33] Such a vision was typical of most writers on the Left, regardless of their specific political affiliations at any given moment.

The Loose Enders, an informal, New York–based group of writers, illustrators, editors, and others who forged initial connections in the Authors Guild, typify the shared commitment among progressives and radicals in the field of children's literature. Originally getting together to discuss book contracts, they began to meet periodically for dinner, whenever they felt at "loose ends," and collectively they became an important force in the field. Several members of the group had lost their teaching jobs or had found other sources of income drying up as a result of McCarthy-era purges, and they reestablished themselves as authors of children's books. Others had entered the field not because other avenues had closed to them but simply because they discovered they liked to write for children. The specifics of their political affiliations varied: as Loose Ender and author Mary Elting Folsom noted, some were "more radical than others, but that didn't even cause discussion." Elting says that "we just took it for granted that each of us shared with the others what I can only call a sort of basic liberal code." All were opposed to the war in Korea and, later, the war in Vietnam. All were deeply concerned about the effects of racism upon children. And none of them, she insists, "could possibly have been an informer during McCarthy times."[34] Several Loose Enders wrote books that were national or even international bestsellers, but most of their names remain unfamiliar to lay readers; few authors of children's books—no matter how well the books sell—achieve the celebrity status of a Dr. Seuss or a Margaret Wise Brown. And in that sense, this is a project of recovery, not of obscure historical artifacts, but of texts and voices that had an important impact in their day.[35]

The Loose Enders, individually and collectively, turn up throughout this study. But more broadly, the geographic, ethnic, racial, and religious backgrounds of the figures I examine is typical of the Left more generally, except that, as one might expect in a study of children's literature, women are overrepresented. Many of the writers and illustrators were secular Jews; several were the children of immigrants; and a few were immigrants themselves. Others, like the midwesterner Meridel Le Sueur, could trace their roots to native radical traditions. A significant number were African American.[36] While many of these individuals lived, at some point, in New York City, *Learning from the Left* also discusses people who lived and worked in Massachusetts, Illinois, Minnesota, Missouri, Iowa, Vermont, Florida, Ohio, California, New Jersey, Connecticut, Washington state, Virginia, and Colorado.

• • •

Tony's "wonderful door" is a useful metaphor for understanding how and why leftists were able to play an important role in the children's book field in the mid-twentieth century, but we can gain a fuller sense of the "system of social relations that sustain[ed]" children's books by leaving fiction for a moment and turning to an actual historical event.[37] In June 1941, the antifascist League of American Writers devoted a session at one of its periodic writers congresses, held since 1935, to the "juvenile" craft. Children's literature had not been on the agenda of earlier congresses at all, but the 1941 session devoted to the topic suggests a growing recognition of the medium's importance for the Left. Speaking on the topic of "Socially Constructive Literature for Children," writer Mary Lapsley encapsulated a fundamental concern of all progressives when she framed the issues in terms of a larger battle against fascism and a far-reaching educational agenda. "Our problem is this," she said. "How do we educate our children so that they will be anti-fascist, and not fascist?"[38] In other words, how were adults going to raise children actively opposed to fascism or, at the very least, not in support of it? While fascism was the overarching concern in 1941, Lapsley's question had implicit corollaries, which were understood by those listening to her talk: how to educate children to reject racism, to support the rights of labor, to embrace an international community, and to condemn imperialism? How to cultivate children's imaginations, their critical thinking abilities, and their sense of history?[39]

Although Lapsley argued that all literature, including children's literature, is a form of propaganda, her colleague Ruth Kennell was quick to insist that "we don't mean [the child] should be given economic treatises, nor sermons about class injustices."[40] In the early 1930s, or not so long before Kennell's address, the CP had briefly promoted exactly this sort of children's literature, but Kennell's comment reflected leftists' recognition that few children would want to read economic treatises or sermons, and, perhaps more important, few "child guardians" would let such material get into children's hands.

Kennell not only rejected treatises and sermons as viable children's reading, but she also denied having any interest in taking over the means of cultural production. "We do not demand direct outlets for our 'social message' (Heaven forbid!)," she insisted. Yet in truth, Kennell's concerns, and the concerns of all those in the League of American Writers, were *precisely* these things: social messages and outlets for them. Thus, when Lapsley declared, "the problem is how to get our kind of stories across to them and not another kind," her focus went beyond writing or illustrating and entered the arena of production and dissemination. As Kennell put it, in more apocalyptic terms, "How can we write honestly, holding fast to enduring social values, when at this time the forces of destruction are in the saddle, and sell what we write?" The challenge, then, was how to make the "social message" of cultural workers on the Left palatable to those controlling the field of children's book publishing, that is, the librarians, teachers, and assorted experts whom Kennell called "child guardians." An even greater and perhaps more pressing challenge was how to reorient or challenge that power structure, how to transform its very nature, or "refunction" the whole children's literature field by literally "infiltrating" it (to borrow a term from McCarthyism) with more progressive people.[41] This concern was reflected in the fact that discussions at the congress's juvenile session included not just authors and illustrators like Wanda Gág, Alfred Kreymborg, May McNeer, Howard Simon, Eva Knox Evans, and Marshall McClintock, but a range of people involved in the production and dissemination of culture for children, including editors (among them Daniel Melcher of Viking Press), publishers, teachers, librarians, and a labor organizer in the publishing union—as well as folksingers, a puppeteer, and a member of the Works Progress Administration's Federal Theater Project.[42] That the son of Frederic Melcher, owner of *Publishers Weekly* and founder of the prestigious Newbery Medal, was part of the discussions suggests that the "cultural front" extended almost to the very core of the children's literature establishment.

Those in attendance recognized that in order to change the nature of children's literature and the conditions of work in that field, progressive cultural workers needed to understand the particular mechanics of children's book publication and distribution as well as the social meanings attached to the field.[43] A children's book author must write for at least two audiences: adults—that is, parents, teachers, and librarians—who buy the books, and children, who read the books or to whom the books are read. The primary market for children's books was, and still is, institutional, meaning libraries and schools, and this was particularly true before advances in printing and the advent of juvenile paperbacks made children's books easily affordable. Given the importance of institutional markets, selling children's books entailed marketing to the "child guardians" who influenced school and library (as well as parental) purchases through lists of recommended books and awards. Finally, as the generation of new titles began to be heavily influenced by school curricula and by local and federal educational policies, writers looking for viable markets had to be attuned to what was happening in schools, as well as in the critical establishment.[44]

The particular status of children's books as cultural objects also made them unique, offering a measure of protection from scrutiny while simultaneously guaranteeing sales. As they were widely believed to be good for children, children's books escaped the stigma attached to commercial culture and often maintained an aura of purity that could ward off would-be censors, especially when books appeared to conform to general standards of acceptability.[45] The outcry over popular titles like *Are You There God? It's Me, Margaret* (in the 1970s) or, more recently, over the *Harry Potter* books obscures the fact that most children's books tend to receive very little attention, critical or otherwise.

The fact that children's books were viewed as outside the literary establishment—beneath it, actually—did much to explain how the field could inconspicuously "harbor" significant left-wingers throughout the McCarthy era, despite concurrent concerns about the "seduction" of "innocent" youth by violent comic books, rock and roll, television, and "un-American" schoolteachers.[46] Historically, this devaluation was reflected in poor contracts and limited or no royalties for authors, a condition that limited the field's appeal to potential writers and reinforced its literal feminization.[47] Given the prevailing image of the field and its gendered nature to the present day, it is perhaps unsurprising but still necessary to point out that almost all of the juvenile editors, youth services librarians, elementary school teachers, and, by and large, even booksellers involved with the day-to-day business of children's books were women. In 1950, 97.5 percent of all youth services librarians were women. And for many years, the field of juvenile editing was entirely composed of women, even while men dominated the rest of the publishing field, especially at the executive level.[48] Although some of the most familiar names in twentieth-century children's literature are men's—Dr. Seuss, E. B. White, H. A. Rey—children's literature was a field largely controlled by women, which contributed to both its devaluation within a hierarchy of literary production and its "inconspicuousness."[49] As the field was undervalued, it was, likewise, overlooked. As writer Mary Elting commented, "It's a curious thing that our trade was so looked down upon that nobody bothered with us."[50]

But the children's literature field was not simply overlooked. It was also protected by the unquestioned authority of the "child guardians," who vouched for the moral, educational, psychosocial, and literary qualities of children's books and who were themselves generally liberal in orientation (except in matters of race, where the pressures exerted by southern markets had an undeniable effect).[51] The children's book field was small enough that many actors within it had close connections and, in most cases, responded to one another on a personal level, usually not bothering with the technical details of a person's political affiliation. In effect, a tightly knit network of professional women held positions in nearly all levels of the field and, as such, exerted tremendous power. Indeed, one woman might gain a foothold in several arenas, beginning as a teacher or librarian, then going into editing, and then writing her own children's books. These women's specialized knowledge concerning children, and the feminized position of children's literature within a literary hierarchy, allowed the field to operate with low visibility.[52]

Beyond the public perception of children's literature as a field set apart, protected, and not really worth examining, trade children's books were, in fact, much more difficult to monitor than school textbooks, which were subject to intense scrutiny at the state, local, and even national levels. The random usage of trade books made them harder to track than textbooks, which would be used by every student in a class or grade. Individual titles of trade books were also bought in much smaller quantities. Although a library would carry hundreds or thousands of books, it would have only one or two copies of a given title. Since the number of different trade children's books published in any given year often reached the thousands, it was virtually impossible for cultural watchdogs to investigate each one.

A combination of factors brought concrete opportunities for people on the Left to influence the field at all levels and helped leftists to recognize the potential for juvenile literature to reach the broad masses of children. A progressive common sense on the subject of children began to become apparent early in the twentieth century, and more democratic models of parenting and education gained momentum in reaction to the rise of fascism in the 1930s. By the time Dr. Spock and Dr. Seuss became household names in the 1940s, the popularity of what came to be called "permissive" or "progressive" parenting signaled the decline of an authoritarian relationship between parents and children and a widespread desire to make imagination, free expression, cooperation, and commitment to social justice hallmarks of American childhood.[53] This shared perspective on childhood created opportunities for alliances between people who in other contexts might not have cooperated with one another. Thus organizations like the Progressive Education Association and the Child Study Association helped to extend the Left's influence in the children's book field by the 1940s, a period during which radicals from the working class were attaining prominent positions in many media, including film, theater, and radio. And whereas cultural workers in other fields often paid dearly in the postwar period for political positions that challenged the Cold War status quo, in most instances children's literature remained a "wonderful door" for those who could imagine a society arranged in a different and, from their perspective, more egalitarian, more just, and more fulfilling way.

Trends in publishing and in education after World War II also helped leftists at the very moment other avenues were becoming closed to radical cultural producers. New nonfiction series such as the First Books, the Real Books, the All-About Books, the Landmark books, and various biographical series built upon the successes of mass-market publishing while usually managing to secure the institutional markets traditionally denied to fiction series like Nancy Drew and the Hardy Boys. Many, if not most of these series had a significant number of left-wing contributors. And in the most striking irony, Cold War educational policies—from "civic education" programs designed to foster patriotism and anti-Communism, to initiatives like the National Defense Education Act, designed to build strength in defense-related subjects—further bolstered markets for the kinds of books leftists were eager to write. Particularly sought under these initiatives were books about history and society and about science and technology. Such subjects coincided with the agenda of radicals pressing for books that would "reveal something about the world to children," and, indeed, leftists in the juvenile field made their greatest contributions in these areas.[54]

Those inclined toward conspiracy theories might imagine a vast network of people on the Left engaged in a variety of potentially subversive activities aimed at indoctrinating children: authors writing books with hidden messages and illustrators creating pictures inflected with subliminal content; radical literary agents obtaining book contracts for writers who disguised their identities (and their politics); librarians recommending certain political books to unsuspecting children; editors in children's book departments soliciting left-wing authors to write books or recommending certain kinds of editorial changes; bookstore buyers ordering and featuring certain kinds of materials. There were, in fact, politically committed people in all of these positions, and there was a real effort by leftists to promote "socially constructive" literature for children.

But the juvenile "red network" was neither as clearly present nor as subversive as a conspiracy hunter—or a contemporary scholar seeking sites of resistance—might imagine it to be. This was not only because of the basic limitations of children's literature as a genre, but also because leftists' main impact on children's literature came about not as a result of organized left-wing activity. Perhaps not surprisingly, most of the popular books by radicals are decidedly *not* revolutionary, in the sense of rejecting American forms of government or economics. Most of the books that receive extended treatment in the latter chapters of this study, which were linked to Cold War–era curricular initiatives—and, generally speaking, geared to an eight- to fourteen-year-old age group—give expression to a tradition of anticapitalist thought in American intellectual history, one that was certainly out of fashion after 1945 but that was still the product of an American, that is, not an alien, intellectual tradition.[55]

The books place high value on the American values of democracy and free expression. While they are often openly critical of past or present injustices, they point toward solutions that affirm the possibility of reshaping American society and institutions to embody the nation's democratic promise; that is, they show individuals and communities actively working against injustice and toward enlightenment, a model that is true to native traditions of dissent and reform. At some level, this conformity to basic generic conventions and adherence to an implicit liberal code gives testimony to the conservative nature of the Old Leftists: they truly believed the Popular Front slogan that "Communism is twentieth-century Americanism."[56] But they believed in an Americanism that was inclusive, democratic, and egalitarian. Their work also points to how the Old Left's views about childhood and education contributed to shaping the New Left generation: the older generation of radicals and progressives believed that children were to be taught, at the appropriate age, truths about the world in which they lived. They were to be taught that they could and should work to improve existing conditions and to challenge injustice. Most of all, leftists wanted to provide children with hope and the sense that the system, though imperfect, was open to change and improvement.[57] So it should not be a total surprise that children raised on these books grew up to reject the Cold War status quo.

Simply put, the Popular Front Left played a major role in shaping the character of twentieth-century children's literature. A wide variety of positions in the children's book field were inhabited by people on the Left, a fact that cannot be entirely separated from the more general effort represented by the cultural front—or the cultural arm of the Popular Front social movement—to transform the means of cultural production as well as culture itself. Changes in the children's book field in the 1930s and 1940s opened space for left-wing writers and illustrators—and many of their philosophies—even in the 1950s. Thus the history of the children's book, considered in light of its intersection with the history of the Left, complicates and challenges traditional understandings of each.

• • •

This book is divided into three major sections. Part I, "Progressive and Proletarian Precedents," looks at the 1920s and 1930s, examining, on the one hand, the coincidental development of juvenile publishing, progressive education, and the nonsectarian Lyrical Left and, on the other hand, the early work of Communists in children's literature, most of which was geared toward a limited audience of working-class children. Chapter 1, "Lyrical Leftists, Juvenile Publishing, and the Politics of Progressive Education," focuses on an impulse toward "child liberation" among progressive educators and nonsectarian leftists. This impulse dovetailed with the development of juvenile divisions in publishing houses and rapidly expanding markets for children's literature in the 1920s. Chapter 2, "Books for 'Young Revolutionists': Children's Literature and the Communist Milieu, 1925–1935," looks at the brief attempt (paralleling the "proletarian renaissance" in adult publishing) to create radical literature for working-class children, an approach that was quickly superseded beginning in the mid-1930s by new efforts to create a body of literature for the broad masses of children.

Part II, "Producing Dissent," looks at the push and pull factors from the dawn of the Popular Front in 1935 through the years of the Cold War consensus (or roughly up to President John Kennedy's assassination), which set limits on leftist expression and also created certain opportunities in the children's literature field. Chapter 3, "Work and Sing: Children's Literature and the Cultural Front, 1935–1965," reveals how the depression and World War II influenced beliefs about what ideas children should be exposed to and what they should be taught. A general antifascist common sense, along with the entry of radicals into the expanding culture industries, brought increasing left-wing influence on the production and content of children's books. Chapter 4, "'Pink-Tinged Pages'? McCarthyism and Children's Literature," and chapter 5, "Countering the Cold War: Social Significance versus Social Pressure," address the impact of McCarthyism and the Cold War on schools, libraries, and publishing houses, as well as on specific individuals. These chapters also explore the factors that made possible the extension of an alternative, counterconsensus tradition in children's literature at a time when so much of American culture was marked by the ideology (or the anti-ideology) of the Cold War.

Part III, "Science and History for Girls and Boys," offers case studies of works in the thematic genres to which leftist cultural workers, particularly those influenced by Marxism, made the most substantial contributions. Chapter 6, "The Tools of Science: Dialectics and Children's Literature," and chapter 7, "Ballad for American Children: History, Folklore, and Leftist Civic Education," focus, respectively, on books about science and books about history and folklore. An epilogue looks at the long-range impact of the Old Left in the children's book field, focusing especially on the Council on Interracial Books for Children, an influential organization created in the 1960s by several former radicals. I argue that the sea change that scholars have recorded in the children's literature field beginning in the late 1960s—when children's books became more realistic and more reflective of American cultural diversity—had roots in the Old Left's influence in previous decades.[58]

Just as it took some time for Tony's teacher, his parents, and other authority figures to believe in Tony's wonderful door, it took time to transform children's literature from a genre overdominated by sweetness and light, by didactic lessons, and by moral precepts to a genre that actually spoke to the experiences of childhood in all their diversity, presuming a child reader who would eventually—if not right away—be capable of making the world anew.

PART I

Progressive and Proletarian Precedents

1

Lyrical Leftists, Juvenile Publishing, and the Politics of Progressive Education

In 1927, poet, puppeteer, and Lyrical Leftist Alfred Kreymborg published *Funnybone Alley*, a loving portrait of a crooked street in Ballyboo. Ballyboo, just in case you were wondering, "lies somewhere under the sun by day, somewhere in the moonlight at night and somewhere between the Battery and the Bronx, with a river for a necklace, a lake for a bracelet and a pond around the middle finger."[1] This imaginary place in the real city of New York seems at one level timeless: the adults go to work, the children play, and at night parents tell young ones stories, or sing them lullabies when they cannot sleep. But something distinguishes Funnybone Alley—and the people who live there—from the modern world that surrounds it, a world of skyscrapers, busy streets with automobiles, and businesspeople rushing off to make important deals.

Kreymborg notes of the folk on this zigzagging lane:

> They have the same insignificant stores their forefathers had, the same impractical methods and the same bank accounts. If they have any bank accounts. This poverty in money matters had kept the alley from keeping up with Bullyfine Boulevard, where the marvelous mansions parade, or Solemnity Street, where the banks and bankers play together, or Triangle Square, where the trusts are built on those pillars: Vim, Vice and Victory.

This is a place where the regular rules of commerce seem not to apply, a place where a different set of values dictates the terms of human relationships. The people on Funnybone Alley have no head for business (they refuse to charge more for their goods than they are worth "and often charge less"); they are, moreover, infinitely distractible, inclined to stop working to watch a parade

23

or an organ grinder. Nearly all of them, says Kreymborg, are "afflicted with tenderness." At community events, like concerts by the Ballyboo band, "each and every shopkeeper" contributes (with vaguely Marxist undertones), "in accordance with his profession and economic capacity," refreshments, furnishings, or whatever is needed. These kind, common folk—like Peter Pringle the shoemaker and Pa Peppermint the confectioner—fashion small pleasures and rich fantasies from the poverty of their existence and instinctively look out for each other.[2]

The children of Funnybone Alley are good but not too good, mischievous but never malicious. Lonesome Sam Pumpernickel, *Funnybone's* principal protagonist, is a dreamy boy filled with yearning, who lives with his Uncle Adolph and Aunt Ada, proprietors of the local delicatessen. Sam loves his aunt and uncle, but he is most content when on his own, or when adventuring with his "cronies," William Roe, "alias Bolivar Bill," and Gustav Gullible, "alias Raspberry Red." The children alternate between the worlds they imaginatively create and the here-and-now world of the city, with its barges, taxis, trains, derricks, and tall buildings and with all its sounds and smells. They roam freely through Ballyboo but they habitually avoid Solemnity Street, that avenue of capital and commerce, for "there is nothing anywhere that can possibly appeal to their fancy."[3] Once in a while, however, Sam and his cronies will swing on the telegraph wires or hang from the fire escapes around Solemnity Street, just because they know they should not do so.

When sent on errands, the boys often get distracted and forget what they were supposed to bring home, but the shopkeepers on Funnybone Alley seem unconcerned with selling their wares anyway, and they often give things away for free. If asked about it, more reflective residents of Ballyboo would scratch their heads and struggle to articulate the ethic that made their community seem so different from the society that surrounded it:

> Uncle Adolph, no doubt, being friendly enough to listen and courteous enough to answer, would have said something like—"Camaraderie? Brotherhood? Who can tell? Selfishness? Unselfishness? Who can say which? Possibly they go together. To get you have to give. To give you have to get. I don't know. I never thought of it before."[4]

The Lyrical Left

Funnybone Alley provides us with a starting point for linking the history of the children's book—especially as it became tied to educational imperatives—with the history of the Left. In their anticapitalist, whimsical vision of things and in their romantic reverence for children, and irreverence for just about everything else, especially the establishment—the people of Funnybone Alley seem unself-consciously to embody the spirit of what John Patrick Diggins has called the "Lyrical Left." Or perhaps more accurately, *Funnybone Alley*'s cast of characters represents an idealized fantasy of that playful, antiorthodox leftist generation of the 1910s and 1920s.

While they supported socialist principles, Lyrical Leftists' critique was directed as much against the "genteel tradition" as against the economic order that supported this tradition. Like the New Left of the 1960s, which, at least initially, "saw itself as the first generation of existential radicals who could live without doctrinal illusions," this earlier generation of Leftists "rose up in revolt against abstract doctrine, embraced a pragmatic socialism that was as open-ended as free verse, and proudly heralded itself as conqueror without a creed."[5] They tended to gather around magazines like the *Masses*, a radical, nonsectarian journal of art, literature, criticism, and commentary, whose contributors and readers often combined "Freudianism, feminism, socialism, syndicalism, anarchism, and bohemianism in a heady but precarious blend."[6]

Most chroniclers of the Lyrical Left date its demise around 1917, when the First World War and the Russian Revolution combined to produce seemingly irreparable factionalism among radicals, or 1919, when the "red scare" drove a significant portion of the Left out of the country or underground, and the new American Communist Party (CPUSA) stifled some of the free-spirited, nonsectarian debate characteristic of Leftists in previous years. By the 1920s, the triumph of consumer capitalism seemed as though it would channel all of the remaining energies of the revolt against economic injustice into what Frederick Lewis Allen called the "revolution in manners and morals." However, despite the many forces that dissipated radical energies in the 1920s, remnants of the Left remained united during those years by "the idea of salvation by the child," described by Malcolm Cowley in *Exile's Return*, a memoir of bohemian Greenwich Village in the 1920s. According to this "doctrine," Cowley says, "each of us at birth has special potentialities which are slowly crushed and destroyed by a standardized society and mechanical methods of teaching." Cowley and other cultural and political radicals of his era believed that "if a new educational system can be introduced, one by which children are encouraged to develop their own personalities, to blossom freely like flowers, then the world will be saved by this new, free generation."[7]

Alfred Kreymborg's own trajectory bridged the social, cultural, and political worlds of the 1910s Lyrical Left and the Popular Front Left of the 1930s and early 1940s. A prolific writer of poetry, prose, and plays, he was in some ways the prototypical Lyrical Leftist. A New York City native, born in 1883, Kreymborg circulated among the prominent literati, artists, and rebels of his day.

Based primarily in Greenwich Village, in the 1910s, Kreymborg mingled with and befriended members of the *Masses* crowd like Max Eastman, John Reed, and Floyd Dell; experimental photographers like Man Ray and Alfred Stieglitz; modern artists like Marsden Hartley and William Zorach; and spirited socialist reformers like birth control advocate Margaret Sanger and Walt Whitman's younger disciple Horace Traubel. In the 1920s Kreymborg spent time in Chicago around the poets and writers of the Chicago Renaissance: wandering the Loop and tossing a baseball in Lincoln Park with Carl Sandburg; trading notes with Vachel Lindsay and Sherwood Anderson; and hanging out in the offices of Harriet Monroe's *Poetry*. Kreymborg did a brief stint with the Provincetown Players, a radical theater troupe on Cape Cod, and he spent the obligatory period in Paris with other American expatriates before returning to Greenwich Village in the mid-1920s. During his career, he helped found or edited several literary magazines—among them *Broom, Others*, and a short-lived experiment in promoting "great American literature" that he called *American Quarterly* (pre-dating the academic American studies journal of the same title). Making the transition from the bohemian scene of the 1920s to the revolutionary milieu of the 1930s, Kreymborg would join the John Reed Club, which supported the talents of "proletarian" writers. In the late 1930s, he joined the Executive Committee of the League of American Writers, and in 1946 *Funnybone Alley* would be remade as a record album, becoming a kind of cult classic among children of the Popular Front.[8]

Lyrical Leftists' belief in salvation by the child and their faith in the revolutionary power of education helped to transform modern understandings of childhood. In conjunction with wider trends in education, these factors helped to set the terms for key developments in the juvenile field as it became a separate and significant sector of the American publishing industry in the 1920s and early 1930s. Individually and collectively, in their philosophy and in their work, the Lyrical Left and a broader cohort of progressive educators offered a usable past for Popular Front Leftists, who aimed to reach a wide audience of children with their message.

On the one hand, fanciful or imaginative books like *Funnybone Alley*, Carl Sandburg's *Rootabaga Stories* (1922), and Wanda Gág's *Millions of Cats* (1928) encouraged children to imaginatively extend the limits of the possible and implicitly criticized the competitive, acquisitive spirit of capitalism. On the other hand, informational books like Lucy Sprague Mitchell's *Here and Now Story Book* (1921)—and all the books it (and Mitchell herself) helped to inspire—embodied a different though related spirit of children's liberation: the simple stories of everyday life in the modern city were meant to empower children with an understanding of social relationships, giving them the power to change and improve the world around them. A corollary genre to the category of books that taught children about social relationships was the culturally sensitive book that represented an attempt—however flawed in practice—to eradicate social prejudices through education.

The imperative to protect children could be used to criticize imaginative literature, especially fairy tales (for containing frightening or confusing fantasies), as well as here-and-now or "social studies" literature (for its depiction of a "real world" that children were emotionally or cognitively unprepared to confront). However, nonsectarian leftists of the 1920s were strong voices for protecting not children's morals or their innocence, but their right to dream and their right to know something about the world. Overall, the common cause among members of the progressive education community and the Lyrical Left milieu helped to predict the key role that educational imperatives would play in creating opportunities for leftists in juvenile publishing. Moreover, this common cause also pointed to the political power of imagination and play. Efforts at cultural sensitivity among progressive educators likewise had an important impact on children's literature and school curricula, and this impulse would animate the Popular Front in fundamental ways. However, the unconscious racial biases of many Lyrical leftists, doctrinaire socialists, and progressive educators represented a past less usable for the Popular Front generation.

Modernity, Politics, and the Development of Children's Book Publishing

Both the Left and the children's book as we know it today are products of the modern industrial era. Children's book publishing developed as a specialized field at a moment of immense technological and demographic changes, political unrest, and intellectual upheavals that redefined the family, gender roles, and childhood itself. The rise of what came to be understood as the modern era, characterized by industrialization, urbanization, immigration, mass education, and technological and commercial revolutions, coincided with the dawn of a new view of childhood. Indeed, in 1909 Swedish feminist Ellen Key declared that the twentieth century would be "the century of the child."[9] The distinctly modern idea that all children had the right to read and to enjoy good books shaped the development of the children's book field in the early twentieth century.

Key's focus on children was part of a much wider preoccupation that arguably culminated in the 1920s with the popularization of Freud. Historian Carolyn Steedman argues that one of the most dramatic reconceptualizations at the turn of the century was the change in the position of the working-class child from a component of the labor force to a subject of education. Developmentalist or evolutionary thought suggested that, unlike their parents (who were already corrupted), even poor and immigrant children could be "saved" and "Americanized"; under this logic, *all* children had the right to childhood, something previously reserved for children of the middle and upper classes. This new view of childhood went along with the expansion of library services to children and the growth of public education around the turn of the century, and it was evident in the changing character of children's literature, which gradually shifted away from heavily didactic and moralistic stories to works written purely for children's amusement.[10]

Library services to children developed in the late nineteenth century to assimilate the growing body of books and magazines for children from the United States and abroad, to keep unsavory publications like dime novels out of circulation, and to raise standards of quality in children's literature. Library schools began special training programs for children's librarians at this time, and increasingly libraries set aside sections or whole rooms for children. These would be staffed by a new cadre of educated women, most of them unmarried, who had emerged as key figures in professions related to child welfare, including social work, settlement house work, teaching, and children's librarianship. Women's interest in developing library services for children went along with their social role as nurturers, and it also tapped into elements of the social purity crusade, of which women were leaders. Indeed, as library historian Christine Jenkins notes, the librarian, and particularly the youth services librarian, tended to see herself as a "protector of public morals in print."[11]

Librarians, along with other professional women who became editors, book reviewers, educators, and other specialists in child welfare (those Ruth Kennell would term *child guardians*), assumed tremendous power as arbiters of children's reading. First, they established lists of recommended books that influenced purchases by bookstores, parents, and libraries. Likewise, review journals, like the *Booklist* (established 1905) and the *Horn Book* (established 1924), and awards, like the Newbery and Caldecott medals (established 1922 and 1937, respectively), ensured that librarians and others with expertise would uphold the standards of trade children's books and maintain control of the field. As historian of American publishing John Tebbel notes of early children's librarians, "[T]hey represented a body of organized opinion, backed by purchasing power, that had a major effect on the development of children's literature."[12]

Librarians' demand for quality children's literature and for professional expertise among those publishing children's books provided the impetus for separate divisions in publishing houses. The movement to create quality children's books from within literary publishing houses also came partly in response to the perceived corruption of childhood by profit-oriented commercial media. In 1913, Franklin K. Mathiews, the chief librarian of the Boy Scouts, bemoaned the quality of reading material available to his charges in a talk called "Books as Merchandise or Something More." Mathiews's complaints led to the first Children's Book Week, which, by 1919, had become a national event (simply known as Book Week). Book Week, still in existence, typifies the unique status of juvenile publishing among commercial enterprises, as it manages to turn a massive annual sales event into a kind of moral imperative: every year, schools, libraries, and other community organizations enthusiastically trumpet the benefits of childhood reading and openly promote the sale of children's books as a cultural good.[13]

Book Week demonstrated the marketability of children's books in a child-oriented consumer culture, and publishers began to make a serious effort to gain access to the juvenile market. The first juvenile division of a publishing house was established at Macmillan in 1919, and by the end of World War II, thirty-two publishers had specialized departments, nearly all headed by women.[14] From the beginning, children's book editors and librarians had close ties, not only because so many children's book editors had begun their careers in the library field, but also because public and school libraries represented the primary market for children's books, which most parents could not afford to buy. Publishers regularly turned to children's librarians for suggestions, and librarians worked closely with the American Book Publishers Association, offering criticism and commentary. Book Week's origins had little to do with politics, but the fact that both the American Communist Party (CP) and the American Legion (AL) were established in the same year that it became a national program—and the same year that presses began to establish juvenile divisions—does point to the ways in which politics would increasingly become intertwined with children's culture in the twentieth century.

Both the Right and the Left saw children as key to the future, and this interest in children was manifested in children's programming as well as in literature for children. For instance, the KKK and the CP had junior programs, and Communists, Legionnaires, and Christians all created special publications for children. In the educational realm, right-wing groups like the American Legion waged a popular and, in many ways, effective campaign to keep public schools free of radical influence. In addition to monitoring textbooks and teachers, the AL sponsored programs like American Education Week, which had as its goal not only "eliminating illiteracy," but also "combating forces of pacifism, radicalism, and un-Americanism among our Nation's children at their most impressionable age." The AL's two-volume history textbook, *The Story of Our American People*, "did not find a ready market," according to one historian of the AL, but neither, it must be said, did Socialist or Communist Party publications for children. What patriotic groups like the AL did not count on was that progressive educational thought—which was, to some extent, radical in its origins and implications—would reshape school curricula, practices, and, ultimately, "supplementary" materials like children's books, in ways that were beyond the control of the Right.[15]

Learning Freedom: The Politics of Progressive Education

Just as Kreymborg serves as an apt representative of the Lyrical Left—and several of the leftist strands that followed it—so *Funnybone Alley*, which came out at a critical moment in the history of American publishing, speaks to a Lyrical Leftist sensibility that combined a romantic faith in the child's potential to redeem society with faith that education, in and out of school, could produce a more democratic and egalitarian future. *Funnybone Alley*'s school aptly represents the new sensibility that influenced progressive educational philosophy and practices in the early twentieth century. The community's free-spirited children do their best learning outside the school's walls and among the sights and sounds of the city, but school still plays an important role in their lives. It is egalitarian (the teachers are called "aunt" and "uncle" instead of "mister" and "missus"), cooperative, and child-centered. It is a place children attend with pleasure, rather than by compulsion. The school principal's guiding philosophy is: "Without self expression no human being is free and without freedom no human being can live."[16]

Rather than a cage to tame young boys and girls, *Funnybone Alley*'s school has been developed to accommodate the children and *their* interests. And rather than learning competition, the children learn to help each other out:

> Lonesome Sam had a mighty poor head for arithmetic, but an excellent ear for spelling. Right and wrong created a balance which nobody praised or censured. If Sam stuttered that four times thirteen are forty-two and forgot to carry one—and Bolivar carried it and corrected him—no one blamed Sam or praised Bill. Bill could spell a word doe when it should have been dough, or coff when it should have been cough. And stumbled over other words throughout the language left by our ancestors. Sam rarely made such mistakes. Nor did Aunt Jones laud him or scold Bill.[17]

The children can come late and leave early if they need to, and they can spend their days doing exactly what it is that interests them. As Kreymborg notes, "If Sam felt like writing what he had seen, Bolivar like modeling, Raspberry like painting, Strawberry like singing, Christopher like composing—there was a private room for these needful activities."[18]

Although *Funnybone Alley*'s school represents a utopian ideal, the emphasis on self-directed activity among the children was characteristic of practices widely promoted by advocates of progressive or "experimental" education.[19] This had important consequences for children's book publishing as well as for the content of children's literature. New teaching methods that deemphasized textbooks and gave greater weight to children's independent learning meant increased demand for trade children's books to supplement the curriculum in the 1920s and 1930s. Educators and librarians sometimes referred to changing educational methods, which became widespread during this period, as the "new curriculum" or the "new education," and they remarked upon the role of books and librarians in this transformed mode of study. As librarian Margaret Girdner noted in 1929:

> In the days when we were in school, we were assigned certain pages
> in a textbook to read and the next day we came back and repeated the
> facts to the teacher, who supplemented our information from her own
> experience. How different it is today! Now the class, influenced by
> the teacher, selects a subject in which they are interested; the teacher
> assigns certain phases of the subject to groups of students and the chil-
> dren are turned to a collection of books to find the facts which are
> then reported to the entire class for discussion and analysis.[20]

This shift in educational methods contributed to the rapid expansion of school library services in the 1920s and 1930s, which, in turn, fueled the explosive growth of children's book publishing in the first half of the twentieth century. Schools were now spending large sums of money on children's books, particularly nonfiction, to supplement the formal curriculum. Rising demand from educators made publishers increasingly attentive to curricular needs when shaping their juvenile lists.[21] Authors themselves often shared the same impulses that gave rise to experimental education, producing a new sensibility that was reflected in both imaginative and nonfiction American children's literature.

An agenda of social transformation was implicit in many aspects of progressive educational philosophy. Drawing heavily upon the philosophies of John Dewey, progressive educators held that school should serve the whole child, that it should be a laboratory and model for the outside world, teaching democracy and cooperation and providing children with tools for confronting social problems. This dimension of progressive educational philosophy would become increasingly apparent in the 1930s, as many educators were infected by the radical spirit of the age.[22] Dewey himself would argue that education was the essential tool for solving the problems of society, and that in a rapidly changing industrial civilization, rote memorization was less useful than learning methods of thinking that could be applicable to all problems. Dewey's philosophy of education looked forward rather than aiming to preserve the existing social order. As he would argue in 1928:

> If one conceives that a social order different in quality and direction from the present is desirable and that schools should strive to educate with social change in view by producing individuals not complacent about what already exists, and equipped with desires and abilities to assist in transforming it, quite a different method and content is indicated for educational science.

The content of progressive education, as well as the methods, presumed a new model of schooling. Socialist presidential candidate Norman Thomas argued in 1932:

> [W]e should encourage teachers in the schools deliberately to stimulate thinking and discussion on the cause and extent of poverty, the reasons for war, the difficulties in the way of peace, the meaning of liberty, and what justification, if any, there is for a system in which ten million are unemployed because they are alleged to have produced too much.[23]

Progressive education was not necessarily radical in its implications, but the basic proposition that education should respond to the child's needs and interests represented a new and arguably radical mindset.[24] As Agnes De Lima, who worked closely with progressive private institutions, including the Little Red Schoolhouse, Walden School, and Elizabeth Irwin School, argued in her book *Our Enemy, the Child* (which came out just after the infamous Scopes trial):

> A teacher recently prophesied that the next heresy hunt will be directed against the rapidly growing number of people who believe in "experimental" education. Some canny sleuth will discover that there is a direct connection between schools which set out deliberately to train children to think, and to develop creatively, and the radical movement. . . . The dangerous centers are those directed by people who have a vision of a new social order, and who believe that the way to prepare for it is to bring up a generation of free thinking, self-directing young people whose spontaneity, originality, and native curiosity have not been stifled nor confined within narrow grooves of conformity.[25]

Influenced by progressive pedagogues like Dewey as well as by Freud and Marx, Lyrical leftists were drawn to the imaginative realm because they believed that the imaginative, creative, artistic, and playful traits inherent to childhood represented a model for the liberation of society as a whole. In his 1919 book, *Were You Ever a Child?* Floyd Dell argued that what children need from school is "not a new flock of parents." What they do need, he said, is to be taught the "lesson of freedom and friendship" by adults who are willing to treat children as their equals. Dell maintained that society's failings could be traced to an educational model that "presents our participation in adult life as meaningless toil performed at the bidding of another under coercion." He believed children must learn that "work can be play ... [and] adult life can be a game like the games of children, only with more desperate and magnificent issues."[26]

Anticipating cultural critics like Paul Goodman—who in 1960 would tell a budding New Left that "growing up" had become "absurd" in a society that provided few opportunities for meaningful work—Dell argued that growing up should not mean trading the vitality of childhood for the drudgery that was daily life for most adults. As Dell put it, "[T]he object of a genuine democratic education is to enable [the child] to remain always a child."[27] The goal was to grow up while still maintaining the spirit of childhood. Thus, childhood play—and the imagination, artistry, and creativity inherent in it—represented for Dell and for other Lyrical Leftists perhaps the most fundamental aspect of education.

Liberation through Imagination

"All power to the imagination" was a slogan of 1960s French student radicals that was adopted by the New Left in the United States, but it was equally applicable to members of the Lyrical Left. And although resonances between the Lyrical Left and the radicals of the 1960s may seem more obvious, echoes of the Lyrical Left's imaginative vision can also be found in the work of Old Left authors and illustrators, such as Crockett Johnson, Ruth Krauss, P. D. Eastman, Syd Hoff, Leo Lionni, Lilian Moore, and William Steig. The radicals of successive generations who embraced this vision wished to preserve rather than tame the child's "uncivilized" impulses, and they sought to raise questions—even in an ostensibly playful manner—about the deeply held values of civilization itself. Writers and artists working in the 1920s such as Alfred Kreymborg, Carl Sandburg, and Wanda Gág appealed to children's imaginations and their desire for free expression while implicitly—and sometimes explicitly—critiquing the social order. Their work and their lives would inspire a later generation of politically committed authors who recognized the radical potential of a free-thinking young person.

In a survey of American children's literature through 1922, Gillian Avery argued that Carl Sandburg's *Rootabaga Stories*, published that year, "launched America's own golden age, in which it was accepted that literary worth should be the criterion in what was written for children and that pleasure was as important as moral profit." The stories are informed as much by Sandburg's socialist politics as by his distinctive literary sensibilities. While they are not self-evidently "protest poems" in the manner of the poetry in *Smoke and Steel* and other works by Sandburg, throughout these tales one finds the same spirit that inspired Sandburg to work for socialism, to write poetry, and to raise children (whom Sandburg called "the anarchs of language and speech"). Sandburg's biographer Penelope Niven claims that Sandburg's socialism was "personal, instinctive, and eclectic . . . more than a formal theoretical philosophy." However, this open-ended approach did not diminish Sandburg's commitment to the cause: he campaigned for Eugene Debs when he ran for president on a Socialist Party ticket in 1908; he worked briefly as a private secretary to the socialist mayor of Milwaukee; and he wrote and edited for numerous socialist publications before becoming a labor editor for the *Chicago Daily News* and then making a living as a writer.[28]

The *Rootabaga Stories* (1922) and *Rootabaga Pigeons*, which followed a year later, take place amid an imagined midwestern landscape that might be read as a rural counterpart to the urban Funnybone Alley. Although Sandburg was separated by geography from the primary Lyrical Left milieu of New York City, he shared many ideals with Village radicals, and he was convinced that he "would have fitted in Greenwich Village."[29] Thus it is worth reading the *Rootabaga Stories* as a document of the Lyrical Left, paying special attention to the ways in which Sandburg represents and imagines children as subjects of and witnesses to the possible worlds he envisions.

In the collection's opening story, "How They Broke Away to Go to the Rootabaga Country," a father, Gimme the Ax, who lives in a house "where everything is the same as it always was," decides "to let his children name themselves" with the first words they speak. The boy is thus named Please Gimme, the girl named Ax Me No Questions. Tiring of the land "where everything is the same as it always was," the father and two children trade in all of their earthly possessions ("pigs, pastures, pepper pickers, pitch forks, everything except their ragbags and a few extras") and go to the railroad station. "Do you wish a ticket to go away and come back or do you wish a ticket to go away and never come back?" the ticket agent asks them, to which Gimme the Ax replies: "We wish a ticket to ride where the railroad tracks run off into the sky and never come back— send us as far as the railroad rails go and then forty ways farther yet."[30] After days of traveling, the family finally lands in the Village of Liver and Onions, in Rootabaga Country, where the other stories—"About the Deep Doom of Dark Doorways," "About the Ways the Wind Went Winding," "About Corn Fairies, Blue Foxes, Flongboos and Happenings That Happened in the United States and Canada"—unfold.

Rootabaga Country is a mostly rural landscape with gophers, jack rabbits, nail-eating rats, and boys with "secret ambitions." It is a land where Henry Haddlyhoagly will walk for miles in the icy winter night to play the guitar with his mittens on for Susan Slackentwist, and where "limber prairie girls" hum "little humpty dumpty songs" by the light of the moon.[31] It is a nowhere land of irreverent nonsense but also somehow familiar and very American; it is at once nostalgic and utopian, backward-looking and future-oriented. It simultaneously embodies an anarchic sensibility and a clearly socialist vision. In one "dippy little town," boomers and sooners used to sing songs and make jokes and dig each other's post holes and fetch water for one another and give one another gifts, until suddenly, when the "pigs, pigs, pigs, and more pigs" came, they began to make wars. There was a war to decide "whether the pigs should be painted checks or stripes" and then one over "whether peach pickers must pick peaches on Tuesday mornings or on Saturday afternoons" and then a long war over "whether telegraph pole climbers must eat onions at noon with spoons, or whether dishwashers must keep their money in pig's [sic] ears with padlocks pinched on with pincers." In this way, the town became embattled, friends became enemies (calling each other "pie face mutts, bums, big bums, big greasy bums, dummies, mummies, rummies, [and] sneezicks"), and soon no one was left.[32] In this way, we see the ridiculousness of war.

But if this story posits a socialist utopia in the past before the corrupting effects of modernity, Sandburg can also imagine a thoroughly modern utopia in which technology really does bring progress. In a story about two skyscrapers in the Village of Liver and Onions, Sandburg articulates the socialist ideal of harnessing the power of technology for human good, a vision that here is also linked to feminism and children's liberation. When these iconic edifices of modern commerce decide to have a child, they tell each other, "[I]t must be a free child. . . . It must not be a child standing still all its life on a street corner. Yes, if we have a child she must be free to run across the prairie, to the mountains, to the sea. Yes, it must be a free child."[33]

The daughter who comes to them is the Golden Spike Limited, "the fastest long distance train in the Rootabaga Country." They were glad to have a child who was "strong" and "lovely" and "useful," and "they were glad, the two skyscrapers were, glad to have a free child running away from the big city, far away to the mountains, far away to the sea, running as far as the farthest mountains and sea coasts touched by the Northwest Wind." Their young Golden Spike is like the mythic Atalanta, who can outrun her male peers and who was celebrated in the 1970s film, book, and record *Free to Be You and Me*. This sleek, powerful railroad train evokes a modern, young "new woman" who rejects traditional gender expectations and revels in a world of limitless possibility.[34]

Like *Funnybone Alley*, Sandburg's *Rootabaga Stories* are as much for adults as for children.[35] The stories speak both to an imagined child reader and to an adult fantasy of the child's liberated imagination. Sandburg acknowledged this dual purpose to New York public librarian Anne Carroll Moore, who could appreciate the stories for their poetic whimsy even if she was, apparently, somewhat confused about their intended audience:

> Some of the Rootabaga Stories were not written at all with the idea of reading to children or telling. They were attempts to catch fantasy, accents, pulses, eye flashes, inconceivably rapid and perfect gestures, sudden pantomimic moments, drawls and drolleries, gazings and musings—authoritative poetic instants—knowing that if the whirr of them were caught quickly and simply enough in words the result would be a child lore interesting to child and grownup.[36]

In combining the "chick chick-a-chick, chick-a-chick, chick-a-chick" of the train into Rootabaga Country with the subversive pleasures of nonsense and a Whitmanesque romance of landscape, Sandburg spoke to something that went beyond the categories of the imaginative or the real, the child or the adult. In a most playful fashion, Sandburg acts as both "the artist" and, quite subtly, "the agitator," two qualities Sandburg attributed to his friend and hero Eugene Debs. In later work, Sandburg would continue to celebrate a landscape of prairies and skyscrapers, of tough girls and big-shouldered men. His poetic, rooted, and socially conscious vision would powerfully influence the sensibility of other writers, including Langston Hughes, Meridel Le Sueur, and Milton Meltzer, all of whom were drawn toward both radical politics and children's literature as vehicles for their views.[37] And Sandburg's three-volume portrait of Abraham Lincoln, published in installments beginning in 1926, was perhaps the single key work that helped to establish Abraham Lincoln as a people's hero and an icon of the Left.

Radical politics and children's literature would likewise attract Wanda Gág, winner of two Newbery and two Caldecott honors and author of one of the most popular children's books of all time, *Millions of Cats*. Like a number of other artists—among them Peggy Bacon, Crockett Johnson, Lynd Ward, James Daugherty, Syd Hoff, and Elizabeth Olds (with whom Gág attended art school in St. Paul)—Gág moved from producing socially conscious art to creating picture books for children. In Gág's case, the two were clearly connected, and, indeed, her career as a writer and illustrator of children's books owed much to her leftist associations.

Gág, whose immigrant father had a failed career as an artist, grew up in a Bohemian community in New Ulm, Minnesota, and came from a family of freethinkers. She attended art school in St. Paul, where she got involved with the John Ruskin Club, whose members "debated the merits of abstract art, the artist's social responsibilities, religion, women's suffrage, realist literature, and political philosophy." Her close friendship in Minnesota with the radical artist Adolf Dehn primed Gág to join the Lyrical Left milieu in New York, where she moved for a fellowship with the Art Students League. In Greenwich Village, she got to know members of the *Masses* crowd, among them Art Young, Floyd Dell, and Robert Minor. She began to create prints and drawings that explored, according to historian Richard Cox, themes of "alienation from one's own culture and disorientation within a de-personalized urban, technological, society."[38] Her works were published in radical journals like the *Masses*, the *Liberator*, and the *New Masses*.

Although Gág herself had no children, she partly raised her brothers and sisters, and she taught in a progressive one-room school in which each child was given "freedom and responsibility in their studies." Cox says that Gág "believed that children were blessed with forthrightness and innate good sense and need not be shielded from reality." Even so, she also would defend fairy tales and the imaginative realm more generally, agreeing with writers who saw the need to "lead children beyond the limited circle of their lives." Unlike Anne Carroll Moore, who promoted imaginative literature as a haven for a protected childhood world (and who gave high praises to Gág's work), Gág was less interested in protecting children from the real world than she was in encouraging children's capacity to imagine a different world.[39] Her interest in and concern for children was part of her larger concern for the powerless.

In the late 1920s, Gág's pictures in the *New Masses* would attract the attention of Coward McCann's new juvenile editor, Ernestine Evans, herself something of a radical. Evans had worked as a news correspondent in the Soviet Union and maintained a strong interest in that country's ambitious plans to build socialism and to create a literature for children that would support socialist goals.[40] Thus it is not a coincidence that Evans helped to launch Gág's career as a writer for children. After attending an exhibit of Gág's drawings in 1928, Evans agreed to publish *Millions of Cats*. The book sold more than 10,000 copies in its first months, and it has remained in print ever since.[41]

Millions of Cats subtly communicates some of the social messages that Gág brought to her more explicitly political art. A landmark book in its closely coordinated text and illustrations—Evans called it "a marriage of picture and tale that is perfectly balanced"—*Millions of Cats* tells a very disturbing story about the barrenness of bourgeois living, greed, competition, environmental degradation, and senseless violence.[42] But the story's rhythmic language, hand lettering, and soft, almost cuddly pictures of rolling hills, fluffy clouds, and, of course, all those cats lend a seemingly innocent playfulness to the story, making it appeal primarily to the senses rather than to the conscience.

In the story, a very old man sets off into the hills to find "a sweet little fluffy cat" for his wife, who was "so very lonely" despite their nice clean house with "flowers all around it." After walking for "a long, long time" over the hills and through the valleys, the man comes to gaze upon a hillside, where he sees a sight beyond his wildest dreams:

Cats here, cats there
Cats and kittens everywhere,
Hundreds of cats,
Thousands of cats,
Millions and billions and trillions of cats.

The picture accompanying this text shows several cats in the immediate foreground displaying evidence of their individuality: one, large and grinning, dances for the old man like a Jazz Age hip cat; another rubs up against the old man's leg; and a rather fat cat, off to the side, stands upright in a halo of light, surrounded by kittens, staring at the old man. In the background, toward which the old man gazes in awe, an enormous crowd of anonymous cats blends into the hillside, giving the scene the appearance of a political rally or a strange religious revival. Cats, known for their willful individuality, here meld into an overwhelming mass (see figure 1.1). But the man is dazzled, unaware of the ominous nature of his encounter.

Thrilled with his luck at finding so many cats, the old man assumes he now has only to choose "the prettiest cat," but each one he sees strikes his fancy, and of each new cat he finds himself proclaiming, "I simply must take it!" And so, "before he knew it, he had chosen them all." In Gág's illustrations, we see the man proceeding across the hills, literally herding an endless procession of cats. The trouble that lies ahead quickly becomes apparent: when the old man and the cats come to a pond, the cats declare they are thirsty. Although there seems to be "a great deal of water," after "each cat took a sip . . . the pond was gone." Likewise, when they become hungry, the cats eat every blade of grass on the hills.

When the old man proudly arrives home with his feline entourage, his wife points out that the couple cannot possibly feed all these cats. "I never thought of that," the old man responds innocently. "What shall we do?" She suggests that they let the cats decide which one the couple should keep, so the old man

Figure 1.1. Illustration by Wanda Gág from *Millions of Cats*. The very old man is awed by the image of so many cats. Gág contributed work to the *New Masses* before launching her career in children's literature. Copyright 1928 by Wanda Gág, renewed 1956 by Robert Janssen. Used by permission of Coward-McCann, a division of Penguin Young Readers Group, a Member of Penguin Group (USA) Inc., 345 Hudson Street, New York, NY 10014. All rights reserved.

calls out and asks the cats which one of them is "the prettiest." The question inspires a ferocious quarrel, "for each cat thought itself the prettiest." Eventually the cats destroy one another, all but a "thin and scraggly" kitten, "a very homely little cat" who, knowing he certainly wasn't the prettiest, had not attempted to compete with the other cats. The "homely little cat" who "nobody bothered with" turns out to be, for the very old man and the very old woman, "the most beautiful cat in the whole world," more beautiful, that is, than the vain cats, the competitive cats, the violent cats, and the fat cats. The story ends with the little kitten, grown pretty and healthy, playing with the old woman's ball of yarn. But the happy ending is betrayed by the carnage that has come before it and, in a sense, makes the story's moral message not only more palatable but also less self-evident and more ambiguous.

The plain little kitten who was not interested in fighting was a typical Gág hero. Fellow artist and radical Lynd Ward noted of Gág in 1947, shortly after her death, "[D]espite the great success that her books brought her, her spiritual home was always among those . . . who were pushed around by circumstance and less than well treated by a world that in our lifetime has too often seemed patterned more for the strong and ruthless."[43] Like Kreymborg, Gág participated in the juvenile session of the 1941 Writers Congress of the antifascist League of American Writers, and her children's books would consistently be recommended by the Communist *New Masses*.

Here and Now: Liberation through Knowledge

While Kreymborg, Sandburg, and Gág highlighted the child's imagination in reaction to the numbing effects of modern civilization, many progressive educators responded in the opposite way, celebrating children's creativity but emphasizing everyday experiences and the richness of the world around them. Unlike traditional education, which, radicals believed, taught children to be obedient cogs in a machine, progressive educators focused on giving children the tools to understand and control their environment. As Dell put it:

> In the school-workshops of capitalism the child is taught how to work for somebody else, how to conduct mechanical operations in an industrial process over which he has no control; in the democratic workshops of the school he learns to use those processes to serve his own creative wishes. In the one he is taught to be a wage-slave—and bear in mind that this refers to the children of the poor—for the rich have their own private schools for their own children. In the other, the child learns to be a free man.[44]

Lucy Sprague Mitchell was probably most responsible for applying the principles of progressive education to children's reading. She had an enormous influence on the development of juvenile literature in general and on writers in the Communist milieu more specifically. Mitchell's here-and-now philosophy and books were widely appreciated and adapted, and many writers, including committed leftists, were trained by her.

Dewey's emphasis on process and on teaching children to understand the relationships within and among social, ecological, and physical elements would translate fairly directly into Lucy Sprague Mitchell's own pedagogical philosophy, out of which her writings, as well as her writing instruction, grew. The other major influence on Mitchell was the radical educator Carolyn Pratt, who aimed to put into practice a revolutionary ideal of education in which children would be liberated in the classroom and thus inspired to change the world outside. Pratt imagined a school that would give children room for the freest possible expression, and she regarded the community around the school as a laboratory for children to accumulate experiences and learn "the facts of 'industrial and distributive processes.'" Like Pratt, Mitchell believed that this knowledge could changes ways of thinking and being in the world and ultimately transform the "industrial system of which we so disapprove."[45]

Like Gág and Kreymborg, Mitchell was close to the *Masses* crowd. She was sympathetic to Marxism and highly critical of capitalism; she was interested in Freud and psychoanalysis; and, like Pratt, she was committed to breaking down traditional gender roles, using the classroom as a model for the larger society. And she, like many educators, was strongly interested in the "Soviet experiment." Still, she did not formally join any political organization, and "she believed in the power of education, rather than political revolution, to end exploitation." Although not as radical as Pratt, it was Mitchell who "would ultimately propel Pratt's theories about socialist education into the progressive mainstream."[46]

After working at Pratt's Play School in Greenwich Village and at a number of other progressive schools and helping to organize the Bureau of Educational Experiments, which conducted research, sponsored programs, and acted as a clearinghouse for progressive schools, Mitchell eventually founded a cooperative school for experimental teachers. This school, which became the Bank Street College of Education, trained teachers in progressive educational theory and practice. In Mitchell's view of things, "social education" was one of the most important aspects of her teacher-training program. A teacher "must care," she said, "both about children and the world. He must have convictions. He must have a definite approach to life situations which include what he wishes children to become and what he wishes the world to become." Mitchell insisted that a teacher must "take on some of the problems of his generation," ranging from "situations in his home town," to "national policies, conflicts in the world of industry, or international and global relations." Internships for students at Mitchell's school with groups like the radical League for Industrial Democracy strengthened links between progressive educators and the organized Left. Mitchell also founded the Writers' Laboratory, which taught writers to produce children's books that would serve the goals of progressive education. Margaret Wise Brown, author of *Goodnight Moon* (1947) and *The Runaway Bunny* (1942), was among those who studied there, along with leftist authors whose works were popular in the 1940s, 1950s, and 1960s, among them Helen Kay, Ruth Krauss, Eve Merriam, Nina Schneider, and Lilian Moore, all of whom would become Loose Enders.[47]

Mitchell is, somewhat unfairly, remembered as a rather strident opponent of fairy tales for young children, a position that made her a controversial figure among librarians and other proponents of imaginative literature. Challenging the idea that fairy tales were important for cultivating the child's imagination, Mitchell argued that the genre tends to confuse young children "because it does not deal with the things with which they have had first-hand experience and does not attempt to present or interpret the world according to the relationships the child himself employs." Mitchell believed that once a child was oriented in the physical world, say at six or seven, "fairy lore" could be a great gift to her imagination, and she acknowledged that "fairy stories cannot be lumped together and rejected *en masse*." However, she did believe that "brutal tales like Red Riding Hood" and "sentimental ones like Cinderella" were inappropriate for all children. Mitchell insisted that what a child needed to cultivate her imagination was room for free expression: "it is only the jaded adult mind, afraid to trust the children's own fresh springs of imagination, that feels for children the need of the stimulus of magic."[48]

Mitchell believed that stories should "further the growth of the sense of reality" and help the child to interpret relationships in the world around him, helping him to "develop a scientific process of thinking." In 1921, she put together her first *Here and Now Story Book*, aimed at two- to seven-year-olds, by adapting actual stories from children with whom she worked. What began as an experiment became a kind of gospel. As Mitchell would note in the foreword to *Another Here and Now Story Book*, published in 1937, "In 1921 stories for young children about their familiar everyday environment were regarded by us and by others as experiments. Now every new list of children's books shows a larger and larger proportion of this type."[49]

The original *Here and Now Story Book* went through twenty-four printings and was translated into several languages, becoming especially popular in the Soviet Union, where educators found much to praise in the stories' emphasis on concrete experience and the relationships among human beings, industrial processes, and the built environment. Mitchell followed this with *The Here and Now Primer: Home from the Country* (1924) and *Another Here and Now Story Book* (1937).[50] She wrote a number of other books, including *The Taxi That Hurried* and *A Year in the City*, stories that were part of the *Bank Street* series of Little Golden Books, which Mitchell helped to supervise and which were widely praised for their educational value as well as their affordability.

The most successful of the *Here and Now* stories connected the child, as one reviewer noted, to "the processes by which the things he needs are produced." The playfulness of language, mimicking children's own verbal utterances, the attention to simple details, and the emphasis upon mechanical relationships and the child's embeddedness in an industrial society distinguished Mitchell's stories from much of the existing "informational literature" for children, "of which very little," Mitchell contended, "is worthy of the name." The stories' vivid depictions of children's everyday surroundings and experiences made them models for writers for years to come.[51]

Like Kreymborg, Mitchell tended to focus on the modern city, but rather than portraying children's imagined worlds, she excelled at showing the drama of the actual urban landscape, with all of its sounds, sights, and smells. This is evident in "The City!" from Mitchell's *Here and Now Primer*:

> The city! Hear it!
>> Rattle clatter rattle, wagon!
>> Rumble grumble rumble, truck!
>> Patter patter, pitter patter,
>> Hear the many city feet.
> The city! Smell it!
>> Smoking, smoking, smoking chimneys.
>> Whiff! A breeze from off the bay.
>> Smell the autos, smell the stables.
>> Smell the busy city streets.[52]

Several stories about a boy called Boris in the original *Here and Now Story Book* use the fresh perspective of a young immigrant to defamiliarize the city, thus highlighting its energy and intricacy and pointing to the presence of immigrants in urban America:

> In [Russia] he had never seen a city, never seen wharves with ocean steamers and ferry boats and tug boats and barges—never even seen a street so crowded you could hardly get through, had never seen great high buildings reaching up, up, up to the clouds. . . . And he had never heard a city, never heard the noise of elevated trains and surface cars and automobiles and the many, many hurrying feet.[53]

Though particularly attuned to the sensory experiences of the modern city, Mitchell also believed that the actual mechanics of industrial production were fascinating to children. Demystifying these processes of production could give young people a sense of connection to the labor that produced the consumer goods they used in daily life. "The Children's New Dresses," for instance, describes the process of a storekeeper getting dresses from a factory, the factory owner getting cloth from the weaving mill, and the weaver getting cotton from the cotton plantation.[54]

Mitchell's attention to the sounds, sights, and operation of machinery in the modern city inspired many books about machinery and industrial processes. Such books, which became a fixture of publishers' lists and popular classroom tools, explained the mechanics of how derricks work, how steam functions as a power source, and how water moves from an underground aquifer to your kitchen sink. Many of these stories tended to glorify industrial labor, as in *Mike Mulligan and His Steam Shovel* (1939), a story that melds an imaginative and an industrial sensibility, reminding us that it was Mike Mulligan and his steam shovel, Mary Ann, "and some others" who built the canals for ships to go through, who dug the tunnels for trains to pass through, who made the roads for cars to drive on, and who built the foundations for the great skyscrapers.[55]

Illustrations in books like *Diggers and Builders* (1931), *How the Derrick Works* (1930), and *A Steam Shovel for Me!* (1933) display the strength and skill of manual laborers in ways evocative of early 1930s proletarian art and Soviet constructivism, and they highlight the work of racial or ethnic minorities (*Steam Shovel for Me!* shows African-American and white workers together, and *Diggers and Builders* features ethnic workers such as Tony the Steam Shovel Man and Pedro the Road Builder). The industrial aesthetic in books such as these are also suggestive of the labor of cultural production and the affinity that cultural producers would come to feel with manual laborers (see figure 1.2).

The *Here and Now* stories provoked intense reaction, in part because of their profound impact upon children's literature. Educators, on the whole, were thrilled with the stories, citing the great value of books describing city life and familiar elements of the child's world. Lyrical Leftists were excited as well: Floyd Dell, for instance, insisted that Mitchell's *Here and Now Story Book* "contains the best stories for young children that I have ever seen." But skeptics included not only those like Anne Carroll Moore, who wished to shield children from the real world for more or less conservative reasons, but also defenders, as Kreymborg put it, of "children's capacity to dream." He declared that the popularity of the *Here and Now* books, or books on "the social sciences," "smacks of standardization and regimentation under a commercial oligarchy." He feared that this "practical and humorless" trend in literature (and toys) for children was designed to help "twist our children into little businessmen."[56]

Yet much of this literature, or perhaps most of it, was written not to reproduce social and economic hierarchies but to create a basis for challenging them. Gág, for her part, saw the value of books about modern science and industry, acknowledging in 1939 that "children are fascinated by stories concerning the modern miracles of science." Even so, she insisted that "modern children" also need "fairy lore," because "their lives are already over-balanced on the side of steel and stone and machinery—and nowadays, one might well add, bombs, gas-masks and machine guns."[57]

In actuality, Kreymborg and Mitchell (and Sandburg and Gág) shared many of the same concerns about contemporary society and its effects upon children. Moreover, the line between fanciful and factual stories was actually less clear

Figure 1.2. Illustration by Romano from *A Steam Shovel for Me!* by Vera Edelstadt. The images of muscular workers communicate a proletarian aesthetic, and the girders and skyscrapers draw upon the Soviet avant-garde style of constructivism, which visually corresponded to the idea of building a new world. This picture shows the visual conventions of the production book, but it is also a reminder of the labor of cultural production and the child audience for that labor. New York: Stokes, 1933.

than Mitchell's condemnation of the fairy tale and Kreymborg's lament about "the decline of Mother Goose" would have us believe. Many factual books display the same desire to fuel children's imaginations that motivated the fanciful writers of Mitchell's day. In fact, Mitchell's own *Here and Now* stories are often imaginative to the point of abandoning realism altogether. Like Mike Mulligan's steam shovel, Mary Ann (as drawn by Virginia Burton), many of Mitchell's stories use anthropomorphism—animals, water, trains, and other objects display consciousness—in a way that, by Mitchell's own logic, would tend to confuse young children. The point is that her notion of realism still encompassed a view of childhood that depended upon children's ability to imagine possibilities beyond the everyday.

In general, both the imaginative fantasy of Carl Sandburg's *Rootabaga Stories* and the everydayness of Mitchell's tales shared a utopian desire for children to transcend the alienated drudgery of modern industrial life. All of these books tend to show working people in control of their lives and taking pride in what they do. The influence of Mitchell and other progressive educators on, for instance, Alfred Kreymborg, is evident both in Lonesome Sam's fascination with the world around him (especially sounds) and in *Funnybone Alley*'s cooperative, child-centered school. Reviewers praised *Funnybone Alley* both for its "charming world of imagination" and because it should "stimulate a new interest in skyscrapers, city lamp-posts, in streets and parks, in sandwich men and brokers in silk hats and other personages and familiar sights of the Here and Now."[58] The authors of *Funnybone Alley* and the *Here and Now Story Book*, of *Millions of Cats* and *How the Derrick Works* hoped both to set children free and to ground them in the everyday, to educate them and to liberate them.

"Educating for Peace": Internationalism, Racism, and Limits to the Progressive Vision

Part of teaching children about the here and now also entailed an education in what would now be called "cultural diversity." An emphasis on "cultural gifts" in children's literature of the 1920s reflected the dawning of new attitudes about racial and ethnic traits (as cultural rather than biological) and about prejudice (as something learned rather than innate). This new sensitivity on matters of race, ethnicity, and religion had an important influence on American leftists, particularly with the rise of fascism and its doctrines of racial purity, in the 1930s. However, the inability of progressive educators to recognize and overcome their own racial biases ultimately limited the extent to which their work would serve as a usable past for members of the Popular Front Left.

Progressive educators' belief that schools should tackle real social problems and provide a laboratory for social change helped to put "intercultural understanding" at the top of educators' agendas beginning in the mid-1920s. Race riots, the increasing prominence of the Ku Klux Klan, a wave of lynchings, new immigration restrictions, and the targeting of "foreign agitators" by the American Legion and other right-wing groups spawned a countermovement among educators to highlight the cultural gifts of racial and ethnic minorities.[59] Influenced by the insights of anthropologists and psychologists into the culturally conditioned aspects of racial prejudice, the movement built upon progressive traditions—especially marked in the settlement house movement from the turn of the century—of celebrating the distinctive cultural contributions of the nation's immigrant groups.

However, cultural-gifts proponents' optimism about the extent to which ethnic, racial, religious, and even class conflicts could be resolved simply through education was tarred by reformers' own limitations. As historian Diana Selig notes, many of these advocates held simplistic understandings of group identity, and their approach encouraged a focus upon transforming "individual outlook" rather than upon getting at the structural roots of prejudice.[60] These educators and authors were, of course, themselves influenced by the prevailing prejudices of their day. In particular, racism against African Americans was so entrenched in the 1920s and early 1930s that many well-intentioned educators and authors found themselves perpetuating harmful stereotypes; indeed, the nonstereotyped portrait of African Americans was exceptional during this period. Even works by socialists were so often tarred by racism that a key feature distinguishing later works produced by members of the Communist Left from that of their forebears was a conscious (if still often problematic) antiracism.

At least two dozen of the Newbery Medal and Honor books published between 1922 and 1940 concerned children in other lands (e.g., South America, Poland, Portugal, England, Italy, France, Japan, Switzerland, China, Scandinavia, Africa, the South Seas, Bulgaria, Albania, India, Hungary, Ireland, and Greece) or minority characters in the United States, such as American Indians and Alaskan "Eskimos." Other books, like Annie E. S. Beard's *Our Foreign Born Citizens*, which contained biographical sketches of distinguished immigrants, including Andrew Carnegie, Louis Agassiz, Mary Antin, and Samuel Gompers, were self-consciously geared toward the Americanization of foreigners and breaking down anti-immigrant sentiment among native-born Americans.[61]

Despite all of this attention to diversity, only one of the Newbery Honor books (and none of the actual medal winners) published during this period focused on African Americans. This book, Hildegarde Hoyt Swift's *Railroad to Freedom: A Story of the Civil War* (1932)—a fictionalized account of Harriet Tubman's life—showed limitations characteristic of its times, despite its sympathetic intent. Nowhere is this more evident than in Swift's self-consciously antiracist author's note at the end of the book, in which she notes that "the words 'pickaninny'—'nigger'—'kinky'—'darkie' and all similar words *are nowhere used in this book as expressive of the viewpoint of the author*" but simply for "realism" as "they would have been used by the different kinds of people whom this book concerns." One might read Swift's note as a weak attempt to assuage liberal guilt for indulging in the stereotypes she claims to be challenging. Swift also uses dialect, as was common practice. The book ends with Tubman expressing incredible sadness and remorse when visiting her dying former mistress and belatedly appreciating qualities of the mistress's late son, "Marse George," who in life had been consistently cruel and merciless toward Tubman. Such remarkably conciliatory scenes betray the author's compromised position as a liberal attempting to condemn the past injustices of slavery without offending contemporary white southern readers.[62]

Other than Swift's book, the general absence of African-American protagonists in the Newbery Award and Honor books was perhaps preferable to negative characterizations, but strikingly negative portraits of African Americans were the norm in children's books prior to the 1940s. This was so common as to escape comment, other than in the Communist press.[63] Indeed, a 1931 discussion in *Progressive Education* of "books for boys and girls," which praised a number of books about children in other lands (including the Soviet Union), recommended several books that to today's eye are strikingly racist, including *The Pickaninny Twins* by Lucy Fitch Perkins and *Miss Jimmy Deane* by Rose B. Knox, described by the reviewer as "another pleasant story of Southern plantation life eighty years ago." Along with these two books, the reviewer also recommended the sensitive and sympathetic story by the white socialist and activist for the National Association for the Advancement of Colored People Mary White Ovington, *Zeke*, which concerned a boy studying at Tolliver (Tuskegee) Institute.[64] It may be that all of these books were deemed praiseworthy by progressive educators because they seemed to convey, in accessible terms, the everyday life of Americans in various cultures and times to the imagined reader—presumably a northern, urban, white child. No matter that the two former books described a "reality" that was more a segregationist's fantasy than actual truth; in the 1920s and early 1930s, that fantasy was the common wisdom.

Considering Perkins's and Knox's books as texts praised by educators because of their cultural sensitivity is revealing, and Perkins's *Pickaninny Twins* is a particularly interesting example. Perkins began writing her *Twins* series of books (twenty-six books in all) beginning in 1911, as a conscious effort to foster "mutual respect and understanding between people of different nationalities." The series included *The Dutch Twins* (1911), *The Eskimo Twins* (1914), *The Japanese Twins* (1912), and so on, continuing until 1935. In this spirit, the *Pickaninny Twins* ends with an afterword to teachers in which Perkins notes:

> Children in the third and fourth grades have studied and become familiar, in part, with the life of children of our own and other lands . . . but little has been written in books to acquaint them with the life and play of the children of Negroes, living in our own country, who have a history and culture of their own. The reading of this story will help all children to a broader understanding of the Negro.

She suggests that schoolchildren try "making and dressing Negro dolls" or "making a miniature cotton plantation" to further lessons from the book. This liberal attempt at cultural appreciation seems to assume that the southern cotton plantation is the natural locale for African Americans, that black children all speak in dialect, and that all black mothers wear kerchiefs on their heads, look like Aunt Jemimah, and are tough but loving. Moreover, Swift's note at the end of *Railroad to Freedom* would suggest that the negative connotations of the

word *pickaninny* were well understood by the early 1930s. Books romanticiz-
ing the "old South" like *Miss Jimmy Deane* or *No Surrender* (1932) by Emma
Gelders Sterne, which a reviewer in the *New York Times* praised for having
"caught perfectly the atmosphere of the period," are far more strikingly offensive by today's standards than Perkins's book, and they too seem to have been
perfectly acceptable to most reviewers at the time.[65] Sterne's nostalgic portrait
of loyal slaves and the evils of Reconstruction was a familiar story in the era of
Gone with the Wind.

Lucy Sprague Mitchell herself indulged in the stereotyping of racial and
ethnic minorities, particularly Africans and African Americans, and she generally assumed that her readers were white, urban, and middle class. Although
Carl Sandburg's populist portrait of Abraham Lincoln and his milieu (written
originally in the 1920s but later partially republished in an edition for children)
condemns slavery, it is certainly dehumanizing to Indians. The limits of Mitchell's and Sandburg's visions prove them to be products of the era in which they
wrote: in the 1920s, there were few antiracist models to emulate.[66]

The *Brownies' Book*, a creation of W. E. B. Du Bois for "the children of the
sun," or the children of Africa, was one brief exception. The magazine was published for just two years, from January 1920 through December 1921; according to literary scholar Katharine Capshaw Smith, it was most likely inspired by
the violence of the "red summer" of 1919.[67] An announcement of the magazine
proclaimed that the publication "will be a thing of Joy and Beauty, dealing in
Happiness, Laughter and Emulation, and designed especially for Kiddies Six
to Sixteen. It will seek to teach Universal Love and Brotherhood for all little
folk—black and brown and yellow and white." The humanizing portrait of African Americans in the *Brownies' Book* was unusual and highly significant, but its
audience consisted almost entirely of urban, middle-class, African-American
children whose parents were members of the NAACP. The magazine's articles
and stories tended to highlight outstanding black individuals and to subscribe
to the doctrine of "racial uplift," thus avoiding the realities of life for the many
urban and rural poor African-American children. Langston Hughes, who
began his writing career with the *Brownies' Book*, would insist as late as 1932
that "the need today is for books that Negro parents and teachers can read to
their children without hesitancy as to the psychological effect on the growing
child mind, books whose dark characters are not all clowns, and whose illustrations are not merely caricatures." And, he added, once the books are written,
African-American children, especially those in the South, would need access to
libraries in order to read them.[68]

While only parts of the progressive educational tradition would thus be
useful to Popular Front Leftists—for whom antiracism was a priority—the
impulse among educators and their literary allies to fight prejudice, however

limited, would eventually move cultural sensitivity, including sensitivity toward African Americans, to the forefront of publishers' agendas, especially as the rise of fascism and World War II showed the potentially dire results of overzealous nationalism, racism, and hostility toward foreigners.

From Progressive to Proletarian

Educational historian Lawrence Cremin notes that radicalism flourished in the pedagogical milieu of the 1920s "though in a decidedly minor key." If most schools still supported what Upton Sinclair called the "goose step," new practices and new notions about education's purposes gained a significant following in the 1920s. They were increasingly accepted as the Roaring Twenties gave way to the Great Depression, placing strains upon the nation's underfunded schools and convincing a significant number of educators that schools should not only provide children with tools for solving social problems, but should actively work to change the social order.[69] Even children's librarians, traditionally more concerned with protecting children's virtues than fostering their critical outlook, began to use some of the radical rhetoric commonly voiced by intellectuals during the depression. As one librarian put it in 1932, "In their own proper capacity as molders of thought, librarians are in a position to give a tremendous forward impulse to the enlarged understanding of economic and social problems and of international relations on which today's children may build their participation in adult affairs a few years hence."[70]

For the most part, trade publishers did not immediately realize the market potential of what came to be called the "problem book," or a book dealing with real-world issues. However, as the next chapter explores, the literal proletarianization of many children under the conditions of the depression helped to inspire a body of literature whose politics were explicit rather than implicit, a literature designed not simply to enlighten children and set their spirits free, but to radicalize them. Although limited in their audience, these texts not only mark the initial entry of the Old Left into the children's literature field, they also reveal the explicitly political possibilities of the here-and-now, or production, book as well as the fairy tale. Perhaps most significantly, they link an antiracist tradition of children's literature to the priorities of the Communist Left.

2

"For Young Revolutionists"

Children's Literature and the Communist Milieu, 1925–1935

> Interesting literature which is now skillfully used only by the
> bourgeoisie must be replaced by cheap but good revolution-
> ary literature.
> —Young Communist League,
> *The Road to Mass Organization of Proletarian Children*

Helen Kay's *Battle in the Barnyard: Stories and Pictures for Workers' Children* (1932) was the first American-authored book for children published by
a Communist press. Envisioned as fare for the "proletarian child," the book
was inspired by the German *Fairy Tales for Workers' Children* (1925) and was
intended for use by the Young Pioneers, the principal Communist organization for children in the late 1920s and 1930s.[1] In the title story, a rich rooster
gains control of the henhouse and puts his fellow chickens to work, keeping
them docile and productive through police coercion and a hired preacher who
celebrates the rewards of submission to a higher authority. "As time went on,"
Kay writes:

> the chickens slaved harder and harder and the rooster grew richer
> and richer. They began to believe whatever the preacher chickens told
> them. They thought that conditions must always be as they are. That
> the greater amount of chickens should be poor and that a privileged
> few must live off the wealth that the poor chickens scratched up.

Things go on this way until a "young and energetic cock" begins to think about
their situation. He talks to the other chickens about how they might better their

51

lot, and ultimately he decides the chickens must rebel against the rooster and his aristocracy: "Secret leaflets were printed and spread over the colony for the chickens to read and to learn the truth. Huge mass meetings were called and the exploited chicks were organized into battalions to drive out their oppressors." As the logic of revolution would have it, the rebelling chickens win, killing the rich rooster and his protectors, while the police and the preachers flee from the farm, never to be heard from again ("perhaps the wolves ate them"). The farm is now a happy place; the chickens have all "learned their lesson, and never again will anyone be able to trick them into slavery."[2]

The moral of the story is not too difficult to discern: workers must band together to keep those in power from unjustly acquiring all the fruits of their labors, and they must not be lulled into believing that their oppression is "the natural order of things." Perhaps children would interpret the story literally and think of its lessons only in terms of animals, but there is enough anthro-pomorphism here that Kay's meaning seems fairly transparent. Moreover, the children who were likely to have read this story had parents who would be sure to make its intended meaning clear. Published in a limited print run by a Com-munist press, the sectarian tone and radical content made it highly unlikely that *Battle in the Barnyard* would ever be made available to children through public schools or libraries.[3] But it is safe to say that Kay's *intended* audience was quite small. A *New Masses* review (1935) of several other books "for young revolu-tionists" took evident pride in the fact that such books "will never be picked by a Junior League Guild or awarded a Newberry [sic]." Yet, the reviewer noted, the authors discussed were "certain to win a more satisfactory reward—to be counted among the founders of proletarian children's literature outside of Rus-sia, and probably to be named as inspirers in the reminiscences of the next gen-eration of revolutionary leaders."[4]

In 1934, Marxist literary critic E. A. Schachner defined the "revolutionary" text as "one which consciously supports the movement for the revolutionary destruction of capitalism and [calls] for its substitution by a dictatorship of the proletariat which will, in the course of its own emancipation, abolish all classes." *Battle in the Barnyard* fits this definition in that it explicitly criticizes capital-ism, encourages sympathy with the working class, and urges active resistance to the status quo. But definitions of "revolutionary" and "proletarian" litera-ture were a source of ongoing controversy in the 1930s, and while Schachner's definition is a useful starting point, it is a bit too constrictive for our purposes. The term *proletarian children's literature* can be used to refer rather broadly to texts published in the late 1920s and 1930s, usually by Communist presses, that had working-class or poor children as their primary protagonists (or as the indicated audience) and, in most cases, that explicitly challenged the domi-nant social order.[5] Like the proletarian renaissance in adult literature in the early 1930s, proletarian children's literature was a short-lived genre, appearing in the late 1920s and mostly disappearing with the rise of the Popular Front in 1935. Unlike adult proletarian literature, which was published by mainstream publishers, reviewed in reputable journals, and available in libraries, proletarian children's literature, because of the popular belief that children should be shielded from the political realm and from the harsh realities of society and economics, was published almost exclusively by Communist presses and was distributed primarily through Communist or Communist-affiliated organizations and institutions like the Young Pioneers, the IWO (International Workers Order) Juniors, and left-wing summer camps. Its circulation was so limited that proletarian literature for children escapes comment in nearly every scholarly survey of proletarian literature.[6]

Approximately thirty children's books with explicitly radical messages were published in English and were available in the United States in the 1920s and 1930s (additional books were published in Yiddish, Finnish, and other languages).[7] The majority of these books were originally published in other countries—usually Germany, England, or the Soviet Union—and of the few books originally published in the United States, several were published only in mimeograph form.[8] As the "ABC for Martin" (figure 2.1) from *Martin's Annual* would suggest, this literature tended to be sectarian in tone and was therefore limited in its audience. Thus although several authors in the Communist milieu consciously attempted to create a body of proletarian children's literature in the late 1920s and early 1930s, the Left's real impact on American children's literature came after this period. The primary goal of this chapter is to explore how proletarian children's literature produced in the United States—and, to some extent, its cousins produced in the Soviet Union and Europe—served as a bridge between older leftist traditions and the Popular Front.

With a few notable exceptions, when American Communists began to write literature for children in the early 1930s, they tended to follow their predecessors in Socialist Sunday Schools who wrote highly ideological literature. To the extent that the Socialist or Communist parties directly supported the writing and publication of children's literature, a central aim was to create a body of children's literature uncorrupted by commercial imperatives or public school politics. Despite this aversion to mainstream media and institutions, in the early 1930s Communists did take lessons from more popular literary models, among them those of the Lyrical Left and progressive educators. Even in the CP's most sectarian phase, roughly 1929 to 1934, Communist authors did not write only revolutionary books, and Communist critics did not tend to recommend such books as the sole source of children's literary diet.[9] This suggests that even in its most "revolutionary" phase the Communist Left was, first, not monolithic nor as ideologically rigid as many of its critics would argue, and

A B C
FOR MARTIN

$$A$$ stands for Armaments—
war-mongers' pride;

$$B$$ is for Bolshie,
the thorn in their
side.

$$C$$ stands for Capitalists,
fighting for gold;

$$D$$ for Destruction
they've practised of
old.

Figure 2.1. "ABC for Martin" from *Martin's Annual* by Joan Beauchamp, an example of revolutionary or proletarian children's literature. New York: International, 1935. Used with permission courtesy of International Publishers Co., Inc., New York.

second, that its members were, from the beginning, considerably more open-minded and likely to cooperate with progressive and liberal allies on matters concerning children than in other realms of practice. These attitudes and practices were ultimately critical to the success of Communists and fellow travelers in the children's book field, where their influence continued into and beyond the McCarthy period. Beyond the revolutionary messages and sectarian tone of proletarian children's literature, what most strikingly distinguished American-authored literature in this genre from literature produced by many progressive educators, socialists, and even European Communists (including those in the Soviet Union) was its particular concern with racial justice, which would become even more pronounced among writers in the Communist milieu in later decades.

In the early 1930s, Communists sought to give children a vision of inter-racial, working-class solidarity, a sense of history, and tools for understanding (in Marxist terms) how the world operates. Communist writers endowed their child protagonists with a spirit of independence and autonomy, and they imag-ined their ideal audience of proletarian children in these same terms. Children's literature produced in the American Communist milieu in the early 1930s (and its socialist and Soviet relatives) set significant precedents for later, less-sec-tarian works that would achieve widespread distribution. Moreover, several writers who cut their teeth writing more openly ideological children's literature (Helen Kay among them) went on to join the children's literature mainstream. Most important, this work reveals how the Old Left came to view children's lit-erature as a significant medium for its message.

The Proletarian Child

The same 1930 anthology on "the intimate problems of modern parents and children" that contained Alfred Kreymborg's "The Decline of Mother Goose" included an essay by Mike Gold on "The Proletarian Child." The proletarian, or poor, laboring child was a lightning rod that not only drew Communists into children's literature, but also helped to link the concerns of the Communist Left with many other Americans in the depression years. Gold's dire portrait of poverty-stricken, undernourished working children, forced to leave school in order to help feed their families, may have been somewhat exaggerated to jus-tify Gold's radical political views, but it speaks to a dramatic shift in the public's perception of children and in children's actual lives. Dorthea Lange's haunt-ing photograph of the "migrant mother" and her children, the iconic image of the Great Depression, suggests something of how children became prominent markers of national and individual duress during this period.

The widespread suffering of the depression triggered spontaneous, inde-pendent organizing efforts by non–wage earners—unemployed men, women, and children—who generated "a new awareness of home, family, and neigh-borhood" as political spaces, according to historian Van Gosse. This organiz-ing helped the CP, a small, largely secretive, and basically insignificant orga-nization until the late 1920s, gain in influence as it expanded its focus beyond industrial workers to include the working class in general, including women and children.[10]

The Communist press was quick to play upon a national concern with the suffering of innocent children, especially in the party's drive to recruit women.[11] In the early 1930s, Communist publications frequently called for the improvement of child welfare and condemned child labor; implicit, and often explicit, in this discourse was that the suffering of working-class and poor children was endemic to the capitalist system, in contrast to the "happy children in the Soviet Union."[12] The Soviet example was consistently upheld because Communists believed that the entire system must be changed before the conditions facing children in the United States could be improved.

Given that "the educational problems of the proletarian child are different from those of the child coming from a middle-class environment," Gold maintained that "educational theorists . . . concern themselves with the needs of a favored minority of American youth." Criticizing John Dewey in particular, Gold pointed out that there was nothing intrinsically liberating about a school "organically fitted" to the needs of industrial civilization, particularly when the needs of those controlling civilization diverged so strikingly from those at the bottom. The hopeful optimism of early progressive educators was challenged as the quality of education diminished severely under the strains of the depression. As the Communist press was quick to point out, schools in poor districts and those serving black students were notoriously deficient in staffing, materials, and physical structure, and more than 2,500 schools were closed in the early 1930s due to lack of funds. But many children never even made it into the schools that were open. As of 1930, 18.7 percent of children ages five to seventeen were not enrolled in school, and more than 2 million children between the ages of ten and seventeen, or one out of nine, was gainfully employed.[13]

In a school system supported by a capitalist state, the Communists maintained, children could not have the liberty to think freely. Thus in the years prior to the Popular Front, Communists created special organizations for children, most notably the Young Pioneers, to build class consciousness in the proletarian child. Modeled after the Soviet Young Pioneers, the Pioneer organization in the United States took on its own character. Leaders consciously crafted the program as a radical alternative to the Boy Scouts: the Pioneer motto was "Always Ready," and the uniforms and outdoor activities could be taken as a left-wing rip-off of the Boy Scouts. However, instead of "training children to be soldiers of capitalism" (as per a critic of the Scouts), the Young Pioneers marched in May Day parades and joined picket lines; they organized school strikes for free school lunches or carfare; and they lobbied mayors and city councils for better playgrounds and for relief. They were also urged to "try to win over the adults, especially working-class mothers" and to "struggle in the family against backward ideas (religion, petty bourgeois tendencies)."[14] Most children who became involved in the Pioneer organization came from left-wing families and joined Pioneer troupes with other children who shared their ethnic backgrounds, despite the fact that the Pioneer organization was meant to provide an alternative to ethnic ties and family allegiances, both of which were originally seen as having conservative implications.[15]

Communists viewed the class-conscious proletarian child as intelligent, feisty, committed to social justice, and entitled to know "the truth" about the way the world really worked. A 1934 pamphlet, *Who Are the Young Pioneers?* told children:

> We think most of you have brains and want to use them. We think you know how to think for yourselves, too, in spite of the fact that in the schools and newspapers and movies they try to make you think the way they want you to. We think you should know about serious things and talk about them. And we know you have enough sense to understand them and enough spunk to do something about them.

Understanding "the child" in a new way and forgoing notions of "protection" for an ideal of radical preparation—and activism—Communists also called for a new kind of children's literature that would, in Gold's words, help "the child of a worker . . . grow into the mass spirit that can alone save him from despair in his situation."[16]

Fairy Tales and Five-Year Plans: Socialist, Soviet, and Other Radical Models

For socialists in the early twentieth century, the poor child and the working child represented blighted possibility, imminent social decay, and the basic unworkability of the capitalist system. Socialists drew upon the popular romantic notion of the innocent child as a redeemer of corrupt adulthood, but presented children robbed of their innocence by poverty or "premature toil" as evidence of the need to reform the system as a whole (see figure 2.2). While the image of the suffering child was used to rally adults to action, socialists also addressed children themselves as subjects, viewing them not simply as helpless victims but as natural radicals and the seeds of a great and growing movement.[17] Unlike Communists prior to the Popular Front, who focused their energies on working-class children, socialists worked to nurture this spirit of rebellion in children of all class backgrounds.[18] Also, unlike Communists, they did not believe that children should be activists in their own right. As *The Child's Socialist Reader* (1907) put it, "[W]e look to you to carry the Red Flag forward in your strong, young hands when you reach manhood and womanhood."[19]

Figure 2.2. "Nest of Special Privilege." Drawing by Ryan Walker. While the mother bird feeds her hungry children in their nest, child laborers feed the fat capitalist sitting in the "nest of special privilege." Socialists frequently commented upon the evils of child labor. Cover illustration for *The Coming Nation: A Journal of Things Doing and to Be Done* (July 13, 1912).

Recognizing the power of public schools as well as recently established organizations like the Boy Scouts and Girl Scouts to indoctrinate children with the values of the dominant culture, socialists sought to create alternative institutions that promoted an entirely different set of values.[20] Socialist Sunday Schools—which sometimes cooperated with anarchist Modern Schools—used literature, along with songs, festivals, theatrics, and more or less traditional recitation to teach children to think in a "logical" and "scientific" fashion, to encourage them to question authority, and, most important, to build a feeling of solidarity with an international working class. As socialist educator William F. Kruse put it in 1917, "If we can get our young people to feel these two great principles—reason and comradeship—we need never fear that the masters will be able to hoodwink them."[21]

Although teachers in Socialist Sunday Schools, like teachers in anarchist Modern Schools, tended to argue that they were not out to "indoctrinate" or "propagandize" children, they did, in fact, teach children the basics of socialist doctrine. And even very young children were seen as able to comprehend basic lessons about the class struggle, as is apparent from texts like Nicholas Klein's *Socialist Primer: A Book of First Lessons for the Little Ones in Words of One Syllable* (1908), which had lessons explaining, for instance: "The child is in the shop to make the fat Man rich. Is it good for the child? See the Shirk, who lives on the work made by the poor child." Although a number of texts created for use in Socialist Sunday Schools, including Klein's, were quite didactic, lessons about socialism were more often than not couched in other subjects. The schools also used popular socialist-authored books like Jack London's *Call of the Wild* and *White Fang*, which had more subtle messages about competition and the struggle for survival.[22]

As with later children's literature by Communists, much Socialist Party literature for children emphasized history and science. The *Little Socialist Magazine for Boys and Girls* contained a regular column on the "History of Our Country" and another on scientific themes such as "The Sun and the Stars" and "Gravitation and Inertia," offering basic information about astronomy, gravity, and various aspects of nature (with particular emphasis on evolution), along with moral and economic rationales for science study. As William Gundlach explained to young readers in 1910, "Ignorant people are the best wage slaves, for they know nothing about the rights of human beings, and their hope lies in the fantasy of a happiness hereafter."[23] Communists shared with their Marxian forebears the urge to teach lessons of scientific and historical thinking and the need to question authority. But both groups also recognized the power of imagination.

Though works like Carl Sandburg's *Rootabaga Stories* and Kreymborg's *Funnybone Alley* denaturalized the existing social order, writers addressing children in an explicitly radical context could go even further. Both socialists and Communists in Europe and in the United States employed fairy tales—traditionally used to enforce the values of the dominant social order—to convey moral lessons about the corrupt nature of capitalism and the ideal of cooperation for the common good. The inclusion of the "fairy tale" "Happy Valley" as the opening story in *The Child's Socialist Reader* indicates that socialists were attuned to the potential of this genre to appeal to young people with critical moral and political lessons. In this story, the gallant Fairplay defeats the giant,

Monopoly, and, in so doing, releases Capital, an ugly dwarf, from Monopoly's spell, transforming the dwarf into a beautiful princess, who marries Fairplay so they can together work with and for the people of Happy Valley.[24]

The first stories for children published by the CP in the United States were a translation of German fairy tales by Hermynia Zur Mühlen, one of a number of German Communists who "proletarianized" the classic fairy-tale genre during the Weimar period.[25] Despite the attraction of American Communists to these stories, as materialists—and as followers of Lucy Sprague Mitchell's here-and-now gospel—they felt the need to justify the value of fairy tales to proletarian children, as is apparent from translator Ida Dailes's introduction to the American edition of Zur Mühlen's *Fairy Tales for Workers' Children* (from which *Learning from the Left*'s cover image is taken):

> You have read many fairy tales, some of them very beautiful and some that frightened you with their horrible giants and goblins. But never, I am sure, have you read such lively stories about real everyday things. You see poor people suffering around you every day; some of you have yourselves felt how hard it is to be poor. You know that there are rich people in the world, that they do not work and have all the good things of life. You also know that your fathers work hard and then worry about what will happen if they lose their jobs. Comrade Zur Mühlen, who wrote these fairy tales . . . shows us that the rich people who do not work but keep us enslaved are our enemies; we must join together, we workers of the world, and stop these wrongs.[26]

Dailes emphasizes that these fairy tales are about "real everyday things" and that their lessons are directly relevant to Zur Mühlen's intended audience of working-class children.

In all of the stories in Zur Mühlen's collection, the powerless—a rose bush, a sparrow, little boys, a dog—bemoan their suffering, learn the truth about capitalism, and come to express allegiance with other oppressed peoples and creatures. The final story in the collection, "Why?" concerns a little boy, Paul, who gets punished for always asking questions, especially questions about why all good things seem to go to rich people. All of the people (and the animals) tell him that his questions are silly, and he becomes desolate, until a beautiful dryad living in a birch tree tells him he is not alone in wanting to know these things. She tells him to put his ear down to the earth to listen for other people's questions, and he hears a boy asking why he is hungry, a woman asking why she must work all day for wages that are barely enough to live on, and a man asking why "have the idlers everything and the workers nothing." The dryad tells the boy that when enough voices start asking why, "there will be an end to the misery and poverty and to those lousy parasites." She tells him to keep asking questions and to encourage other poor people to ask questions, until the questions "fall on the structure of injustice like a hammer and smash it."[27]

Fairy tales such as this provided a model for how the content and meanings attached to familiar literary forms could be transformed to radical ends. This is likewise seen in books like *Bows Against the Barons*, a radical version of the Robin Hood tale by the British writer Geoffrey Trease (1934), and in later leftist versions of American folktales. But while Communists appreciated the radical potential of fairy tales, like many progressive educators, they felt a certain uneasiness about them. In an otherwise effusive review of *Fairy Tales for Workers' Children*, which upheld the collection as a model for American writers, Mike Gold criticized the stories for having "a slight atmosphere of slave wistfulness, depression and yearning about them." Gold maintained that "the proletariat must grow away from the mood of Christian slave revolt; it is already doing so in Russia, it must do it elsewhere." Exhorting his fellow radicals to teach practical lessons for an industrial age, Gold insisted that "we must teach proletarian children that they are to be the collective masters of their world, and that the vast machinery of modern life is to be their plaything."[28]

The echoes of Lucy Sprague Mitchell and Floyd Dell, the reference to Russia, and the discussion of proletarian children—all in the same breath—reveal more than the Communist preference for factual literature or, as Gold would put it in 1930, "facts are the new poetry."[29] Gold's comments on Zur Mühlen's book also suggest the way in which Soviet children's literature served as a model for Communists and as an important link between Communists and progressive educators. The Soviet example showed the value and viability of making children's books "socially constructive" but also popular, and here affinities with educators and others controlling the children's literature field would turn out to be crucial.

Red Schoolhouse

American debates over the appropriate form and content of proletarian fiction were significantly influenced by developments in the Soviet Union. Although it is unlikely that they were actually subservient to Soviet cultural policy, in the early 1930s many writers in the Communist milieu consciously crafted their work to conform to principles outlined by Soviet cultural policy makers. In particular, calls in critical organs like the *New Masses* for a literature of fact paralleled the vogue of documentary texts, especially texts by workers, in the era of the Soviet cultural revolution. Soviet children's literature, which was likewise dominated in the 1920s and 1930s by nonfiction, especially the production book—"stories about how things are made," "stories about trades," and books about industrial topics and machines—also served as an important example for American writers in the Communist milieu.[30]

Soviet work in the juvenile field demonstrated the extent to which children's literature could be harnessed at all levels of production and dissemination toward the goal of the "recreating of the individual."[31] Moreover, Soviet authors like the engineer Il'ia Marshak (known to readers as M. Il'in) demonstrated the potentially radical implications of seemingly apolitical production books, which provided step-by-step information about the workings of the world. Finally, although Communists were fairly adamant (prior to the Popular Front) in their rejection of potential progressive and liberal allies in education and publishing, a mutual admiration for certain aspects of the Soviet Union in the early 1930s demonstrated a shared interest, among people of varying political allegiances, in creating "socially constructive" or "significant" children's literature. The Soviet example provided a model for creating books that were cheaply produced, widely available, acceptable to authorities, and popular with children.

While American Communists often used the Soviet Union's example as a foil to emphasize problems in the United States and to point to the government's inadequate response to these problems, Soviet children's literature also made American Communists turn a critical eye on themselves. When asked why American Communists became interested in writing and publishing children's books, Betty Bacon, who initiated a series for children at International Publishers, the Communist Party publishing house, replied:

> A lot of it was because people went to Russia. And they were very interested in what was going on in Russia. Some of it was very awful, and some of it was very good. The interesting thing was that during this period in Russia, they published more children's books, and better children's books, than ever before or since. To the point where a new one would come out, and you'd try to get ahold of it, and it would be sold on the street corners, and you would not be able to get it. The children's books were very popular, and they were not bad at all. So that aroused a lot of discussions. If they could do it, how come we can't? What are we doing that's wrong?[32]

American writers, illustrators, librarians and editors—and not only those in the Communist milieu—praised Soviet children's literature for its quality and affordability, and they marveled at the resources devoted to the creation, production, and dissemination of children's literature in a country still struggling to meet basic human needs.[33]

Without a doubt, Soviet children's literature was explicitly geared toward the project of "Communist character-education."[34] Foreign admirers were either enamored with the goals toward which the Soviet Union was working, or they were simply struck by the fact that books could be ideologically driven, yet beautiful, amusing, educational, and popular with children. As Ernestine Evans (Gág's editor at Coward McCann) observed in 1931, "[T]he gusto and zest with which . . . they [the Soviets] can recruit the young to think about economics rather than business, engineering projects rather than private claims, astonishes the rest of the world."[35]

The lesson for Americans—whether they wanted to strengthen American values or to create revolutionary consciousness—was obvious. Especially during the period of Lenin's New Economic Policy (NEP, 1921–1928), the field of Soviet children's literature was remarkably dynamic, attracting some of the country's best writers and becoming a favorite genre of avant-garde constructivists. Although Stalin's orthodoxy destroyed much that was innovative in Soviet children's literature, even under his rule Soviet authors of children's books still had considerably more freedom than did adult writers.[36]

The Soviet preoccupation with the machine, science, and production reflected not only a modernist machine aesthetic, but also the utopian optimism of the new Soviet society, whose architects believed in the power of science and technology to bring about an equitable, prosperous, and efficient society that would be the envy of the rest of the world.[37] Soviet adulation of the machine and all things scientific resonated with the New Deal inheritors of the 1910s progressive reform tradition. Like their Soviet peers, these advocates of state planning hoped science and technology could eliminate inefficiency and waste and foster social equality. Likewise, progressive educators interested in a science of education geared toward the whole child avidly watched what one writer for *Progressive Education* called "the only *nationwide* experiment in progressive education in the whole world."[38]

Numerous progressive educators, including John Dewey, George Counts, and Patty Smith Hill, visited the Soviet Union in the 1920s and early 1930s and sent home mostly glowing reports about Soviet pedagogy and about the ways in which education served the task of social planning. Testimonials by American Communists like Scott Nearing and Anna Louise Strong echoed these reports in more uncritical terms but were similar in substance.[39] The self-evident horrors of agricultural collectivization and Stalin's series of show trials in the 1930s, designed to eliminate opposition to his regime, eventually made all but the most committed Communists highly critical of Soviet policies. But prior to this time, many educators joined with committed Communists in their admiration for Soviet children's literature.

Given the context in which these books arose, Soviet production books can be seen as modern fairy tales that celebrated the miraculous qualities of science and engineering. They reflected, as Steiner puts it

> an uncritical and (in its own way) religious faith in the triumph of social organization by means of correct theory plus cutting-edge technology. And just as any religion needs its miracles, so too the constructivist-Socialist faith hailed as miraculous all those wonderworking machines and devices meant to hasten the advent of the materialist paradise.[40]

Under Stalin's first five-year plan, which emphasized realizing the promise of the machine, the production book was elevated to center stage. The most widely hailed author in this genre was M. Il'in, who had mastered the art of creating books that were "politically acceptable, technologically focused, and genuinely appealing to young readers."[41] Il'in published more than a dozen books, the majority of them in the 1930s and 1940s, and most of them discussed the historical development of technical or scientific phenomena. Although all of Il'in's books received rave reviews in the Communist press, quite a few were also singled out by progressive educators as exemplary instances of modern pedagogy, and Il'in's books were sold directly to readers by the *New Masses* as well as by *Progressive Education*.

Reviewing *Black on White* and *What Time Is It?* (both published in 1932) in *Progressive Education*, Nora Beust commented that "both books will give any child—or adult for that matter—more interest in and respect for the evolution of the intellectual tools of the human race than can be gained from the crowded, uninteresting pages, filled with involved, condescending sentences, of our American schoolmasters." These two books very simply and entertainingly describe the development of time-keeping devices and the history of the book by using amusing anecdotes designed to cater to a child's fancy.[42] For instance, in *What Time Is It?* Il'in notes:

> I remember in my early childhood before I knew what clocks were for, the pendulum of our big clock seemed to me something like a stern person who never stopped repeating some admonition, as "You mustn't, mustn't / Suck your thumb!" Later, when I had mastered the difficult science of knowing by the position of the hands what time of day it was, I could not get rid of a certain feeling of fear which the clock roused in me. The complicated life of the many wheels seemed to me a secret which I could never understand. But the construction of a clock is, after all, not so complicated.[43]

Books such as this one had no self-evident political message; indeed, as a reviewer for the *Times* of London noted, "[T]here is no attempt at propaganda." Even reviews of Il'in's books in Communist publications seemed to struggle to find a political message. For instance, a review in the *New Pioneer* of *What Time Is It?* and *Black on White* primarily uses the books as evidence for why "in the Soviet Union . . . children do not hate their school books," in contrast to the United States, where school and books "are all crammed full of propaganda and lies to make the children hate the workers of other countries, especially of the Soviet Union." But there were deeper lessons in the books that were obvious to students of Marxism. As a reviewer for the *New Masses* observed, "Il'in . . . manages to convey a feeling of the sweep of history and the interrelation of forces that should be an excellent foundation for dialectic thinking in a child as well as a stimulant to the average adult."[44]

All Soviet literature for children (indeed, all of the Soviet arts) was bound to the doctrines of socialist realism—including the requirement of having "ideological content."[45] However, much of Il'in's work suggests how very subtle that ideological content could be.[46] While his production books attracted the attention of American educators for pedagogical reasons, the books made Communists see the value of ostensibly apolitical work explicating "the vast machinery of modern life."[47] Thus Communist journals like the *New Masses* and the *New Pioneer* would recommend that children read texts such as Lewis Hine's *Men at Work*, Thomas Hibben's *Carpenter's Tool Chest*, and Vera Edelstadt's *Steam Shovel for Me!* as well as Lucy Sprague Mitchell's books.[48]

Unlike several of Il'in's other books, *New Russia's Primer: The Story of the Five-Year Plan* (1931) makes the politics of the production book explicit. It was intended primarily for Soviet schoolchildren, but Il'in also expected his books to be read by uneducated adults. Throughout the book, which describes the ways in which engineering would, and had already begun, to transform Soviet society, the United States is held up as an example of what makes capitalism unworkable and socialism necessary. As Il'in notes, "[I]n a country boasting millions of machines, store rooms are bursting with food, corn is burned in place of coal; milk is poured in the river. And at the same time in this very country, thousands of people go hungry." Asking, "[W]hat is the matter here?" Il'in diagnoses that "all these magnificent machines, belong not to all Americans but only to a very few." While the machine tended to be an enemy of the American worker, Il'in asserted that in the Soviet Union, "the more machines we have, the easier will be the work, the shorter will be the working day, the lighter and happier will be the lives of all. We build factories in order that there may be no poverty, no filth, no sickness, no unemployment, no exhausting labor—in order that life may be rational and just." What Il'in was suggesting was that the real glory of the machine could be realized only under socialism. And ultimately, we can infer, the very project of gaining in knowledge and understanding—when set up as a project for the masses of people and not just for the elite—is a step on the road to socialism. Thus, the giant task of construction involved not only changing nature but also changing human beings: "We must root out uncouthness and ignorance, we must change ourselves, we must become worthy of a better life." Finally, Il'in insisted that "this better life will not come as a miracle: we ourselves must create it. But to create it we need knowledge: we need strong hands, yes, but we need strong minds too."[49]

Nora Beust, writing in *Progressive Education*, hailed *New Russia's Primer* as the book that "took America by storm." Indeed, the book was a bestseller in the United States. Reviews of the book, which suggest that its readership extended well beyond educators, librarians, and young people, express a range of reactions from unqualified excitement (Ernestine Evans called the book "a dazzling engineer's chart for creating more than enough to go around"), to dismay at "the child-like naïveté with which the Communist leaders are putting their trust in the power of machines." But even reviews calling the book "propaganda" often acknowledged its "genius," "charm," and "finesse." As a writer for the *Yale Review* noted, "Lenin once remarked that if he could get hold of the children in the period of their formative years, he would be able to win them over to his principles. Of all the textbooks prepared to carry out this 'precept' of Lenin's, this volume is one of the best."[50]

Although more explicitly political than books such as *Black on White* or *What Time Is It? New Russia's Primer* was also published by a commercial press (Riverside). Its enthusiastic introduction by "Frontier Thinker" George Counts presented the book as a challenge to American educators, not just in terms of the example it set for "how textbooks might be written," but also because after reading this book, "the American teacher will be forced to put to himself the question: can we not in some way harness the school to the task of building a better, a more just, a more beautiful society? Can we not broaden the sentiment of patriotism to embrace the struggles which men must ever wage with ignorance, disease, poverty, ugliness, injustice?" Counts's antagonism toward the Soviet system would later become as pronounced as his initial enthusiasm for it, but the fact that leading American educators praised the book and did so in an appeal to "patriotism" reveals the temper of the times. American recovery from the Great Depression seemed to depend upon public willingness to actively consider alternatives—or at least adjustments—to the system in place, and this idea filtered, at some level, into educational discourse.[51]

Despite their apparent affinities, more orthodox Communists were not quite ready to accept progressive educators as potential allies and, indeed, they rejected George Counts's controversial 1932 treatise, *Dare the School Build a New Social Order?* as flawed in its logic. As Gold's portrait of the proletarian child suggested, Communists believed that very little social change could be expected to come from schools as long as they were part of a capitalist system.[52] But the appeal of Soviet books to American educators did reveal to American Communists the value of the educational marketplace, where there was growing demand for children's literature that implicitly—and, in rare cases, explicitly—raised questions about dominant institutions, values, and practices.

American Fare for the Proletarian Child

Prior to this moment of recognition in the mid-1930s, most Communists who tried their hand at children's literature attempted to write proletarian children's literature.[53] In the United States, the primary outlet for this literature was a magazine for children, the *New Pioneer*. As an organ of the Young Pioneers, it was consciously geared toward serving the goals of the Communist children's movement, and it contained a variety of stories, articles, pictures, jokes, games, puzzles, book and film reviews, and letters to the editor.[54] The magazine launched careers in children's literature for a number of authors and illustrators, including Helen Kay, Ben Appel, William Gropper, Ernest Crichlow, and, most famously, Syd Hoff, who, as A. Redfield, served as art editor for the *New Pioneer*. Hoff later published at least six bestselling children's books that mimic the style if not the content of "A. Redfield's" work, such as *Mr. His* (1939) (figure 2.3), a book about "a very rich little man" who owned everything in "Histown" and spent his days eating well and tallying profits until workers in Histown got wise and revolted.[55] A shift in tone and address in the *New Pioneer*, coinciding with the Popular Front, predicted the broader shift in children's literature by writers in the Communist milieu (from A. Redfield's *Mr. His* to Syd Hoff's *Danny and the Dinosaur* and from *Battle in the Barnyard* to later work by Helen Kay such as *One Mitten Lewis*), as well as the eventual obsolescence of the *New Pioneer* itself.

The *New Pioneer*'s editors worked carefully to combine child appeal with political content. The magazine's first issue (May 1931) spoke enthusiastically and directly to its imagined readers, and the magazine's ideological bent was made explicit at the outset:

> I might as well tell you right now, there's just two kinds of people. Bosses and workers. And I stand four-square for the workers and the workingclass children. We have to fight together with our parents for the things we want and that belong to us. And say! I bet many of you fellows and girls work after school or maybe all day long, because your parents are out of work or underpaid. Well, you and I both are against

Mr His
BY A. REDFIELD

HIS TOWN

O NCE upon a time there was a fat little man whose name was Mr. His. He was a very rich little man and he lived in a little town which was called His-

Figure 2.3. *Mr. His: A Children's Story for Anybody* by A. Redfield (Syd Hoff). Hoff would go on to write many bestselling children's books, such as *Danny and the Dinosaur* (1958), *Sammy the Seal* (1959), and *Julius* (1959). Copyright 1939 by *New Masses*. Used with permission courtesy of International Publishers. Photographic reproduction courtesy of Spencer Research Library, Josephson Collection, University of Kansas.

child labor. Let's get together and make the bosses cash out of their profits to maintain children who now must work.[56]

Stories such as "From Boy Scout to Pioneer" (August 1931) and "Sammy and the Buy [*sic*] Scouts" (January 1933) reiterated the message that the Boy Scouts were servants of "the bosses" and enemies of "the workers." This message was evidently absorbed by young readers such as Hazel Hakola, a budding Marxist from Brantwood, Wisconsin, who warned her peers in a letter to the editor not to "swallow all the bunk that capitalism is trying to force in you." Hazel reminded "workers' children" that they should "stay away from . . . Scout camps."[57] The many contributions to the magazine from children—in the form of letters describing Pioneer activities or commenting on social conditions, or in jokes, puzzles, stories, and poems—can be said to mimic in form the proletarian "collective novel," composed by workers and popular in both the Soviet Union and the United States in the early 1930s.[58]

In general, the *New Pioneer*'s stories and articles tended to be more factual than fanciful, with a heavy emphasis on historical and scientific themes, which would be true for the bulk of leftists' output in the juvenile field in later

Figure 2.4. "American History Retold in Pictures." Drawings by Bill Siegel, with script by Jack Hardy. Text reads: "There are two ways of looking at history. One is the way the textbooks and public schools go at it. This is history as Wall Street and the owning class want you to see it. Facts and events are set forth in a false way and other facts are left out, so that wrong ideas are given you of times in the past, the present world, and what the future holds. The other way of looking at history, our way, is from the standpoint of the workers and toiling masses. This is the only true, scientific way of studying history and finding out what will happen in the future." From *New Pioneer* (June 1932). Used with permission courtesy of International Publishers Co., Inc., New York. Photographic reproduction from Tamiment Library, New York University.

decades as well. Biographical sketches, for instance, featured Industrial Workers of the World (IWW) leader Big Bill Haywood; the revolutionary intellectual John Reed; and Ada Wright, mother of one of the African-American Scottsboro Boys accused of raping a white woman. These sketches provided children with models of revolutionary activism. Historical vignettes and discussions of current events, such as the Scottsboro struggle, Tom Mooney's imprisonment, and the rise of Hitler, and a regular cartoon showing "American History Retold in Pictures" (figure 2.4) were intended to make children politically aware and engaged and to give them a sense of historical precedent and evolution.[59] Likewise, a regular column on "Nature and Science for Johnny Rebel" was meant to teach critical and scientific thinking and to highlight the misuse of science under capitalism.

Other articles put a new twist on the production story, describing not simply where things come from and how they are made, but also the exploitation of workers involved in a product's creation and importation to the United

States. For instance, in "The Story of Sugar," a bowl of sugar describes the painful knowledge he acquired in the process of his transformation from cane to granules and in his importation from Cuba:

> I learned who owns the land I grew on, who starves the people that cut me down, who owns the machinery in which I was ground, who owns the ship I came on and the factory in which I was refined. And do you know who it is? Americans—bankers—profiteers who were never near that field except maybe to look at it from a distance from under the shade of an awning.[60]

Stories like this present a striking contrast not only to Mitchell's here-and-now stories, but also to most of Il'in's production books. The popularity of the latter, in contrast to sectarian texts like "The Story of Sugar," predicted the shift in the mid-1930s toward work that could have broader appeal.

Most fiction in the magazine was realistic, usually about children coming to class consciousness or inspiring such consciousness in adults. The magazine attempted to play on children's natural rebelliousness to challenge all authority figures, especially teachers, although teachers could also be objects of sympathy especially when they declared their solidarity with the working class (as a fair number did in the 1930s). In "Our Teacher Learned Something" by Grace Hutchins, the storyteller, Tom, is a Pioneer who always stirs up trouble with his patriotic history teacher, Miss Markham, who is a member of the Daughters of the American Revolution (DAR). When Miss Markham praises George Washington, he tells her that Washington was a slave holder and "only interested in the rich." When she says America is a great country, he tells her about hungry children in his neighborhood who eat nothing but garbage. At first, Miss Markham calls Tom a "Bolshevik." But as teachers' salaries are cut to starvation wages, teachers, following their students' lead, begin marching in the streets. Miss Markham holds out, but at the end of the story she tells Tom, "I'm resigning from the D.A.R. I know now—I belong with the working class."[61]

Despite the seriousness of these themes, writers and editors often told stories in a playful tone, which is perhaps most evident in parodies on standard children's stories and poetry, such as "Mother Goose on the Breadline" or "Alice in Hunger Land." In the same way that radical German fairy tales adapted standard narrative structures and retold familiar stories with working-class rather than aristocratic heroes, so American Communist authors adapted Mother Goose and other familiar rhymes and stories to invest them with new meaning. For instance, "Pioneer Mother Goose" poems in the December 1934 issue included:

This bloated Pig masters Wall Street,
This little Pig owns your home;
This war-crazed Pig had your brother killed,
And this greedy Pig shouts "More!"
This Pig in Congress shouts "War, War!"
All day long.
These Pigs we'll send to market—
And will they squeal? You bet!
Down with Capitalism!
Long live the Soviet![62]

Other stories attempted to debunk treasured American myths. For example, "A Kitchen of Heroes," published in February 1932 (on the occasion of Washington and Lincoln's birthdays), declared all of the wonderful tales about Washington and Lincoln to be bunk:

It is as plain as the nose on an elephant's face that if the capitalists can teach every kid to believe that a dead president was a man who was so honest and correct in everything that every kid must take off his hat and look respectful when that president's name is mentioned, why it is a lot easier to make the same kids believe that the president who is living RIGHT NOW is also a "great and good" guy.

If Washington never told a lie, author Harrison George declared, "he was the only president of this country that never did." And Lincoln was no hero either: he was looking to save northern white capitalists by maintaining the union. When the slaves were "freed," they were only "changed from plain slaves into wage slaves." George notes that "the Negroes of the South are still the worst enslaved [sic] of all the poor people. The Southern landowners still rob and murder them and allow them no real freedom. So the workers and farmers, black and white, still have the job of really freeing them, which the capitalist president Lincoln pretended to do, but didn't."[63]

As is readily apparent from reading the *New Pioneer*, the Communist line on Lincoln—and on the Boy Scouts—would change dramatically during the Popular Front, as Lincoln was refashioned into the quintessential "people's hero" and as the Boy Scouts were invited to join the Pioneers in "the struggle against war and fascism, the struggle for the life, liberty and happiness of the American people."[64] During the Popular Front, as Communists looked beyond their traditional working-class constituency and sought recruits from the middle class, they also crafted material to appeal to middle-class children. In doing so, they precipitated a shift not only away from sectarian, Communist-sponsored children's literature, but also a move to a more widely disseminated progressive children's literature that had only an indirect relationship to the organized Left. The shift in approach characteristic of the Popular Front is apparent in the *New Pioneer*'s changing editorial slant: "Dear Comrade Editor" became "Letters to the Editor"; "Science and Nature for Johnny Rebel" became, simply, "Science"; and instead of addressing the magazine to "the Boys and Girls of the Workers and Farmers," the *New Pioneer* became, simply, "An Illustrated Magazine for Boys and Girls." Ultimately, the magazine's attempt to mainstream itself would render it obsolete, and the *New Pioneer* ceased to exist in 1939.[65]

As one might guess from the tone of Hazel Hakola's letter, readers of the magazine tended to come from radical families themselves, and most were already active in children's organizations like the Young Pioneers.[66] However, editors also intended that the magazine be used to recruit new children to the movement, and although even middle-class readers of the magazine were likely to come from politicized families, the magazine may have been passed around in schools, particularly in progressive schools that encouraged social consciousness in children. This is certainly suggested by the experience of Dahlov Ipcar, née Zorach.

When I first met with Ipcar, an award-winning and widely read children's author, she seemed skeptical of my reasons for talking to her and several times emphasized that her parents, the Lyrical Leftist artists William and Marguerite Zorach, who had been hounded during the McCarthy years, had been "apolitical." But several months after our original conversation, my discovery of a poem by a fourteen-year-old Dahlov Zorach, published in the *New Pioneer* in 1936, prompted Ipcar to comment more openly about her political socialization. She maintains that young people at the progressive schools she attended were highly conscious of politics and concerned with national and international issues. A number of the teachers held radical political views, and quite a few classmates, likewise, came from families involved in organized left-wing activity.[67] Dahlov's best friend from age eleven on came from a politically active family, and, she claims, it was through this girl that she came into contact with the *New Pioneer*.[68]

Young Dahlov clearly was impressed enough by the magazine to pen her own, heartfelt poem, "The Miners," which was published in the July 1936 issue of the *New Pioneer*. Though the poem has a melodramatic quality typical of a fourteen-year-old's literary sensibility, it displays a stirring solidarity with the striking miners and suggests heightened awareness of contemporary labor struggles:

The winds are cold and the nights are long,
But the strikers sing as they march along
Though the winds blow cold

Through the day and night
The strikers march on the picket line;
March, march to a steady time . . .
We shall not starve for we shall fight![69]

The revolutionary zeal of Dahlov's poem, which was published after the declaration of the Popular Front, suggests that children did not bother to keep track
of changing "party lines." Moreover, the fact that it was published in a Communist magazine suggests that attracting socially conscious, middle-class children
to the movement was given more emphasis than any quest for doctrinal purity.[70]
Does the poem therefore represent Communist successes at recruiting children
of the middle class? Certainly a child of bohemian artists would be more open
to radical politics than a child of a businessman. But "Miners" appears to be
as radical as Dahlov ever got. Ipcar's children's books (her own and those she
illustrated, including several by Margaret Wise Brown), show little hint of her
childhood radical consciousness. Even so, they do reflect a lifelong respect for
physical labor and working people. And Ipcar herself attested that "almost all of
our friends who gave up the political world remained liberal in their hearts and
minds."[71] Thus, while the *New Pioneer* did not turn Ipcar into a Communist, it
does seem to have contributed to an enduring sympathy for poor and working-
class people, what Michael Denning calls a "plebeian sensibility."

"Black and White, Unite and Fight"

In contrast to earlier working-class movements, under the guise of Communism, this sensibility would unite poor and working-class people across
racial lines.[72] While changes in the *New Pioneer*'s tone, content, and readership would tend to reflect the new focus and rhetorical strategies of the Popular Front (Ipcar's proletarian poem notwithstanding), emphasis on black and
white unity would consistently characterize children's literature by American
writers in the Communist milieu. From the 1930s into the 1960s, children's literature by authors in—or once in—the American Communist milieu was strikingly marked by antiracist politics or, at the very least, by a conscious attempt
to reject racism. In this sense, American proletarian children's literature stood
in marked contrast to literature produced by many progressive educators and
socialists, whose racial prejudice was typical of their times. Even proletarian
children's literature from Europe failed to register the antiracist sensibility of its
American counterparts.

Proletarian literature was not particularly exemplary in its gender politics,
however. The Girl Scouts, for instance, never received the attention devoted to

the Boy Scouts, and boy protagonists far outnumber girls in the literature. Still, a number of stories in this genre do have strong and feisty female protagonists (for example, girls are activists alongside boys in stories in Kay's *Battle in the Barnyard* and in the *New Pioneer Story Book*). On the other hand, though by no means immune to the prejudices of their day, Communist-authored texts, particularly those by American writers, do show a marked effort to challenge the racial bias that is so apparent in mainstream children's literature of the 1920s and 1930s.[73] Still, Communists' authentic commitment to eliminating racial discrimination and promoting interracial unity did tend to come at the expense of attention to ethnicity. Especially in the 1920s and early 1930s, the majority of American Communists were immigrants (though their children were often native-born), and among them Jews were overrepresented. Although Communists' ethnic identities were often inseparable from their radical politics, in the 1920s and early 1930s party policies held that strong ethnic identifications would detract from members' identification with the international working class. Under the logic of the CP's "Bolshevization" policy, which held until the mid-1930s (when the Communist Party "reconciled itself to the perception among many of its members that revolutionary politics could be linked to ethnic identification"), every effort was made to subsume ethnic or religious identities under that of class.[74]

This dynamic was reflected in Communist children's literature, where, prior to the mid-1930s, there was minimal discussion of the ethnic groups prevalent in the party. Even Yiddish textbooks published in the early 1930s for secular Jewish schools run by the International Workers Order (IWO) had very little that was "Jewish" about them. For instance, a second-grade Yiddish textbook called *Workers' School* (1933) emphasizes that this is a *workers'* school—rather than a Jewish school:

> Sidney is studying in the Workmen's School. Sidney is studying in a Yiddish school. The name of his school is Jewish children's school, associated with the International Workers Order. His father is a worker. Sidney knows how difficult life is for the workers the world over. He reads books and he writes also some pretty stories about workers. When he walks in the street and he sees workers repairing the roads he stops and watches them. Near them stands a foreman. The foreman does nothing. He just looks and sees how other people work. Sidney does not like him. He goes home and he writes a little story about bosses and their workers.[75]

Presumably, young Sidney's story would have helped workers—not necessarily Jewish workers—to realize their predicament and to challenge a system where some people work and others sit back and collect profits.

As efforts were made to subsume ethnic loyalties under the rubric of class solidarity, in the early 1930s attention to racial discrimination and difference came to substitute for attention to ethnic difference. More specifically, blacks, who seem to be everywhere in American proletarian children's literature, became a stand-in for Jews, who were almost entirely absent from English-language proletarian children's literature (despite their prevalence in the Communist Party). Unlike ethnicity or religious identity, sensitivity to race was seen as an aid rather than a hindrance to class consciousness.[76]

Representations of African Americans in American proletarian children's literature can, on the one hand, be understood in the context of what Evgeny Steiner calls "proletarian internationalism." This internationalism, which emphasized the key role of national minorities in the revolutionary struggle, grew from the important role of minorities from the Russian empire in the Soviet revolution. Russian revolutionaries' successful play on minority groups' discontent contributed to the thesis that colonized and oppressed national groups could form an important basis for revolution in other countries. Thus African and, to some extent, Asian characters are common in the proletarian children's literature published in the Soviet Union, Germany, and England.

Steiner argues that Soviet literature about children in exotic lands—usually Africa or China—at best subsumed race issues or conflated them with class concerns and at worst was paternalistic or even sadistic in its representation of darker, primitive, innocent peoples' abuse and exploitation at the hands of white capitalists and imperialists.[77] While far tamer than a number of Soviet books from the 1920s that Steiner discusses, even Il'in's *Black on White* uses "a negro named Sambo," both as a device to describe the development of communication from primitive oral methods of communication to use of the written word and as an opportunity to mention the unjust capture and enslavement of an innocent African by an American slave holder. Despite the attempt to comment on the injustice of slavery, the story highlights Sambo's naïveté and his vulnerability in the face of his literate master. Moreover, it produces for readers less of a feeling of sympathy than a feeling of superiority: unlike Sambo, we are literate and understand the power of the written word.[78] Likewise, while well intentioned, "The Little Grey Dog," a story in the German-authored *Fairy Tales for Workers' Children*, paternalistically describes a little slave boy so helpless that he depends upon, first, a dog, who helps him to escape, and then a kindly white man, who takes him in. The story is a lesson in the double oppression of poor blacks (it seems to be set in the United States), but the slaves themselves are helpless victims, with fewer resources than the wise animals who aid them.[79]

The story "Little Black Murzuk" from the *Red Corner Book for Children*, originally published in England, strikes the twenty-first-century reader as particularly infected with an almost Kiplingesque case of paternalistic sympathy for the little people in Africa. Hailed by the American *New Pioneer* as the most outstanding story in this collection, the tale describes a happy native boy in the jungle, who lives with elephants, monkeys, and hippopotamuses. Illustrations show Murzuk and the other natives as woolly-headed, big-lipped, and childlike. They panic at the arrival of a steam ship—"a strange beast"—but turn joyful when the white missionaries and imperialists on the ship give them trinkets and promise to make their "nation live happily ever afterwards." The "negroes" put on their new beads and finery and sing all night, "just like children," but are astonished when the whites force the natives to work for them, killing those who do not cooperate.[80]

Driven to weeping by all the violence, Little Black Murzuk asks his elephant friend, "Why do the white people beat the blacks so hard? . . . Why is it that the blacks are treated so badly—tell me why, my elephant, my one and only elephant?" The elephant does not answer. The story ends by asking, "Well, children, rebel children, is this fair? What do you think about it?" Of course the British origins of the story might explain its striking "imperialist nostalgia,"[81] but recommendation of the story in the *New Pioneer* (and American republication of it) suggests its fit with the dominant American racial ideology as well. Still, the story's depictions of blacks are strikingly different from those in literature by American Communists, due to the special status of African Americans in Communist policy.

Soviet policy on the "Negro question" in the United States grew out of Comintern strategy vis-à-vis "national minorities," but it assumed special importance in an American context. In the United States, African Americans were the largest and clearly the most oppressed minority group, and their unequal treatment, in many cases backed by the force of law, provided evidence of the hollowness of American democratic rhetoric. African-American visitors to the Soviet Union were treated like heroes, and a number of black intellectuals, artists, and writers were drawn toward Communism because what they saw and heard of the Soviet Union seemed to suggest that in a Communist state, prejudice would vanish and interracial cooperation could flourish.[82]

The Bolshevization of the American party in 1925 also helped the position of African Americans in the CP. This policy dissolved foreign-language federations and forced members of the party to join interracial units, either street units where they lived or shop units where they worked. While this policy alienated some immigrant members, it helped blacks in the party to work closely with groups that had previously been insular and exclusive. Finally, a 1928 Comintern resolution on the "Negro question," which declared American blacks to be an oppressed "nation within a nation," with the right to self-determination, held that the success of revolutionary movements in the United States depended upon the support of African Americans. This resolution asserted that "the Negro problem must be part and parcel of every campaign conducted by the Party" and that "white chauvinism" within the party must be countered by a "thorough educational campaign."[83]

For American Jewish Communists, whose traditions had historically attracted them to radical movements, including Communism, the struggle for black equality became an important path toward Americanization. The majority of the white Communist organizers in Harlem were of Jewish ancestry, as were white experts on the "Negro question" and white activists involved with the Scottsboro defense.[84] Thus the struggle for black equality assumed particular significance for American Communists, especially Jews. These special American conditions helped to distinguish the treatment of blacks in children's literature by American Communists from minorities' treatment in European children's literature.

The *New Pioneer* was filled with articles and pictures emphasizing struggles against racial discrimination and highlighting interracial cooperation, with special emphasis on the campaign to free the Scottsboro Boys, which became a focus of interracial organizing efforts in the United States and internationally (see figure 2.5).[85] Articles and fiction also presented scenarios where black-white cooperation was essential to the workers' struggle and where children—thought to be born free of prejudice—were key to adults' enlightenment on the subject of race. For instance, Myra Page's "Pickets and Slippery Slicks," originally published in the May 1931 issue of the *New Pioneer* (with illustrations by Lydia Gibson) and reprinted in the *New Pioneer Story Book* (1935), highlighted a friendship among two white and two black working-class children in a southern mill town. The story begins with two sets of siblings playing separately on the banks of a creek. The white brothers Billy and Sam eye the black sister and brother Myrtle and Charlie as they play "slippery slicks," that is, as they slide down the mud bank into the creek, with tumbles and laughs. The white boys eventually join in the black children's game, and the four become friends and play together by the creek every day. "For children, like nature, know no color line," Page writes. "Humans are human to them. Of race and class they know nothing and care less, until their elders, trained in the ways of a world divided into classes, take them in hand." Billy and Sam get themselves into trouble during a lesson in Sunday school on the "Brotherhood of Man" in which the teacher explains that the mill owners and workers are "really one big family." Billy asks the teacher, "[I]s black and white folks brothers too?" The teacher, thrown by the inquiry, insists that they are not. When she learns that Billy's questions come out of a friendship with Myrtle and Charlie, the teacher makes clear that they are a "disgrace" and have "done a shameful thing." Billy and Sam are punished by their parents and forbidden

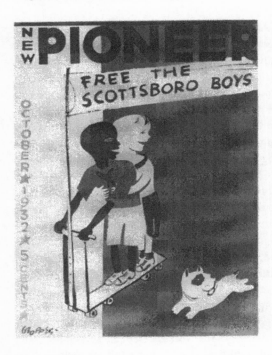

Figure 2.5. "Free the Scotts-boro Boys." Cover illustration by William Gropper for *New Pioneer* (October 1932). The image of interracial friendship and the banner supporting the Scottsboro Boys (a group of African-American youths accused of raping a white woman) represent typical images and concerns of the *New Pioneer*. Gropper also frequently contributed art-work to the *New Masses*. Used by permission courtesy of Gene Gropper. Photographic reproduction from Tamiment Library, New York University.

to return to the creek, and when Myrtle and Charlie finally get the courage to come to the white part of town to see whether something has happened to their friends, they are called "lil' niggers" by Billy and Sam's parents and are told to go away and never come back. "Charlie and Myrtle, like Billy and Sam, had been taught their first lesson in race prejudice. Never again was the shaded lane of over-hanging trees to be a care-free place in which to play. Part of the glamour of the creek was gone forever."[86]

But new circumstances bring the children back together. When the mill announces a wage cut, black and white union organizers come to town to build the union, and they emphasize the need for interracial solidarity among the workers. Suddenly all four children are out picketing with their parents and singing "Solidarity Forever." Now it seems okay for Billy to ask Charlie and Myrtle: "as soon as this here picketin's over, how 'bout we go down to the crik, 'n' have a game of Slippery Slicks?"[87]

Two of the seven stories in Helen Kay's collection *Battle in the Barnyard* have African-American characters. "Us Alley Kids" concerns a black boy who gets into trouble by venturing into the luxurious gardens of the rich white peo-ple living nearby; "A Night's Adventure" describes an interracial group of Young Pioneers leafleting in a poor, black neighborhood in Washington, D.C. In the latter story, a group of children enter a black church and incur the rage of the preacher, who wants the children thrown out, but members of his congregation, placing class solidarity over race or religion, stand behind the children. Upon reconvening with the other Pioneers, the children explain, "[T]he old guy [the preacher] wouldn't let us give out our leaflets. He just wouldn't budge, but the workers were with us. They just turned right over in our favor when they saw that one of us was Negro and the other white."[88]

None of Kay's black characters speaks in dialect. While the black characters in Page's story do, so do the white characters, and the depictions of the black children and their parents are in no way caricatures, as in *The Pickaninny Twins*. While these stories and most of those in the *New Pioneer* focus more on black-white cooperation than on black culture itself and are most often by Euro-American rather than African-American authors (the *New Pioneer* did count among its illustrators the African-American artist Ernest Crichlow), the characters depicted appear human, plausible, and sympathetic, in contrast to representations of African Americans in the books by liberal authors mentioned in the previous chapter and in contrast as well to much of the proletarian internationalism in European Communists' children's literature.

Thus, American Communists perhaps most distinguished themselves from many of their peers in the progressive educational field—as well as their socialist predecessors—in the arena of race, and it is in this realm that proletarian literature represented the most usable past for post-1935 leftists. However, in contrast to writers like Lucy Sprague Mitchell, whose books became a staple in schools, prior to the mid-1930s, only a few authors identified with the Communist movement created books that schools and libraries would buy.

"A True Conqueror": Popo's Proletarian Possibilities

The commercially published *Popo and Fifina: Children of Haiti* (1932) suggests how a book could combine a radical perspective on race and class with sensitivity to the child audience and the children's book marketplace. Early models of commercially viable children's books by authors in the Communist milieu were rare,[89] but *Popo and Fifina*, a book that remained in print for decades, showed the real potential of American children's books to be popular yet politically engaged. It is certainly no stretch to call the book's protagonists proletarian, and while the book's politics are quite subtle, the story offers a radical critique of labor practices, of the dominant racial ideology, and of American economic policy, and it presents a model of autonomous, free-thinking children.

Popo and Fifina came out of a collaboration between Langston Hughes— at that time active in a number of Communist-sponsored causes—and his friend Arna Bontemps. In the spring of 1931, Hughes had spent several weeks in Haiti, at that time under occupation by the United States, where he collected the impressions that would become the basis for this children's story, which Bontemps largely wrote and edited.[90] *Popo* described the daily life of two children in Haiti, using sensual and poetic descriptions of the landscape, the foods the family ate, and the daily tasks they performed, repeatedly showing the children's delight in small pleasures, like the taste of a mango from their grandmother's tree or the sight of colorful fishing boats in the harbor. The family is obviously poor: their house is a one-room shack with a tin roof, and the family sleeps on beds of straw laid out on the floor. However, Hughes and Bontemps never directly comment upon the poverty itself, and one senses that nearly everyone on the island is poor as well. Still, islanders are extremely generous toward one another; they tend to share what they have and to work cooperatively. For instance, when Popo's family arrives in Cape Haiti from the country, the fishermen share their catch with Papa Jean, who has not yet been able to go out fishing himself. We see the constancy of work in the lives of the family members: Papa Jean's daily trips in the fishing boat (he hesitates to take even one day off from work) and Mama Anna's washing, preparing food, and keeping house.

Despite the simplicity of the scenes and the beauty that clearly surrounds this poor family, their lives are not romanticized, and the discourse on labor in the book is subtly laced with political commentary. One scene comments both on labor conditions in Haiti and on the country's dependence upon the U.S. economy:

> A little further down the road they passed the only important factory of the town, where pineapples are canned and prepared for shipment to the United States. Here Popo saw many black men working. They did not move about leisurely, like other workers, and Popo thought he wouldn't enjoy working so hurriedly.[91]

Just as this comment upon labor conditions is subtly couched in a child's musings, so the book contains no explicit discussion of race. All of the characters in the book are black, and the story comes from their perspective, not from that of an outsider.

Commentary upon class and race is at once everywhere and nowhere in this book, and as such the book's politics never attract attention. What is striking, however, are the autonomous and independent child characters. In one of the most vivid scenes in the book, Popo, hearing the sound of drums in the distance, decides to follow men walking down to a place on the main road where the drums are playing and people are dancing under the moonlight. "Nobody paid any attention to the little black boy walking along by himself. Popo didn't mind that, for children in Haiti are used to walking alone in the dark. . . . And near at hand were dancers, drummers, and drums!"[92] Popo is never punished or even scolded for his wanderings (although a cousin he meets sends him home so his mother won't worry) nor is there any sense of shame attached to the sensual dancing that Popo witnesses.

There is only one scene in the book that uses explicitly revolutionary imagery, but the scene apparently aroused no negative comment.[93] Popo, who asks for few material things from his parents, decides he wants nothing more than a kite that he can fly all day and evening. Papa Jean stays up late one night after work, and the children awaken to find a red kite with yellow and green trimmings (red, of course, is associated with revolutionary strength, while yellow and green are associated with Pan-Africanism). The children launch their kite with great excitement, watching as it goes up like "a big scarlet star rising." But as the children walk along the beach, their kite flying high above, the fun is suddenly threatened. A "strange kite, a dull brown thing," held by another boy who "was very proud of his rude misbehaving kite," becomes entangled with Popo's. As Popo struggles to recover his "red star-kite," he suddenly feels a cord snap: "But it was not his cord. His kite pulled and sang as steadily as ever; but the other one, the hawk, was falling to the earth like an evil bird with a broken wing. Down, down, down it sank. A moment or two later it dropped into the ocean. Popo's big red star climbed the sky proudly, a true conqueror."[94]

In a sense the entire book is a proud, true conqueror. Like Popo's scarlet star, whose symbolism is difficult to dismiss, *Popo and Fifina* remained on Macmillan's prestigious list for more than two decades, meriting multiple foreign translations; it was also excerpted in anthologies of children's literature and used as a model for aspiring writers of children's books, not as "black-authored children's literature" and certainly not as "Communist children's literature," but as great children's literature.[95]

As producers of culture in the Popular Front Left ultimately became more attentive to the possibilities (and limits) of trade children's literature as a genre, they began to write more books like *Popo and Fifina* and *What Time Is It?* and fewer like *Battle in the Barnyard*. What was key from the standpoint of the Left's ability to affect children's literature was timing: at about the same moment that left-wing authors stopped producing sectarian books for "young revolutionists" and began creating books that regular kids would want to read, educators, librarians, and publishers started calling for real-world books that addressed the economic and social conditions of the day in terms accessible to a child reader. As problem books—along with general nonfiction—gained new cachet among publishers, members of the Communist Left were poised to find an audience and a market in children's literature. The remainder of this book explores the output of leftists as they moved into all levels of the children's literature field, as they responded to a changing social and political climate, and as they created books that would be read by millions of children—at home, in libraries, and in schools.

• • •

Perhaps one final caveat is in order so that the *Battle in the Barnyard/Popo and Fifina* distinction is not set up as a false dichotomy. Proletarian or revolutionary children's literature demonstrated that children's books, like books for adults, could have an explicit political message. However, when leftists looked for models of how to write books that would actually sell, they more often looked back to the Lyrical Left and progressive educators. Moreover, while far more popular than proletarian children's literature produced by the Communist Party, most of the books examined in this study have not become classics in the usual sense of the term—although many of these books remained in print for decades. The anarchic sensibility of the Lyrical Left did predict imaginative works like Crockett Johnson's *Harold and the Purple Crayon*, Syd Hoff's *Danny and the Dinosaur*, and William Steig's *Sylvester and the Magic Pebble*—books at the core of the children's literature canon—as well as popular animation such as *Mr. Magoo* and *Gerald McBoing Boing*.[96] All of these texts were products of the Old Left, but they also resonated with the spirit of the 1960s New Left and counterculture, offering an obvious bridge across leftist generations. But it was the here-and-now philosophy of progressive education that had the greatest impact on the Old Left in terms of cultural production, most likely because it fit with a Marxist, materialist outlook. Building on a tradition established in the United States by Lucy Sprague Mitchell and made synonymous with the Soviet project by Il'in, the vast majority of children's books produced by members of the Old Left were works of nonfiction or works of realist fiction, and the most popular subjects treated were science and history. Many of these books reached a massive audience through schools, and yet they have been easy to overlook as cultural productions of the Left.

PART II

Producing Dissent

3

Work and Sing

Children's Literature and the Cultural Front, 1935–1945

In Harry Granick's *Run, Run! An Adventure in New York* (1941), two white ten-year-olds from the Midwest, Ruth and Tony, arrive by train in New York City as winners of a contest sponsored by the Fruity Cereal Company. Waiting for the other children and the corporate sponsors to join them at Grand Central Station, the children, noticing a creepy man with a patch over one eye who seems to be watching them intently, decide they'd be safer on the city streets than waiting around in the station (figure 3.1). Ruth and Tony venture off into the city, and here is where the plot, as they say, thickens. A reviewer for the *New Masses* summarized the children's adventures:

> They run into a bootblack. An artist. A Chinese family in Chinatown. The captain of a fishing boat. A Negro family in Harlem. A singer. . . . The ten-year-old children discover parts of New York many well informed persons don't know exist—like the forge in the sub-basement of the New York Public Library; the Aquarium where immigrants were once held for investigation as they are now held at Ellis Island. The youngsters were guests in fire traps and discovered what sub-standard tenement buildings are like. They join a demonstration and picket on the line. They are part of a people's parade. They sleep wherever they find themselves at the end of a strenuous day evading the detectives frantically searching for them. They even find refuge under the Statue of Liberty and on Ellis Island.[1]

In each of the children's many adventures, there is either a knowing child or an adult at the fringes of mainstream society who acts as a guide for the children: a streetwise shoeshine boy and his class-conscious father, an artist living

Figure 3.1. Illustration by Gregor Duncan from *Run, Run! An Adventure in New York* by Harry Granick. Ruth and Tony, two ten-year-old children from the Midwest, run through Grand Central Station (under the watch of "One-Eye") as their adventures in the city commence. The flat and conventional character of the illustrations serves to disguise the radical nature of the story. New York: Simon and Schuster, 1941. Used with permission courtesy of Granick family.

on the Lower East Side, a black musician who lives in Harlem. These guides supplement the children's own wisdom and provide truthful answers to their questions. In one scene, for instance, Ruth and Tony encounter a shoe shiner being forced off the sidewalk by a policeman. As the policeman tells him to move on, the man turns to Ruth and Tony. "'No like to see poor man on rich street,' said the little man, bitterly. 'You know what? I make this side-walk! Yes, I make it! I mix the cement. I lay it. Me! With these hands! Now, no allow to stand on it!'"[2] The immigrant worker is literally forced off the ground that he has helped to create, and the children learn that this is not what America is supposed to be like.

The children's natural curiosity leads them to ask questions about the things they see on their adventures, whether it is substandard housing conditions or racial discrimination, both of which they see in Chinatown, in Harlem, and throughout the city. In concert with the children's own observations, honest adults, usually from the working class, paint a picture of society for these presumably naïve (but open-minded) midwestern children, a picture that crosses into territory rarely broached in popular children's books published prior to the 1960s. When, for example, Tony asks an exiled Austrian writer, who acts as a kind of sage to the children during their stay on Ellis Island, why a group of men are sitting quietly in a corner of the room, away from the rest of the group and encircled by guards, the Austrian answers:

> "Those poor men have lived in your country. Now they are being sent back to their old countries. . . . Many are criminals, some came to your land without permission, and some, I have heard, are not wanted by the rich men of your country. They have organized farmers and workers to be together strong."
> "Why is that bad?" ask[s] Tony.
> "It is not bad," sa[ys] the Austrian thoughtfully. "It is only bad when you are not a citizen."[3]

Although the story takes place in New York, it is a New York that is representative of the nation, as viewed through the lens of Popular Front Americanism. In other words, it represents the nation in all of its racial and ethnic diversity, in its contrasts between rich and poor, and in its dominance by corporate capitalism. And yet the book's critique is playful, always attentive to its child protagonists and audience. For instance, on the way to the Statue of Liberty, the children stop to look at a statue of Giovanni Verrazano. Tony is shocked to learn that Verrazano landed there nearly a hundred years before Hendrick [sic] Hudson, and yet he was never mentioned in Tony's history book. Ruth, sharing his outrage, remarks, "We ought to do something about this." Thinking through the issue further, she decides, "[W]e ought to get another frankfurter."[4]

After their night camped out on Ellis Island, Ruth and Tony miraculously come across the group of children and Fruity Cereal folks with whom they were supposed to have convened the day before. At first they are pleased to have found the others, and they happily board the tour bus. But they soon learn that the other children have had to "promise to eat Fruity Cereal every morning for the rest of their lives." And after listening to a guide talk monotonously through a megaphone, directing attention to various corporate landmarks, they quickly realize that "there were better ways of seeing New York."[5] Ruth and Tony manage to slip away from the group and spend the rest of the story avoiding the detectives sent to find them. (The one-eyed man, who appears throughout the story, turns out to be a former Fruity executive with antiauthoritarian, anticorporate, and somewhat voyeuristic tendencies, who had concocted a plot to give two of the contest winners a chance to see the "real" New York while never far out of his surveillance.)

The book's reconfigured Americanism, celebrating workers, racial minorities, and immigrants; its rejection of traditional authority figures; and its populist, anticorporate sensibility make *Run, Run!* a representative document of the Popular Front in terms of the text's thematic emphases. Perhaps even more significant, the book as an object represents a reimagining of the children's book medium by someone savvy to the operation of the modern culture industries. Granick, a self-educated Russian-Jewish immigrant of working-class background, published only two children's books, but he was a member of the League of American Writers who wrote extensively for radio (and later television), often with children as his audience.[6] Compilers of his FBI file were never able to ascertain with certainty whether Granick was a Communist; an ostensibly reliable informant told the FBI that "he always suspected subject of being a Red but never had any proof of this; however, subject acts and looks like a Communist."[7] Whether he was, in fact, a Communist (or just looked like one), evidence does suggest that Granick gave careful consideration to the question of how children's books could be effectively used to serve the interests of the Left.[8]

Upon superficial examination, *Run, Run!* is unremarkable, and this is arguably what gives the book its power. The illustrations are flat, mundane, and give no hint of the radical themes expressed in the text. The first twenty or thirty pages are the stuff of a rather banal preadolescent series novel, with these typical, midwestern children chatting on the train about the dry details of their ten-year-old existences. Thus an adult quickly perusing the book would be unlikely to pick up on its political perspective. However, Ruth and Tony, who initially seem like run-of-the-mill children's book protagonists, introduced 1940s readers to a cast of characters and situations that were far from the children's literature norm.

On a broader level, the book itself is a comment upon the ways in which commercial culture might be adapted and transformed to more progressive ends. "One-Eye," for example, uses his power to mock the company to whom he owes his livelihood. Ruth and Tony, of course, only got to New York City in the first place by the good graces of the Fruity Cereal Company, which had intended to create loyal customers by chaperoning a flock of impressionable children through the marvels of corporate America via Wall Street, shopping sprees, and other appropriately consumerist "adventures." As Harry Granick managed to convince a commercial publishing house to publish a book that mocked corporate America and that celebrated a hidden side of New York—and the nation—so would other cultural workers on the Left become important players in the field. Likewise, children's books that critiqued the status quo in subtle, and sometimes not so subtle, ways began to gain a popular audience.

This chapter considers how the conditions of production and dissemination of children's literature changed beginning in the mid-1930s, and it looks at the particular ways that leftists, in response to these changes, began to reshape the field and its output in the years prior to the onset of the Cold War. Beginning in the mid-1930s, the Popular Front against fascism brought Communists into cooperation with liberals, independent radicals, and others who shared Communists' commitment to defeating fascism, challenging racism and imperialism, and supporting the labor movement. Efforts on the part of a previously sectarian Communist Left to expand its influence and appeal to democratically minded members of the middle class entailed a shift in rhetoric that reframed Communism as "twentieth-century Americanism," or as rooted in native revolutionary traditions. More broadly, the rhetorical and tactical shifts characteristic of the Popular Front linked the playful, nonsectarian, and antiauthoritarian consciousness characteristic of the Lyrical Left (and its allies in education) to the strongly prolabor, antiracist, and anti-imperialist views of the revolutionary Old Left. This confluence had several important consequences for children's literature.

The first consequence had to do with work. Beginning in the late 1930s, radical cultural workers, in cooperation with their progressive allies, arrived at a new understanding of children's literature as a medium: a medium situated within a matrix of intellectual (and physical) labor, subject to a variety of social, economic, and political forces, and enormously powerful as a tool to reach "the broad masses of children." Once it got their attention, children's literature could be a tool to "educate children so that they will be anti-fascists and not fascists."[9] The rise of a progressive formation in children's literature—in which cultural workers in the field began to see themselves as intellectual *laborers*, with a stake in the labor movement and democratic struggles more generally—influenced both the output of children's book publishers and the actual mechanics of the field's operation.

The second consequence had to do with literary expression. Children's books began to embody some of the key themes of the Popular Front, including an antiracist, prolabor, internationalist Americanism; a celebration of work and workers; and a faith in technology and science as the basis for more equitable distribution of resources, improved health, and diminished social conflict. Leftists took the lead in extending the antifascist common sense of the Popular Front and Second World War to children's books that celebrated the heroics of common folk and the patriotic struggle to defeat fascism in the United States and also abroad (especially in the Soviet Union). A corollary to this antifascist common sense was that an antiauthoritarian impulse in children's literature implicitly linked the cause of antifascism to a more democratic vision of adult-child relations. Along with this more democratic vision of adult-child relations came a waning belief in childhood innocence and more children's books that grappled with real-world issues.

As the leftist agenda coincided with national imperatives—especially during the war years—there arose striking opportunities to openly use children's books on a broad scale as agents of political socialization. Although the political climate would change dramatically after the war, the work of leftists in the children's literature field—though now necessarily less explicit in terms of politics—would not only continue but increase as other avenues of cultural production became subject to increased policing and as the Cold War ironically brought new opportunities for leftists in the children's book field.

Social Messages and Outlets for Them

In conjunction with the annual Christmas flurry to buy children's books, the December 24, 1935, issue of the *New Masses* featured an article by Jean Simon entitled "Which Books for Your Children?" The ostensible inspiration for Simon's piece was a letter to the editor received some weeks earlier from a mother who despaired of explaining to her boy "in his own terms, the world of conflict and contradiction in which he is growing up." Simon suggested that this mother's problem was one faced by many parents: how to make children aware of what is going on in the world around them; how, that is, "to reconcile the history-book America, of plenty and equal opportunity for all, with the hunger and privation which meet [children] on every hand outside and, only too often, inside the school walls." Though Simon acknowledged that there were finally a few decent books that explained *sexual* functions to children, "for the present we must despair of finding ready-made answers, with diagrams, to questions about the simple *economic* facts of life."[10]

Simon's article was the first in a series of articles, reviews, and booklists published in left-wing venues with increasing frequency in the 1940s, which were concerned with identifying and publicizing progressive children's books that had broad marketability. Simon's piece, and those that followed it over the years, also urged progressive writers to venture into the world of children's book writing.[11] Eventually, along with discussions of what kinds of content such books might encompass, came thoughtful consideration of how progressives could most effectively influence the field of children's publishing to ensure that what Mary Lapsley would call "our kind of stories" reached as many children as possible. First, however, came simply a call for "good" books. Later, with cues from schools, libraries, and publishers that the time was right and with inspiration (though almost certainly without direction) from the Soviet Union came more concrete strategies.

Simon made positive reference to a "small but sturdy collection of children's books" that were "springing up on the Left," but pointed out that such books were "not readily accessible to the masses of children" because they were kept out of libraries and most schools. Discussing a range of children's books published in Europe and the United States, she praised the work of Soviet author M. Il'in, British author Geoffrey Trease, and German writers Liza Tetzner and Alex Wedding. Simon argued that the "children's proletarian literature" created by the Young Pioneer movement in the United States had an advantage over the radical children's literature coming out of Europe, in that it concerned itself with problems familiar to working-class American children, and she singled out Helen Kay's *Battle in the Barnyard* as especially worthy of praise: "It ought to be an excellent supplementary text in Class Struggle, expressing the struggle between exploiter and exploited in terms of ants, chickens and pelicans." Still, she conceded, "children of picture-book age would probably fail to make the desired and necessary association between the barnyard and its human counterpart."[12]

More important, Simon maintained that literature created for children in "working-class organizations" like the Pioneers was not only hard to find, but it also "retains the mark of sectarianism." As such, it would be neither meaningful nor interesting to children already "corrupted" by "the recent products for children."[13] As Simon put it, "[W]e cannot plead too strongly for honest children's books created . . . for the broad masses of children who are threatened by the poison generated by the commercial children's presses which are constantly flooding schools and libraries." Simon called for a literature that would "unite all children, not only working-class children and children of the unemployed," a literature that would bring attention to pressing social issues without putting off young readers (or those "child guardians," to use Kennell's terminology, who controlled their access to books). Overall, Simon insisted:

> Our children's literature must have at its heart the feeling that human beings—children too—deserve sunshine and fun and warm clothes and good things to eat and above all, peace; and that men must organize to fight for these things and to fight against such things as poverty and imperialist war and exploitation; and against inequality of black and white, men and women, Jew and Gentile. But most important: it must use none of the words which by their strangeness would frighten children away from the real issues.[14]

She was referring here not simply to words per se—words like *proletariat, capitalism, Communism,* and *class struggle*—but to a *language* that could be inclusive and familiar to most American children. Indeed, she urged writers to draw upon "an immense American revolutionary tradition," reminding her peers, "if we want Daniel Boone to belong to us we all first have to make him come to life for ourselves."

Between 1935 and 1945, leftists became attuned to the value of trade children's literature as a medium for their message. The move to create a far-reaching children's literature with progressive influence entailed a move away from the sectarian character of much of the early socialist and Communist-authored children's literature and toward the creation of a commercially viable literature that was still "socially constructive," if not revolutionary. In this sense, it was appropriate that Lyrical Leftists Wanda Gág and Alfred Kreymborg were part of the League of American Writers' juvenile session in 1941, because their work from an earlier period suggested how this could be done. Once again, education was key.

Winter Soldiers: Children's Literature in the Battlefield of Schools

In the context of schools, several sometimes competing trends helped to build the market for children's books that dealt with the social, political, and scientific issues of the day. On the one hand, new methods of teaching adopted under the influence of progressive education, a new emphasis on democracy and social justice in school curricula, and a new political/class consciousness among teachers helped to create a welcome climate in classrooms and school libraries for the kinds of books leftists were interested in writing. On the other hand, a growing reaction against "creeping socialism" in the educational realm led to the monitoring of teachers and textbooks and, in many cases, precipitated the removal of what were deemed to be "subversive elements" from schools. But rather than depoliticizing the realm of education, right-wing pressure on schools ultimately helped to convince leftist cultural workers to shift their energies away from classrooms and textbooks and toward libraries and juvenile trade books, realms that were less visible but still central to the experience of schooling. Fears among progressives of "fascism goosestepping through the quiet halls of your children's schools" show the initial rumblings of a battle that would become full blown during the years of the Cold War and in which children's literature would quietly become a vital weapon.[15]

Increasing emphasis on democracy, citizenship, and social justice in education helped to precipitate the market for children's books supporting such imperatives. This new thrust reflected the growing popularity among educators of ideas once embraced only by a few frontier thinkers like George Counts: that the school had a part to play in the remaking of society along more equitable lines and that social, political, and economic conflicts could be prevented through the education of future leaders and citizens. As the director of Lincoln School (of Columbia University's Teachers College) put it, "If the words 'progressive school' are to have any genuine significance, their utterance should call to mind a school intensely interested not merely in method but in the social outlook of its members, critical of contemporary life and deeply concerned with its improvement."[16]

The pedagogical trend toward student-generated learning complemented the new antifascist common sense for it rejected an authoritarian model of adult-child relations and emphasized freedom, democracy, and cooperation as desirable traits.[17] Alongside a changing model of adult-child relations, the self-image of teachers changed with the broader "laboring of American culture" during the Popular Front. A growing number of educators came to agree with the idea that "in economic status the teacher's position is much closer to the ditch digger than to the college trustee." Encouraged to "discard the educational philosophy of neutrality," many teachers began to identify with the working class and its struggles. Beginning in the mid-1930s, teachers increasingly cast their lot with unions. And union activists tended to argue that they had the duty to do more than improve the economic status of teachers. As the director of the New York Teachers Union asserted in 1935, "We must of necessity take a stand on current social problems, especially educational problems, which are fundamentally social in origin. In this respect, we are not different from other unions, for the labor movement is a mass movement that involves the whole social order."[18]

Despite the Marxist critique of public schooling voiced by Mike Gold and others in the Communist milieu in the early 1930s, they increasingly acknowledged affinities with progressive educators, who were themselves profoundly affected by the Popular Front structure of feeling. Communists and their allies believed in the power of education to transform consciousness and, ultimately, public practice, as is evident from an extensive array of schools and programs aimed at both adults and children.[19] As they began to see the value of reaching "the broad masses of children," they eventually turned to the public schools, which, though decidedly unwelcoming to radical teachers and textbooks (especially in the years following World War II), would prove a viable market for Left-authored children's books.

Closely tied to the new economic and social orientation of many teachers—and its impact on pedagogy—was a growing liberal consensus on the subject of race. Partly in reaction to the racial ideology of fascism, partly as a result of new social-scientific findings about race and prejudice, and partly in response to the need for national unity in wartime, the somewhat patronizing "cultural gifts" movement, which began in the 1920s (and which helped to inspire works like Lucy Fitch Perkins's *Twins* series and the foreign-lands books), evolved into "intercultural education" programs, which aimed to strengthen democracy and alleviate social conflict by celebrating American cultural diversity.[20] Despite the movement's tendency to paper over the deeper structural issues involved in racial conflict, benign liberal efforts to celebrate "diversity" (sometimes taking the form of inviting several African-American students to an all-white class for a day or introducing students to interesting ethnic foods) could take on a distinctly radical edge.[21]

Clearly geared for use in white or predominantly white classrooms, Marion Cuthbert's *We Sing America* (1936) not only celebrated the achievements of outstanding African Americans but also pointed to the grave and repeated injustices suffered by the majority of blacks in a racist system. Cuthbert comments, for instance, upon the injustice of segregated schools:

> The Negro children are supposed to have schools just as good as those of the white children, but in only a few places are they as good. What happens is that most of the money is spent on white schools. The Negro schools get what little money is left. Many people feel that it is unfair for Negro children not to have as good schools as white children.

Presenting this situation to children, Cuthbert points to the fundamental dilemma created by the Supreme Court's *Plessy* decision: "Even if some day the schools for Negro children are as good as the schools for white children, is it a good thing to have separate schools for Negro and white children? That is something for you to think about. Some very wise grownups are trying to find the right answer to that question."[22]

During the Second World War, despite pressures toward unquestioning patriotism, many educators took the nation's struggle against fascist dictatorships as an opportunity to teach students about democracy and the right to embrace minority views and cultures. As historian William Tuttle notes in his study of the Second World War's impact upon children, "[R]epeatedly, home front educators expressed apprehension that without the democratization of schooling worldwide, there would soon be another generation of fanatics plunging the world into yet another war."[23] In New York City, many teachers were already predisposed to movements for social change and thus even more likely to adopt a "democratic, pluralist interpretation of World War II."[24] The New York Teachers Union actively promoted the pamphlet *The Races of Mankind* by anthropologists Gene Weltfish and Ruth Benedict, which blamed uneven wealth and achievement among various racial and ethnic groups on environment and inequality of opportunity rather than on inherent racial difference. The union claimed to have sold 1,500 copies of the pamphlet within a month of its publication. William Taft High School in the Bronx purchased 4,000 copies of the pamphlet, and its English department used it "as the basis of a unit on 'working toward brotherhood.'" At other schools, science classes, drawing upon information in *Races*, "did laboratory tests of blood types, demonstrating the absence of correlations with race or religion. They then publicized the results in their communities, to pressure the Red Cross to end blood bank segregation." Although *Races* was initially used in army training, it was barred by the War Department after members of Congress condemned the pamphlet for aiming to create "racial antagonism." Several classes wrote letters to Congress protesting the army's banning of the pamphlet, perhaps recognizing the dangerous precedent that had been set. That Ethel Rosenberg would ask her lawyer to buy *The Races of Mankind* as a gift for her sons while she was in prison in the early 1950s attests to the way in which sentiments that were mainstream during the Popular Front and Second World War would move into the marginal world of the far Left during the Cold War.[25]

Despite the ultimate banning of *Races*, the war was a kind of watershed for intercultural education programs in schools throughout the country. Springfield, Illinois, offered perhaps the most prominent example, and by 1946, 4,000 schools in twenty-two states had created programs modeled on some aspects of the Springfield Plan, which, according to historian Daryl Michael Scott, "called for the schools to teach multiracial democracy" throughout their classroom curricula. Other schools instituted special units on such subjects as "Negro history and culture" or distributed comic books, produced by the East and West Association, which had intercultural themes. The Common Council for American Unity, publishers of the journal *Common Ground*, sent Langston Hughes on a month-long tour of twenty-five schools in 1944 to spread the council's ideas. Such efforts were meant to counter the very real cultural conflicts aroused by the war, which often overshadowed American rhetoric of democratic pluralism.[26]

While the war's tendency to inspire what we would now call "multicultural" curricula was unmistakable, an opposing conservative impulse encouraged instituting curricular programs applicable to practical military imperatives (e.g., science programs geared toward serving projected defense needs) and adopting school disciplinary models borrowed from the military. Such efforts, of course, challenged the emphasis on independent, critical thinking and democracy fostered by progressive pedagogy and intercultural education.[27] Likewise, the antifascist wartime agenda did little to quell long-running pressures on school boards to root out "subversive" teachers and textbooks, and interracial books were frequently the target of wartime censorship efforts.

The National Americanism Commission of the American Legion had begun an earnest campaign against Bolshevism in schools and colleges in 1930, noting that teachers "are making regular breeding grounds out of the classrooms for their un-American teachings . . . under the guise of so-called 'new thought, liberalism and academic freedom.'"[28] The *New York Teacher* reported that by 1934, under pressure from an alliance among the Daughters of the American Revolution, the Veterans of Foreign Wars, the American Legion, and Hearst Press, fourteen states had passed legislation requiring teachers to take loyalty oaths; by 1935, eight additional states had passed such legislation; and by 1936 bills had been introduced in eleven of the remaining twenty-six states.[29]

The National Association of Manufacturers (NAM) took the lead in investigating American textbooks, seeking out any that were "prejudicial to our form of government, our society, or the system of free enterprise." Perhaps the most famous textbook controversy concerned Harold Rugg's enormously popular series of social studies textbooks, which sold more than a million copies between 1929 and 1939. Rugg's textbooks openly and candidly discussed slavery, described the United States as a nation of immigrants, challenged traditional gender roles, advocated social planning, and made vivid the pressing social problems of the day. The textbooks were attacked with increasing frequency and intensity beginning in the late 1930s. One official from the Daughters of Colonial Wars, for instance, complained that the books "tried to give the child an unbiased viewpoint instead of teaching him real Americanism."[30]

The combination of local attacks and a national campaign by the NAM dramatically reduced the sales of the books, foreshadowing even more widespread textbook controversies in the late 1940s and 1950s and precipitating self-censorship among textbook authors and publishers who wished to avoid such crises. In August 1941, Governor Eugene Talmadge of Georgia announced that he would burn any books that advocated interracial cooperation, singling out Cuthbert's *We Sing America* and promising "to get rid of that book and all books of that kind." Progressive and intercultural education would become even more suspect in the milieu of the Cold War.[31]

Although the most notorious and widespread instances of teacher dismissals occurred in the 1950s, the investigation and suspension in 1941 by New York's anti-Communist Rapp-Coudert Committee of thirty-three professors on the faculties of City College and Brooklyn College (including Max Yergen, the first African-American professor on the faculty of a New York City university and instructor of the first class on Negro history and culture) precipitated an outcry from the New York Teachers Union and from educators around the country. Their protests did little to restore the teachers to their classrooms. But a group calling itself the Committee for the Defense of Public Education did produce a striking book, *Winter Soldiers*, in response to the dismissals. In content and form, this book anticipated something of the way in which pressures on teachers and textbooks would ultimately precipitate a shift of radical educators' energies to children's literature.

The text of *Winter Soldiers: The Story of a Conspiracy against the Schools* by author and fired teacher Louis Lerman, starkly describes a battle between "progressive" and "reactionary" forces being waged over the bodies of the nation's children. In his foreword to Lerman's text, the prominent anthropologist Franz Boas—a strong voice against fascism and racism in the late 1930s—articulates the basic confrontation between the educational values of the Left and those of conservative and business organizations like Chambers of Commerce, the American Legion, and the National Association of Manufacturers. Boas insists:

> [T]he attacks upon our schools . . . are intended to curtail schooling and to indoctrinate the young with the idea that . . . every attempt to adjust the old ways to new needs is subversive and will lead to disaster. They are opposed to fundamental needs of our times, to the education of the masses to independent thinking, to clearing away of prejudices and to a tolerant understanding of the needs and aspirations of the various groups constituting our society.[32]

More striking than the book's text are its illustrations by prominent artists, several of whom—including Julian Brazelton, Ernest Crichlow, William Gropper, Rockwell Kent, Elizabeth Olds, and William Steig—would go on to write and/or illustrate children's books (see figure 3.2). Indeed, *Winter Soldiers* looks, and in some ways reads, like a children's book, and it addresses itself explicitly to children as well as to working-class adults (who were the implicit audiences of much Left-authored children's literature). It also suggests that the values of the "real America" are being threatened. As Lerman notes in the book's opening:

> LET ME TELL YOU the story of a strange thing that is happening in America. I tell you the story in pictures so that even you children, who cannot read the honey poison speeches of the destroyers of your schools; so that even you men and women who work in the shops and the factories, the offices and farms, and perhaps have no time for the luxury of reading, may read as you run your lathe, as you wash dishes in the kitchen, as you sell groceries over the counter, as you march on the picket line . . . —so that you may know what is happening in America—America the free and the beautiful.[33]

Though an attempt to maintain a progressive influence in schools, *Winter Soldiers* foreshadowed a movement of leftists out of teaching and into trade children's literature.[34] The field offered ample professional opportunities to edu-

Figure 3.2. Illustration by William Steig from *Winter Soldiers: The Story of a Conspiracy against Our Schools. Winter Soldiers* (1941), which contained pictures by a number of people who would go on to illustrate children's books, was published to protest the initial wave of teacher dismissals in New York City following the Rapp-Coudert hearings. In this picture, Steig shows Rapp-Coudert, among others, standing on the backs of young children. Steig would later become a bestselling children's author with books like *Sylvester and the Magic Pebble* (1969). Used with permission courtesy of Jeanne Steig. Photographic reproduction from Tamiment Library, New York University.

cators who had come to feel unwelcome in public school classrooms, despite educational demands for material that grappled with contemporary problems and issues. Public and school librarians increasingly made the effort to stock their shelves with sources answering this demand, and publishers, in turn, scrambled to add socially constructive literature to their lists.

The Problem Book

A changing view of childhood in light of children's actual lives in the 1930s and 1940s translated into changes in the ways in which many "child guardians" came to understand children's literature and their role in relation to it. As Ruth Kennell said of many juvenile editors, librarians, and publishers in her remarks to the juvenile session of the Writers Congress:

> They recognized that during the years of the depression when a majority of American youth had neither a beautiful nor a secure environment, it was not presenting a true picture to publish only books about happy, sheltered children. Such a conspiracy of silence about actual conditions merely postponed the inevitable disillusionment from year to year until the youth is no longer a youth, and must face the grim realities of life unprotected.[35]

The Second World War intensified the sense among librarians and those in the publishing business that children could no longer be, or should no longer be, shielded from the "truth." Alice Dagliesh—author, children's book editor at Charles Scribner and Sons, and book reviewer for *Parents* magazine—noted in 1941, "I still hear quibbling over whether a book is 'too sad' or 'too realistic' for children." Dagliesh lamented that "our children have been wrapped in cellophane by well-meaning adults, they have been carefully and overzealously protected from the unpleasant. Now they can no longer be. They are part of a world at war, and they must be strong enough to be a part of it along with adults." Similarly, in a widely cited piece in the *Library Journal* called "Making the World Safe for the Janey Larkins," Julia Sauer, author and head of the Department of Work with Children at the Rochester (New York) Public Library, noted: "It has been said that there are at the moment only two kinds of people in this country—those who are conscious of the world, and those who are not." Sauer expressed an urgent need for books dealing with the present: "When children in other parts of the world are sacrificing their lives, their health, their security, is it asking too much that America's children should sacrifice some of their carefree childhood?" She claimed that instead of thanking his or her parents for a carefree childhood, a young adult confronted with "tomorrow's chaos" was more likely to ask her parents, "Why wasn't I told?"[36]

Such comments represented a growing consensus among people in the children's book field that children's literature contained too much "sweetness and light" and not enough "red meat," as child expert Josette Frank was quoted as saying in a 1941 article in *Publishers Weekly* on "The Problem Book." "During the last year we have heard increasingly about 'books with social significance' written especially for young people," the article notes. "Stories involving the adventures of migratory workers, the underprivileged, and other problems heretofore regarded as taboo for young people have been successfully issued by many publishers." The authors asserted that while such books are rarely presented with "any special ballyhoo as to their social content, subsequent discussions, lectures, and conferences have revealed them as vital sociological documents."[37]

The problem-book article presented the results of a survey with "twenty four men and women who are outstanding and representative in the juvenile field," including "editors, teachers, social workers, librarians, educators, authors, publishers, book sellers, critics and parents." These professionals and parents were asked "what their views are on the 'problem' book for young people, and what the market and esthetic [sic] value of such works may be." While the article's authors acknowledged that the term *social significance* could be off-putting (especially in the context of children's literature, which is often imagined as a realm apart from pressing social and political issues), their terminology was not accidental. In a playful gesture that tied this growing trend in children's literature to a larger "movement culture," the top of the article's first page featured a musical bar with letters dancing along the lines instead of notes, the letters spelling out, as though a tune, "Sing us a Song of Social Significance," words taken from the hit Popular Front musical *Pins and Needles*.[38]

Likewise, if Sauer's reference to "those who are conscious of the world's problems and those who are not" reminds us of the workers' song "Which Side Are You On?" or of the 1930s manifesto "Writers Take Sides" or of other left-wing rhetoric, it is because many people in the children's book field were profoundly affected by the structure of feeling characteristic of the Popular Front. So it is perhaps not surprising that one of the people consulted for the problem-book article in *Publishers Weekly* was Elizabeth Morrow (Betty Bacon), juvenile editor at McBride, an active member of the Communist Party, and a reviewer of children's books for the *New Masses*. "Average young people do not think of social significance in abstract terms," she reflected. "What they want above all are good stories. Given good stories, they will take what comes with them. . . . The social significance must arise naturally from the conditions of the story . . . or else it becomes propaganda. Young people have no use for propaganda as current coin among themselves," she maintained.[39] Bacon's consciousness of the delicate relationship between children's books and propaganda reveals a great deal about the Left's changing view of children's literature. Likewise, the inclusion of Bacon in this survey of "representative and outstanding" men and women in the children's book field further suggests the entrance of leftists into the children's literature mainstream.

The library field showed tendencies similar to juvenile publishing. Just as the cause of antifascism and U.S. involvement in the war dramatically affected the priorities of American educators, book burning, censorship, and the creation and enforcement of explicit racial hierarchies under fascist regimes precipitated a new emphasis on diversity (in terms of content and viewpoints) in U.S. library collections and a shift in librarians' priorities from the "protect[ion] of public morals in print" to advocacy for intellectual freedom.[40]

In 1939, for instance, the American Library Association (ALA) passed the Library Bill of Rights, beginning, as library historian Louise Robbins notes, "a process of establishing the defense of intellectual freedom as a primary tenet of librarianship."[41] This bill did not, until the 1950s, extend to children (because librarians still took seriously their role as protectors when it came to children), and it did not necessarily represent a political statement on the part of librarians other than a defense of the traditional liberal notion of a free marketplace of ideas. But it did signal a real shift in the role of librarians away from protection and toward advocacy, which gradually encompassed library services to children as well as adults.[42] Moreover, a segment of those in the library profession, including children's librarians, *were* radicalized, not only by the rise of fascism, but also by Congress of Industrial Organizations' (CIO) unionization drives encompassing teachers, librarians, and white-collar workers in publishing houses.[43]

"Going out on strike affected the ideology of a lot of people," writer Rose Wyler reflected, mentioning a strike of Disney cartoonists in 1941 and union activity at Columbia University Teachers College, where she taught elementary science education (before finding other work in anticipation of being investigated for her political views). "Many professionals had the idea that people who went on strike were factory workers and truckers, but problems created by the Depression changed professionals' attitude[s] toward unionization or organization of some kind."[44] Betty Bacon pointed to the importance of the United Office and Professional Workers' Union for establishing a kind of community among leftist children's book folk: "that's how you got to know all the good left-wing people from all the different publishers, because we all belonged."[45]

Librarians on the Left joined together in 1939 to form a Progressive Librarians Council (PLC), which went well beyond supporting the ALA Committee on Intellectual Freedom. It advocated for many "progressive causes" within the library field, including fighting racial discrimination in the profession (and in libraries, which were segregated in many cities), supporting tenure and acting against unfair dismissals, cooperating with labor organizations by "providing labor literature of all kinds and bringing it to the attention of librarians," and promoting unionization efforts within libraries. Though the Progressive Librarians Council did not directly address services to children in its resolutions, a number of children's librarians were active in the PLC and in other organizations through which they connected left-wing activism with library services to children. Several of these women and men became very important in the field and were instrumental in pressing for changes in library services to children and in children's literature more broadly. Charlamae Rollins, an African-American librarian who ran the children's department at the George C. Hall branch of the Chicago Public Library from 1932 to 1963, was one significant player. As a PLC member, Rollins began a letter-writing campaign in 1941 in which she complained to publishers about the lack of books that spoke to the experience of African-American children. Positive responses from teachers led Rollins to compile the landmark book *We Build Together*, one of the earliest guides to books about African-American children.[46] Those active in the PLC and in related organizations were well aware of the role they played in the nation's cultural and educational apparatus, and they took seriously their part in "the defense of culture and democracy." Though the PLC did not survive the McCarthy era, by the 1960s new organizations, such as the Social Responsibility Roundtable, had taken its place, and some of the same individuals joined these organizations.[47]

New children's books about industrial labor that took the implicitly prolabor politics of the *Here and Now* books a step further reflected the affinity that white-collar intellectual laborers began to feel with members of the working class. Lavinia Davis's *Adventures in Steel* (1938) valorized the vital and often dangerous jobs performed by steel workers and described the importance of unions as protection against unfair labor practices. Mary Elting's *Lollipop Factory and Lots of Others* (1946) briefly describes a speed-up and explains the need for unionization in the midst of teaching young children how ice cream, lollipops, and other products are made and distributed. Notably, Jeanne Bendick's illustrations subtly challenge norms in two ways: they show black faces (something she and Elting had to press for) and also show women on the assembly line (see figure 3.3). Even more explicit in its politics, Elie Siegmeister's paean to manual labor, *Work and Sing* (1944), included the songs of sailors, cowboys, railroad linemen, farmers, and other workers, linking these bards of "the folk" to a tradition of protest singing ("Joe Hill sang such work songs of all mankind twenty years ago: Leadbelly, Woody Guthrie, Aunt Molly Jackson, Earl Robinson and many others sing them today. And tomorrow all kinds of people in all kinds of places will be singing them together").[48]

One of the few texts for children from this period that deals very explicitly with the conflict between capital and labor is Henry Gregor Felsen's story for young adults *The Company Owns the Tools* (1942), which he wrote under the pseudonym Henry Vicar. In this story, an honest young mechanic from a small town in Iowa gets a job in Motor City (Detroit), building cars for the war effort.

Figure 3.3. Illustration by Jeanne Bendick from *The Lollipop Factory and Lots of Others* by Mary Elting. This picture operates on several levels, showing assembly-line labor, workers of different races, and also women workers. The latter two were unusual sights in children's books of this time period. The book tells children how lollipops, ice cream, pencils, and other common goods are produced. Garden City, N.Y.: Doubleday, 1946. Used with permission courtesy of Jeanne Bendick.

There he receives a humbling lesson in assembly-line mass production, quickly deciding that the only way to maintain any dignity in his work as an individual is to band together with the other workers, despite the company's harassment of the union and its efforts to divide workers along racial lines. The logic of the union is dictated by the logic of mass production, in which each individual unit is essentially the same as any other. As one of the men puts it: "They can do without any one of us, but they can't do without all of us."[49]

That such books could earn praise from librarians and others among those Kennell called "child guardians" is clear evidence of shifting criteria for judging the value of children's books. Julia Sauer's article "Making the World Safe for the Janey Larkins" pointed to librarians' new interest in promoting "socially constructive" children's literature. The daughter of a migrant laborer, Janey Larkins was the protagonist of *Blue Willow*, a 1940 book by Doris Gates that was sometimes referred to as the "juvenile *Grapes of Wrath*." Her family has almost no money, and Janey herself has no possessions other than a plate picturing a blue weeping willow tree, given to her by her mother before she died. Despite the conditions in which she grows up, Janey is optimistic, headstrong, and determined to get an education. The squalor of Janey's existence, as the book matter-of-factly describes it, is striking for a children's book of the time (as is the fact that Janey's best friend is a child of Mexican migrants). The book earned praise from both liberal and radical reviewers for its portrayal of poverty and for the extent to which it helped to expand the range of experiences represented in children's literature.

Along with Doris Gates's *Blue Willow*, other realistic books for children by liberal authors such as Lois Lenski, John L. Tunis, and Florence Crannell Means similarly embraced the populist, antiracist, prolabor, and antiauthoritarian politics characteristic of the Popular Front. And like *Blue Willow*, these books were met with acclaim by members of the children's literature establishment as well as by reviewers in left-wing outlets.[50] In the 1940s, Lois Lenski began to publish the regionalist stories for which she would become famous. These books, including the Newbery Medal–winning *Strawberry Girl* (1945), focused primarily on poor or working-class children of different races or ethnicities and usually centered on strong, feisty female protagonists.[51] Tunis's strongly prolabor and antiracist sports books, which were popular among adolescent boys, used sports as the subtext for confronting racial and religious discrimination or labor conflicts.[52] *Keystone Kids* (1943), for instance, told of struggles to unite a baseball team torn by prejudice against a Jewish rookie catcher. Finally, Florence Crannell Means's books dealt with American children of various minority groups, including American Indians, African Americans, Jewish Americans, and Japanese Americans. Her most controversial book, *The Moved Outers*, which describes the wartime internment of a Japanese-American family, was selected as a Newbery Honor book for 1946.[53]

United through Books

The trend toward realism in children's literature reflected a growing belief that children were autonomous beings, independent-minded, concerned with social justice, and entitled to know something about the way the world works—ideas fundamental to the social vision of the Left. As liberals began to recognize their common cause with radicals on certain issues, especially where children were concerned, so radicals broadened their own notions of what kinds of books were good for children. By the 1940s, left-wing venues began to regularly review and recommend children's books, and their lists also became quite expansive. In addition to praising books by writers in the Communist milieu, lists of recommended children's books printed in the *New Masses* and the *National Guardian* or distributed by the Marxist Jefferson School of Social Science consistently praised books by Lenski, Means, Tunis, and Dr. Seuss, as well as by Lucy Sprague Mitchell and other liberal writers. In general, lists and reviews in these forums eschewed the ideological rigidity that could often be found in other realms of leftist literary criticism. Indeed, as Betty Bacon said of the lists of children's books she compiled for the *New Masses*, "[W]e weren't so worried about the politics of the author as the politics of the book."[54] In other words, if a book positively portrayed labor or taught something about race relations or technical processes, if it promoted critical thinking or poked fun at authority figures, it had a good chance of earning a stamp of approval from Bacon and other left-wing critics (as well as from the liberal establishment). Leftists even made lists of books that were just "for fun."[55] Bacon believed that both laughter and poetry were essential elements of growing up; she insisted that "if you don't laugh you can't grow" and that there is a "kind of understanding that you get in poetry and nowhere else."[56]

At the same moment that leftists like Bacon were expanding their notions of what books were good for children, new awards and booklists created by liberal librarians, educators, and others concerned with children translated into incentives for children's books of "social significance." The Child Study Association (CSA), for instance, inaugurated an award in 1943 for a story dealing with "the contemporary scene . . . in a way that will help clarify vexing—perhaps controversial problems." As the chair of the association's Children's Book Committee noted:

> We believe that children want to know and are entitled to be told what is happening in relation to such present problems as social-economic differences, labor relations, and race prejudices in our own country, and good neighbor relations abroad. If our children are asked to preserve this precious thing we call "a democratic way of life" they will certainly have to know first what it is.[57]

The award's announcement in 1943 provoked an immediate response from publishers, which recommended books for the award.[58] Several other awards and booklists that recognized social messages as well as literary merit would follow in the coming years; the educational journal *Common Ground*, for instance, published regular lists of children's books that would be useful in combating prejudice and xenophobia.

That trade children's literature was becoming a safe medium for characters like Janey Larkins represented a significant victory for those wishing to see more "socially constructive" juvenile fare, but the victory was incomplete, to say the least, as an article surveying the field for the *New Masses* in 1942 attested. Harry Taylor (in all likelihood Harry Granick, who sometimes wrote under this pseudonym) argued that the field "still produces too many of the over-charming, cushioned tarts of sheer pilf for pelf and too few packages of the real and the present."[59] Taylor/Granick would join liberal critics in singing the praises of books like *Blue Willow*, but he also pointed to the limits of such "realistic" books by liberal authors, noting the moment when *Blue Willow* loses its radical social critique, with an ending that clearly embodies a good dose of wishful thinking. When Janey's father runs out of work and her stepmother becomes gravely ill, the Larkinses realize they will have to move away from the town where Janey finally feels she is settling in. But here is where the story becomes like a fairy tale: at the last minute the rich and kindly Mr. Anderson, who owns the shack where the Larkinses live, learns that his foreman has been charging the Larkinses rent and keeping the money for himself; Mr. Anderson decides to offer Janey's father the foreman's job and to give the Larkins family a real house, with all the free eggs and butter they can eat. The book never provides realistic solutions to the plight of migrant workers and, moreover, does nothing to suggest the reasons that the Larkinses' situation exists in the first place. Granick argued that children deserve a more honest explanation: "I have had a thirteen-year-old tell me that though she liked *Blue Willow* . . . she thought its author, Doris Gates, should have been honest to the last page, and not blamed the suffering of the Larkins[es] on a farm foreman."[60]

Similarly, although her choice of subject matter in *The Moved Outers* was fairly remarkable for its time (as was her consistent focus on ethnic and racial minorities), Florence Crannell Means's position in that book clearly tends toward liberal integrationism as opposed to a more cutting critique. Means portrays the Oharas as patriotic Americans who are very much assimilated in their community prior to their internment. Although life in the camps is shown to be difficult, they make the best of things, and by the end of the book, they exhibit great hope and optimism about the reintegration of Japanese Americans into U.S. society.

Granick and other leftists were by no means dismissive of such books, however. They recognized that the publication of a book like *Blue Willow*, and its critical acclaim, marked new understandings of childhood and changed conditions in the children's book field. Reviewing developments in American children's literature, Granick noted that vast improvements in the past twenty years coincided with, on the one hand, recognition on the part of publishers that there were "profitable opportunities in juvenile book making," and, on the other hand, with "grave disillusions [that] caused progressive people in all fields to reexamine the basis on which a better world might conceivably arise." This reexamination, he said, turned attention to children, producing a "mounting conviction that children are a tremendously vital portion of the nation and must be treated with imagination and honesty."[61] In other words, the development of modern children's book publishing in the United States coincided with the development of the organized Left; Granick asserted that they might fruit-

fully intersect, with politically committed cultural producers consciously placing children's literature on their agendas.

Granick complained, "progressive educators as well as the children themselves are still calling for stories that bear a direct relation to socio-economic
reality. But the rate at which this wish is being gratified, though accelerating,
remains a trickle." Considering the question of whether there was any untapped
"force" that could "appreciably swing writing and editorial choice into a wider
democratic channel," Granick argued that this force was "implicit in the largest
and most progressive mass organization in the country, the trade union movement of over 11,000,000 members, many of them parents." He insisted:

> If once the trade unions recognized that the children of today are the
> trade unionists of tomorrow and that in a very important measure
> children are daily being subjected in class room, cinema, radio and
> reading matter to distortions and suppressions of the truth and the
> real world into which they are growing, the unions would try to cor-
> rect this condition as strenuously as they seek to improve any other
> conditions of labor.[62]

Certainly union organizing among teachers, librarians, and publishing
workers already linked to the juvenile field contributed to recognition by leftists
of the part that children's literature could play as part of the cultural front. But
the movement of leftists into all levels of the field came less as the result of an
organized effort on the part of unions (or the CP) and more as a result of interest
intersecting with opportunity, especially for young women. Indeed, as to why it
took nearly seven years for the League of American Writers to place children's
literature on its agenda, Ruth Kennell speculated that "a natural reason why
adults do not recognize our literary work is that they do not read it, except as
mothers, teachers and librarians"—all predominantly "feminine" professions.[63]
But this lack of visibility and the lack of "literary legitimacy" (as Bacon put it)
made the field particularly hospitable to radicals, especially women.[64]

As Bacon put it, "[P]ublishing was very different in those days. There were
a lot of publishers, and they were not all owned by the same people. There was
a lot of variety in publishing. So there were a lot of little 'chinks' so to speak,
that you could get into." Many young radicals, she says, had gotten jobs in publishing, where "there was . . . a lot of possibility." This was especially the case
for the rapidly expanding field of juvenile publishing, which expanded even
more rapidly in the years of the baby boom, from the mid-1940s to the mid-
1960s. "We got out of school and we got jobs and we got assistant this, that
and the other thing, and we were able to exercise a certain amount of influence," Bacon recalled. "Eventually people got to be the heads of whatever it was

they were working on."[65] Groups like the League of American Writers—which also sponsored writers' schools—and editorials by people like Jean Simon and Harry Granick encouraged progressive writers to create books for children. But perhaps even more important was the overall climate of the field.

Though they may not have been open about their politics, radical cultural workers operated comfortably in the children's literature mainstream, not just as writers, but as influential "child guardians," working in publishing houses, libraries, and bookstores; reviewing children's books; compiling booklists; and otherwise overseeing the field's output. Clara Ostrowsky, for instance, who ran the library and bookstore at the Marxist Jefferson School of Social Science, reviewed books for the *New Masses*, worked with the Progressive Librarians Council, and was also a member of the CSA's Children's Book Committee and wrote reviews for its journal, *Child Study*.[66] Betty Bacon, for her part, believed that the work she was doing in the children's book field and in the party supported both her concern for children and her interest in building a more socially just society. "I never separated them and that was the whole point. The two were together, just like that," she told me, crossing her fingers to show their interconnectedness.[67] Thus, when she wrote lists of recommended books for the Communist *New Masses* or for the trade journal the *Retail Bookseller*, she singled out many of the same books for praise.

Left-wing writers and editors were active in organizations like the Book Mobilization Committee, the Writers' War Board, and the Bureau for Intercultural Education, which had an important influence on the field during the war. The Book Mobilization Committee, of which Bacon was a member, set up a subcommittee on children's books in 1943, with the goal of extending library services to children and obtaining the cooperation of trade unions in the distribution of children's books.[68] The Writers' War Board and the Bureau for Intercultural Education developed extensive programs to combat prejudice in children's literature, an issue of paramount concern to writers on the Left, who aggressively pressed for changes in this area.[69]

Members of the CSA's Children's Book Committee took an active role on issues of racial, ethnic, religious, and class representation, using their connections and clout to directly confront publishers or to open dialogue with librarians about objectionable aspects of various books, and they recommended books with strong social messages (Josette Frank, for instance, singled out *The Company Owns the Tools* to a woman looking for recommendations). Their journal, *Child Study*, even praised a book with a "frankly Marxist point of view." Committee chair Josette Frank even went so far as to make direct appeals to authors, writing, for instance, to Lavinia Davis in 1948 about the need for children's books on the subject of labor and asking if Davis might revive *Adventures in Steel*, which had gone out of print. "I find," Frank wrote, that there is no book which takes its place and, in fact, no other book on this whole general subject."[70]

It is perhaps ironic that the Child Study Association, a group of upper middle-class women, was one of the primary levers for a marked shift in the merit criteria for children's literature. In sometimes not-so-subtle ways, the criticisms decrying the lack of "red meat" in children's literature could be interpreted as an implicit attack on, as author Howard Pease put it, the "tenderminded feminine control of children's books" by women editors, librarians, educators, and authors.[71] But it was exactly this "tenderminded feminine control" that made the genre seem so unthreatening and thus a place where social issues could be confronted, even during the Cold War, by individuals whose political views, in other contexts, were deemed threatening to the "American way of life." The general acceptance of radically minded people in influential organizations like the Child Study Association and in publishing houses literally helped to create common cause in the children's literature field.

Such momentum was built around efforts to create books of "social significance"—books fostering "brotherhood," "good will," "democracy," "understanding," respect, and peace—that Clara Ostrowsky and Elizabeth Morrow would claim that the 1944 Book Week luncheon showed "a new point of view toward children's books." Writing in the *New Masses*, they proclaimed, "the editors and booksellers and writers and librarians are taking seriously their part in building a united nation and united world." Book Week's slogan in 1944 was "United through Books," a theme that explicitly connected the vision of a postwar international community to children's reading; it also, though inadvertently, aptly represented the coalitions being built in the United States around children's books. Considering the range of organizations sponsoring the 1944 Book Week luncheon—including the Child Study Association, the Women's Committee of the National Council of American Soviet Friendship, and the Book Committee of the Women's Council for Post-war Europe—it is fair to say that the moment represented the culmination of a united front in the children's book world. Ostrowsky and Morrow claimed, "Never before had such a variety of interested groups gathered to talk about children's reading, and never before was the talk so aware of the responsibilities of children's books in a democracy."[72]

Recognizing children's books' embeddedness in a matrix of physical and intellectual labor was a key step in transforming or refunctioning the field, from the mechanics of book production to the content of books themselves. This is made evident in *Here Is a Book* (1939), a story about book publishing. Recalling the long road from idea to printed page, the book's author, Marshall McClintock, notes:

Thousands of people had something to do with making that book. The men who cut down trees to make pulp for the paper, the men who shipped the logs, the men who made the paper at the mill, editors, advertising men, stenographers, shipping men, the men who mined the lead for the slugs of the linotype machine, and the men who made that machine and all the others used in bookmaking. And there were linotype operators, pressmen, ink makers, proof readers, binders, and the men who ran the trucks and trains that carried the books all over the country. Booksellers, salesmen, clerks, librarians, teachers, reviewers—and of course the author and artist.[73]

Here Is a Book has no explicit political message, but it indicates an awareness of the full circle of production and dissemination that would have to be encompassed in any effort to make children's literature more progressive (although in its catalog of the "thousands of people [who] had something to do with making that book" it neglects to mention women, who would almost certainly have played key roles). He may have had some issues relating to being a man in a female-dominated field, but it is clear that McClintock, who worked as an editor at Vanguard, at Whitman, and at Messner (and whose wife, May Garelick, also worked as an editor and author), was attuned to the political potential of children's books and children's book publishing. When he spoke at the 1941 Writers Congress on the progressive potential of mass-market children's books, McClintock noted Whitman's successes in publishing cheap, popular books with a serious message, like the antifascist *Betty Boop in Miss Gulliver's Travels* (1935).[74]

McClintock's comments on the progressive potential of mass-market children's literature came at essentially the same moment that Western Printing was launching the twenty-five-cent Little Golden Book series. Like the British Puffin Picture Books, the Little Golden books may well have been inspired by Soviet success at publishing good, cheap books in massive quantities, an accomplishment that seemed to predict "something like a revolution in children's books."[75] Certainly many committed leftists—as well as the progressive educators who worked with Lucy Sprague Mitchell on Golden Books' early *Bank Street* series of readers—recognized the opportunity presented by Little Golden Books for reaching the "broad masses of children" as they signed on as writers, editors, and illustrators.[76]

McClintock's reference to the "thousands of people [who] had something to do with making that book" indicates a real consciousness among members of the Popular Front Left that far-reaching changes in American culture would require changes in the means of cultural production. To the extent that the Soviet Union had mobilized every possible cultural institution—libraries, schools, bookstores, and museums—to promote children's reading, many people took notice.[77] In the United States, as white-collar workers like "book-sellers[,] . . . teachers, and librarians" as well as authors and artists, began to join the "miners," "linotype operators," "shipping men," and other blue-collar workers in embracing the Popular Front structure of feeling, they were able to change the kinds of books that were written for and ultimately read by children.

Books as Weapons in the War of Ideas

The Second World War provided the crucial context for linking the agenda of the Communist Left to Americans more generally. At the same time, it brought attention to the power of children's literature as an agent of political socialization. The war against fascism brought new meaning, for instance, to the nation's folk heritage and history, as it required defining *Americanism* as something diametrically opposed to a racist, imperialist, and authoritarian fascism. Thus a book with no apparent connection to the war, Irwin Shapiro's *John Henry and the Double-Jointed Steam Drill* (1945), was enlisted as a tool of antifascist education.[78]

On the frontispiece of the book, which was illustrated by James Daugherty, a striking image sets up the reader to bring a whole set of associations to the archetypal story of a single (black) man's struggle against the power of the machine (figure 3.4). The picture shows the muscular, shirtless John Henry, holding a sledge hammer across his shoulders and stepping forward, as though he is about to emerge from the picture. He is flanked on one side by an African-American solider dressed for combat and, on the other side, by an African-American woman reading to a young boy, presumably her child. Both the soldier and the woman are placed in the background in relation to John Henry, and their eyes are cast downward, in striking contrast to John Henry's determined upward gaze.

Below this triad of folk hero, soldier, and mother/child are a pantheon of twentieth-century African-American celebrities, all of whom are associated with the black struggle for civic, cultural, or economic equality: Joe Louis, the celebrated boxer and World War II soldier; George Washington Carver, the scientist and inventor; Paul Robeson, the actor, singer, lawyer, and activist (who would soon be blacklisted for his political views); singer Marian Anderson; educator Booker T. Washington; and writer Richard Wright. We are invited to understand these figures as continuing John Henry's legacy, as real-life heroes who, through their accomplishments, have defied seemingly insurmountable odds.

Figure 3.4. Illustration by James Daugherty from *John Henry and the Double-Jointed Steam Drill* by Irwin Shapiro. The image of the African-American soldier and the mother and child reading alongside John Henry link this story to the Double V campaign of World War II and to the child readers who represent America's future. Placing the folk figure John Henry above outstanding contemporary African Americans ties his larger-than-life heroics to ongoing struggles in the present. New York: Messner, 1945. Used with permission (to the extent that they may own the rights) courtesy of Charles M. Daugherty Estate.

If this pantheon of black celebrities invites us to consider the contemporary significance of John Henry's story, the image of the black soldier, directly beside John Henry's towering figure, explicitly urges us to consider the story's significance in light of the war being waged at the time of the book's publication. This was a war that African Americans fought on two fronts; the Double V campaign linked the battle against fascism abroad (in which black soldiers participated, in segregated units), with the battle against racism at home. Finally, placing the image of the woman and child reading alongside the soldier and the larger-than-life folk hero puts education on a par with brute physical force in the battle against a dehumanizing enemy, a literal or a metaphorical machine. Indeed, the child reading this story, alone or with a parent, joins cause with the soldier fighting fascism; with the intellectuals, artists, and athletes, whose individual expressions are associated with an entire people's struggle for freedom and dignity; and with John Henry himself. Ultimately, the illustration underscores, it is children who will determine fascism's future. In this context, children's literature, and education in general, took on a new significance.

Moreover, even more fundamentally than the initial declaration of a Popular Front in 1935 (when vocal antifascist expressions, especially in the form of supporting Spanish loyalists in their civil war, were deemed "premature" by the establishment), the war helped to propel members of the Communist Left into the cultural mainstream and provided a unique opportunity to educate children to be "anti-fascist and not fascist," the imperative that Mary Lapsley had set forth at the 1941 Writers Congress. If literature were to be socially constructive at this historical moment, it had to, first and foremost, reject the central premises of fascism. And antifascism had become the American way.

The Second World War drew members of the Communist Left into the armed forces, into core arenas of American propaganda making (most notably, into the Office of War Information), and into the culture industries (where, for example, left-wing filmmakers were paid by the government to make pro-Soviet films). Moreover, the nation's wartime struggle against fascism allowed leftists to articulate aspects of their political and social vision under the banner of protecting the institutions and ideals that the United States had gone to war to defend; in other words, it created a way to demonstrate the Popular Front claim that "Communism is twentieth-century Americanism." In contrast to the situation in Hollywood, where most makers of antifascist films were blacklisted shortly after the war, the lesson in the children's literature field was that careers could be made, not broken, through stories that celebrated the struggle against fascism, as well as the American-Soviet alliance.[79]

The wartime struggle against fascism entered children's literature in explicit and implicit ways, and it weighed heavily upon the minds of those working in the field. As Vernon Ives, an owner of Holiday House publishers and chair of the

Council on Books in Wartime, would ask in a 1943 article in *Publishers Weekly* on "Children's Books and the War": "Caught between material and manpower difficulties on the one hand, and an unprecedented demand for books on the other, are we giving sufficient thought to our responsibilities as merchants of knowledge and ideas?" This concern was especially pronounced for those in the field with strong political convictions. Betty Bacon, writing that same year for the *Retail Bookseller* (as Elizabeth Morrow), made a strong connection between work in the field of children's literature and the struggle against fascism, arguing that recent American children's books "reaffirm our faith in victory over an enemy whose 'children's books' are an instrument of regimentation and hate." To create books that supported the values for which the nation was struggling was, according to Bacon, "our challenge and responsibility. If we who work with children's books meet it fully and honestly, we are doing our job toward winning the war and the peace."[80]

Historian Bill Tuttle has argued that there were few war-related titles published and that "librarians' lists of recommended children's books were relatively devoid of war-inspired stories."[81] It is true that seemingly apolitical classics like *Make Way for Ducklings* (1941) and the *Betsy Tacy* books are products of the 1940s. Yet so many books of the era, from Esther Forbes's Revolutionary War story *Johnny Tremain* (1943), to H. A. Rey's caper about an adorable and mischievous monkey, *Curious George* (1941), can be understood as products of the antifascist imagination, inseparable from the war years that produced them (*Johnny Tremain*, which was illustrated by radical artist Lynd Ward, had obvious lessons about fighting for democracy, and *Curious George*, written by a refugee from fascism, told of a little monkey whose insatiable curiosity and independence typified an antifascist ideal of childhood).

Bacon and others, likewise interpreting the idea of "war-related titles" broadly, would argue that there were war-related lessons to be taken from many children's books published in the early 1940s. Bacon even suggested, for instance, that how-to books are especially important in wartime, when children exposed daily to a climate of violence ought to learn that "making things is much more exciting than destroying them." Likewise, books about history and folklore could give children "roots" and "a sense of continuing history [that] can be very reassuring." Both Bacon and Ives pointed to the importance of books about foreign lands; Bacon singled out as an example Arkady Gaidar's *Timur and His Gang*, a Soviet book that inspired a legion of "Timurites," or children dedicated to helping the families of soldiers in the Red Army. "American children can find points in common with children all over the world in the many books that make Latin America or the Soviet Union as homely and familiar as New Jersey or Texas," Bacon/Morrow maintained. Finally, both Ives and Bacon pointed to the value of books that highlighted, as Bacon put it, "the fundamental principles of the democracy for which we are fighting."[82] Thus, in addition to inspiring "war titles" like Mary Elting and Robert Weaver's *Soldiers, Sailors, Fliers and Marines* and *Battles: How They Are Won* and McBride's *He's in the ___ Now* series (Henry Gregor Felsen wrote *He's in the Coast Guard Now* and *He's in the Marines Now*), the war provoked much deeper grappling with the ideological issues raised by the war and their implications for children and education.

Author Mary Elting (Folsom) says that World War II "was an especially complex time for some of us." Elting herself had been a "vehement pacifist," but in this struggle she, like many others, felt compelled to take sides. "When I began hearing conflicting stories about Hitler, the Nazis, Stalin and his sins, I had to sort out whose side to be on," Elting notes. "My husband finally convinced me the Nazis were the enemy and the Soviets were our ally. . . . Anyway, all my leftist writer friends became devoted anti-Nazis." Elting, who was married to the League of American Writers' secretary, Franklin Folsom, became politicized around the Sacco and Vanzetti trial and execution in the late 1920s. She began a long career in children's literature in the early 1940s, working first in a number of editorial offices and then becoming a founding member of a short-lived venture called Planned Books for Young People that coordinated cooperation among writers, illustrators, editors, designers, salespeople, researchers, and others involved in the process of creating and disseminating children's books.[83]

The first book that Elting herself wrote (with Robert Weaver), *Soldiers, Sailors, Fliers and Marines*, came out of the demand that she and others at Planned Books identified for a simple children's book that could answer children's questions about the armed forces. After publishing this elementary-level picture book in 1943, the first of a number of books that Ives would recommend on the armed forces, Elting and Weaver followed up with *Battles: How They Are Won* (1944), which used both contemporary battles fought in the Second World War as well as historical conflicts—from those of cave men to ancient Israel's battle with the Philistines and Hannibal's victory over the Romans—to illustrate lessons about military strategy and its effectiveness.

Several things about the latter book are striking. The first is the amount of technical knowledge it effectively communicates on a level comprehensible to a relatively unsophisticated reader. Life-and-death issues of war are discussed matter-of-factly in terms of tactics and the coordination of various elements in the armed forces. The ideological aspects of the book are far more subtle. At a very basic level, all of the modern examples of successful military strategy are illustrated with battles fought by the United States or its allies. Although the book contains a number of extended illustrations—from the Battle of Madagascar to confrontations in the Pacific—one of the longest and most engaging sections of the book concerns the Battle of Stalingrad, which Elting and

Weaver call "one of the strangest, fiercest, and most heroic battles that was ever fought." All of the odds, the authors say, favored the Germans, who expected an easy victory against a smaller, technologically disadvantaged Russian force operating under unusually difficult circumstances. In their view, the hard-won surprise Soviet victory came not just because of superior leadership and careful coordination among all levels of the military and civilian populations; they contend that "the city held out because of the Russians' high morale. They were so determined to stop the Germans that they did not behave as people usually do. They worked and fought long after ordinary endurance would have been exhausted."[84] Although this rather impassioned moment in *Battles* is notable for its divergence from the rest of the text, which dwells more on the tactical aspects of battles than on the actual reasons that wars are fought, it points to a common sense of "conviction" (to borrow Ives's phrasing) in Left-authored children's books on the "impact of war."

Among the half dozen books in this category that Ives singled out for special praise, the "really outstanding war stories for children—those that have been written with depth and feeling and conviction"—were two books that won honorable mention for the first CSA Award: Henry Gregor Felsen's *Struggle Is Our Brother*, "with its realistic story of a Russia that knows what the sacrifices of war really mean," and Emma Gelders Sterne's *Incident in Yorkville*, which "courageously poses the problem of the re-education of Nazi youth—a problem that will be very much the concern of tomorrow's citizens."[85] These were books for older children, that is, children old enough to understand the issues at stake, but young enough to be deeply impressionable.

Struggle Is Our Brother (1943), which went through six printings in three years, focuses on the bravery of young Soviets defending their village against the Nazis (see figure 3.5). The book seems to suggest that Soviet success in inculcating children with the values of the society has meant that young people there understand and believe in the fight and will give everything to protect their country's way of life. As a partisan leader protecting the AmSov Dam insists, "[T]he best fighters are those who know why they are fighting."[86] By this logic, he confidently asserts that if Germany were invaded, there would be no grassroots guerrilla groups to defend it. The oppressed German citizens would see no reason to fight, unlike the Soviet civilians—even the children—who will give everything to defend their homeland.

Two related assumptions are implicit in the book: first, that Soviet bravery must come from citizens' unified commitment to a clear set of principles, and, second, that Nazism had no appeal to the masses of Germans. Both assumptions represented wishful thinking on Felsen's part, given the clear dangers of dissenting from Soviet orthodoxy and the mass base of support that Hitler was able to rally (partly through his own system of violent coercion). But the under-

Figure 3.5. Illustration by Woodi Ishmael from *Struggle Is Our Brother* by Henry Gregor Felsen. The book is dedicated to "the boys and girls in the countries invaded by the Nazis, who have given their lives that the boys and girls who read this book might live." This image typifies the book's celebration of Soviet children's bravery in defense of their homeland. New York: Dutton, 1943.

lying message, an important one for American children, was that if you really understood fascism, you would do everything to reject it. Felsen's rosy view of the Soviet people was partly tied to his desire to show that "Russia's enemies [i.e., fascists] are the enemies of civilization," and this fit with other wartime books that showed strong sympathy for the Soviet allies in the battle against fascism.[87] Felsen's depth of feeling and conviction are readily apparent here, as is his belief in the moral imperative of educating young people to reject a politics of hate. As the soldier Sergei tells his younger brother:

We must hate fascism as much, if not more than we hate fascists themselves, because fascism is hate of the vilest kind. Under fascism it is not
normal to love your neighbor; it is normal to despise him, make a slave
of him, or kill him. Fascism is the enemy of decency, of freedom, and
of hope for the future of mankind. So when we defeat the Nazis, little
brother, we are doing more than beating an army that has attacked us.
We are striking a blow for the bright future of all the world.[88]

In negatively defining the terms of an ideal of "civilization" for which the
children in *Struggle* fight, Felsen does not focus on his characters as communists but, rather, as enemies of fascism, just like the Americans. He is able to
describe in loving detail the small village and its people as long as their struggles are explicitly linked to those of Americans. The book itself becomes an
agent in the struggle, a tool to assure that child readers know why their country—and its allies—are fighting.

In Felsen's *Submarine Sailor* (1943), which concerns an American submarine crew on a mission in the Pacific, education and socialization are again what
divide the Americans from their enemies, because Americans, in theory, are
raised to respect the individuality and autonomy of all human beings. The submarine's diving officer, Ken, reminds the skipper that what makes the enemy
different is not his "nature" but, rather, his upbringing. This means that the
issues go much deeper than merely "winning" the war. As Ken puts it, "Unless
we can wipe out the *teachings* of Fascism, and its whole bloody record of hatred,
we've lost the fight. As long as there is a place in the world, no matter how small,
where a man can stand up and teach others to hate and kill, our job isn't done."
Submarine Sailor suggests that the American soldiers dedicated enough to put
their lives on the line for their country are still able to question the motives
and decisions of those in power. Ken complains that fascism "could have been
wiped out without the loss of a single life. But we, by our indifference, and
our fumbling politics, helped it to grow and get strong." Moreover, the fight
for "democracy" is shown to involve an internationalist vision of human dignity, rather than a narrow nationalism: talking to Ken, the skipper, Cleve, "saw
clearly for the first time that the democracy he was defending was more than
being able to live as a free human. It meant keeping vigilance to insure that right
for others, as well as for himself."[89]

Beyond these moments of philosophical reflection in the book, other small
details in *Submarine Sailor* communicate what Felsen clearly felt as an imperative to educate children in antifascist terms, that is, to condemn authoritarian-
ism and racism and to promote democracy, cooperation, and an internationalist, humanitarian ethic of social justice. Contrasting with a popular image of
infallible military commanders, the skipper, Cleve, is thoughtful and aware of

the responsibility that comes with his power. The mess man, the only African American on the ship, is a hero who voluntarily puts himself in great danger, swimming to shore to rescue a Japanese-American man who has been sent to Japan as a spy for the Americans. A *New Masses* review of the book singled out the scene, noting that this "Negro mess man" was "joining the children's favorite heroes and heroines of the past." The ship's crew seems to function so well in crisis situations in part because of the spirit of camaraderie that operates in circumstances where everyone is respected for the skill they bring to their work. "Even in appearance, there wasn't much difference between officers and men," Felsen notes. "All had work to do, and dressed for it. Dungarees were the order of the day and night."[90] Even in a military context bound by hierarchy, the spirit is democratic and egalitarian. Black-and-white photographs of actual submarine crews lend a feeling of authenticity to the story, bolstering the "truth" value of this fictional account.

Though explicitly patriotic in spirit, *Submarine Sailor* manages to combine support for the war and its soldiers with a critical, democratic, internationalist, and antiracist notion of Americanism. Likewise, Vicar/Felsen's *The Company Owns the Tools* rejects the practice of cloaking a xenophobic, racist, and labor-baiting stance in flag worship. In this story, Hollis, the idealistic Iowa-bred mechanic who has come to the big city to make automobiles for the war, is furious when he sees that a mob is waving American flags while preparing to burn a "Negro" in effigy (to protest African Americans "stealing" jobs). For Hollis, "to see such a gathering try to cloak itself with the protecting folds of the symbol of free America was maddening." Moreover, he feels like a stranger in his own country after witnessing the white mob's violent rampage through the city's black section: "When men are equals they don't have to stand by and see their homes burned," Hollis thinks. "Equal men aren't hunted with clubs. 'Life, Liberty and the pursuit of Happiness' didn't add anything about the right to organize mobs to terrorize other Americans, or divide the country into groups of 'real' and synthetic Americans."[91] Here, both racial violence and the repression of valid union demands, both of which detract from the war effort, are characterized as un-American.

Born in Brooklyn in 1916 and the child of Jewish immigrants, Felsen became politicized as a teenager during the depression. As a college student, he quickly became known around the University of Iowa as a campus radical. In his sophomore year, Felsen was arrested on the charge of "committing communism on the public street" for putting posters up that announced a rally "against war and fascism." When Felsen ran out of money to pay tuition, he dropped out and got a job as an officer's mess boy on a ship traveling to South America. His best friend on the ship was an African American who may have been the source of the "Negro mess man" hero in *Submarine Sailor*. Back in the United States, a friend from Felsen's college crowd (presumably another campus radical) helped him to land several freelance jobs and finally a position as a staff writer for the company that published the Christian children's magazines *Young People's Weekly*, the *Girl's Companion*, and *Boys' World*. Felsen's energetic fiction in the magazines, which was probably in sharp contrast to the religion-oriented material, attracted the attention of Norman Carlisle. Carlisle was Mary Elting's partner in Planned Books, a program that, as noted earlier, connected authors and illustrators with publishers seeking books on particular topics. With Carlisle as his agent, Felsen published nine books between 1942 and 1944, jump-starting a long and successful career as a writer for young adults.[92]

If educating children to be antifascist is the subtext of several of Felsen's books, it is the central issue in Emma Gelders Sterne's *Incident in Yorkville* (1943), published the same year as Felsen's *Struggle Is Our Brother* and *Submarine Sailor*. Unlike Felsen, Sterne had already been writing children's books for years when she published this book. However, *Incident* was one of the books that most clearly marked Sterne's own antifascist education, as she shifted from writing books reflecting her origins in the racist South to writing vociferously antiracist stories and portraits in the 1950s and 1960s.

Emma Gelders Sterne was born in Birmingham, Alabama, in 1894 to a well-to-do German-Jewish family. Although Sterne's own Jewishness might have given her an outsider's sympathy toward other marginalized groups, she embraced the white-skin privilege bestowed upon her by southern culture. All of her relationships with African Americans as a child "were solely on a master and servant basis." Living in a city that was one-third African American, she knew no black person as a peer and was shocked in her freshman year at Smith College in 1913 to hear a black man, W. E. B. Du Bois, introduced as the commencement speaker (years later, she would write a biography of Du Bois for young people). She was stunned by the eloquence of his speaking and the power of his words, and she would say that day marked a turning point in her life, though it would be many years before she renounced the white supremacist ideas that defined her relationship to the "Old South." It was not until the 1930s that Sterne, then living in New York City, witnessed terrible poverty firsthand and gradually became more sympathetic to causes espoused by her radical brother, Joe Gelders. In 1942, Sterne would describe herself in *Twentieth Century Authors* as "a left-wing New Dealer and internationalist." She was an active supporter of the war effort, writing pamphlets for the Office of War Information, the Writers' War Board, and other organizations. Unlike those who took the classic path of replacing their youthful radicalism with hard-headed realism after the war, Sterne would only become more radical as the years wore on, joining the Communist Party in 1950, around the same time that she began working as a juvenile editor at Aladdin Books.[93] Raised in the racial hierarchy that was the South in the early twentieth century, Sterne would find the struggle against fascism personally transformative. As was the case with Felsen, this personal commitment brought great passion and "conviction" (to use Ives's word) to Sterne's writing.

Incident is set in the Yorkville section of New York City, an area populated primarily by German immigrants. At the core of the story are the Hersheys, an Anglo-American family whose members strongly support the war and who seem to be models of neighborliness and tolerance. The fourteen-year-old Hershey twins, Mike and Mary, provide a sharp contrast to Erich Braun, an American boy of the same age, whose German-American father took him and his sister to Germany for several years to train with the Hitler youth movement. Returning to the United States after his father's death, Erich and his sister join their mother in the apartment of the children's aunt and uncle, who happen to live in the same building as the Hersheys. Erich's mother, the American-born Helena Braun, is more than a little ambivalent about Erich's pro-Nazi sympathies, but her sister, Minna Kulner, and her German-born husband are loyal Nazis, like Helena's deceased husband. The conflict of wills in Erich's family mirrors the larger conflict Erich will increasingly feel between the German fatherland and the American motherland, neatly symbolized by a picture of Hitler on the wall in the Kulners' home, which can be quickly flipped over, if necessary, to reveal a pastoral Wisconsin landscape from Helena and Minna's childhood.

Erich's aunt and uncle do all they can to dismiss the appeal of what the United States has to offer, but Sterne seems to imply that just living in this country makes it impossible to avoid a powerful democratic sentiment. This idea is perhaps best expressed in a striking Popular Front moment, when a radio broadcast of Paul Robeson singing the "Ballad for Americans" at a pro-Russia rally in Madison Square Garden proves both irresistible and infuriating to the Kulners and their young charge. When Erich arrives home from school one day, Minna Kulner is listening to the radio. She tells her nephew that the radio tells only lies, but they keep listening, and, moreover, Erich sees that what she tells him is not true. The radio *does* seem to tell the truth, for instance, when it tells listeners that the Nazis are winning (Erich wonders, would a German radio station tell as much if the tables were turned?). Erich's uncle declares that the Nazis' enemies are too stupid to know when they are beaten and that not even the Russians realize it yet. To prove his point, Kulner has his wife turn the radio to a meeting in Madison Square Garden "where ten thousand people were gathered in praise of the foreign Russian army, and somebody was singing a ballad.

"'A Negro, he is,' Kulner whispered, and when his wife would have turned it brusquely off, he said, 'No, leave it. I want Erich to hear the applause. Then he will see what fools we have to deal with.'"

Erich's reaction is appropriately dismissive, but what he hears sets up the conflict that will occupy the rest of the book, a conflict about the meaning of *America* and *Americans* in this moment of wartime:

The words were a lot of nonsense about liberty and nobody believing in it. Nobody but Washington and a lot of other dead people. And words about uncertainty and doubting, of which Erich knew America had plenty, but they must, the way the man sang, have no uncertainty at all. It was as if this Negro knew the Master Race was winning all these battles and it wouldn't make any difference in the end. The self-confidence of the Americans was appalling.[94]

Robeson's name and the "Ballad for Americans" are never mentioned, but the reference to the "Negro" singing about "liberty and nobody believing in it," and "words about uncertainty and doubting" would have unmistakably recalled Robeson and the "Ballad for Americans" to most 1940s readers. In this song about "the et ceteras" and "the and-so-forths that do the work," Robeson, identifying himself as "an Irish, Negro, Jewish, Italian, French and English, Spanish, Russian, Chinese, Polish, Scotch, Hungarian, Litvak, Swedish, Finnish, Canadian, Greek and Turk, and Czech and double Czech American," asserts his hybridity even as he affirmatively answers the repeated question, "Who are you? . . . Are you an American?"[95] The coded reference to the song and Robeson would have added another layer of meaning to the story for contemporary readers, and it served to align Sterne's book with Earl Robinson's ballad and Paul Robeson's booming voice—all weapons in the war of ideas.

If Erich's education at home is primarily geared toward keeping him loyal to the Nazi cause, his education at school occurs not through an authoritarian, hierarchical system of rules to be followed and facts to be accepted and memorized but, instead, through an open program—characteristic of progressive educational practices—that emphasizes questioning, critical thinking, and multiple viewpoints. Indeed, what Erich is least prepared for is the informality, freedom, and camaraderie in the American school. He is surprised to find that girls are permitted in school, as are Jews and "Negroes," and he is also shocked to learn that many of the teachers are women. When Mike and Mary refer fondly to "Old George," Erich is amazed when he realizes that they are talking about the school principal and not "some menial."[96] And he is taken aback when he is asked (rather than told) what subjects he will study.

His teacher, Peggy Wolfe, becomes consumed with the challenge of reversing the education that Erich Braun has received in Germany; she is keenly aware that "to ensure the future [Hitler] depended most of all on the children whom he taught to despise the very idea of human worth." The problem is that she cannot simply replace Erich's authoritarian upbringing with authoritarian, i.e., fascist, methods of teaching; she must show Erich by example why he himself should choose "the American way of life." Goading Erich by telling him that Nazis, unlike Americans, are afraid to read anything but their own ideas, she dares him to read *The Adventures of Huckleberry Finn*, reasoning to herself that Huck was probably the least Nazi-like person in American literature.[97] Erich accepts her challenge. Contemptuous at first of this boy in shabby clothes with bad grammar, he unwittingly begins to sympathize with Huck, and even Jim. And the fact that Huck could decide for himself that the law under which he was raised was morally wrong offers a powerful challenge to the idea that received authority should never be questioned.

In another key scene, Peggy asks her class to do a writing exercise on what the Declaration of Independence means to them. Erich, as expected, rejects the Declaration's premises entirely. "I have read the Declaration of Independence and it is not correct because in all nature there is no equality," he writes. "The strong must rule, therefore the inferior people cannot be equal." His response is just what Peggy was looking for: "You believe then, that men are unequal? That the stronger shall rule the weaker? That might is right?" she asks him. As Erich explains the logic of Nazi principles, the class becomes more and more uneasy until Erich is finally physically attacked by several of the students, and he is deeply shocked and humiliated to find himself the weaker one. He is only saved because Stanislaus, a Polish refugee, whose hate and fear of Nazis is deeper than anyone's, suddenly takes pity on Erich and lets him go. Peggy, for her part, is horrified by the violence that she has helped to unleash, concluding, "Germans will have to change themselves from within. . . . from without we cannot help them."[98]

But Peggy's little experiment has an impact on Erich, and it is one of a series of factors that proves Germans are not invincible, nor is their profascist training. By the end of the book, Erich decides he does not "want to die for Hitler." Still, Erich's conversion is punctuated by ambivalence, as Erich tries to cover for his uncle, a German spy who is about to be caught by the American authorities, and as he berates himself for caring, as he reads *Huck Finn*, about what happens to Jim, whom he knows is of "an inferior race."[99] The battle for the hearts and minds of fascists would not be an easy one, and it would, presumably, continue after the war, as Felsen had suggested.

. . .

The frontispiece to *Incident in Yorkville* declares, "Books Are Weapons in the War of Ideas." According to Sterne's FBI file, this was a conviction Sterne further supported by donating proceeds from the sale of *Incident* to the Joint Anti-Fascist Refugee Committee, a Left-sponsored organization. The FBI documentation of this "Good News for Anti-Fascists" points to a strange irony that would become even more apparent after the war, when anti-Communism and children became twin obsessions for many Americans.[100] Although the climate for left-wing cultural producers in most fields would chill dramatically, children's books would become even more important weapons in the war of ideas in the postwar period. As passionate and vocal supporters of the war, left-wingers benefited from a growing consensus that children could no longer be shielded from reality and that they needed to understand something about why the war was being fought. Working as writers, illustrators, editors, and librarians, leftists helped to make an antifascist sensibility basic to American children's literature, and in so doing they also found a niche for themselves in the field. They recognized that "the company owns the tools," but they discovered affinities with those controlling children's book publishing—at a time when the field was undergoing great expansion (the baby boom meant new schools and, likewise, new markets for children's books).

Incident earned Sterne recognition and brought ideological and material support to left-wing causes, but it also attracted the attention of the FBI. Yet this attention had little impact upon Sterne's career. In both of these senses, *Incident* is instructive. Even in the relatively few instances that the anti-Communist network bothered to monitor children's book writers, effective suppression of them was the exception rather than the rule. The next two chapters explore this surprising dynamic: first, we consider the impact of the Cold War and McCarthyism on the field of children's literature, and, second, we explore how leftists managed to sustain the values and sensibility of the Popular Front through children's books.

4

"Pink-Tinged Pages"?

McCarthyism and Children's Literature

On November 28, 1954, the front page of the *Milwaukee Sentinel* contained a sensational headline: "New Lincoln Book Has Pink-Tinged Pages." A lengthy story, accompanied by a review and an editorial, described how Communist propaganda had wormed its way into the innocent world of childhood through the misuse of a popular hero by Meridel Le Sueur, "one of the pillars of communist literature in the United States." About a month earlier, Le Sueur had paid a visit to Milwaukee, where she spoke on a local radio program about her most recent book, *River Road: A Story of Abraham Lincoln*, and then read from the book for an audience of children at the Milwaukee Public Library. That night, according to the *Sentinel*, she attended a party to promote the *Worker* and the *Daily Worker*, "the Sunday and daily editions of the newspaper of the communist apparatus in the United States." Finally, sleuthing *Sentinel* reporters discovered that just three weeks after Le Sueur's visit to Milwaukee, her writing could be found in the *Worker*, in an article saluting the thirtieth anniversary of the CP publishing house, International Publishers.[1] The *Sentinel*'s exposé of *River Road*'s purportedly pink pages seemed to suggest that Popular Front Americanism had no place in the profoundly altered cultural climate of the Cold War.

The left-wing movement against fascism—though ostensibly patriotic in the context of the Second World War—spawned a reaction from the Right that echoed many elements of fascism itself: the banning and sometimes even the burning of books; the dismissal of teachers, librarians, and many others whose affiliations or beliefs challenged those deemed to be acceptable to people currently in power; and the general closing down of dissent. "McCarthyism," a phenomenon pre-dating the rise of Senator Joseph McCarthy himself, which institutionalized the process of defining certain beliefs, affiliations, and people as "un-American," affected nearly every arena of cultural production: Holly-

wood, television, radio, libraries, schools, universities, newspapers, and publishing houses.[2] Thus it is no real surprise that McCarthyism had an impact on
the production, content, and reception of children's literature, from the ways
that authors came to approach their work to the choices that librarians made
when stocking their bookshelves.

Although the field of publishing was traditionally very progressive, this
began to change with the Cold War in response to accusations coming from the
far Right. In January 1951, for instance, the *American Legion* published an article by Irene Kuhn on "Why You Buy Books That Sell Communism," which was
reprinted in the *Catholic Digest* and widely circulated, with predictable effects
upon many publishing houses. In August of that same year, *Counterattack: The
Newsletter of Facts on Communism* printed an "exposé" of the well-respected
publisher Little, Brown, citing what appeared to be an extensive list of red-
authored titles published by the firm and fingering the left-wing editor in chief
and vice president Angus Cameron as a possible explanation. Little, Brown
issued a statement attempting to counter the charges and confirming Cameron's resignation, which signaled that McCarthyism truly had come to American
publishing. Henry Holt, taking even more drastic measures, summarily fired all
staff who had helped to publish work by Langston Hughes. Radical authors, in
general, began to find fewer and fewer outlets for their work.[3]

As Le Sueur's experience suggests, children's books were, at times, singled
out and targeted for banning in libraries, especially school libraries. *Counterattack*, for instance, "exposed" Howard Fast's contribution to a Knopf-published
collection of stories called *Yankee Doodle: Stories of the Brave and the Free* and
asked its readers, "Would you want your children ... or any children ... to
learn about American history from a CP member whose writing is featured
in a recent issue of the Moscow-published *New Times*?" There were incidents
throughout the country targeting libraries and school materials. In Bartlesville,
Oklahoma, a librarian was fired for allowing the *Nation* and the *New Republic*
in the local library, and in Montclair, New Jersey, the Sons of the American
Revolution proposed that libraries segregate works by Communist authors into
a "subversive" reading room. Even more ominously, the mayor of San Antonio proposed that "red-authored" books be removed from public libraries and
burned (no children's books, incidentally, appeared on a mimeographed list of
"red reading" circulated by local San Antonio red-hunter Myrtle G. Hance).[4]

It was in this atmosphere that Le Sueur found herself under attack for her
supposedly subversive biography of Abraham Lincoln, *River Road*. Although
not advocating a "public burning of this book," the editors of the *Milwaukee Sentinel* maintained that "intellectual freedom," a fine idea for educated, discrimi-
nating adults, should not apply in the same way to children, who are not yet
schooled "in the manly art of intellectual self-defense." Criticizing the librarians

who placed Le Sueur's books on the shelves and invited her to speak before an audience of young children, the *Sentinel* editors insisted, "libraries and schools have a grave responsibility to devise reasonable restrictive standards in regard to this and all other literature cleverly designed to poison the young mind." The reference to the "manly art of intellectual self-defense" suggested not only that children were ill equipped to do battle with Communist propaganda masquerading as children's literature, but also that those female "child guardians" in the business of protecting children from evil influence in their reading, namely, librarians and teachers, were lacking the requisite "manly" virtues as well. Such apparent naïveté on the part of these women might explain why, prior to the Milwaukee incident, Le Sueur's children's books—on Johnny Appleseed, Sparrow Hawk (an adopted son of Black Hawk), Nancy Hanks (Abraham Lincoln's mother), Davy Crockett, and including *River Road* itself—had received nothing but praise from reviewers, who used words such as "poetic" and "beautiful" to describe the books. A review of *Sparrow Hawk* in the *New York Times*, for instance, called it "history not found in textbooks."[5] Such history, according to people like those staffing the *Sentinel* in the mid-1950s, had no rightful place on library shelves, at least not in the children's section.

Librarians in Milwaukee (and, presumably, elsewhere) did keep Le Sueur's books on their shelves, very consciously rejecting the implications of the *Sentinel* articles.[6] Although Knopf did not reprint *River Road*, the firm kept the rest of Le Sueur's juvenile books in print through the 1970s, and these kept selling, particularly to schools and libraries.[7] But the *Sentinel* exposé had unmistakable effects nonetheless, which rippled well beyond Milwaukee. NBC's "Carnival of Books" canceled a prerecorded reading of the book and a conversation with Le Sueur, citing the Milwaukee affair as a rationale for doing so.[8] More important, Alfred A. Knopf published no new book by Le Sueur, even after *Chanticleer of Wilderness Road: A Story of Davy Crockett* (1951) experienced a surge of popularity in 1955 with the nation's Crockett craze.[9] The outcry in Milwaukee effectively closed one of the few remaining doors to Le Sueur's commercial success as a writer for at least a decade, during which time only left-wing outlets like *Masses and Mainstream* and Howard Fast's Blue Heron Press would touch her work.[10]

The outcry over Le Sueur's Lincoln book was chilling but fairly unusual; the only thing typical about her experience is the support she received from people sympathetic to her situation. The more common experience for leftist cultural workers was to find something of a refuge in the children's literature field, which, except in rare instances, tended to operate below the radar of red-hunters. The industry was controlled in significant measure by sympathetic people, from editors like Harper's Ursula Nordstrom to librarians like the Milwaukee Public Library's head of children's work, Norma Rathburn, who opposed the anti-Communist purges of that period. Even Alfred A. Knopf, a lifelong Republican, was a vigorous critic of Senator McCarthy and defender of free speech, despite his apparently equivocal support of Le Sueur following the Milwaukee incident.[11]

How then did McCarthyism affect children's literature and those who produced it, and to what extent were liberals, progressives, and radicals in the field able to resist McCarthyism's logic? To what extent might the particular imperatives and assumptions governing the field of children's literature have allowed it to maintain a progressive structure of feeling, despite competing right-wing imperatives? This chapter points to the pressures exerted by the Cold War and McCarthyism upon children, teachers, authors, publishers, editors, and librarians. The chapter that follows focuses more concretely on the dynamics of cultural production and dissemination in a Cold War context, highlighting ways in which people in the children's literature field were able, within limits, to challenge the Cold War consensus.

"They're Not What They Used to Be"

To understand how political dynamics actually played out in the 1950s requires going back to the end of the Second World War. The many children's books reflecting the antifascist common sense of the Popular Front and Second World War appeared to offer proof that campaigns by the *New Masses* and the League of American Writers to recruit progressive authors into the field and to promote "socially constructive literature for children" had been largely successful. In October 1946, *Parents* magazine published an article on current children's books entitled "They're Not What They Used to Be." As its author, Jean Van Evera, noted, "[T]he never never land of children's books is a different place from what it was in your young days." "Realism" and "social significance" had become the new catchwords for children's books. Noting the differences between books popular in the early twentieth century and those compelling to contemporary readers, and singling out books (all by radicals) such as *Two Is a Team* (1945) by Jerrold and Lorraine Beim, which was hailed as the first interracial picture book (figure 4.1), *Navy Diver* (1942) by Henry Gregor Felsen, *Let's Find Out: A Picture Science Book* (1946) by Herman and Nina Schneider, and *Paul Robeson: Citizen of the World* (1946) by Shirley Graham, Van Evera concluded that "today's writing gives youngsters a healthier, saner and more interesting approach to the world and everything that's in it than you ever gained from your own youthful reading."[12]

Less than a year later, Jay Williams, a relatively new writer of children's books, surveyed the field for the left-wing *New Masses* and reached conclusions

Figure 4.1. Illustration by
Ernest Crichlow from *Two
Is a Team* by Jerrold and
Lorraine Beim, copyright
© 1945 by Jerrold and
Lorraine Beim, renewed
1973 by Andrew L. Beim,
reproduced by permission
of the publisher. This book
is often considered the first
interracial picture book.
Although the illustrations
make it very clear, nothing
in the text indicates that
one of the two friends is
white and one is black.
Throughout the story, the
two boys play together
and learn that everything
works out better when they
cooperate.

similar to Van Evera's about how the field had changed. While Van Evera had pointed to World War II as the event that "brought the outside world to the doorstep of the nurseries," Williams linked developments in children's literature to industrialization, the consolidation of corporate capitalism, and challenges posed by the "progressive movement." "Fifty years ago, or thereabouts, young people were brought up to believe that their elders knew the answers to everything, that a child was the property of his parents and that he must submit in everything to parental authority," Williams asserted. He proceeded to relate this authoritarian stance toward children to "the great era of capitalist expansion" at the turn of the century. "America was the golden land of opportunity, of Horatio Alger's young heroes, the *Elsie* books, the *Little Colonel*, and eventually of *Penrod*, the youthful Babbitt (the antithesis of Huck Finn, as it were)." However, if children's books published early in the century reflected the new international hegemony of monopoly capital, at the end of World War II, children's literature looked very different, in Williams's estimate:

> Today a vigorous, progressive working class, led by men who have
> learned lessons in strategy and organization, challenges this empire

as never before. A war against fascism lies behind us. The very fundamentals of pedagogy have changed; it is no longer possible to conceal
the science of history and evolution, and daring souls everywhere are
speaking out against the divine right of the capitalist oligarchy. It is
inevitable that this tendency should find soil in juvenile literature.[13]

The similar testaments from Van Evera and Williams—that is, from liberal and radical sources—suggests a progressive common sense on the matter
of children's literature in the immediate postwar period. The variety of books
for children published just after the war that were authored by leftists or that
supported a left-wing agenda is quite striking, from Williams's own *The Sword
and the Scythe* (1946), describing a medieval peasant rebellion with fairly open
reference to current struggles against unjust authority; to Arna Bontemps's collective biography, *We Have Tomorrow* (1945), which included a glowing portrait of the Communist New York City councilman Ben Davis; to Lorraine
Beim's *Sugar and Spice* (1947), which, a *New Masses* reviewer noted, "brings the
woman question into modern juvenile literature for the first time." The market
for such work can be seen as the logical extension of a trend toward socially significant children's literature that was established during the depression and the
war.[14] Certainly Le Sueur's folk histories can likewise be seen as extending the
democratic, populist spirit of the Popular Front into the Cold War.

Through the 1940s, progressive influence in the children's book field was
more and more in evidence, not only in books themselves, but also in the criteria for awards and in discussions about the state of the field. The Child Study
Association (CSA) helped maintain the momentum that the war had given to
"socially significant" literature for children by continuing to sponsor its award
for a book dealing with the "contemporary scene" and addressing "vexing, perhaps controversial problems." It also published "Let Them Face It" booklists
and held regular forums that brought together children's book editors, authors,
labor organizers, librarians, teachers, and representatives of liberal and progressive groups. In a November 1947 CSA program on "America in Books for Young
People," Howard Fast, Eva Knox Evans, and James Daugherty (all progressive
or radical in their viewpoints) gave presentations. Fast, already a controversial
figure who had begun to feel the effects of the red scare firsthand, spoke of the
importance of teaching children "the folk lore of democracy," which "will some
day be made true and living and lasting."[15] Implicitly praising groups like the
Child Study Association, which had helped to foster a progressive climate in
the field, Fast claimed that "children's books are a freer market. They are in a
freer area where far more ideals are tossed around than you will ever find in
adult books."[16] Illustrator Ernest Crichlow, reflecting back on this period several decades later, would make a similar comment, noting that issues, particu-

larly racial issues, were subtly tackled in children's books long before they were addressed in books for adults.[17]

That children's books would be a "freer market" is, of course, counterintuitive, given the imperative of "protection" vis-à-vis children. One way the comparative freedom in the children's book field after World War II can be understood is in relation to the "new liberalism" of the postwar period, which, according to those who embraced it, was "tough-minded" and "realistic" in contrast to the "immature" idealism said to be characteristic of the "old" (read: Popular Front) liberalism. If the old liberalism was immature, a logical (and unsuspicious) outlet for it was the world of children. But the logic of the Popular Front also continued to play a role in the Cold War. Belief in interracial and international cooperation formed the basis for the sentimental logic of integrationism that undergirded American relations with our less modernized (i.e., younger) friends in the Third World. Like the democratic spirit of the New Deal, these remained values that many Americans wanted their children to learn, even if in practice a more cynical view of things dictated the terms of foreign and domestic policy. More concretely, those controlling and mediating children's book publishing tended to share the Popular Front common sense articulated by people like Fast. This may partially explain why only work by the most visible left-wing authors of children's books ever came under open attack. In many ways, children had become the repository for the social vision of the 1930s, the last hope for it, as Fast's children's story *Tony and the Wonderful Door* and his address to the CSA, would suggest: "In childhood they have the vision of Robinson Crusoe," Fast asserted to the audience at the CSA program. "They need that vision, the vision of man, master of the elements, who determines his future, who makes his future, who fights against adverse circumstances and though he be beaten down, comes up again."[18] Fast made a point of noting in the lecture his pride in the fact that some of the most avid readers of his "adult" books were adolescents. Although his own books were widely banned, his claims about children's literature being a freer market were largely true.

The Child Study Award and lists like "Let Them Face It" did, as author Howard Pease had hoped, signal a real shift in merit criteria for children's books beginning in the early 1940s, and the trend continued for some time, in part because what Pease had dismissed as the "tenderminded feminine control" of children's books was both virtually complete and seemingly unassailable.[19] More organizations—from the National Conference on Christians and Jews to the "intercultural education" journal *Common Ground*, to the New York Public Library—began to publish lists of children's books for "democracy," "brotherhood," and "international understanding."[20] Likewise, in addition to new booklists, more awards, with similar criteria, followed the Child Study Award, including the Julian Messner Award for a book "promoting racial or religious tolerance," which was announced in 1944 by the publisher Julian Messner, with the 1947 award going to the radical writer Shirley Graham for her biography of Frederick Douglass. The Committee on the Art of Democratic Living sponsored a children's book contest (with Josette Frank, head of the CSA's Children's Book Committee, acting as a judge) in 1949; in 1955 the progressive Downtown Community School (the school of choice for many radical New York parents) inaugurated the Nancy Bloch Award for a book "that furthers understanding and appreciation among peoples of different racial, religious and cultural backgrounds." The Jane Addams Award, presented annually since 1953 by the Women's International League for Peace and Freedom—"for a book that most effectively promotes the cause of peace, social justice, world community, and the equality of the sexes and all races"—is still given.[21]

The Cold War and American Childhood

The progressive structure of feeling in children's literature in the postwar period is striking particularly because so much of the anxiety, fear, and panic that characterized the discourses of the Cold War and McCarthyism—which were a constant undercurrent in American life from the late 1940s into the early 1960s—centered around children. In a time of rapid social and technological change, atomic insecurity, and great uncertainty about the future, the child became a focal point for national anxiety: anxiety about violence, social control, changing sexual norms, and "alien"—both extranational and extraterrestrial—influences. Congressional hearings over the effects of comic books and television on children were a sideshow to the McCarthy hearings, both symptoms of the same cultural malaise, an effort to contain and control unpredictable forces that individually and collectively threatened the nation's carefully crafted image of democracy, prosperity, and consensus.[22] Perhaps the most striking show of the nation's psychological weakness, the Communist "brainwashing" of American GI's captured in Korea, called into question the very fundamentals of American childrearing: how would Americans "meet the world challenge" if young people were so susceptible to the "disease" of Communism?[23]

The family itself was seen as the first line of defense against Communism, but it was also seriously threatened in the postwar period—by a loss of parental control, by changing sexual mores and gender roles, and by apparently declining birth rates (witnesses to an "'international sit-down strike' against motherhood" failed to recognize that they were in the midst of an unprecedented baby boom). Communism itself, which was said to advocate the abolition of the family, was perhaps the greatest threat of all to the American family. The family represented the nation in miniature, and proper childrearing was the basis for good citizenship, the first and last line of national defense. Thus, when Julius and Ethel Rosenberg were convicted for passing "atomic secrets" to the Soviets, the primary (and ultimately fatal) evidence against Ethel was her supposed lack of maternal instinct, or her willingness to make her sons orphans for the Communist cause.[24] As a "bad mother" she was, logically, a "bad American," and Ethel's supposed lack of mother love evidently proved her capacity for treason.

Making explicit the links between parental control and affection in the home and the maintenance of American hegemony in the global arena, a 1947 editorial in *Life* magazine on threats to the American family declared, "J. Edgar Hoover's No. 1 job is protecting our atomic secrets; No. 2 is curbing juvenile crime." As the Rosenberg example and Hoover's obsession with juvenile delinquency suggest, at some level both national security and juvenile crime could be linked to bad parenting or, more broadly, poorly socialized children. Juvenile misbehavior suggested both a lack of parental control as well as a more general softening in the nation's moral fiber, which had made possible Communist "infiltration" into all levels of American society and culture.[25]

In contrast to the dominant discourse blaming parents, the media, or children themselves, leftists argued that juvenile crime came from young people growing up in a "dog-eat-dog" culture of greed, violence, and fear, and they argued that the focus on juvenile delinquency was merely a convenient way to distract attention from the structural causes of youthful rebellion and crime. Likewise, in contrast to arguments blaming youthful lawlessness and a general breakdown of traditional family life on forces like Communism, left-wing sources repeatedly drew upon what we would now call family-values rhetoric to condemn McCarthyism as un-American. A long-running series in the *National Guardian*, for instance, focused on the unjustified trauma suffered by the two Rosenberg sons and their "beloved and respected American parents." Likewise, campaigns to challenge arrests and deportations enacted under the Smith and McCarran-Walter acts repeatedly showed smiling, wholesome-looking parents and children whose idyll had been disrupted by Cold War purges. The implication, again, was that good parents were, *ipso facto*, good Americans and that un-American forces threatened the family's stability as a unit.[26]

Fears that the mass media were "seducing" innocent children were not confined to the Right or the Left, but the nature of the criticisms often reflected particular political biases. Albert Kahn, whose *Game of Death: The Effects of the Cold War on Our Children* represents the most sustained discussion of leftists' anxieties vis-à-vis children and youth in the postwar period, shared the critique of comic book violence made famous by Frederic Wertham's sensational exposé, *Seduction of the Innocent*. Kahn, however, linked violent comic books to a broader "culture of violence" and "the over-all Cold War atmosphere of crime, corruption, cynicism, brutality, and resort to force." Similarly, at a 1951 conference on "the ideological problems faced by children from progressive homes," sponsored by the Marxist Jefferson School of Social Science, several parents noted that their children were "confused and intimidated by the incessant anti-Communist and anti-Soviet propaganda they meet in school, comic books, over the radio, and television."[27]

The American system of public education was a focal point for Cold War anxieties vis-à-vis children. Voices coming from both the Right and the Left expressed deep concerns about what was happening in the nation's classrooms and its effects upon children. Like the family, education was an essential line of defense against Communism. As one commentator on the Korean brainwashing phenomenon noted in 1959, "[T]he teen-age prisoners of war were unable to defend America because they lacked patriotism, and this void was in turn due to their limited knowledge of American democracy and how it works." But if education was essential to socializing young people to be loyal to "the American way of life," many people also saw schools as potentially dangerous conduits for Communist ideology. The booklet *100 Things You Should Know about Communism and Education*, prepared by the House Committee on Un-American Activities in 1948 and distributed widely to community groups and schools, warned that Communists posed a deadly danger to the nation's students: "by slipping propaganda into classroom work and textbooks and by leading gullible students into red-sponsored campus activities," Communists (often "frustrated females," according to the report) threaten children's "future as . . . independent American citizens."[28]

By 1953, the majority of American states required teachers to take loyalty oaths, and many states passed legislation like New York's Feinberg Law, which empowered the regents to compile a list of "subversive" organizations and to dismiss teachers who belonged to any of these groups. Thousands of teachers lost their jobs, whether through outright dismissals, resignation under pressure, or refusal to take loyalty oaths. Teachers who remained in classrooms during this time often found themselves steering clear of controversial subjects, and they tended to shy away from union activism, given the investigation of many union activists. A widespread, grassroots network of individuals and groups, such as the Daughters of the American Revolution, the Defenders of American Education, and the Church League of America, used a campaign against Communist influence in the schools to promote a narrowly defined vision of education, geared toward promoting unquestioning patriotism and free enterprise, and they urged citizens to join in their efforts by keeping a close watch on teachers and by carefully scrutinizing their children's textbooks.[29]

Although red-baiting projects like the *Educational Reviewer*, a quarterly review of school materials, were usually undertaken by right-wing fringe groups (some of whose members had fascist associations), they exerted a real influence in schools and communities around the country, where whole courses of study were deemed to be subversive.[30] Pressure groups in Los Angeles, for instance, successfully called for the banning of UNESCO materials. In 1953, the state of Texas passed a law requiring that prior to the adoption of any textbook for use in public schools, the textbook's author must take an oath attesting that he or she was not (and had not for five years been) in any of the groups on the attorney general's list of subversive organizations. Because of the sheer size of the California and Texas textbook markets, such actions virtually assured that almost no schools in the country would purchase textbooks authored by Communists.[31]

As the number of teacher dismissals around the country would suggest, the idea that Communists and their writings should be kept out of classrooms was widely accepted. However, anti-Communist purges did far more than simply remove Communist teachers and Communist-authored textbooks from classrooms. In practice, the targets of red-hunters in schools included not just Communists and Communism but all forms of "collectivism"—from Communism and socialism to New Dealism—as well as the broad set of practices loosely understood as "progressive education," which the *Educational Reviewer* called "a vicious, un-American system." Moreover, in a political climate in which interracial alliances and civil rights activism were repeatedly linked to Communist influence, intercultural education likewise became a target of the Right. A school in Birmingham, Alabama, for instance, banned *Senior Scholastic* because it had a special issue on Brotherhood Week.[32]

Leftists, on the other hand, saw schools not as radical hotbeds but as training grounds for fascism. Vague wording in New York's Feinberg Law, calling for dismissal in the event of "seditious and treasonable utterance," effectively eliminated most controversial material from classrooms. As a 1949 article in the left-wing *Jewish Life* noted:

> Any kind of objective and mildly progressive teaching becomes more difficult than ever. As a substitute for many-sided free discussion of current issues the children will get propaganda for the Cold War. The end product of this new pro-fascist dispensation is to convert New York's public school children from thinking human beings to Nazi-like robots.

Radicals viewed anti-Communist measures in schools as an effective way to roll back curricular innovations, to justify racial bias in school curricula, to make schools into "instrument[s] of national policy," and to deflect attention away from underfunded, segregated, overcrowded, and increasingly militarized schools where very little actual learning took place.[33] But right-wing pressures on schools also had unintended effects that wound up helping some of the very leftists who were purged from schoolrooms, by drawing them into less visible fields like children's literature and, ironically, creating markets for the kinds of books they wanted to write.

"The Commies Go after the Kids"

In this age of anxiety concerning children, the mass media, education, and the slipping authority of parents, cultural production geared toward children, including children's books, would seem particularly likely to come under careful scrutiny. However, both the Right and the Left seemed to view children's literature as an innocent realm uncorrupted by the forces that had defiled mass culture and education. Thus children's books and their radical-minded creators usually met dramatically different fates from textbooks that showed a liberal orientation or teachers whose associations or, far less often, whose teaching suggested a left-of-center orientation.

J. B. Matthews's exposé "The Commies Go after the Kids," published in the *American Legion* magazine in December 1949 and then reprinted for mass distribution by the right-wing National Council for American Education, offers an overview of the "methods" used by "communists to win over and indoctrinate our children." It provides a revealing case study in the logic of red-hunters in this realm. It also suggests how and why children's books managed to achieve privileged status as texts often viewed outside of the realm of politics. The article touches on music, theater, afterschool programs, summer camps, comic books, and, of course, schools and school textbooks, but children's books are (almost) entirely absent from the discussion. Matthews singles out the Young People's Record Club ("to which hundreds of elementary schools have subscribed"), giving the club particular attention because "everybody prominently connected . . . has a record of affiliation with communist organizations." The only example he gives of the club's subversive fare is the song "Building a City," which celebrates manual laborers but fails to offer "even a hint that manufacturers, construction companies, bankers, architects, draftsmen, or capitalist enterprisers [sic] have anything to do with 'Building a City.'" This is apparently evidence enough to make the popular record club "a striking illustration of the fact that the 'comrades' do not miss a trick. They work away night and day at the business of infiltrating and indoctrinating, a little here and a little there. Even the smallest assault upon the 'system' is not neglected."[34]

Pictures accompanying Matthews's article show children (all boys, incidentally) listening to a man in a straw hat playing a guitar ("the musical commies mouth the words, but the Kremlin masterminds call the tune," the caption reads); a group of roughhousing boys, one of whom appears to be African American, being directed by a young man wearing a YCL (Young Communist League) T-shirt ("Commie-run youth camps are not generally concerned about sound minds in healthy bodies"); and boys looking at comic books being handed out by kind-seeming men ("the comic books ground out by the fun-loving commies are not put out just for laughs").[35]

Matthews's vision of a conspiracy targeted at the kiddies was based on very limited and arguably outdated evidence.[36] Still, though not as centrally coordinated as Matthews would have it, especially as the Left came under siege after the war, it could be argued that children *did* become the focal point for an alternative culture organized around summer camps, experimental schools, afterschool programs, concerts, and other cultural events. And, as the example of the Young People's Record Club would suggest, this progressive culture also had some fairly mainstream routes to reaching children, among them children's books that reached a wide market.

The Jewish Left sustained a particularly vital culture into the 1950s, though Jewish radicalism arguably lost some of its steam as Jews became more assimilated into American life.[37] Secular Yiddish schools, emphasizing the links between left-wing politics and a progressive Jewish tradition, were maintained by the Workmen's Circle, the Labor Zionists, and the Communist-dominated International Workers Order and offered classes after school or on weekends. Independent day schools like the Little Red Schoolhouse, the Walden School, the City and Country School, the Downtown Community School, and the Hessian Hills School (all in the New York area) often taught the children of radicals, and a fair number of teachers in these schools were political refugees of the public schools.[38] Summer camps like Camp Kinderland and Camp Wochica (*Workers' Children's Camp*) taught similar lessons and values, and Left-run institutions like the Jefferson School of Social Science offered programs for children and youth as well as classes on parenting and children's book writing.[39] Some of these alternative institutions also produced publications, and a network of left-wing bookstores—from the Progressive Book Shop in Los Angeles to the Francis Scott Key bookshop in Washington, D.C.—distributed many of these publications.[40] But Matthews's attention to organizations and institutions like the Jewish People's Fraternal Order and Camp Kinderland made them seem more influential than they probably ever were; their influence was more indirect, to the extent that values learned through institutions and organizations like these could be carried into the cultural mainstream. (The Young People's Record Club, on the other hand, was enormously popular.)

Matthews does assert that "their primary drive for children has been in our schools and school textbooks," but his evidence for this actually disproves his point, suggesting, on the one hand, that he was overlooking the obvious, that is, children's literature, and, on the other hand, begging the question of how subversive the educational material produced by left-wingers actually was. Matthews claims to have identified a three-pronged plan to enlist teachers and administrators, to disseminate propaganda through textbooks and instruction, and to organize students, but never details this plan or gives evidence for its existence. But he does single out one "textbook" as proof of his claims, Mary Elting's *We Are the Government* (1946). His criticisms of the book have more to do with its author than with its content; the worst he can say about the book is that Elting noted the "excitement" that other countries, including the Soviet Union, had about the U.S. Constitution. Matthews insists that "the only 'excitement' the Soviet Union has ever had with respect to the Constitution of the United States is to destroy it and the freedoms which rest upon it."[41]

Matthews claims that Elting was an instructor in the Communist Workers School, which was untrue, but his assessment of her political inclinations was accurate enough. Still, his targeting of *We Are the Government* as a school textbook is somewhat misleading. The book was actually conceived as a trade children's book, or a "classroom library" book. But because of the information this book was uniquely able to provide, it was sometimes used as a textbook. *We Are the Government* was one of the first texts to explain the workings of the U.S. government for a young audience, detailing the workings of the Executive Branch, the Legislative Branch, the Judicial Branch, the Department of State, the Veterans Administration, and other federal offices and programs and explaining processes such as how a bill becomes a law. The politics in the book are very much New Deal politics: the section on the National Labor Relations Board, for instance, highlights the Wagner Act and notes that prior to its passage workers were sometimes fired or "their names were put on blacklists" if they tried to join unions, and "sometimes thugs were even hired to break up union meetings, and leaders were put in jail." Elting comments on the Wagner Act's success, noting that "the law began working in the simple way it was supposed to because almost everybody now took it for granted that unions are an important part of American life." Similarly, a chapter on the Tennessee Valley Authority—often targeted by the Right as a socialist undertaking—celebrates its achievements: putting unemployed people to work, reclaiming farm land and waterways, and producing low-cost electricity for farms, towns, and industries.[42]

What first led to trouble for the book was Elting's discussion of how a bill becomes a law. Elting used the example of a congressman who "believes there should be a law providing free medical care for everybody in the country," a plan that, in this hypothetical example, generates disagreement, controversy, and amendments, but eventually becomes law.[43] The president of the American Medical Association, who happened to be another Doubleday author and for some reason got hold of the book, objected to this example and demanded that it be changed, calling the hypothetical bill "socialized medicine." Elting's editors at Doubleday stood by her. The book was then attacked in the *American Legion* magazine (by Matthews) and then denounced by Paul Harvey, a radio host. Elting's brother got wind of the controversy and, shocked to learn that his sister was a "red," stopped speaking to her for decades (thereby supporting the argument that McCarthyism destroyed families). The state of Texas banned the book from purchase by schools. But despite all of the fuss, Elting's editors remained supportive, not only keeping the popular book in print, but also putting it into new editions. And they continued to offer her new book contracts.[44]

If Elting's book had not been adopted as a textbook, Matthews—and the others—probably would never have noticed it. Despite his careful attention to "even the smallest assault upon the system," other than the mention of Elting's "textbook," Matthews never explicitly mentions children's literature, children's book publishing, or libraries. The lack of attention to children's literature on the part of red-hunters was thus one part of an equation that made the children's book field a viable home for the Left during the Cold War; the other crucial piece of the equation is that the few authors who *were* called to justify their Americanism in most cases managed to find strong supporters in the children's book field.

The Right Goes after the Reds

Although many of the leftists who wrote children's books were monitored by the FBI because of their political involvements or were cited in various legislative hearings investigating un-American activities, few were actually called to testify, and rarely were children's books themselves at issue. Children's books are usually mentioned only incidentally in authors' FBI files, if at all. Typical is a 1952 entry in Helen Colodny Goldfrank's (a.k.a. Helen Kay) lengthy FBI file that describes "subject" as "unemployed and a housewife" who "occasionally writes children's books."[45] In 260 pages, Kay's work as a writer of children's books is probably mentioned five times or fewer. Langston Hughes, Helen Kay, and Leo Huberman were among those called to testify before a committee investigating the politics of authors whose books could be found in overseas libraries. According to the *New York Times*, the inquiry was meant to determine whether "public libraries set up throughout the free world . . . to counteract Soviet propaganda" actually contained books by authors sympathetic to Communism. The distribution of books was at stake, but the line of questioning had remarkably little to do with the content of those books and far more to do with their authors' political inclinations and affiliations. As the *Times* put it, "It does not matter whether books are on chess or on the care of goldfish. If the author of a chess book or a goldfish study has a Communist record, his book goes out [of the libraries]."[46]

Langston Hughes was certainly not subpoenaed because of anything in his children's books; indeed, he turned to writing children's books when he found himself in political trouble, again suggesting the medium as a kind of refuge. Hughes became an easy target for the Right as a well-known African American who had vocally supported radical causes in the 1930s. The relationship between Hughes's career as a writer of children's books and his run-ins with McCarthyism are discussed in greater detail in the next chapter; in brief, however, Hughes "cooperated" with the committee in order to save his career, managing to disavow a connection to the Communist Party without actually disavowing a connection to the broader progressive movement and its ideals. Huberman and Kay, by contrast, were unfriendly witnesses: Huberman, though he answered the committee's questions, insisted that it was possible to be a communist but not a member of the Communist party and, moreover, that it was possible to believe in socialism and to be a good American, testimony that may have given him the moral high ground but did not help his career as an author.[47] Huberman had been a teacher in progressive schools and in adult-education programs, was a member of the human relations commission of the Progressive Education Association, had worked as an editor of *Scholastic* magazine, and had recently cofounded the socialist journal the *Monthly Review.* Two of his books, *We, the People* and *Man's Worldly Goods*, were intended for young people as well as working-class adults. It is not clear whether his books were banned from overseas libraries.[48]

Kay was relatively unknown as an author at the time of her testimony. However, she received a great deal of publicity for taking the Fifth Amendment before the investigating committee, becoming one of fourteen Fifth-Amendment authors whose books were singled out for removal from overseas libraries. Her *Apple Pie for Lewis* (1951) may have been the only book for young children to be removed.[49] After *Battle in the Barnyard* (1932), Kay's *Insects* (1939), a Little Wonder Book, introduced her work to the educational marketplace and survived a second printing but made very little splash.[50] *Apple Pie for Lewis* had been a kind of breakthrough book for Kay, as it was listed in the "Recommended Books of 1951" published by the *Library Journal.* The book was cited in the hearing but never actually discussed (Kay would not admit she had written it). Based on the experiences of Kay's son (actually named Lewis) visiting his grandmother's apple orchard, in the story Lewis eagerly anticipates the ripening (or, you might say, the reddening) of the apples, but this is about as political as the book gets.[51]

The daughter of Russian immigrants who supported the Bolshevik cause, Goldfrank/Kay had been an activist since childhood. She had been a leader of the

Young Pioneers and an editor of the *New Pioneer*, and prior to having children she had worked as a labor journalist and Communist party activist, organizing miners in Pennsylvania, for instance, and earning a place in Lauren Gilfillan's roman-à-clef, *I Went to Pit College* (1934). In her twenties, Kay had worked for the Communist party as a courier taking supplies and funds into Nazi Germany, playing upon her good looks, language skills, and the kind of fearlessness born out of commitment to a cause. The FBI clearly suspected that she was involved in something more sinister, as is evident from repeated attempts to link her to notorious "spy ring" figures like Elizabeth Bentley and Whittaker Chambers, but it never seemed to gather conclusive evidence. Her file does suggest that she was no longer active in the party by the time *Apple Pie for Lewis* was published (which did not make any difference as far as efforts to ban it were concerned), and the terror produced by years of surveillance and the call to testify in Washington meant that most of Kay's children's books show almost no trace of her once-radical sensibilities.[52]

Kay pleaded the Fifth Amendment to almost every one of the committee's questions, including the question of whether she had even *heard* of her book *Apple Pie for Lewis*. She did admit to having been born in New York City and to having attended a school where the Pledge of Allegiance was recited, but she declined to answer "whether that pledge mean[t] anything to [her]." She acknowledged being an American citizen and claimed to be proud of it. Still, she declined to tell the committee whether she had "carr[ied] money from Moscow to Germany for the Communist party," and her silence on this matter must have seemed particularly sinister at a time when the entire country was up in arms about Communists having passed "atomic secrets" to the Soviets. It would take several years and an oppositional sensibility to recast Goldfrank/Kay's activity—or activity like hers—as heroic rather than as traitorous, as in the 1977 film *Julia*, which makes a heroine out of a friend of Lillian Hellman's, possibly modeled on Kay herself, who smuggled money and supplies into Nazi Germany.[53]

While Hughes had appeased the committee just enough to keep his career, and Huberman essentially gave up on the idea of mainstream publishing, Goldfrank/Kay was able to salvage some of her career without giving any information at all to the committee. She and her entire family were humiliated by the national news attention that her appearance in Washington brought, but a few sympathetic editors were willing to continue publishing her work. And there were no incidents akin to Le Sueur's experience with the *Milwaukee Sentinel* that focused on particular books.[54] Arguably, she might have been more successful had she not had the run-in with the McCarthy committee (Goldfrank/Kay herself certainly believed this to be the case), but she did publish more than thirty books after her appearance before the committee, several of which—like

One Mitten Lewis (1955)—sold quite well.[55] Few Hollywood radicals who defied HUAC fared so well without disguising their identities (Helen Kay's real name was never a secret). There was no blacklist per se in juvenile publishing, as there was in other fields. But then again, the stakes were never very high.[56] Moreover, as noted earlier, few left-wing authors had the visibility or the kind of record of activity like that which brought such humiliating attention to people like Hughes and Kay. McCarthyism may have helped to suck the politics out of some children's books, but it destroyed few careers. Moreover, as later chapters discuss in greater detail, many children's books continued to carry the progressive values of the Popular Front, and politically minded authors tended to find support among those controlling the field of children's book publishing. Thus they were able to go on working with impunity.

"I Don't Care, as Long as He's Not a Republican"

The response of editors working with Mary Elting and Helen Kay was fairly typical in terms of their attempt to stay above the fray of McCarthyism. Ursula Nordstrom at Harper and Richard Walsh at John Day explicitly told authors who were under investigation that they were not interested in their politics, just their writing. When Millicent Selsam told Nordstrom that her husband was being called before the McCarthy committee, Nordstrom apparently responded by saying, "I don't care, as long as he's not a Republican." Nancy Larrick at Random House, who was married to the labor journalist and sometime juvenile author Alexander Crosby, recognized the considerable risks she was taking by publishing Anne Terry White, whose husband, Harry Dexter White, had been secretary of the Treasury and accused of espionage, but Larrick felt that White's writing merited such risks.[57] Priscilla Hiss, the wife of Alger Hiss, eventually made a living as a copy editor at Golden Books some years after being let go from her teaching job at the Dalton School; a number of the staff members at Golden Books were probably sympathetic to the position into which she had been thrown by the accusations leveled against her husband.[58] And although the record is not entirely clear on the subject, it is quite possible that even prior to the whole Milwaukee incident, Knopf—an outspoken opponent of McCarthy—knew Le Sueur was blacklisted from most publishing venues but made a conscious choice to publish her children's books.[59]

Librarians were especially likely to take a stance in favor of intellectual freedom. Former teachers like Irving Adler, Sarah Riedman, Hyman Ruchlis, Rose Wyler, May Edel, and others could find their books featured prominently in school libraries even after they were no longer welcome in the classroom. Part of what made the attack on Le Sueur's book stand out was the implication that librarians had somehow failed in their jobs by allowing Le Sueur and her books into their bastions. Librarians, however, had come to believe that they had a more pressing calling than "protecting" children. The American Library Association issued several statements in 1953 defending intellectual freedom in public and school libraries, rejecting the practice of labeling "subversive" litera- ture, and condemning censorship in overseas libraries, citing "free libraries as the enemies of enslaved minds."[60] And although individual librarians certainly practiced self-censorship of their collections, others, including the librarians in Milwaukee who had invited Le Sueur to speak, bravely came out against attacks on school and public library collections, defending not just their right but also their duty to do so. As Edwin Castagna, director of the Enoch Pratt Free Library in Baltimore (and former member of the Progressive Librarians Council) asserted in 1963:

> If the public library is not a place for the dissenting, the heretical, the unorthodox, the critical, for offbeat books with ideas not likely to be found in the mass media, it is not the right kind of place. If the public library does not aggressively seek out and make readily avail- able this kind of material, distasteful as it often is, it is not serving its function.[61]

But despite rhetorical support for "the dissenting, the heretical, the unorthodox, the critical," an aversion in the 1950s toward openly controver- sial books, especially books dealing with present-day conditions, followed the 1940s emphasis on "socially significant" literature for children. Changes in the Child Study Award, which had been given to a book for young people that grappled with pressing social problems, give some indications of a new climate in the field. In 1951 the Child Study Association found "no book" that "seemed to fulfill the special purposes of the award." After this point, the CSA began to shift its criteria, giving the award "to books about both personal and univer- sal problems."[62] The change suggests that tackling social issues head-on had become a trickier task for authors and more difficult for "child guardians" like those in the Child Study Association to promote.

In the 1950s, we find no more commercially published books with politics so open as those in *The Company Owns the Tools* or *Run, Run!* The "political" aspects of works published in the 1950s were, with some exceptions, channeled through realms providing some distance from the present-day context, particu- larly history or science, which had a natural appeal to cultural workers embrac- ing a Marxist, materialist sensibility. In other cases, politics were expressed through the imaginative and the fantastic, in books like Crockett Johnson's *Harold and the Purple Crayon* (1955), in which a boy has the capacity and tools to literally create his own world; and Ruth Krauss's *A Very Special House* (1953), which describes a house where "everywhere is music," where animals run freely, and "NOBODY ever says stop stop stop." As children who "ducked and covered" became increasingly mistrustful of adults who said this activity would make them safe, they found in children's books further evidence that authority was often arbitrary and unjust and that critical, independent thought and activism were fundamental to good citizenship.[63]

Fighting "Adult Chauvinism"

In his 1947 *New Masses* piece on the state of the children's literature field, Jay Williams suggested that progressives had not been giving children's literature the attention it deserved. He insisted that "literary critics and progressive publications—whose aims are free from commercialism and opportunism—begin to recognize the value of juvenile writing." In Williams's view, "[U]ntil this is done left-wing critics have no right to call themselves opponents of chauvinism, for to ignore the young people and their literature is to be guilty of a kind of adult chauvinism as detrimental to our own future as any other kind of discriminatory practice."[64] As an author who may have wished to get more recognition for his own recent venture into the juvenile field, Williams's comments are understandable, but they are misleading, to the extent that they minimize the real inroads that leftists had already made into the field. Children's books may have never garnered the critical attention they deserved in the leading publications of the Left, but this might have helped to limit the attention they received from red-hunters, who were some of the most avid readers of these publications.

Even the muted politics in children's books of the 1950s did not mean that leftists had moved out of the field; indeed, they had become deeply entrenched in it. The next chapter considers more concretely some ways in which radicals and their allies resisted, negotiated, and even sometimes benefited from Cold War pressures, a phenomenon that explicitly played out in the demand for science and history books, discussed in the final chapters.

5

Countering the Cold War

Social Significance versus Social Pressure

In the fall of 1945, International Publishers—"long dedicated," as Clara Ostrowsky put it in the *New Masses*, "to serious books which cast new meaning on our world"—launched a juvenile series called Young World Books. Inspiration for the series came from Betty Bacon, who had joined the staff at International Publishers after working in the juvenile divisions of several trade publishing houses, including Bobbs Merrill, McBride, and W. R. Scott. Promotional material for Young World Books noted that the series' goal was to "open the door to a wide world of ideas that will help the young readers of today to become the good citizens of tomorrow." According to Ostrowsky's article, the books were "designed to answer questions young people have about the world today and to equip them to play their part in achieving a better world."[1] This rhetoric was right in line with the current children's literature discourse around realism, "problem books," and "social significance," and it appeared to effectively position Young World Books to fill an important niche in juvenile publishing.

Of course, Young World's focus on "serious books" that "cast new meaning on our world" was not the only thing to distinguish the series. As a venture of the CP's principal publishing house, its links to the political program of the party were both implicit and explicit. Although the books were identified as "Young World Books," they were openly associated with International Publishers. Unlike previous efforts sponsored by the Communist Party, Young World managed to access a mainstream market, gaining the positive attention of reviewers, librarians, teachers, and other cultural arbiters. These books were never bestsellers, but several were reprinted numerous times (as of 2005, at least two of the books remain in print with other publishers). Moreover, the series launched careers in juvenile writing or illustrating for several folks who did go on to write or illustrate bestsellers. Most important, Young World Books was tied to a conscious effort by radicals and progressives in the immediate postwar period to make children's literature a core part of the "cultural front," especially as other avenues of cultural production—most notably Hollywood, broadcasting, and teaching, but also much of the publishing industry—became closed to leftists. Although the series was an important undertaking, its demise in 1952 was actually relatively insignificant, given the fact that so many other publishing houses were, by this time, publishing left-wing authors whose books essentially performed the same cultural work. The latter books were not part of a CP program, but they were, nonetheless, products of the Popular Front structure of feeling.

International had been publishing children's books for at least a decade, mostly reprinting books originally published in England, Germany, and the Soviet Union. Eric Lucas's *Corky* (1938), a collection of contemporary and historical short stories about streetwise, feisty children, echoed offerings in the *New Pioneer* and probably reached a similarly limited market. What made the Young World series different from International's previous juvenile undertakings, and Communist literature in general, was its relatively wide distribution and critical success. The head of International Publishers, Alexander Trachtenberg, was initially unenthusiastic about starting a juvenile series, but Betty Bacon convinced him that the effort was worthwhile, pointing out that books simple enough for children would be accessible to workers with little education or for whom English was a second language.[2]

Bacon was key to Young World's success, but her efforts went well beyond Young World Books. She started the book series and personally recruited most of the writers and illustrators. She also literally taught people to write children's books, offering a class at the Jefferson School of Social Science on writing for children. Among her students were Millicent Selsam, who published her first book, *Egg to Chick*, in the Young World series in 1946 (and later taught her own Jefferson School class on writing children's books); Shirley Graham; and Helen Kay, who went from writing proletarian "fairy tales" like *Battle in the Barnyard* to books earning recognition from the Junior Literary Guild. As Mary Elting, who helped edit some of the Young World Books, said of Kay, "Betty Bacon came along and taught Helen how to form her books in a way suitable for libraries and schools (some of the credit may also go to Lucy Sprague Mitchell, who taught Kay through her Writers' Laboratory)."[3] Experienced in trade publishing and actively maintaining ties to the industry through organizations like the Association of Children's Book Editors, Bacon helped to place a left-wing agenda in the mainstream.[4]

Bacon also taught left-wing parents how to select books for their children. In a series of articles published in 1946 on the *Worker*'s "Women's Page,"

Bacon explained "how to pick a picture book," what children should "get out of books," and how children's books could help "progressive parents" who "want to share their ideals with their children and want their children to grow into courageous, progressive, citizens." In her tips on choosing picture books, Bacon told readers to consider whether the illustrations were "colorful," "well drawn," and clear, as well as whether any were "too scary." Of the text, she asked, "Is it simple? Is it clear? Is the language good? Is the book written in a silly or condescending manner?" She urged parents to think carefully about what books they buy, and yet also cautioned them to think about the child's interests, not their own: "Are you suiting Junior's tastes or your own adult preferences? (Think twice before you answer that one.)" The article reminds parents that just because a book is more expensive does not mean it will be better and it also urges parents to consider whether the illustrations "contain caricatures of Negroes or other races and nationalities." There is otherwise little proselytizing here, and the emphasis is on helping parents to find quality, age-appropriate books at affordable prices.[5]

On the question of what children should get out of books, Bacon expressed the philosophy that undergirded her conception of Young World Books:

In this turbulent world, children must learn early to find their way through complex problems. They must learn early to observe, to draw conclusions, to think. Books are a tool of learning and thinking, and the child who finds this out when he is very young has taken a big step forward. When and how he does this depends a lot on how you introduce him to books.

Echoing Lucy Sprague Mitchell, she encouraged parents to provide the young child with books "about things that are familiar to him," gradually offering the child a range of books that match his or her special interests, whether those be "airplanes, or cooking, or nature study." She recognized that many *Worker* readers were limited financially, but suggested that if possible they should "let [the child] buy a book or two for his own." But she emphasized the value of teaching a child to look things up in the library, for there is no greater "thrill," she said, than being able to discover the answers to one's questions. More important than how much a child reads or even what a child reads ("he will inevitably bring home a lot of trash") is what he gets out of books, she insisted. "Your job," she concluded, "is to supply him with books that really say something to him—and show him by experience that the right kind of books can give him something he wants."[6]

The final article in Bacon's series for the *Worker* speaks more directly to the factors that apparently made Young World Books seem like a necessary undertaking to Bacon. Noting the desire of parents involved in "trade union and political activities" to explain "just what they are doing and why," and the dearth of books dealing with American workers and unions, Bacon claimed that "it was so that such books could be published that International Publishers established Young World Books last year." The article highlights a new book in the Young World series, *The Story of Your Coat*. Written by Clara Hollos and illustrated by Herbert Kruckman, the book, Bacon explained, highlights the contributions of workers and the important role of unions. Perhaps most important, "by telling this story in terms that are both understandable and exciting to children, the book gives them an idea of the co-operative nature of labor in our society."[7]

This series of articles in the *Worker* makes it clear that a left-wing audience was important to Bacon when she conceived of Young World Books. However, in contrast to Communist literature published in the 1920s and 1930s, Young World Books was created more for a mainstream audience. Fourteen books were published through the series between 1945 and 1952, most of them dealing with science or history and all by people close to, if not in, the Communist Party. One book, *How the Automobile Learned to Run*, was a translation of a story by the Soviet writer M. Il'in, but all of the others were original books by American authors. Nine of the books were on scientific or technological themes; *Swamp Fox Brigade: Adventures with General Francis Marion's Guerrillas* by Eric Lucas (1945) dealt with an episode in American history; *Voyage Thirteen* (1946), also by Lucas, told a story about a multiethnic crew on a World War II freighter; *Reunion in Poland* (1945) by Jean Karsavina dealt with post–World War II reconstruction in Poland; and *Tree by the Waters* (1948), also by Karsavina, was about labor struggles in a working-class town in Massachusetts. In addition, Young World put out a collection of Walt Whitman's poetry called *I Hear the People Singing* (1946), with an introduction by Langston Hughes. Meridel Le Sueur contracted with Young World to write a book on tools, but the book was apparently never completed.[8]

Other than the Whitman/Hughes book and the Il'in book, most of the titles were by relatively unknown or first-time authors, and other than Lynd Ward, who illustrated *Reunion in Poland* just two years after illustrating bestseller and Newbery Award–winner *Johnny Tremain*, the illustrators generally had relatively little previous experience in children's literature. Most of the Young World books were positively reviewed in the mainstream reviewing establishment; several were included on recommended booklists.[9] At least four of the Young World titles were reprinted by commercial publishers. On the other hand, several were offered as premiums with subscriptions to the *New Masses*, promoting them among leftist readers.

Young World is unique as a relatively mainstream series directly connected to the Communist Party, but those connections limited the scope, content, and quality of the books, as well as their distribution. Even so, with few exceptions, Young World books are not didactic or dogmatic; they are well written, engaging, and informative. That they would be otherwise presumes that political work must necessarily be preachy or of limited artistry. Like many other books by left-wing writers, Young World titles were well received by librarians and teachers because they were good books. But it also seems that few teachers, librarians, or educational supervisors made the connection between International Publishers and the Communist party, or, perhaps, few thought the connection was relevant. Still, International was not equipped to publicize its children's books nor to promote them to the extent that other publishing houses could, so their distribution was ultimately limited. Likewise, although most of the Young World books achieved some level of success because of their high quality (and, especially in the case of the science books, their relatively muted politics), it is only logical to assume that Communist connections hurt the books' prospects for achieving a mass audience (even the Young People's Record Club, which had no direct Communist connection, was repeatedly subject to censorship efforts because its directors and many of its contributors were left-wingers). Young World was ultimately a casualty of McCarthyism: Alexander Trachtenberg was jailed under the Smith Act in 1952, and International's operations were reduced to a bare minimum. Not surprisingly, children's books were not the press's top priority.[10]

The example of International Publishers' venture into the world of trade children's book publishing only begins to suggest the ways in which leftists in the children's book field challenged the Cold War "consensus." This is true not only because Young World Books was a relatively short-lived venture, but also, more important, because most left-wingers in the field worked at commercial presses. Moreover, the conscious or unconscious cooperation of liberals was an essential element of leftists' ability to maintain a role in the field.

In his 1947 *New Masses* article on the children's literature scene, Jay Williams brought attention to children's literature itself and the labor of its production, as well as the informal and formal networks of cultural workers in the field. He asserted that "it is no accident many of the writers for young people are active in progressive organizations, or in the Authors Guild. Their convictions are inseparable from their work, and that young people like these convictions is shown beyond doubt by the popularity of their work."[11] Although McCarthyism made it increasingly less likely that people would forge connections through openly political institutions and organizations, like-minded people also had a way of finding each other through the Authors Guild as well as in informal and often unlikely locations. The story of how Lilian Moore and Rose Wyler met is telling: a long-lasting friendship and professional collaboration between the two women began in the ladies' room at Golden Books. They recognized each other from the Authors Guild, where both women were quite outspoken. Moore asked Wyler pointedly, "Are they trying to screw you like they're trying to screw me? Let's get together and talk contracts!" Eventually both women would become major figures in the field and leaders of an effort by the Authors Guild to improve book contracts for juvenile authors.[12]

Such tales of ladies' room networking are probably more true to actual experience than images of plots hatched in dark Communist-cell meetings, but the lack of a coordinated program makes it much more difficult to accurately assess the impact of the Left in publishing houses. Still, an anecdotally compiled list would suggest that the influence was significant and that a number of people in the field consciously worked to counter the logic and effects of McCarthyism. In addition to Bacon, several leftists, of varying political affiliations, worked as juvenile editors or in other capacities as arbiters of work published, reviewed, or disseminated.[13] A number of agents, perhaps most notably Maxim Lieber, worked with left-wing writers or illustrators, several of whom were suffering from the blacklist.[14] Several publishing houses were known for their owners' liberal or even radical sympathies. Scott, Vanguard, Capitol, Schuman, Harvey House, Messner, Day, Golden, Simon and Schuster, Doubleday, and Random House all had this reputation at one time or another.[15] Writers themselves were sometimes able to secure contracts for people suffering from blacklisting. One indication of how open the children's book field was is the fact that even openly political children's book writers usually used their own names.[16]

Betty Bacon acknowledged that there was something of a push among writers close to the party to write for mass-market operations like Golden Books, as they recognized "a great opportunity to reach many kids." Although commentators like Harry Granick would call for publishing ventures sponsored by the "labor movement," beyond Young World Books and the short-lived though self-consciously progressive Children's Book Club (which offered books such as Alex Novikoff's *Climbing Our Family Tree* and Margret and H. A. Rey's *Spotty*, a tale of interracial mixing told through "a brown-spotted bunny in a family of white rabbits"), most leftists worked in mainstream institutions, as authors, illustrators, editors, librarians, and booksellers.[17] Moreover, most activism related to children's literature was through organizations like the Authors Guild rather than the CP. Some concrete examples tell a bit more about how left-wing authors, librarians, editors, booksellers, and others, in cooperation with liberals who (consciously or unconsciously) helped them, navigated the politics of the Cold War, within the generic constraints of children's literature.

Protecting Writers versus Protecting Children (and Sales)

Meridel Le Sueur, whose work was directly attacked, presents a useful starting point for this discussion. Knopf took considerable risks by giving Le Sueur a book contract in the first place, even in 1946. Le Sueur had always been quite open about her politics, and as the relatively progressive wartime climate gave way to the Cold War, her record of publication shows she began to pay a price: Knopf was the only commercial publisher that would touch Le Sueur's work between 1947 and 1961. That Knopf's editors were aware of Le Sueur's politics is evident from correspondence urging her to tone down potentially controversial elements in her manuscripts; for instance, in September 1953, editor William N. Hall at Knopf wrote Le Sueur to suggest that controversial elements of her Lincoln book be "eliminated" or "rephrased." His rationale for this editorial suggestion was the desirability of avoiding material that would "militate against sales." But others in the firm were clearly enthusiastic about her presence on the Knopf list. For instance, a letter dated May 21, 1954, from a new and progressive Knopf editor, Rachel D'Angelou, expressed great enthusiasm about Le Sueur and her work and encouraged Le Sueur to submit future projects to the press.[18]

Whether she did so is unclear, but after the editors at Knopf were alerted to the cancellation of Le Sueur's reading on NBC's "Carnival of Books," she probably knew it was not really worth the bother. Even so, Le Sueur's situation was not hopeless. A letter dated January 16, 1955, from Genieve Fox at the Children's Music Center, a Left-run distributor of children's records and books, suggests something of the way in which left-wing networks operated to maintain a progressive presence in the field. "I may be naive at this point," Fox wrote, "but have Borzoi [Knopf's imprint] and Messner refused publication of recent or future books by you?" Fox mentioned several juvenile publishers that were still publishing radical authors: Scott, she noted, was still publishing Millicent Selsam, and Messner was still publishing Shirley Graham. And Watts was still doing books by Langston Hughes. She also passed on the names and addresses of outlets with a conscious or de facto specialty in work by progressive writers and artists: Cameron and Kahn Publishers, Howard Fast's Blue Heron Press, and Folkways Records.[19] Le Sueur would, in fact, turn to Howard Fast's independent press, which was expressly created to help victims of the blacklist. This raison d'être distinguished Blue Heron Press, but the commercial presses Fox mentioned were not publishing radicals simply by some coincidence. Each of these presses had editors who were actively opposed to McCarthyism: May Garelick at Scott, Gertrude Blumenthal at Messner, and Helen Hoke Watts at Watts. Still, the commercial imperative placed practical restrictions on publishers and limited the extent to which they could resist the pressures of McCarthyism.

Watts, which published not only Langston Hughes, but also Mary Elting, Franklin Folsom, Rose Wyler, Harold Coy, and a range of other left-wing authors, represents an especially interesting case. The relationship between Franklin Watts Publishers and Langston Hughes suggests the dilemma faced by liberals and progressives in publishing: although they wished to demonstrate a liberal, antiracist position, they felt forced to grapple with McCarthyism and its implications. As a visible target of McCarthyism, Hughes was a political liability whom other publishers were afraid to touch.[20] But he was also a talented author with a track record of writing for children. Helen Hoke Watts was critical of McCarthyism and supportive of civil rights for African Americans, and these principles surely had something to do with her support for Langston Hughes. Undoubtedly she wanted to publish Hughes in part because she knew he was good and his books would sell, but it also seemed to be the right thing to do. Even so, while it is true that Watts published work by Hughes throughout the 1950s, the firm found it impossible to do so without demanding some kind of public statement addressing his political past. But when it came to the books themselves, far from forcing Hughes to tone down his politics, Hoke Watts actually pressed him to be more forthright in his discussion of racial relations in the United States.

In the early 1950s, Mary Elting Folsom and Franklin Folsom complained to the publisher Franklin Watts that his lists of children's books included nothing about African Americans and no work by black writers—a common complaint voiced by left-wing writers, who consistently pressed for the integration of children's literature.[21] Watts's *First Books* series had soared to popularity in the mid-1940s; Franklin and Mary Elting Folsom had contributed to the series' success by writing, individually and sometimes in collaboration, *The First Book of Boats* (1945), *The First Book of Automobiles* (1949), *The First Book of Indians* (1950), *The First Book of Cowboys* (1950), *The First Book of Baseball* (1950), *The First Book of Firemen* (1951), *The First Book of Nurses* (1951), and *The First Book of Eskimos* (1952). Franklin Folsom also had written several titles in the *Real Books* series for Watts, including *The Real Book about Abraham Lincoln* (1951), *The Real Book of Great American Journeys* (1953), and *The Real Book about Indians* (1953). And the Folsoms also had referred a number of other authors to Watts, thus becoming some of the most prolific writers on Watts's juvenile list and an important connection for the publisher.

Anxious to prove to these income-producing authors that they were not racists, Franklin Watts and his wife and editor, Helen Hoke Watts, told the Folsoms that they would gladly publish a *First Book of Negroes* and that they would even be happy to have an African-American writer do the book if the Folsoms could suggest a writer. Helen Hoke Watts, who had coauthored the 1941 "Problem Book" article in *Publishers Weekly* (discussed in chapter 3), was politically progressive and very much part of the effort to make children's books more reflective of pressing social issues. She had worked with a number of Left-leaning editors at Messner before joining her new husband's firm and had even made playful references in the mid-1940s to her "left-wing causes."[22]

The Folsoms would test just how far Helen Watts was willing to stand by her left-wing causes when they suggested Langston Hughes as an author for *The First Book of Negroes*, for Hughes was at that time already beginning to find himself in political trouble. While probably never actually a member of the CP, Hughes's support for progressive and "Communist front" causes was well known: the right-wing publication *Red Channels*, for instance, published a four-page list of Hughes's radical associations in 1950, and the American Legion had begun a smear campaign against Hughes as early as the mid-1940s, exposing Hughes's "long communist front record" and widely circulating two "atheistic" and "communistic" poems by Hughes, "Good-bye Christ!" and "Revolution." The AL's campaign had sharply curtailed Hughes's income from high school speaking tours, which he undertook as a representative of the Common Council for American Unity (publishers of the intercultural journal *Common Ground*). The opportunity with Watts—which accepted the Folsoms' suggestion—came as Hughes was scrambling for income and struggling to distance himself from his left-wing associations because of the effect they were having on his livelihood. Thus Hughes was in no position to refuse the less than generous contract that Watts presented to Hughes's agent, Maxim Lieber, "with a take-it-or-leave-it ultimatum."[23]

Arnold Rampersad's discussion of the Wattses' relation to Hughes's politics and their efforts to censor *The First Book of Negroes* fails to fully or accurately represent the complexity of the situation or the resulting text itself. Rampersad points to the statement Hughes prepared, at the Wattses' request, "denying past or present membership in the Communist Party," and maintains that they "clearly pressed him to make his book as inoffensive to conservatives as possible."[24] While Franklin and Helen Hoke Watts did, indeed, ask Hughes to prepare a statement in response to accusations about his radical politics, most of their suggestions, rather than making the book "inoffensive," actually made it more politically charged. And most of the calls for changes represented the Wattses' efforts to keep other, even more radical, authors happy.

Almost all of Helen Hoke Watts's editorial suggestions were directly drawn from Mary Elting's comments on the manuscript. As Hoke Watts put it, "Because Mary Elting has written so many of the First Books (under such an array of names!) . . . and because I knew of her interest in this manuscript from the very first, I sent this draft to her for further criticisms and suggestions and she came up with some good ones." The commentary from Mary Elting was quoted almost in its entirety within Hoke Watts's letter, though Hoke Watts periodically interjected statements of agreement (or occasional disagreement), elaborated on various points made by Elting, and appended suggestions from "F.W." (Franklin Watts) at the end of the letter.

In general, Elting's comments, seconded by Hoke Watts, asked Hughes to more explicitly acknowledge racial discrimination and racially based economic disparities in both the American South and the North, the home of Hughes's middle-class, African-American protagonist, a boy named Terry who lives in New York City, where his father is an interpreter for the United Nations. Elting noted:

> I think Mr. Hughes was right in making him a boy who embodies all the good things that exist for Negroes in New York. Although he is typical of only a tiny proportion of northern New York children, he is a reality which all kids are justified in hoping to achieve. But I suspect that the majority of Negro children will be bothered by the feeling that *they*, the ordinary kids, aren't to be found anywhere in the book.

Elting argued that "since the book as a whole is so positive and hopeful, while at the same time it deals honestly with Jim Crow in the South, I think it would be a mistake to leave the feeling that New York is wholly a fairy-tale country." Hoke Watts concurred, noting, "F.W. and I both realize that you get into the subject later on in the book, but he feels (and I do, too—and apparently Mary does too) that it ought to come *earlier* in the book. . . . Not necessarily long-drawn-out—but definite." Hoke Watts added, parenthetically, "Don't worry about the Southern market (not that you would). We have no hopes of it anyhow, except for the enlightened—which is, surprisingly, quite sizable."[25]

Page-by-page commentary ranged from technical suggestions or questions to further advice that Hughes make racially motivated historical and contemporary injustices more apparent in the text. For instance, Elting asked, in regard to the third page of Hughes's manuscript (with Hoke Watts concurring), "'[W]ould it be worth noting that the reason Negro slaves could be captured in great numbers was not because they were dopes but because the superior weapons were on the side of the captors?' (Yes. H.H.W.)." Hoke Watts added Franklin Watts's suggestion that Hughes could point out the fact that because their color made them distinguishable, blacks were particularly vulnerable to slavery. Further comments from Elting asked Hughes to be more explicit in his comment about "problems relating to colonial countries." As she put it, "I don't think there's any danger in adding, that means countries where colored peoples, who have always lived there, have been conquered and are now governed by white people." Of a scene where Terry goes to see a broadcast of Louis Armstrong with his friend David, whose father writes radio scripts, Elting noted, "I assume David will be pictured as a white child." He is, in fact, shown as white in the illustration, with no comment in the text.

Two pages of Franklin Watts's own comments on the subject of segregation were tacked on to the end of Hoke Watts's long letter. Franklin Watts noted that "it is important some place early in the book to explain what segregation is, then to show how silly it is and how it is broken down." He suggested a definition such as "segregation is a device to preserve inequalities by not permitting some people—i.e. Negroes—from sharing eating places, waiting rooms, occupations, hotels, etc." Spelling out segregation in such a way made it clear that Watts was wholly against it and drew attention away from the fact that Watts himself had been accused by several of his authors of participating in discriminatory practices in publishing. Such concerns about image aside, that the firm changed its practices partly because of pressure does not diminish the fact that Watts was actually one of the first publishers to consciously break down color barriers in the children's book field.

The condemnation of Jim Crow in the book is unequivocal and unapologetic, and the central protagonists of the book are educated African Americans who are committed to achieving racial justice. Terry's grandmother, for instance, a graduate of Fisk University, "does not say 'ain't,' or use bad grammar, except when she is reciting folk poems or telling stories." She explains to Terry:

> [T]here have always been white people in America who wanted Negroes to live happily and have the same rights as other Americans. No one has yet been able to wipe out *all* the ugly leftovers of a bad time in our country, but good citizens are trying, and someday there will be no more WHITE or COLORED signs anywhere.[26]

On the other hand, that the book couches its social critique in a discourse of liberal integrationism is undeniable, and it is true that significant but controversial figures like W. E. B. Du Bois and Paul Robeson—who, by all rights should have appeared among the "famous American Negroes" portrayed in the book—are conspicuously absent. Likewise, a picture of Josephine Baker was removed from the book for the second printing after a New York columnist threatened to attack the book if she remained in it.[27]

The Wattses' divergence from Elting on the issue of the book's ending aptly illustrates the need they clearly felt to demonstrate their firm's patriotic stance as they published a radical author and material that challenged the southern status quo. As a conclusion, Elting had suggested having Terry and his friend happily ride home together on the subway, but Hoke Watts maintained that the *First Books* needed "a sort of summary page, to give that satisfied feeling *to the reader*, of having reached the end of a circle, and all the ends tied up neatly." The Wattses' suggested ending tells volumes about the extent to which it was necessary to frame controversial ideas within a conciliatory patriotic discourse in this time period and also demonstrates the extent to which the imagined desires and values of various "child guardians" directly affected editorial choices. As Hoke Watts wrote to Hughes, "F.W. and I suggest (don't groan, please) that you end with a paragraph or two—no more—on *the real value* of being an American. (Again, don't groan) you've no idea how much this sort of country-appreciation is valued by the older people who, after all, select the books young people read, 98% of the time."[28]

The ending of the published book reflects the Wattses' suggestions. After an evening skating at Rockefeller Center, with the flags of all nations waving in the snowy dusk, Terry thinks to himself, "This is the prettiest city in the most wonderful country in the world, and I'd rather live here than anywhere else on earth!" He tells his father this as they drive home, and his father agrees, but also reminds Terry that "our country has many problems to solve." The ending is clearly framed in terms of Cold War liberalism and racial progress. Even so, the book's final message is one urging activism. After pointing out that in some countries "people are governed by rulers, and ordinary folks can't do a thing about it," Terry's dad points out that "here all of us are part of democracy. By taking an interest in our government, and by treating our neighbors as we would like to be treated, *each one of us* can help make our country the most wonderful country in the world."[29]

The majority of the book is openly critical of racial discrimination; it exposes racially based injustices in both the South and the North; and it portrays interracial friendship as natural. Moreover, it describes the rich history and culture of African Americans, with roots in Africa and in America, and recovers a heritage basically unknown to American children, black and white, at the time of the book's initial publication in 1952. Moreover, an edition of *The First Book of Negroes* published sometime in the late 1950s lists six "other books to read," five of which were by left-wing authors or illustrators.[30]

Rather than simply being a sop to the Folsoms in answer to their criticisms of Watts, *The First Book of Negroes* was highly publicized—as Hoke Watts put it at the end of the long letter quoted above, "It's going to be our biggest fall book." Hughes himself worked on publicizing the book in African-American communities, sending to Watts the names of black teachers, librarians, booksellers, journalists, and public figures who should be sent copies. Helen Hoke Watts became a supportive friend to Hughes (as is shown by the tone of their correspondence) even when attacks against him—and *The First Book of Negroes*—

became increasingly vehement.[31] But as letters began to come directly to Watts, the publisher probably felt compelled to ask Hughes to clear his name.

Virginia Stumbough, president of the Children's Reading Roundtable, contacted Watts for clarification in regard to some controversy surrounding Hughes. Enclosing a letter she'd received from William H. Harris of the American Legion's National Americanism Commission detailing Hughes's long list of alleged "Communist front" associations, she asked Watts if he could tell her "anything you have learned about his allegiance to any of these groups," adding, somewhat sheepishly, "I still feel that all this should have little bearing in judging the literary quality of a very fine book. . . . But why is Mr. Hughes' list of memberships so long? And if it actually was not, who was responsible for these lists?" Demonstrating the general climate in which Stumbough felt obliged to make such a query into Hughes's politics, she mentioned that one librarian to whom she had spoken believed, "[N]o matter what the literary quality of a book, it should not be financially supported by Americans, if it is known that the money to its author will be turned over to an anti-American cause."[32]

Hughes *had* been affiliated with many of the "front" groups, causes, and publications that were included on the AL list, including the American League against War and Fascism, the Book Union, the International Labor Defense, the Negro Playwrights Company, the *New Masses*, the *Daily Worker*, and others. Moreover, he *had* written the "atheistic" and "communistic" poems that were quoted in full, and this seemed damning enough for some people. Harris had written in his letter, "It is our belief that no book written by an individual that could write a poem such as 'Good Buy [*sic*] Christ' and 'Revolution' has any place in our educational or literary structure." Despite assorted factual errors in his report (including a claim that Hughes had been a "professed card-carrying member of the Communist Party" for approximately twenty years), condemnations of Hughes by Harris and others were taken seriously enough that Watts politely urged Hughes to straighten out any confusion as to his alleged associations with Communist or Communist-front groups. Hughes did so in a statement that Watts made available to anyone needing proof of Hughes's patriotism.[33]

When Hughes was finally called to appear before a congressional committee, he decided to cooperate in order to save his career, although as a "cooperative" witness, Hughes was remarkably skillful in negotiating the committee's questions.[34] Hughes publicly disavowed any connection to the Communist Party in the present or past, but he managed to do so while still affirming the dignity of his struggles for social justice. Likewise, in the statement he prepared for Franklin and Helen Hoke Watts denying his membership in the Communist Party, Hughes asserted that his "goal as a writer was to effect social change in a free, harmonious America." He added: "If my little book, *The First Book of Negroes*, can help to that end, I'll be grateful."[35]

Sales of *The First Book of Negroes* may certainly have been affected by the controversy, but it also brought the book increased publicity.[36] And Watts continued to publish new *First Books* by Hughes throughout the 1950s and into the 1960s. Interestingly, Hughes's race may well have actually benefited him in terms of how the Wattses handled the controversy around him. In contrast to Hughes's experience, Watts revoked Irving Adler's contract for a book on weather after Adler was fired from the New York City schools for refusing to answer questions about his political affiliations. Ironically, the book was then assigned to another radical, Rose Wyler, whom Adler knew from the teachers' union.[37]

If Le Sueur's negotiations with Knopf say something about the world of fine literary imprints and if Hughes's negotiations with Watts says something about an institutionally oriented series, the negotiations around the *Kathy Martin* books speak to the particular dynamics of publishing a mass-market, girls' fiction series. Because series books of this genre tended to be formulaic and quickly written, publishers often were more concerned with maintaining a series' rate of production than with an individual book's merits, the specific details of its plot, or the particular beliefs of an author. Usually kept out of libraries in light of their perceived low quality, series books published for the mass market were subject to even less scrutiny than were trade books. Certainly these factors may have had something to do with why a number of radicals (anarchists, socialists, Communists, etc.) wrote mass-market series books; for instance, Mildred Wirt wrote the *Penny Parker* series and several early *Nancy Drew* books; Walter Gibson wrote the *Biff Brewster* series; Sam Epstein did the *Ken Holt* series (as well as many of Watts's *Real Books*); Leslie MacFarlane wrote many early *Hardy Boys* books; and Franklin Folsom wrote the *Troy Nesbit* series. Franklin Rosemont says that these authors critically approached "questions of crime, legality and illegality" and "probably had a radicalizing influence on many readers."[38]

As a distinctive genre, mystery series such as those mentioned above deserve a full study of their own and therefore are not explored in any depth here. However, surviving editor-author correspondence relating to the *Kathy Martin* books offers a fascinating glimpse into the politics of these texts as well as those of the authors and editors who created them. These exchanges suggest that some "censorship" took place not so much for political reasons but simply because of generic constraints. Despite certain freedoms offered by the debased series medium, that genre had its own peculiar limits.

Emma Gelders Sterne and her daughter Barbara Lindsay wrote most of the *Kathy Martin* series, which is about an enterprising and sometimes-sleuthing young nurse, under the name Josephine James (several of the books were written by a blacklisted friend and relative by marriage, Louis Hartman). During the years they worked on the *Kathy Martin* books, the late 1950s and early 1960s, both Sterne and Lindsay were intensely involved in the Civil Rights movement. Sterne was active in a California chapter of the Council on Racial Equality (CORE) and other organizations, and she was also writing children's books like *I Have a Dream* (1965), which highlighted the efforts of pioneering civil rights activists. The last four books in the *Kathy Martin* series—published in the mid-1960s when Lindsay was ill and Sterne was overburdened with other work, including civil rights activism—were written by Louis Hartman.[39]

Several things about the authors' relationship to the *Kathy Martin* books and about their relationship to the editors with whom they worked are clear from surviving correspondence in Sterne's papers. First, it is evident that these books were written primarily as a source of income while Sterne was writing more "serious" and time-consuming children's books about African-American history, and both she and Lindsay were involved in political work. Though their motive for writing the *Kathy Martin* books was largely financial, it is clear nonetheless that Sterne and Lindsay thoroughly enjoyed writing them and felt great affection for the characters and the scenarios they created in the books. Kathy Martin and her friends—African-American Faith Channing, Mexican-American Jenny Ramirez, and Japanese-American Yo Nakayama—are young women more interested in pursuing careers than in getting married (and when they do marry usually insist they will continue to work). They find themselves having unlikely adventures that defy the traditional conventions and typical sexism of series books, even as the books employ the requisite conventions of romance and mystery.

Second, editors at Artists and Writers Press, a subsidiary of Western Printing that published the *Kathy Martin* books under the Golden Press imprint, were not only aware of their authors' politics, but in fact, largely shared them. The series' primary editor, Caroline "Carrie" Lynch, for instance, talked in letters to Sterne and Lindsay about her own volunteering with Harlem children during the riots in 1964 and about going to anti–Vietnam War demonstrations. She also encouraged Sterne's involvement with CORE. In the same letter in which she mentioned CORE, Lynch urged Sterne "godspeed with the two civil rights books," referencing children's books that Sterne was writing for another publisher. Likewise, editors working with Sterne on the *Kathy Martin* books knowingly published Hartman when other media would have nothing to do with him, allowing him to work on several *Kathy Martin* books without actually signing his name to the contracts.

The situation that got Hartman involved in the first place highlights how small the network of children's book writers and editors was. When Sterne initially decided that she and Lindsay could not do all of the *Kathy Martin* books alone, one of the substitutes Sterne initially suggested to Lucille Ogle (of Western Printing and Golden Books) as a Josephine James stand-in was Betty Bacon, whom Sterne knew through the Bay Area left-wing community. The person finally chosen for the job was not only blacklisted but, in fact, had no experience writing children's books; however, Sterne's word was apparently enough to bring Hartman on board.[40] Overall, there was a kind of Left-inclined, intellectual consensus among the writers and the editors of the *Kathy Martin* books. Still, there was also a subtle struggle for full control of the books' contents.

Correspondence surrounding the books among Sterne and Lindsay (and sometimes Hartman) and editors Carrie Lynch and Pete Borden is lighthearted and friendly, with story ideas like sending Kathy to Africa with the Peace Corps (which was eventually accepted as number 13, *African Adventure*) or to Mexico with the Friends Service Committee, or possibly involving her with the Poverty Program in the United States. In a letter to Hartman, for example, Lynch suggested, "Maybe she could be working near an archeological [*sic*] 'dig' that could give mystery or romance or some such. ooh-whee!!!! Kathy Martin at summer camp? In veterinarian service? Rest home nurse? Ambulance chaser? Again, another old idea of yours—possibilities of work in the space program? Space medicine?" Lynch even seemed to seriously entertain what sounds like a fairly implausible story line: "*Another* idea you mentioned—working with teen-age gangs. But don't see how you'd do it. . . . don't you need a social worker to work with gangs?"[41]

The gang idea seems to have been one of many that Sterne, Lindsay, or Hartman suggested just to see how far they could push and get away with it. To give one example, Lindsay and Borden exchanged long, very humorous letters concerning *Kathy Martin* number 7, *Search for an Island*, and the story's characters and situations. Sterne and Lindsay consistently worked to make characters in the *Kathy Martin* books more interesting and less conventional than the usual figures who would turn up in juvenile series books. In this book, Kathy has been invited to serve as ship's nurse for a cruise that two mystery writers, Marco and Mathilda Sobrini, are undertaking in search of an "island of delight," which was identified in Herman Melville's writings. Kathy is no Melville aficionado herself, but she joins the rest of the crew in their combings of various Melville texts to identify the island, and she seems quite at home with the literary Sobrinis as well as the "beat" artist chef.[42]

In response to editor Pete Borden's concern that "Marco and Mathilda Sobrini seem like pretty highly-powered company for Our Girl from the apple-pickin' country,"[43] Lindsay wrote:

About Kathy and the intelligentsia: Kathy (for which read Gentle Reader) may not follow all the ins and outs and convolutions of people like the Sobrinis, but we think it not an unhealthy thing for her—them to discover that Eggheads, Too, Are People (Hath not an Egghead eyes . . .); that the search for the self-other relationship is much the same. . . . remember, she is a taker-of-long-walks. I don't think this will be too much of a problem.

Further responding to Borden's criticism of a flimsy plot device involving a seashell, Lindsay—after explaining her and Sterne's rationale—noted, parenthetically, "We had a bloodcurdling idea at one point—the search, the discovery that the island had been bomb-tested completely out of existence, thereby proving that man can indeed conquer nature, including the part of nature which is man. Now aren't you glad of a mere shell to cope with?"[44] Sterne and Lindsay had been wise enough to recognize that an atomic bomb blast would not go over well in the books; Lindsay was even able to joke with Borden about it.

Editors and writers did not always see eye to eye about what was appropriate material for the books. A letter to Sterne and Lindsay from Carrie Lynch, dated September 16, 1963, followed up on a phone call that we can imagine brought tension to an otherwise warm and friendly relationship. As Lynch put the matter, "[I]t boils down to a difference of opinion between us about the scope and province of these books. Will try, but don't know if further elaboration on my part will really make you agree with our position regarding the Kathy books." Lynch explained that this genre of juvenile fiction series books had historically followed "an accepted and expected pattern." Children, and parents, she said, buy these books expecting "entertainment value," "wholesomeness," "a little romance and mystery." "Because of this expected pattern, clearly proclaimed by the genre," she went on:

they do not expect to find: extreme violence, or, of course, sensationalism. . . . The reader wants to sympathize with patients' illnesses, but she doesn't want to be *devastated* by them. She expects things to be sad at times—but not too sad—and she expects it all to come out all right in the end. This may not be realistic, but *these books* are not expected to illustrate for children all the hard facts of life.[45]

Lynch listed subjects that might upset young readers: "death, incurable cancer[,] . . . drug addiction, perversions, mental illnesses, etc. etc.," all subjects that, furthermore, could not be handled by this genre of book. She went on, getting even more to the point:

Neither does the buyer expect to encounter sermons, lectures, propagandizing, doctrines, pleading for special causes, or political, social or moral counseling. They simply don't expect these books to argue causes or to try to convert. . . . I'm sure there are many *more* things a prospective buyer (parent or reader) does not expect to find in these books (and heaven knows I'm not accusing you of trying to include all such unexpected things!!!!!!) I am just trying to point out what we mean when we say that these books are bought on the clear and reasonable assumption that the buyer knows what he's getting, and that we feel, because of this, that many topics are simply not within the scope or province of these books.

For these reasons, according to Lynch, they "vetoed" drug addiction in an earlier book and mental illness in another: "And now we feel again that the subject proposed in your outline is wholly outside the province of these simple, light books." Insisting that they come to some agreement "about the future direction of these books," Lynch noted that "we're afraid they will get too serious, if not downright depressing, and too adult for their age group." Given the relative explosion of serious problem books in the late 1960s, Sterne, Lindsay, and Hartman were somewhat ahead of their time in their impulses to make the *Kathy Martin* books grapple with serious social issues, but Golden Books was, apparently, not quite ready for such heavy themes. Lynch praised the books for the depth of the characters as well as the books' "sympathetic and sensitive handling of various problems of human understanding, personal relations, values, etc." After making reference to a demonstration in Washington in which they all had participated, Lynch ended her letter by reiterating her commitment to the *Kathy Martin* books—nay, to Kathy herself, who seems almost like a real person in the editorial correspondence—and to Sterne and Lindsay: "you know how I feel about Kathy and about you and Everything and I am so hoping we can all reach a mutually satisfying understanding."[46]

Lynch's objections might be understood under the broad rubric of "protection," although her real concerns seemed more tied to questions of expectation and genre. Lynch was proud to be working with civil rights and anti–Vietnam War activists, and she was proud as well to work with an author who, in another context, wrote books for children dealing with serious issues like racial discrimination and social injustice. Even so, she could not, out of loyalty to readers' expectations and, presumably, out of concern for her own job, let the young nurse Kathy Martin exceed the limits of her own genre.

The examples of Le Sueur, Hughes, and Sterne provide different, but not unrelated snapshots of the ways in which authors, editors, and publishers delicately negotiated particular authors' politics and the politics of various books, within a variety of genres. The snapshots do not, however, provide a complete picture of the Left's role in the publishing field. More often than not, the dynamic was less dramatic and more subtle than in any of the above examples. Furthermore, the dynamics of publication went well beyond publishing houses themselves and were affected by libraries, bookstores, schools, and authors' organizations.

Distributing Books

In the 1950s, radical cultural workers moved into an array of positions in the "communications circuit" traveled by children's books, to the effect that the Left maintained an influence in the field of children's literature even though the cultural climate had changed dramatically from a decade earlier. We find, upon close investigation, that in the 1950s one of the nation's biggest outlets for children's books and records—a store and mail-order catalog serving the educational marketplace—was owned and run by radicals who had left the teaching profession for fear of investigation. We find a number of radicals running the children's book departments in city libraries or in charge of school libraries; we learn of radical activists running book clubs through which books were sold directly to children in the schools. We begin to see networks, formal and informal, untouched or touched belatedly and ineffectually by McCarthyism, which fostered a progressive structure of feeling and a growing labor solidarity among people employed in the world of children's books. Throughout the decade, this amorphous support network, or set of networks, functioned to make what author Mary Lapsley had called "socially constructive" literature for children available and to improve the cultural and financial status of children's book authors and illustrators.[47]

Again, some concrete examples: Genieve and Sidney Fox, schoolteachers, musicians, and among the founders of the teachers' union in Philadelphia, were active in the Communist Party until the early 1950s, when they quit the party, left their jobs, and moved to Los Angeles to escape being subpoenaed to testify before HUAC. Through the circle of radical musicians with whom they were close, they had met Moses Asch, the owner of Folkways Records, and because of this connection they were able to "work their way across the country" selling Folkways records, Young People's records, and recordings of the Children's Record Guild. When they arrived in Los Angeles in 1953, the Foxes started the Children's Music Center in their living room, with the help of the First Unitarian Church—which was, according to the Foxes' daughter, Jennifer Charnofsky, "probably the best-known Communist Party front group in L.A. in the fifties."[48]

Inspired by progressive educational theories and the "people's" music characteristic of the Popular Front and Henry Wallace's campaign, the Children's Music Center's slogan was "Children Need Music to Grow." The store sold children's records, books, and filmstrips, in person or by mail-order catalog to teachers, librarians, and parents around the country. It became the main distributor for Folkways Records (itself an important outlet for left-wing musicians and authors) and one of the first major outlets for "interracial" books and records. The store would often command a school's entire budget for a year's record purchases because it had a vast and diverse selection, and the store's highly trained staff provided badly needed help with schools' music programs.[49]

Though it had a strong focus on music, movement, and child development, the Children's Music Center also had something of a political mission, as its emphasis on multiracial materials would suggest. Genieve Fox had contacted Le Sueur in the mid-1950s concerning a potential blacklist in the children's book field and wrote her on another occasion to see if she would be interested in writing a children's book on Jewish holidays. Thus there was an element of advocacy to the center's work. In the 1950s, the Children's Music Center (which eventually became the Children's Book and Music Center) quickly became widely known as one of the only outlets for purchasing "interracial" materials; by the 1960s, it had become the largest establishment of its kind.[50]

According to Miriam Sherman, who managed the store for the Foxes, "nobody else had ever had a catalog on Black History or Spanish Americans. We were the first to do that. And it was kind of risky for a while." Sherman remembered that the Los Angeles Board of Education had declared that no teacher could use in the classroom any materials related to UNESCO; even so, their store carried "a wonderful album of UNESCO songs" that included "It Could Be a Wonderful World," a song considered highly subversive. Sherman sang me a verse to illustrate:

It could be a wonderful world
If we could consider each other
A friend or a neighbor or brother.
It could be a wonderful world.
It could be a wonderful world.

In addition to this radical fare, the center carried records and books by Woody Guthrie, Leadbelly, Dorothy Sterling, Earl Robinson, Langston Hughes (who advised Genieve Fox on African-American selections), and a range of other leftists from Pete Seeger to Ruth Krauss to Mary Elting.[51]

Sherman was repeatedly followed to work by the FBI, and Charnofsky said that her mother's FBI file indicates that the agency followed her activities on the West Coast closely. But the FBI had no valid grounds for shutting down the store, so it continued to operate. Probably teachers could tell, Sherman says, "from what we were espousing," that the store was run by people on the Left. However, she said, "most of the [school] supervisors didn't pay attention to it." Some teachers, she admitted, were frightened. There was a period when the state of Texas would not accept any of the store's catalogs, and a concerted campaign by the John Birch Society in southern California against Young People's Records and the Children's Record Guild, both of whose products were carried by the store, put local teachers at risk for buying certain records or even for patronizing the store.[52]

Though Sherman called the John Birch Society's allegations about Communist "brainwashing"—via Young People's and other children's records—ridiculous, she acknowledged the effect that these allegations had on the store's business. She recalled that teachers who shopped there said that "they would have to lock [the records] up in either a briefcase or a closet somewhere, because if they were caught with them they could be dismissed." For example, "anything with Pete Seeger was not acceptable at all." Were they "radicals"—these teachers who were hiding books and records on black history, Spanish-speaking Americans, or American Indians; these teachers who were purchasing "books for peace" or Head Start materials (all highlighted in special catalogs by the store) to use in their classes? "They weren't necessarily left-wing teachers," Sherman said, "but they felt the need for bringing this material into the schools. It was a real eye opener for them to see all this material in one place. They'd say, 'Oh, if I'd only known about it before!' They were all conscientious, open-minded teachers who felt the need for this material."

Even when it was risky for teachers to do so, librarians might order from an outlet like the Children's Music Center, given a growing emphasis in the library field on intellectual freedom and social responsibility. A number of leftists who rose to influential positions in children's librarianship in the 1950s brought a social and political agenda to their work and made sure that a variety of viewpoints was represented on their shelves. The field was small enough that children's librarians often knew the authors whose books they carried, and radical librarians were probably aware of which authors shared their political convictions.[53]

Betty Bacon, for instance, who obtained a degree in library science in the 1950s (after moving with her husband to San Francisco to avoid HUAC investigations of his union), became head of the central children's room at the Contra Costa County Library, then headed children's services at the Solano County

Library, and, finally, taught in the library school at the University of California, Berkeley. As a librarian, Bacon said:

> You had this opportunity to bring all kinds of books to kids, which was just a wonderful feeling. And I wanted to be sure that the books that described the world politically, the books that related science and politics, the poetic books which had a political overtone—that all these got to the kids. It was just a marvelous opportunity.

Rose Agree, who had worked as a union organizer for many years, like Bacon changed careers later in life. At age forty-two, she began a degree in library science and shortly thereafter was hired as the school librarian in Valley Stream on Long Island. She became a powerful presence in the state chapter of the ALA and a vocal advocate for multiracial books and for the "freedom to read." Like her colleague David Cohen (a former member of the Progressive Librarians Council who became a school librarian in Queens), she also became active in the Social Responsibility Roundtable and the Council on Interracial Books for Children, both of which began in the 1960s. Minne Motz, whose husband, a professor at Columbia University, was investigated during the McCarthy period, became the head of the New York City schools' library system in the early 1960s. There she worked to expand the range of books available, especially in districts populated by poor and minority students.[54]

Examples such as these suggest that the Left's influence in bookstores and in library services to children was significant and was at times consciously geared toward exposing children to the social issues of the day. Radicals also worked in other agencies of book marketing and distribution but approached this work in a variety of ways, sometimes very consciously trying to *separate* their political activity from their work in the children's book field. Lilian Moore is a case in point.

Most Americans born in the 1950s remember Scholastic's Arrow Book Club, which allowed fifth- and sixth-grade children to order twenty-five-cent, quality paperback books through their schools. Paperback books for children were a groundbreaking idea in the mid-1950s, perhaps even more than the inexpensive Little Golden books had been in the 1940s, as the paperback revolution in children's books enabled middle-school children to choose and purchase books themselves. Arrow thus introduced an entirely new dimension to the marketing of quality children's books. Under the Arrow Book Club's plan, books were reprinted from other publishing houses or directly commissioned from authors. According to Moore, who helped to launch the book club and worked as an editor from 1957 to 1967, the club was extremely successful at disseminating both high-quality and entertaining literature to children from across the socioeconomic spectrum.[55]

Moore herself had been a teacher, but after taking maternity leave in 1950, she never returned to that work, in part because her husband had been very active in his union and Moore did not want to risk investigation herself. Thus it was an opportune time to change professions. She started at Scholastic as a writer for its school newspaper, *Newstime*, and then was asked to consult on the new club for fifth- and sixth-graders that Scholastic was starting on the model of its Teenage Book Club. The Arrow Book Club became so successful under Moore's leadership that two more clubs, for younger readers, were launched: the Lucky Book Club (for which Moore brought in Beatrice de Regniers as editor) and the See Saw Book Club (which Moore recruited Ann McGovern to run). Both de Regniers and McGovern were friends of Moore, progressive in their politics, and part of the Loose Enders.

Though Moore was radical in her own political beliefs, she was well aware that bringing her politics into a children's book club whose fortunes were entirely dependent upon the highly sensitive school market would jeopardize not only her job but the fortunes of her employer as well. "I was a politically conscious, socially conscious person, very much so," Moore told me:

> But you have to understand that when I functioned as an editor for the Arrow Book Club, my thoughts had to be, what would children like, not how socially conscious were the books. I wouldn't have bad books; I certainly wouldn't recommend a book I thought was bigoted, or unworthy of being included. That's one of the strengths of having a person with values and standards.

According to Moore, "having standards" meant resisting Disney tie-ins and other commercialized, low-quality books (though she did bring in mysteries and joke books to entice children who were "reluctant readers"). It also meant that she demanded honesty in advertising the books, whether in Scholastic's newspaper or on the books' back covers:

> One of my big pressures was not to let anybody who wrote that copy oversell a book, because we had to come back to those children, and we had to be perfectly honest with what we told them about the books. I would send the editors who worked on the paper or the jacket copy to rewrite until we were giving an enthusiastic but thoroughly reliable description of the book, so kids would know what they were getting when they bought the book.[56]

Still, Moore did publish a number of writers on the Left through the book club—writers whom she knew personally such as Rose Wyler, Mary Elting, Emma Gelders Sterne, Millicent Selsam, Franklin Folsom, and Dorothy Sterling. But she was extremely cautious about publishing potentially controversial books like Dorothy Sterling's *Mary Jane*, a fictionalized account of school integration in the South. Precisely *because* she had been a radical in other contexts, Moore was in many ways more cautious than, say, Helen Hoke Watts might be. "We couldn't do *Mary Jane* until the time was right," she said. "Because just by offering something where they could mobilize—you know, the whole fever of McCarthy, it was like—like an epidemic, you know. It could have wiped out Scholastic, you have to understand that." Publishing *Mary Jane* "before the time was right" could have banished the Arrow Book Club from the entire southern market, she said. "I fought to do *Mary Jane*," she told me, but admitted to doing Dorothy Sterling "a great injustice" by asking her to change a reference to Mary Jane's "red dress, or something stupid like that. I think Dorothy was sorry she changed it. But she changed it, because it was important to do that book."[57]

For someone like Emma Gelders Sterne, it is clear that politics consumed all aspects of her life and work, to the point that even when writing a presumably fluffy and light girls' series book, she felt the need to inject certain values. In other words, for Sterne, any address to children was a chance to teach them something of the world as she understood it. Other cultural workers on the Left were more sensitive to the political climate in which they worked and thus more cautious and, furthermore, were often convinced that the protection of childhood "innocence" was a worthy goal of adults consciously working to improve the world. In her capacity as the editor of the Arrow Book Club, Moore believed she could make the greatest contribution by getting kids to read and by making sure they had decent, affordable books available to them. "I wanted a world the kids could grow up into that was good for them," she said, "but that didn't mean that they had to start at the age of three learning how to create such a world. It was *our* responsibility, not theirs." She paused and added, "I wasn't trying to empower them to go on a picket line. I wanted them to know how to read so they could *read* a picket sign if necessary."[58]

Moore's position helps to explain why people on the Left were able to thrive in the children's book world: many of these individuals were perhaps more keenly aware than people *not* so consumed by politics of how and where they could, and could not, let politics enter into what they were doing with and for children. Even so, Moore would come to recognize that her world view influenced her work in unconscious ways. One of her own books, *Little Raccoon and the Thing in the Pool* (1963), which Moore described as "a simple humorous tale," tells a story about a little raccoon who is afraid of a "thing in the pool." This "thing" returns every scary face Little Raccoon makes with a face just as scary, sending him home to his mother, all in a dither. Mother Raccoon finally convinces him to try smiling at the thing and, lo and behold, the thing—Little Raccoon's own reflection—smiles back. Published a year after the Cuban missile crisis, *Little Raccoon* was a huge hit in the Soviet Union, where it was published in a paperback edition of 375,000 copies. Looking back in the context of our conversations, Moore says she recognizes now that the book was a plea for peace. Moore's own sense of the relation between her work and her politics, and her after-the-fact recognition that politics may have operated below the surface in her work, reiterates that, on the one hand, radical authors did not necessarily create radical books; on the other hand, it is true that a "political unconscious" pervades many texts that were never meant to be "political."[59]

Loose Ends

Where Moore and others were conscious activists was in the Authors Guild, which was an important clearinghouse of information for children's book authors and a starting point for advocacy. Franklin Folsom, for instance, in 1954 enlisted the help of the Authors Guild in his effort to collect money due to him and his wife (and to other authors as well) from Franklin Watts; he also asked the guild for advice in regard to publishing foreign editions. Along with Herman Schneider, Folsom also helped to launch a children's book committee within the Authors Guild. For one of its initial projects, the committee undertook an extensive survey in 1956 of all children's book writers to determine prevailing contract conditions and the various incomes of children's book writers.[60] As one of the most active members of the Children's Book Committee, Folsom pressed the guild to increase its representation of juvenile authors and to make the guild more democratic in its policies, and he proposed that "a primer on book contracts . . . be made available to *all* writers in the field" so no writer would "depress standards in the field by signing bad contracts."[61]

Members of the guild's Children's Book Committee concerned themselves not only with income issues but also with social issues, sponsoring, for instance, a forum on Children's Books in an Integrating America, with presentations from Dr. Kenneth Clark (whose research on the psychological impact of segregation was key evidence in the *Brown* decision), James Farmer of CORE, and a representative from the U.S. Office of Education. Folsom and others identified significant subjects for which there was a viable market based on school curricula; in the late 1950s these subjects included science, racial integration, and American history.[62] The newsletter of the Children's Book Committee, initiated in the early 1960s, offered advice on contracts, information on the school and library markets, and tips on textbook writing. It also identified subjects eligible for funding under the expanded National Defense Education Act and the Elementary and Secondary Education Act. Articles spoke of the need for better representation of minorities in children's literature and school textbooks, condemned loyalty oaths required of textbook authors (in the state of Texas), and pointed to the ways that children's books helped to promote the "junior feminine mystique"—the ideology that socialized girls to accept traditional gender roles.[63]

Despite the Authors Guild's successes on behalf of juvenile writers, a number of authors found it inadequate as an advocate and disagreed with some of the guild's policies and politics. It is likely that FBI informers in the guild actively prevented radicals like Folsom from rising to positions of leadership. Some of the more politically oriented children's book writers who had gotten to know one another through the Authors Guild, or in other ways, began meeting informally to start discussing contracts and potential action they could take. The dozen or so New York writers and others in the children's book field who got together periodically whenever they felt at "loose ends" were, in one sense, simply a group of friends who had dinner parties at one another's houses or apartments. But these were, in fact, politically minded people, a number of whom had been active in the Communist Party and subject to blacklisting. Furthermore, many were well-known authors who had considerable clout in the field. "Certainly I think some of it was political," Moore said of the Loose Enders:

> We got together because we wanted to talk shop. What kind of contracts were we offered? What could we do to better our conditions? What brought us together was—well, our social viewpoint, of course— but we were friends. It was a remarkable group of people, and some of the best writers of children's books in the country.

They discussed contracts and trends in the field. They sometimes collaborated, and they passed work each others' way. Individually and collectively, the members of the group became an important presence in the world of publishing.[64]

As many juvenile writers began to make connections—through the Authors Guild or networks of friends—working conditions in the field improved. Wyler, for instance, was able to get Golden Books to pay her royalties, which afterward became standard practice. People were emboldened by others' successes. Herman Schneider told me that his wife, Nina, became "the Joan of Arc of kids' book writers" for refusing to sell *Robert and His New Friends* to Simon and Schuster without royalties. As a group, the Loose Enders were galvanized when they went back to meetings of the Authors Guild. Moore mentioned, for instance, that writers had been getting about $25 for the reproduction of a story or poem; she remembered standing up at a meeting of the Authors Guild and telling people to ask for $100. "And then one day a woman called me and said, 'Oh, Lilian, I did what you suggested and got the hundred dollars. But now they want to reprint it somewhere else. Can I ask for anything?' I said, 'Ask for another hundred.' And she got it! It was that kind of activity that the Loose Enders brought."[65]

Thus writers on the Left were not simply interested in *representing* working-class people (along with women and minorities), they actually worked to improve working conditions in the field, and they would ultimately prove crucial in transforming the "all-white world" of children's literature, not simply in terms of the faces in the books, but also in terms of the faces of the workforce itself.[66] Still, most work done by leftists in children's literature tended to be more indirectly political, whether that meant securing contracts for left-wing writers, keeping books by radical writers on library shelves, carrying records by Pete Seeger or books by Howard Fast in their stores, or writing children's books that subtly challenged the Cold War consensus. It is to the latter form of activism, especially as it focused on books about science and books about history, that we now turn.

PART III

Science and History
for Girls and Boys

6

The Tools of Science

Dialectics and Children's Literature

In October 1957, the Soviet Union successfully launched the first space satellite, Sputnik (literally translated as "fellow traveler"), and the United States responded by declaring a "crisis" in American education. Crowning more than a decade of mounting fears about Soviet aspirations for global dominance through technological prowess, Sputnik convinced many Americans that the United States' international position was slipping and that democracy itself was threatened. Both blame and hope for rescue were directed toward the American system of schooling, where young people could gain the technological knowledge and skill—and the intellectual and ideological fortification—to outperform and outwit the "red menace."

Within three years of Sputnik's launch, several left-wing writers, feeding the frenzy for scientific information, published one or more books for children dealing with satellites, rockets, or astronomy. These books about space were only a small fraction of the many science-related children's books written by radicals during this period. Irving Adler, who had recently been fired from the New York City school system for refusing to answer questions about his political affiliations, published a book, *Man-Made Moons: The Earth Satellites and What They Tell Us*, just barely after Sputnik's launch. Because of its timeliness, the book became an immediate hot seller, sent to science and math teachers around the country and snapped up by anxious parents whose children were asking about rocket ships and trips to the moon. Adler's publisher, John Day, was shrewd enough to use Sputnik as an opportunity for publicity. The firm placed a full-page ad for *Man-Made Moons* in the *New York Times*, recognizing that where there was panic, there was money to be made. While this publicity boosted the book's sales to individuals, after 1958 school libraries were even more likely to purchase *Man-Made Moons* (and its revised 1959 edition, *Seeing the Earth from Space*) with grants from the National Defense Education Act (NDEA), which made possible major improvements in school libraries' science collections. Passed less than a year after Sputnik's launch, the NDEA was the capstone of many smaller federal, state, and corporate initiatives designed to strengthen education in defense-related subjects, especially science and math.[1] Such initiatives were, ironically, a great boon to some of the very people being targeted during this time as "subversive."

Initiatives like the NDEA point to a way in which the Cold War politics that purged radical teachers and radical-authored textbooks from classrooms simultaneously created space on school library shelves for books by these very same people. In this instance, an educational program designed to bolster U.S. military and economic strength in opposition to the Soviet Union—and Communism in general—provided major benefits to people who were actively opposed to the Cold War, who were critical of the "military-industrial complex," and who challenged the idea that schools were key components of the national security apparatus. Quite a few of these people were committed Marxists, and several were current or former members of the Communist Party. Adler, for instance, though barred from teaching, found that with all of the subsidies available to libraries for the purchase of science- and math-related books, writing children's books was far more lucrative anyway. Furthermore, he could reach a much wider audience through books than through the classroom. Science was probably the single most popular subject for left-wing writers, and many of the most critically acclaimed and bestselling science books published in the postwar period were by left-wing writers.[2] Leftists certainly capitalized on the great demand for science-related books, but they also were drawn to the lessons that science could offer children.

A subject "ostentatiously objective and intensively value laden," science appealed equally, but for very different reasons, both to Cold Warriors and to political radicals of various stripes. Each group, moreover, believed that science held important lessons for children. In the postwar period, in which the atomic bomb and the baby boom exploded almost simultaneously, children and science represented not only hope for social renewal, but also the uneasy vulnerability of the status quo. A faith in all things "scientifically proven" meant that Americans were eager for "expert" advice on everything from "commonsense" baby care to the construction of a family fallout shelter. However, this confidence in science was mitigated by a creeping fear of what technology had wrought. Such fear was manifested most dramatically in a number of science fiction movies— such as *The Blob, It, The Attack of the Crab Monsters, The Incredible Shrinking Man, Them!* and *Invasion of the Body Snatchers*—in which aliens hatched out of pods or radioactive fallout created mutant monsters. In these films, children were often used to represent the helpless vulnerability of all Americans in the face of natural disasters, extraterrestrial attacks, atomic bombs, and other seemingly uncontrollable phenomena. Still, in contrast to children on movie screens who fled from giant ants or cowered helplessly in dark corners, real American children read about Captain Marvel in comic books, watched Buck Rogers on television, drank milk from "atomic submarine" drinking cups, and played with water-powered toy versions of the ICBM missile, all activities which made technological wonders seem not only controllable, but also fun. Postwar science was both utopian and dystopian, terrifying and child's play.[3]

The success of left-wing cultural workers as authors of science books for children, particularly in the Sputnik era, highlights the way in which initiatives designed to uphold Cold War hegemony may have helped to unravel it. After Joe McCarthy and his minions purged the most visible left-wing scientists, such as Robert Oppenheimer, from professional and academic circles; after scores of high school science teachers lost their jobs in the fallout from various official and semiofficial investigations; and after school science curricula became increasingly geared toward serving the nation's military and corporate needs, there were still a significant number of radicals writing science books for children that encouraged young people to question the Cold War status quo by challenging the logic of racial discrimination, the arms race, and unbridled capitalism and by encouraging children to think critically and to question authority.[4] Many of these books drew upon Marxist categories and dialectical reasoning to challenge the commonsense assumptions of the Cold War. And far from being marginalized, these were some of the most popular and celebrated science books published for children in the postwar period. They were purchased by librarians, used by teachers to supplement their lessons, and read by children. And, quite often, they were paid for with federal funds allocated to fortify American education in the face of the Communist menace.

Although few of these books appear radical or even political to us now, they deserve a more critical examination. Indeed, the basic fact of their publication complicates many widely held views about the limits of public discourse during the Cold War. The politics of Left-authored science books becomes clearer when the books are situated in a number of different contexts. Between the nuclear fallout that followed World War II and the launch of Sputnik in 1957, science assumed a special place in the already politicized postwar educational discourse. To understand the politics of science education—and the role played by children's literature in science education (and its politicization)—requires a closer examination of the educational "crisis" that Sputnik highlighted and, in some ways, precipitated. Furthermore, to understand how and why leftists were able to inadvertently benefit from this crisis requires some understanding of leftists' historical relationships to science and science education. From here we can turn to actual science books by leftist authors that were published in the postwar period.

Eggheads and American Exceptionalism

In March 1958, not quite six months after the launch of Sputnik, *Life* magazine published the results of a new survey that reported on the ways in which "Russia's conquest of space" had altered American attitudes about space exploration, defense spending, science research, and education. Although a range of views was expressed on these various issues, on one point there seems to have been consensus. As the article reported, "Millions of Americans who had taken education for granted all their lives have now turned a sudden and dissatisfied eye upon U.S. schools."[5] In particular, the article suggested that the tide of public opinion had turned against progressive education, that is, against the set of educational practices, by and large institutionalized in American school systems since the 1930s, which focused on developing the "whole child." Critics of U.S. education more vocally argued that Americans had slipped drastically behind the Russians in scientific and technical fields because American schoolchildren were not getting a firm grounding in the disciplines, particularly in math and science.

Articles and reports on the "manpower shortage," the Soviet educational system, and the "crisis in American education" began appearing in magazines, newspapers, and academic journals around the time of the Second World War, but the steady stream turned into a flood after Sputnik. As an article in the *Catholic World* suggested in 1958, by the late 1950s, science had become a "new religion" in the United States. It was a fixation among business, the government, schools, the military, and the media, reinvigorating the sense of national purpose that had temporarily floundered with the censure of Senator Joseph McCarthy in 1954. Clearly, in the national zeal to rout out the internal enemy within U.S. borders, Americans had neglected the external enemy of the Soviet Union, which, in the postwar years, had demonstrated military, scientific, and ideological strengths and the willingness to use them: in the explosion of an atomic bomb in 1949, in the Korean War where Communists had "brainwashed" captured American GI's (never mind that these weren't *Soviet* Communists), in the explosion of a hydrogen bomb in 1953, and in the invasion of Hungary in 1956.[6]

Studies by government agencies, educational researchers, and journalists reported that many, if not most, American students lacked a knowledge of basic scientific facts, that they had few incentives to achieve academically, and that they had little interest in pursuing advanced degrees and careers in the sciences.

Ominous reports on the future "manpower" of the United States showed that the Soviet Union was graduating more engineers and scientists than the United States every year, and this dangerous gap was in itself a severe indictment of American education.[7] The Soviet system of training for "internal Soviet development and for external conquest" was painted repeatedly as "a threat of the gravest kind, and one we must face up to."[8] Not only was training in math and science far more rigorous in the Soviet Union, but a ten-year program, with strong emphasis on math and science, was mandatory for all Soviet schoolchildren. There was little evidence that Soviet students were forced into scientific and technical careers, but incentives for choosing such a path were far greater than in the United States, and the rewards, both material and intangible, were significant.[9]

Scientific and technological achievement became an obsession for Americans, and the way to get there was clearly via the public school system, a controllable intellectual and ideological conduit affecting the life of nearly every young person in America. As a writer for *Senior Scholastic* put it in 1957, "The long-range solution to the problem of the cold war lies in our own classrooms. It lies in the willingness of American students to meet the challenge that has been flung at them by the rise of a new machine-molded generation in Russia—one that has a new religion: science."[10] Americans may have had God, but the godless Russians had "eggheads." American business and government leaders agreed that the nation's schools needed further fortification.

Young people's lack of interest in scientific careers was perhaps most disturbing to those concerned with the manpower shortage in technical fields. And here is where children's books, in theory if not in practice, in hard content if not in ideological underpinnings, fit into a larger educational, military, and corporate scheme. Whatever improvements could be made in teaching, whatever resources and incentives the nation could muster to make scientific careers attractive and lucrative, the fact remained that as a democracy, the United States could not compel young people to pursue careers in the sciences. "Our young people haven't been told the romance of science," complained a reporter for the *Saturday Evening Post* in 1957.[11] What had children been told? Were scientists "romantic" figures in popular culture, or were they crazed weirdos tucked away in laboratories?

A widely cited study by Margaret Mead and Rhoda Métraux of high school students' image of scientists found that although students thought highly of scientists and recognized the value of their achievements, they were less than eager to become scientists themselves or to choose scientists as mates. The survey by Mead and Métraux showed that students thought of scientists as longhaired, "geeky," antisocial "geniuses" who labored long hours at often tedious work. American students were socialized, in contrast, to be "other-directed" (as sociologist David Riesman claimed in his highly influential 1950 study, *The Lonely Crowd*), amiable, and more fun-loving than the kind of person students imagined would choose to become a scientist or to marry one. The study, incidentally, did ask both boys and girls if they would like to become scientists, but only girls were asked whether they would like to marry them. Here, of course, lay another source of national confusion, for while the need for gender equity in the sciences was recognized and even mandated in some quarters (in school science textbooks, for example), male bias in the field was so pervasive that it was simply taken for granted.[12]

Mead and Métraux's survey was, in part, designed to explore how girls as well as boys might become more interested in scientific careers. But even they utterly disregarded the possibility that a woman could be *both* a scientist and a wife. Similarly, in the course of progressive educators' efforts to make science more relevant to students' everyday lives, female students in the 1940s were given the option of replacing traditional science classes with "Girls' Science" or "Kitchen Physics." In these courses, girls learned such skills as how to solder broken toasters and irons, keep coffee warm, and distinguish hard-boiled eggs from fresh ones. Though such courses were created with the positive goal of making science more interesting to girls, like the term "woman doctor," they reinforced the fundamental assumption that science was a masculine realm.[13] Though left-wing writers were instrumental in the effort to make science more interesting and appealing to children, even they did not consistently challenge the deeply held assumption that science was a male realm. The idea of attracting girls to the "hard sciences" was kind of an afterthought in a crisis that focused on a "manpower" shortage in scientific careers, particularly at a time when strictly defined gender roles were so naturalized and, indeed, were taken as evidence that American housewives were more satisfied than the unfeminine Soviet women, who worked in "men's" jobs and left their children in institutionalized daycare.[14]

The first priority for those dictating American educational policy (or diagnosing education's weaknesses) was, as the National Association of Manufacturers put it, how "to keep from passing on to the child, the attitude shared by many of . . . an older generation, that science is something mysterious and magical, understandable only to geniuses and freaks."[15] Many parents, wanting their progeny to be "well-rounded," placed greater value on their children's social success and their athletic achievements than they placed on a report card with high marks. But a number of education reformers felt that this anti-intellectual attitude about childhood achievement would have dangerous consequences for the nation. As Admiral Hyman Rickover, a leading advocate for higher education standards, noted in 1959 in an antiathletic dig against anti-intellectualism, "Everyone who is in any way unusual suffers from the arrogance of mediocre people.... a country neglects its eggheads at its peril. For it is the egghead who ... invents the Sputnik, not the captain of the football team." The discourse encompassing "eggheads," childhood, and national security raised a fundamental question: how could the United States surpass the Russians in the space race, the arms race, and the struggle for international dominance without giving up the cherished freedom in American education and, moreover, without turning American children into "geeks"? Children's books, which young people could choose freely from the library, might hold the key. Yet few of those who successfully lobbied to make more funds available for science-related library purchases imagined that science books could call the logic of the Cold War into question.

While many people, regardless of their politics, believed that it was necessary to introduce children to "the marvels of science" before it was "too late for them to do anything about it," a few considered what might happen if children were taught, via the scientific method, to think for themselves or, even further, to question the values implicit in corporate capitalism. Educational initiatives like the NDEA, which was meant to bolster "the security of the nation" yet also develop "the individual" and support "the furthering of knowledge itself," pointed to a more general ambivalence about education's fundamental purposes, given that schooling in the interests of national security could easily foreclose the possibility of teaching young people many of the habits of mind possessed by well-educated people, such as curiosity, skepticism, and independent thought. The need to be like the Soviets (in achievement) but unlike them ("our" education was democratic; theirs was coercive) furthered the dilemma of how to best turn children on to the "romance of science."[16]

Not only was intellectual strength—that is, knowledge itself—a weapon against the Soviets, but the scientific method itself was also seen as an ideological weapon, for it would enable children to distinguish more clearly the purity, innocence, and beneficence of the American way of life as opposed to life under Communist rule. As the *Senior Scholastic* article "The Cold War Comes to the Classroom" put it, the aim of Russian schooling was "education for conquest," whereas the aim of American schooling was "education for living." According to the article, while the Russians had concentrated on applying science to military endeavors, American scientists had helped Americans to travel, had created a huge array of affordable consumer goods, and, in general, had improved the standard of living in the United States and made life more leisurely and enjoyable. Furthermore, "where U.S. science and technology have been applied in military fields, they have been applied to create weapons for *defense*, not conquest."[17] Like postwar history textbooks—which showed that European nations were imperialist while the United States was not and which recounted a narrative of Anglo-American innocence in contrast to European colonial ambition—science was enlisted to defend the virtuous American way of life against the evil ambitions of the Soviets.[18] On the other end of the ideological spectrum, Marxists, in their own version of exceptionalism, assumed that anyone trained to think "scientifically," that is, dialectically, would quickly reject the logic of capitalism in favor of socialism.

As cultural critic Raymond Williams notes, "The notion of 'science' has often foreclosed analysis of its own assumptions." The great authority of science rests, Williams suggests, upon the belief that there can be such a thing as "positive, scientific knowledge free from the ideological bias of all other observers." As both a method and as pure knowledge, science was a form of power. People from all points on the political spectrum were eager to give to children the powers of science, but for very different reasons. What those in power never anticipated is that their funds to improve science education would help people opposed to many of the values they were trying to uphold. As science for the Cold War came to replace an earlier ideal of science for the citizen, children's books carried a progressive Left vision of science to young people expected to assume the Cold War mantle.[19]

Marxists and Early Science Education

Left-wing authors who wrote science books for children after World War II applied to their books a faith in the scientific method as a tool for rationally solving social problems and their utopian hopes for a new society characterized by cooperation and plenty for all. They wished to give children tools of critical thinking, a distrust of received authority, and insights into the dynamics of biological and technological development and operation. They wanted to share their internationalist, cooperative, and democratic outlook and what they perceived as an ability to rationally evaluate aspects of an irrational society. People on the Left—whether they self-identified as Marxists, Communists, or as left-wing or progressive New Dealers—found books about science to be good vehicles for communicating their social values to children. For individuals under scrutiny for their politics, the ostensible objectivity of science also made it attractive, as did the ready market.

Communists' and socialists' interest in science went back to Marx and Engels, who, in developing the philosophy of dialectical materialism attempted to outline an all-encompassing theory of change and development that would illuminate natural, economic, and social processes, "from the falling of a stone to a poet's imaginings." Dialectical materialism is, in essence, a method of step-by-step interpretation applicable to both science and society. The studiously rational aspects of dialectical materialism are the basis for Marxists' claim to practicing a "scientific" mode of reasoning, one which, like the broader progressive outlook on science, "substitutes curiosity for complacency, deliberate encouragement of doubt for uncritical acceptance of things as they now are." Marxists place "particular emphasis on the inter-connection of all processes" and, perhaps most important, emphasize the extent to which science is "conditioned by the society in which it takes place." One does not need to be a self-professed Marxist to see the primacy of history; Marxists, however, not only view phenomena historically, but also with attention to the ways in which history is shaped by the dynamic struggle between classes. As N. Sparks maintained in a 1948 lecture on Marxism and science commemorating the centennial of Marxism, under monopoly capitalism, profit takes precedence over the good of humanity. Those in power suppress invention in order to safeguard existing investments. Their support of scientific research is primarily concerned with bolstering their own military and economic power, rather than on universal human betterment, and thus science rarely fulfills its potential for improving the world on a grand scale. In contrast, according to Sparks, Marxist scientists consistently emphasize the power of science as a tool for human liberation.[20]

Many scientists were attracted to the rational logic of Marxism, for the appeal of science was almost identical to the appeal of Marxism: both assumed that the world was knowable, that all problems were solvable through rational thought and calculated action. To the extent that Marxism insists upon locating science within society, its implications stretched far beyond committed Marxists. This was particularly the case in the 1930s as the progressive politics of the Popular Front were embraced by a significant portion of the scientific community. Many scientists, science educators, and writers of scientific literature believed that scientific knowledge could empower the young and that scientific modes of thinking could encourage a critical and questioning outlook on the world.[21]

Science education developed in the United States alongside, and sometimes in conjunction with, the development of progressive and radical movements. The "nature study" movement of the nineteenth century, evolutionary thought, and the expansion of education at the turn of the twentieth century all helped to shape the development of high school and elementary sciences and their disciplinary character and strongly influenced early scientific literature for children. The nature study movement, which came into vogue in the United States in the late nineteenth and early twentieth centuries, was closely tied to romantic ideals concerning nature and children. As the only human beings untainted by civilization, children, according to romantics, were wild and perfect nature embodied, and nature study could work to preserve children's inborn wildness for as long as possible. Nature study was seen as a particularly appropriate enterprise for girls, who, through appreciation and understanding of nature, would develop feminine traits of sympathy, cooperativeness, and gentleness.

The influence of the nature study movement on scientific children's literature was apparent well into the twentieth century. Books in this mode emphasized the appreciation of nature over scholarly accuracy, often used anthropomorphism, and employed sentimental language to translate natural phenomena into moral lessons. Some of the "science" titles recommended for elementary readers in the leading science education journal as late as 1944 included *Tim Tadpole and the Great Bullfrog*, *Wallie the Walrus*, *Bozo the Woodchuck*, *Fuzzy and His Neighbors*, and *Clever Little People with Six Legs*.[22] The push to create realistic books for children came largely from Lucy Sprague Mitchell's here-and-now philosophy, which grew out of progressive education.

The importance of science in a program of progressive education had a great deal to do with the influence of Herbert Spencer, who extended Darwinian principles of evolution to theorize more broadly about a science of society. While conservatives, or Social Darwinists, took Spencer's theories to mean that reform efforts were fruitless challenges to the natural evolution of society, socialists and other dissenters insisted that human society could *consciously* evolve and improve through cooperation and planning. Beyond his application of Darwin's theories, Spencer argued that science was "the critical requirement for comprehending and building civilization" and that to ensure its success, a society must train its young people scientifically. Both conservatives and radicals accepted this idea, but conservatives focused upon how science could be used to improve efficiency and productivity, while radicals emphasized how science could bring greater wealth for all and how its methods could be used to create critical thinkers.[23]

Progressives also seized upon Spencer's claim that the development of the individual mirrors or explains the development of the species. Thus the individual, like the embryo, like the species, goes through certain stages of development. This theory had several implications for schooling. Many people believed that through a process of scientific learning—that is, exploration, questioning, and discovery of the natural world—children could best develop as individuals. In the process of confronting change and adapting, the child mind would evolve. Furthermore, through the evolution of the child mind, civilization, informed at its basic level by scientific training, would advance. A corollary of this thinking, which influenced John Dewey and showed up repeatedly in progressive discourse through the 1950s, was that children—curious, enthusiastic, and interested in novelty—were natural scientists, and thus the study of science was highly beneficial to the child.[24]

Progressive educators thus emphasized the child's natural curiosity, and they placed primary importance on the *process* of learning rather than on specific facts themselves. They argued that a chief task of teachers was to preserve the childlike aspects of the child, "to whet his delight in discovery," rather than to project his or her own desires onto the child. "The average boy is something of a scientist, and an artist too," the Marxist scientist J. B. S. Haldane wrote for the *Nation* in an article that was quoted at length in *Progressive Education*. "We grown-ups do our best to knock such nonsense out of him, and generally succeed." Haldane believed that children would easily learn to become scientific thinkers if they were introduced to the "scientific outlook" early in life.[25]

Biology was particularly attractive to progressive educators because of its ability to focus on the human subject, thus translating political and moral issues relating to human society into the (objective) realm of the scientific. In fact, some of the earliest developers of high school biology curricula and textbooks, such as Benjamin Gruenberg, who wrote several children's books in his later years, were socialists or labor activists. (Gruenberg, incidentally, was married to CSA head Sidonie Gruenberg.) Likewise, children's books relating to biology, and especially to human subjects, were those in the science field most likely to be informed by social and political ideas.[26]

Formal elementary school science programs began in the 1920s and 1930s, building upon developments in high school science curricula and strongly influenced by the progressive education movement, but also by radical politics. Progressive educators' theories were closely compatible with those of radical thinkers, and, as we have seen, the distinction is sometimes difficult to make. As the quotation from Haldane in *Progressive Education* suggests, radical thinkers strongly influenced (and were often part of) the progressive education movement and were, in turn, influenced by this movement. This was particularly the case in the late 1930s when many scientists—as well as science teachers—were radicalized by the conditions of the Great Depression and in reaction to the "scientific" racism promulgated by the Nazis. Popular Front scientists believed that if science and social planning were applied to the entire society, there could be plenty of wealth for all, that science could be harnessed for human good instead of destruction, and that prejudices could be eliminated.[27]

Articles in education journals in the 1930s and 1940s often spoke of the relationship between science and democracy and the social implications of science. Many of these articles argued that science study should teach children a questioning attitude toward all received authority, teach them to test all of their hypotheses and to see their limitations, and teach them to see the social and ethical implications of science. Many progressive educators in the 1930s were inspired by the program of science taught in Soviet schools, part of an "educational program," as one American science teacher put it, "by which the Soviet expects to lift the proletariat to new heights of culture and creativeness."[28] The Russians' emphasis on teaching science through immediate, practical applications was particularly appealing to progressive educators (whether or not they self-identified as Marxists), as was their emphasis on teamwork and on science for the public good. Soviet science books for children, especially those by Soviet writer Il'in, likewise had a great impact on American writers, not only those inclined toward Marxism, as they sought models for how science might be employed to teach values like cooperation, democracy, and internationalism.[29]

Some of the first elementary school science curricula were developed at Columbia University's Teachers College, where, for instance, George S. Counts, one of the translators of Il'in's *New Russia's Primer*, was on the faculty. Columbia was at the forefront of the progressive education movement, which, in turn was influenced by a number of radicals who were on the Teachers College faculty. These faculty played an important role in the development of school science curricula, but their influence stretched well beyond this. Rose Wyler, for instance, who was part of the Teachers College faculty in the 1930s, was a major innovator in elementary science curricula. She was a science writer for Columbia Broadcasting's "School of the Air" and then for Encyclopedia Britannica Educational Films (which were shown in schools throughout the country). She later wrote science columns for *Newstime* (published by Scholastic), which was distributed, free of charge, in schools. By the 1950s, she had become an author of Golden books about rockets, astronomy, biology, and other subjects, which sometimes sold in the millions. Likewise, Mary Reed, head of the kindergarten division at Teachers College and part of a group of nursery school teachers who traveled to the Soviet Union in the 1920s, became the chief advisor for the Little Golden *Bank Street* books; her name appeared on the inside of every cover.[30]

The Second World War created new imperatives for science education, and the need to train scientists for defensive purposes challenged the progressive common sense that had characterized the field through the 1930s.[31] Scientists who criticized the atomic bomb and the links between science and the military-industrial state were subject to intense repression beginning in the late 1940s, and science education, likewise, witnessed a trend away from progressive education, which was deemed to be "soft" and "socialistic." But trade children's books, which became increasingly popular adjuncts to formal science curricula, retained this progressive character. A significant number, in fact, reflected Marxism's appeal to scientists. Radicals and progressives had a strong tradition of writing on science subjects for children, and they had been influential in this genre of children's literature from early on.

Nature and Science for Johnny Rebel:
Literature for the Children of Radicals

Socialist children's literature had a strong emphasis on evolution, science, and lessons from the natural world. Drawing upon anthropologist Lewis Henry Morgan (whose work greatly influenced Marx and Engels), as well as Herbert Spencer, socialists of the 1910s and early 1920s argued that children, who would identify with "primitive" peoples, could come to understand human agency in social change by studying the process of evolution. As socialist theorist of education William Kruse put it, "Changes in civilization are the things we wish to impress upon the minds of our students, and the fact that necessity has forced man to think of change and finally, through action, to bring the change about." Numerous socialist books for children dealing with "primitive peoples" used a discussion of early humans to emphasize humans' ability to adapt to different environments, the interdependence of humans and nature, and the ability of human beings to alter their environment.[32]

Although they claimed to be hard-headed materialists, like other writers of their time, many socialists were influenced by the romantic and sentimental conventions of nature study writing, such as the tendency to draw moral lessons from nature. Caroline Nelson's *Nature Talks on Economics* (1912), for instance, written as a set of conversations between two parents and their young children, draws on a conventional format of nature study texts whereby an exchange of letters or conversations between imaginary family members is the premise for teaching children not only appreciation of nature but also moral lessons. In Nelson's book, these moral lessons were applicable to economics and, more specifically, to the conditions of capitalism. For example, in the chapter "Evolution and Revolution," the children learn that the bird they see hatching out of its egg had been in "revolt against living any longer in an egg state." As Father tells little Johnny, "He didn't remain quiet, and say 'it's no use. I have always been in an egg and therefore I shall stay here until I die.'"[33]

Whereas popular nature writers like Anna Butsford Comstock used lessons from the insect world—such as the queen bee's "relentless efforts to care for her young"—to teach children appropriate gender behavior, Nelson emphasized the fact that although good human parents do far more for their young than do birds or insects, under capitalism, the natural conditions of family life are disrupted for the working class. The father does not receive a "family wage" and therefore the mother has to find work outside the home as well. "The mother thus away from her babies suffers terribly," notes Nelson, "and the father loses hope, and the babies cry and pine in cheap, dark rooms, which the mother has no time to clean." Clearly, Nelson's critique of the unnaturalness of capitalism neglected to call bourgeois gender constructions into question.[34]

Science and History for Girls and Boys (1932), a book popular with red-diaper babies, or the children of Communists, was written and self-published by the excommunicated bishop William Brown (who would later publish *Teachings of Marx for Girls and Boys* [1935]). In *Science and History*, Brown contrasted the truths revealed by science with the "fairy tales" taught by religion and argued, "[I]f only the people had more scientific knowledge, they would not be fooled by politicians and preachers and newspapers." Brown's book emphasizes science's utility to the worker and the need to prevent the wealth that science creates from being "wasted in wars or in the fortunes of millionaires."[35]

Brown is at times almost amusingly polemical, calling states that ban the teaching of evolution "ridiculous" and repeatedly scorning religion, but his book is also engaging and appealing to a child's sensibilities. Brown promises to answer the big questions that children have about science and history, questions that never seem to get answered in school or in a way that makes sense to children. He notes that "the books in which your father, perhaps, looks for the answers are very dull and full of big words that you do not understand." Brown insists that science is understandable, interesting, and worth knowing for the power it can give to the worker. He advocates the scientific method—that is, "experience, observation, investigation and reason"—as the road to "truth" and to a better world, and he argues that a childish belief in religion and in the supernatural more generally has impeded progress, for in believing in supernatural beings, humans have, historically, failed to find ways to help themselves. And he suggests that real social evolution, that is, the development of civilization and material progress, comes only when people can exchange ideas freely. Moreover, he attempts to demonstrate, scientifically, that "it is quite silly to regard the features of different races as marks of inferiority or superiority." Finally, Brown insists that as science teaches us to rely on our own efforts, it offers the possibility of creating great abundance and the means to make that abundance available to all. Richard Levins, a red-diaper baby whose grandfather read Brown's book to him as a child, says that "the linking of science and history in the book did not seem at all strange to us. For me, it was all part of an exciting finding-out about the way the world worked."[36] The themes in Brown's book would surface repeatedly in leftist literature about science for the next thirty years, even as radicals shifted their focus from "Johnny Rebel" (who already possessed radical consciousness) to the "broad masses" of children.

In the *New Pioneer*'s column "Nature and Science for Johnny Rebel," Bert Grant (a.k.a. Solon De Leon, a science teacher at a progressive school and brother of Socialist Party leader Daniel De Leon) addressed natural and physical phenomena, "things of interest to every real kid," but he consistently discussed science within a political context. At their most blatantly political, Grant's columns from the early 1930s emphasized children's duty "to help overthrow the capitalist system so that science will be free to banish poverty, overwork, insecurity, and want from the lives of all the workers." But even those columns not explicitly calling for revolution addressed class aspects of science in terms of who benefits from it and who controls scientific endeavor. For instance, a 1932 column on gunpowder, "The Powder of Empire," interlaces the technical discussion with political commentary that is often only remotely related to gunpowder. Explaining the makeup of gunpowder, Grant notes that "three-quarters of it is saltpeter, often used by food manufacturers to preserve their stuff till they can sell it at a higher price. The other quarter is about equally composed of charcoal, and of sulphur [sic] which is what the smelly yellow candles are made of that are used to drive bugs out of tenements." Grant emphasizes the ways in which gunpowder has been used in projects of class domination—from the colonization of the Indians in North America to the German, French, and Belgian control of Africa.[37]

The Popular Front tempered Grant's revolutionary rhetoric—the column's title shifted from "Science and Nature for Johnny Rebel" to, simply, "Science"—but columns still maintained a political dimension, however subtle. While an older column had considered whether the child of a worker could become a scientist, an April 1936 article asked, "Can Girls Be Scientists?" Here, Grant argued that a system of competitive capitalism trained men "in the spirit of individualism and economic rivalry" so that they often prevented women from entering scientific fields. Grant's explanation of why girls were less likely than boys to become scientists repeated Communist logic on the "woman question," which presumed that patriarchy was a product of capitalism and thus an issue secondary to the struggle for socialism. Grant argued, "[I]n a society where all are given an equal opportunity to work, and where the fullest and freest preparation for worthwhile activity is thrown open to all alike, girls will be able to take their place beside young men as scientists of the future." A 1938 column discussing the World's Fair and the exciting technical innovations to be showcased there seems devoid of even this basic critique of capitalism, sounding much like Cold War articles lamenting children's failure to comprehend the romance of science. Many children find science boring, not realizing the deep "fascination" that goes with work in science, Grant tells his readers. However, "the child who takes his velocipede apart or tears her doll to pieces, is an explorer, and is having the same kind of illuminating experience that the scientist has in his laboratory. The scientific professions are fascinating because they engage every talent and every creative impulse to expand the human horizon."[38] Though the emphasis here is on exploration, curiosity, and experimentation, rather than on politics, economics, or social injustice, the messages implicit in Grant's earlier and later science columns are arguably the same. Children are expected to be active, critical, independent thinkers and to question surface appearances.

Young World Books and the Development of Scientific Literature for Children

By the late 1930s, it becomes difficult to see a political dimension in much of the Left-authored science literature for children, but the politics remains an important subtext. Leftists developed discursive strategies for speaking to a large number of children at almost the very same time that demand arose for science-related children's books to supplement formal science curricula: in this sense, International Publishers' Young World Books, which emphasized scientific themes, was particularly well timed. The need for scientific expertise and knowledge during and after World War II not only reshaped school curricula but also created a demand for science-related children's books, and there were few of quality before about 1940. *School Science and Mathematics*, the premium elementary and secondary educational journal in the sciences, began in 1944 to publish regular booklists to aid in the creation of an "elementary school science library," thereby marking an awareness of the role that children's trade books could play in the relatively new field of elementary science education. As publication of juvenile science trade books accelerated by the 1950s, *School Science and Mathematics* updated its recommended booklists annually, indicating that the field had truly blossomed and that children's books on science were considered fundamental to elementary school science study. The existence and proliferation of such lists also suggests that many schools were consciously building school libraries and making efforts to acquire a good collection of science books. By the mid-1950s, many publishers of children's books had recognized how lucrative the science book field was. Prominent series like Franklin Watts's *Real Books* and *First Books*, Harper's *Science I-Can-Read Books*, and the Golden *Book of Knowledge* series (published in conjunction with *Life* magazine) were all products of political and educational developments after World War II. Thanks to growing concerns about "manpower shortages" and the need for technological innovation, there was a thriving market for science books by the mid-1940s and not enough well-written, realistic, and scientifically accurate books available.[39] Given long-running interest in this area on the part of leftists and a real gap in the trade book offerings, leftists were able to establish themselves as some of the most respected authors of scientific literature for children, in part because of the inroads made by Young World Books beginning in the mid-1940s.

The growing number of technically oriented children's books and the increasingly conservative political climate were two factors that led Bacon to emphasize science in the Young World series. As Bacon put it, "[T]o write for children directly about the world in which we live was scary. You didn't write a political novel for kids. And you didn't write a political description for kids.

You just didn't do that. It wouldn't have been acceptable to the society. Whereas if you did it in science it was sort of a step away."[40] But science was not merely a convenient cover for politics. Bacon and other Marxists believed that science offered particularly important lessons, which is why by the 1940s, when left-wing magazines and newspapers from the *New Masses* to the *National Guardian* recommended books for children, they almost always included lists of books about science.

Science books, Bacon believed, could show "the dynamics of dialectical materialism" in a way that would be "really exciting to kids." Under this logic, science books could serve a Marxist agenda without having any explicit political content. But would children reading science books by Marxists—books written from a consciously "dynamic" perspective, to use Bacon's word—become Marxists, or even understand basic Marxist principles? "No," Bacon conceded. And yet she still believed that such books could be radical tools. Children who read really good science books, Bacon maintained, "would understand that they live in a dynamic world where there is a lot of change going on. And it is important for children to understand change. The more we look upon change, the more we encourage it to take place. And encouraging it to take place is often a danger to the status quo."[41]

Understanding radical potential on this very basic level, Bacon took a broad view of literature's political possibilities. A half century after launching Young World Books, Bacon would acknowledge that not all of the science books were entirely successful at offering the kind of dynamic perspective she sought to emphasize. Even so, there was an explicit and sustained effort to communicate, through science, political ideas that one might loosely construe as Marxist, incorporating both principles of dialectical materialism and broader economic and social understandings that drew upon general Marxist categories. The focus in most of the Young World books is upon scientific concepts and the history of science, which makes the politics less visible. Their social critique was firmly within the bounds of American traditions, but the books celebrate anticapitalist, antiracist, cooperative, and prolabor values in an age when corporate capitalism reigned supreme, half the nation was segregated, the notion of "share and share alike" was being called "Communistic," and the labor movement was suffering major setbacks. Young World books were sold to libraries and individuals even as the national political climate became more conservative and despite occasional right-wing attacks that noted the series' emphasis on "evolution" and "pro-Communist themes."[42]

The nine books on science subjects were Young World's most celebrated offerings among librarians, teachers, and reviewers. Reviews praised several of the books for finally supplying young people with scientific information that was clear and accessible as well as engaging. The books were praised for managing to be "charmingly simple" without "talking down" to readers or leaving them "befuddled by an overdose of complicated technicalities." Writing for the *Weekly Book Review*, May Lamberton Becker insisted that *Egg to Chick* "beats the birds-and-the-flowers method to a standstill." Likewise, a review of *Climbing Our Family Tree* exclaimed, "Here at last is a book of science for youthful readers that really rings the bell. It will be a 'best-seller' for youngsters of Junior High School age and it will find a host of grateful readers among the many adults who have never had any systematic scientific training."[43] Four of the nine books were reprinted in later years by other publishing houses, testifying to their quality and longevity.

None of Young World's science writers had previously published children's books, but three went on to highly successful careers as juvenile authors: Millicent Ellis Selsam (a former teacher at Brooklyn College whose husband, Howard Selsam, ran the Jefferson School of Social Science), Irving Adler, and Sarah Riedman (also from Brooklyn College and active in the teachers' union). Several of Selsam's later books, which were published by trade presses, had outstanding sales; she and Adler are also among writers consistently cited as making singular contributions to scientific literature for children. Alex Novikoff, another Young World author, was praised by prominent scientists and children's librarians alike for his 1945 book *Climbing Our Family Tree*, which was exhibited by the New York Public Library as an outstanding book of the year. He also was approached by several publishers to do more children's books but returned to more scholarly venues after his second Young World book, *From Head to Foot*, was published to enthusiastic reviews.[44] Young World thus launched the careers of several major science writers for children. As a consciously political undertaking geared toward a popular audience, it provided a model, with obvious limitations (stemming from its direct links to the CP), for how social concerns could be communicated to a wide audience through science books. Some concrete examples should clarify the social and political dimensions of the texts and thereby suggest thematic patterns for other science books by radicals.

Two books that were the most simple (as they were for the youngest readers) and the least obviously political, Selsam's *Egg to Chick* (1946) and *Hidden Animals* (1947), are perhaps the most explicitly wedded to Marxist logic. *Egg to Chick* describes how an egg is transformed, over the span of twenty-one days, into a chicken. With clear text and easy-to-follow diagrams by Frances Wells, the little book is a valuable source of scientific information not only on the development of the chicken embryo, but on embryonic development in general. A reviewer for the *New York Times* maintained that "because author and artist have combined their talents so well the student from 6 to 10 will unconsciously learn a sound method of presentation of scientific material."[45] The book was timeless enough that it was reprinted by Harper in 1970, twenty-five years after its first edition, and again in 1987. It is still in print. But beyond its utility as a science text and its literary qualities, the "sound method" that *Egg to Chick* offers is a simple lesson in dialectical development.

After showing different kinds of eggs, which can become fish, frogs, turtles, chicks, and dogs, Selsam notes that "people, too, grow from egg cells." Above a diagram (figure 6.1) with a chicken and an egg on the left, a rooster and a sperm on the right, and arrows joining beneath them pointing toward a chick (the whole configuration looking remarkably like the Hegelian dialectic), the text reads: "An egg will not grow into an animal all by itself. It takes two different kinds of cells joined together to start a new animal. One comes from the mother—the egg cell. One comes from the father—the sperm cell. That is why chickens and fish and dogs and people all have both a father and a mother." Selsam links this very straightforward process of development and differentiation to a longer process of evolution: we learn that the young fish embryo, the young turtle embryo, and the young dog embryo "look very much alike even though the grown-up embryos look very different." Engels himself commented upon this phenomenon, also using the metaphor of an egg's development, in *Dialectics of Nature*, noting that "man too arises by differentiation. Not only individually, by differentiation from a single egg cell to the most complicated organism that nature produces—but also historically." Highly precocious children, and the parents supervising their bedtime reading, might consider—as Engels did and as Selsam did too (judging from statements in her other writings and from her very firm grounding in Marxist thought)—that men, unlike animals, make their history *consciously*, thus marking a qualitatively different kind of evolution. Human beings grow and develop without thinking about it, but they change their environment and the conditions of their existence through conscious, rational action.[46]

Hidden Animals, Selsam's second book, illustrates and explains more explicitly and concretely the man-versus-animal, instinct-versus-rational action distinction that Engels makes. She describes the basic principles of animal camouflage, with illustrations that encourage children to find the hidden insect, fish, frog, bird, or other animal in the picture. Again, the book was so well received that it not only won accolades from reviewers upon the book's initial publication, but it also was reprinted by Harper (1969) and by Scholastic (1970), where it could actually be sold directly through schools. Like *Egg to Chick*, it was scientifically accurate and engaging. It, too, is still in print.

Again, rather than pushing children toward any political position, *Hidden Animals* encourages active thinking on the part of children. As one reviewer noted, "[W]ith well-chosen questions, she encourages [young scientists] to think through some of the answers for themselves."[47] But more than simply encouraging children to think, the book suggests a particular way of thinking

Figure 6.1. Illustration by Frances Wells from *Egg to Chick* by Millicent Selsam. The illustration is from a simple picture book about how a chick develops from an egg, but the picture of a chicken/egg joining with a rooster/sperm and creating a chick also illustrates dialectical logic, as "thesis" joining "antithesis" results in a new "synthesis." New York: International, 1946. Permission courtesy of Robert Selsam.

and reasoning. Take one example, more vivid with reference to the illustration (figure 6.2): "This fish is a little SEA DRAGON. It is a cousin of the tiny sea horse. See the streamers of skin on its body that look just like pieces of seaweed. How do you suppose the sea dragon got that way? Keep turning the pages and you will find out." The sea dragon, we learn, "can hide only in sea weed. If it goes to a different kind of place, it has a much harder time." We learn of animals like flounders, tree frogs, and ptarmigans, which can actually change their spots or their colors to blend in with their surroundings, and of trigger fish, which can stand on their heads in a clump of grass to hide. Finally, we see people—two soldiers, that is—dressed in camouflage and remarkably well hidden (in the artist's rendering) in a clump of trees.

Selsam emphasizes that this human camouflage is qualitatively different from the ways in which animals hide. "Stop and think for a moment! Did you notice that all the animals in this book look like the places where they live? Oak leaf insects are shaped like oak leaves. The zebra's stripes make it hard to see. . . . Tree frogs change from gray—like tree trunks, to brown—like stones, to green—like leaves." The fact that these animals look so much like their native environments means that they are better able to hide from their predators. But she emphasizes a key distinction between human and animal camouflage: "Animals have natural camouflage because they are born with it. It is important to remember that they cannot *think* about it or *do* anything about it." A flounder's speckles, for example, do not change because he wants them to, Selsam tells us.

This fish is a little SEA DRAGON. It is a cousin of the tiny sea horse. See the streamers of skin on its body that look just like pieces of seaweed. How do you suppose the sea dragon got that way? Keep turning the pages and you will find out.

Figure 6.2. Illustration by David Shapiro from *Hidden Animals* by Millicent Selsam. The text and picture both encourage children to look closely and carefully and to apply principles they have been learning throughout the book to answer their questions. New York: International, 1947. Permission courtesy of Robert Selsam.

And here Selsam follows with the ultimate lesson, implicit in the principle of natural selection and evolution over time: animal species gradually, through genetic mutations, become more able to adapt to their environment; humans, on the other hand, can *consciously* adapt. By studying animals, human beings can learn enough about natural camouflage to "make their own camouflage to match *any kind* of place."[48]

This simple picture book thus does a number of things besides teach children about how animals' camouflage works. At a very basic level, by asking children to find the "hidden animals," it encourages them to look beyond the obvious, to probe beneath the surface, to question, and to conceive of possible explanations—all rudimentary principles of scientific inquiry. On another level, the book illustrates elementary principles of evolution (principles still very much in competition with creationist theories even today), which fundamentally inform Marxist thinking about development, differentiation, adaptation, and the ability of human beings, unlike other animals, to consciously change the conditions of their existence. The lyrical way in which Selsam describes movement, change, and development in nature also distinguishes Selsam's writing.[49] This poetic appreciation of nature's order, design, and movement is shared by other writers on the Left, especially Dorothy Sterling, whose books on caterpillars, insects, mosses, and fungi read like extended prose poems, marking not the wondrous or divine inexplicability of nature but the beauty of its essential, orderly materiality.

The point of books like *Egg to Chick* and *Hidden Animals* was not to indoctrinate children with political ideology but rather to influence their ways of thinking and reasoning on a very basic level. Young World books for older children had some more overt political messages, but even these books are a far cry from the proletarian children's literature of the 1930s. The notions of development over time and adaptation in relation to natural, social, and economic factors are central in almost all of the Young World science books, suggesting the insistent dynamism Bacon sought to express in the books and, from a Marxian viewpoint, showing dialectical movement as the constant condition of material existence at any given moment and over time.

All of the books also have a historical dimension. *How the Automobile Learned to Run*, by the Russian writer M. Il'in, for example (which is for slightly older readers), deals with the development of the automobile, illustrating dialectical progress through new discoveries and inventions and showing internal changes in the automobile. The book also relates these internal changes to changes in the society as a whole. Furthermore, Il'in inserts a class component: he says that those in power have historically resisted invention and innovation, whereas the workers have been on the side of progress (the displacement of workers by technological innovations is an issue not broached here). All of the Young World science books promote questioning of inherited authority, and each of the authors tends to promote a holistic view of science against the fragmentation caused by overspecialization. The authors emphasize rational, conscious human action as the way people have historically improved their lives and those of others. They emphasize both the liberating potential of science and the dangers of making scientific knowledge and wealth available only to an elite few. Finally, they regard scientific progress as an international, cooperative enterprise, and, using the cover of science, they reject attempts to assert the superiority of one race, ethnicity, or nation. These emphases are explicit in Young World's science books, but they also inform nearly all trade books by left-wing writers.

Clara Hollos's two Young World books, *The Story of Your Coat* (1946) and *The Story of Your Bread* (1950), deal with the processes and labor that go into making everyday objects: the coat a child wears and the bread a child eats. Perhaps the most important (and unusual) thing about Hollos's books (and other books in this vein published contemporaneously or slightly later by trade publishers) was the emphasis on skilled cooperative labor. "Your coat was not made by one worker alone," Hollos reminds children. "It was not made by one machine alone. It was not made in one place alone. It was made by many workers at different machines in different places—all working together." The story itself is more than likely an allusion to the example of coat and linen that Marx used in *Capital* to explain the "twofold character of the labor embodied in commodities": though the same material, the coat is worth more than the linen from which it is made because more skilled labor went into the making of the coat. Illustrations by Herb Kruckman in *The Story of Your Coat* show different workers of different races and ethnicities, as do Laszlo Roth's illustrations in *The Story of Your Bread*. Roth incorporates not only racial diversity in his images, but also the evolution of artistic styles in conjunction with the historical developments being described: thus, for example, the discussion of the Greeks and their bread is accompanied by illustrations in an artistic style attributed to the ancient Greeks, and modern modes of wheat cultivation, flour milling, and so on are illustrated in Roth's own "modern" style. Hollos does more than present an international, multicultural, and developmental view of production in her books. She also shows the difference between those who own the means of production and those whose labor actually creates wealth. In *The Story of Your Coat*, for example, she distinguishes between the few men who own the sheep, the wool, the warehouse, and the factories and the many men and women whose labor transforms the sheep's wool into valuable products and whose labor union fought so that "the workers did not have to work from sunrise until after dark," so they "earned more money," and so that "their children could leave the mills and go to school."[50]

Although Hollos's books were not reprinted, they typify the American version of the production book, which, as Elting's *Lollipop Factory* and a number of others in this vein would suggest, appealed to many left-wing writers. These books helped to demystify everyday objects and processes, investing them with layer upon layer of labor, movement, and gradual development. This form was particularly popular in the 1930s, corresponding to a broader social impulse at that time to gain insight into and control over the mechanisms characteristic of the modern age. (Documentary writing, photography, and film, which were characteristic forms of expression in the 1930s, likewise represented the urge to reveal, explain, and demystify, as well as the desire to know the truth.) Production books, to quote Bishop Brown, reveal "the truth which you do not immediately see with your eyes," but they also give working-class people leading roles in the dramas they present, in contrast to the majority of children's books, which tended to portray a white-collar, middle-class norm with which many children of the working class were unable to identify.[51]

Young World's science books for older children, written by Alex Novikoff, Irving Adler, and Sarah Riedman, shared many of the same themes as those by Selsam, Hollos, and Il'in, although the books for older readers deal with different subjects and undertake more extended analyses. All emphasize the importance of questioning and experimentation by showing something of the development of scientific understandings and the ways in which progress was encumbered during periods when people were not free to question accepted truths. For example, Riedman's *How Man Discovered His Body* (which was reprinted in 1966 by the trade publisher Abelard-Schuman) and Novikoff's *From Head to Foot* both note that Galen's ideas about blood were accepted for hundreds of years and that those who questioned him (and those who questioned other accepted authorities) were punished. As Riedman notes, "If a scientist can at all times question the facts, the error will someday be discovered for all to see. But if questioning is forbidden and curiosity becomes sinful, then errors replace facts and speculation replaces exploration."[52] Both Novikoff and Riedman emphasize that people have, in the past, been forcefully prevented from questioning authority. They also use Marxist frameworks to suggest more subtle reasons for people's tendency, even in the twentieth century, to see the given social order as natural, a tendency that inhibits inquiry and dissent.

Suggesting how hegemony operates to reinforce socially constructed gender norms, *From Head to Foot* gives a contemporary example of a hypothetical great-uncle Ebenezer and great-aunt Hester, who both believe that Ebenezer should work outside the home and that Hester should take care of the house, even though people always said she had a better mind for business. "Of course, [believing] this gave Great Uncle Ebenezer a way of getting his household work done and a chance to feel superior to his wife," notes Novikoff. "Great Uncle Ebenezer wouldn't have liked it if anyone questioned the idea that women were supposed to look after the house while men attended to business. In fact, Uncle Ebenezer would have said it was a law of nature, like gravity or the equinox."[53] This is an example with which children might be able to identify, especially since the return of women to the home after their presence in the workforce after World War II—that is, right around the time of *From Head to Foot*'s publication—required a concerted effort on the part of government, industry, and the media to re-enforce traditional gender roles.

The Ebenezer and Hester example is used to explain the ways in which scientific progress was hampered during the centuries between Galen and Vesuvius:

> Kings and princes, barons and earls, wanted subjects who would be docile and easy to rule. They were afraid of knowledge and science. If people started asking questions about things, who could tell where that would lead? So it became the custom for everyone to believe that the old ideas were laws of nature and could not be questioned.

In what we might take as a prescient reference to a milieu of rapidly constricting freedom of inquiry and expression (Novikoff would lose his job as a professor at the University of Vermont during the McCarthy period, and Riedman,

Selsam, and Adler would also leave or lose their teaching jobs in the late 1940s or early 1950s), Novikoff remarks, "Modern thinkers are not really smarter than people were in the past. Most of us now realize that scientists must be free to doubt and ask questions and figure out the answers, and that the really dangerous characters are those who want to deny scientists that freedom."[54]

Riedman and Novikoff emphasize that not only scientists, but also children themselves, must feel free to ask questions about things they do not understand, including their own bodies. By focusing on human biology, Riedman and Novikoff are able to achieve something of what early high school biology teachers like Benjamin Gruenberg aimed for in developing curricula. In emphasizing adaptation, a significant number of writers and teachers hoped to make the student a "master of life" rather than a passive victim of his or her surroundings. Likewise, they hoped that children would become more comfortable with themselves as physical beings and unashamed of bodily functions, physical sensations, and natural urges. Novikoff's *From Head to Foot* gives a fairly explicit explanation of sexual development and sexual intercourse, for example. The text and accompanying illustrations by Seymour Nydorf are clear and matter-of-fact, but not entirely inattentive to the emotional—what might be called the "unscientific"—side of the physical activity. "The process of inserting the penis into the vagina is called *sexual intercourse*," Novikoff writes, "that is, a sort of communication between a grown-up man and woman in which the sexual organs are used. This action is an expression of deep love between a man and a woman and their means of having a family of their own." This talk of "love" moves sexual activity beyond the mechanical and functional realm of the scientist to the irrational realm of the poet and the philosopher, even as Novikoff continues to place a premium on scientific knowledge. Describing the human body also gives Novikoff, through a discussion of blood types, the opportunity to emphasize that race has no relation to blood: "It is just prejudice, then, not scientific fact, that accounted for the separation of Negro and white blood and plasma in our country's blood banks." Such discussions of human physiology display important parallels to books on anthropology by people on the Left, especially in the attempt to debunk the notion of racial or national superiority.[55]

By showing scientific knowledge, the development of theories, and technological and medical progress as historically evolving in a nonlinear path of errors, questioning, experimentation, and correction (that is, evolving dialectically), the authors—whether describing theories about light (Adler), the evolution of the modern loaf of bread (Hollos), medical discoveries (Riedman and Novikoff), or scientific achievements in general—illustrate, as Engels attempted to show in *The Dialectics of Nature*, "how the scientific attitudes of any society depend on its changing methods, and how science changes the productive methods, and therefore the whole society." Moreover, by discussing science from a historical perspective, it is possible to understand the dynamics of human agency within structural limitations. "That is how history works," Riedman notes of the slow process of overcoming superstition. "Men think with the ideas of their day, and they are limited by the tools and ways of doing things in their time."[56]

One of Marx's most famous statements on historical progress concerns the ways in which inherited tradition limits rational action by individuals. In *The Eighteenth Brumaire of Louis Bonaparte*, Marx suggests (in phrasing that Riedman echoes) that "men make their own history, but they do not make it just as they please; they do not make it under circumstances chosen by themselves, but under circumstances directly encountered, given and transmitted from the past." Though progress only comes through building on the work of previous generations, it is hampered by inherited superstitions and false beliefs. The goal of science is to make man, as Adler puts it, a "giant" who can stand on the shoulders of generations past without, as Riedman puts it, "worshipping at their feet."[57]

All of the radical authors whose work I examine emphasize the liberating potential of science—for example, the power that comes with the knowledge of how to control and use light; the freedom that comes with having bread baked by machines in a bakery rather than by women who are stuck in the kitchen. Part of the materialist world view involves a conscious rejection of any higher power—as Novikoff puts it, "our bodies aren't the way they are because anyone planned them that way"—and an insistence that human power, great as it is, comes from human beings' rationality and abilities to learn and adapt and to use tools. "Only man, with his thinking brain and clever hand, has been able to overthrow the dictatorship of nature and to live as he pleases," Novikoff writes in language that is strikingly political. Science, writers like Novikoff, Riedman, and Adler reiterate, makes man the master of his surroundings. N. Sparks, writing for the Communist journal *Political Affairs* in 1948, similarly insisted, "Science has not, as we so frequently hear from some popularizers and philosophers, reduced man to an insignificant pigmy on a tiny planet in a corner of the universe. On the contrary, it has freed man from superstition and enabled him to establish himself as the true ruler of the earth, his mind able to embrace the complex laws of the universe."[58]

On the other hand, as many left-wing writers emphasized, science's liberating potential is limited, not only by barriers to progress but by the extent to which human beings are willing to cooperate and to share the wealth made possible by science. Science is also limited by the extent to which society can collectively bear the burden of responsibility that necessarily accompanies power. Adler writes in *The Secret of Light*:

[S]cience . . . is not an end in itself, but a tool which people use in the course of their life and work. Atomic energy can be used to destroy a whole city or to make the desert blossom. It all depends on what people do with it. Today, for the first time in history, the great discoveries of the scientists have opened the possibility of giving all the people in the world enough food, clothing, housing and medical care.

Despite this great potential, Riedman reminds children that "millions of people are still hungry, millions who might be cured are still sick. Why? Because science is often harnessed to supply the needs of the few instead of the many. Sometimes, large profit-making corporations may keep some discovery off the market, because it would spoil the sale of older products that are still very profitable." Riedman made similar points in the books she published with trade presses. In *Food for People* (1954), for instance, Riedman posed a persistent dilemma of capitalism: "Why, in shocking contrast, does the rich man enjoy an abundance which is not physically necessary, and which seems appropriate to the man of toil?"[59]

The call to make scientific power and knowledge available to all was not an idle call from people like Riedman and Adler. By writing about science in a way simple enough to be understood by children (Adler in particular is a master at breaking down complex phenomena into clear, understandable, and logically connected elements), writers of science books for children were actively working toward the democratic empowerment of children and of citizens in general.

Lest the Marxist parallels suggest that Young World's authors were teaching not science but dogma, I would argue that although their faith in science and the scientific method might be taken as somewhat overzealous, they do, repeatedly, make a point of emphasizing the importance of questioning *all* authority. They also argue that even the most valid theories evolve over time, so that the whole notion of "hard liners" does not really work here. Novikoff, for instance, notes that Darwin's groundbreaking theory of natural selection has, over time, been somewhat revised, yet Novikoff insists, "This does not mean the theory was wrong. On the contrary, a true theory is alive. Like everything else in the world, it changes and grows. Only a dead, useless theory stays the same down to the last detail." The relationship of Marxism to science could be understood, similarly, as a general, flexible guideline. As J. B. S. Haldane put it, "At best, Marxism will only tell a scientist what to look for. It will rarely, if ever, tell him what he is going to find, and if it is going to be made into a dogma, it is worse than useless."[60]

A rather chilling anecdote related to Novikoff's book on evolution, *Climbing Our Family Tree*, suggests that he, for one, was uninterested in following any party line in his scientific explanations. But the incident also suggests the real limitations of Young World Books and CP functionaries. Mary Elting, who did much of the editorial work on *Climbing Our Family Tree*, tells the story this way:

> There was a time when Stalin came out flat-footedly on the side of Lamarckian evolution, which said that environment was the main thing. There was a sort of scientific, anti-Darwinian mafia in the Soviet Union headed by a man named Lysenko. He did a lot of damage to the really good scientists for a long time. Anyway, the editor in chief at International books, Trachtenberg, called Novikoff in and said that he had to change his discussion of evolution in one of his books to bring it in line with the Lysenko line. Novikoff was absolutely horrified at the idea and refused, of course. So Trachtenberg didn't reprint the book. . . . Novikoff up to that time had been very close to the party, if not a member, but this probably turned him off, as it did a lot of people.[61]

Ironically, the whole Lysenko incident mirrored the very problems with received authority people like Novikoff were writing against. But the fact that Novikoff and Elting were clearheaded about the issue certainly problematizes the whole notion of Communist "dupes."

So just how important was Marxism or dialectical materialism in these books? Was the party line at any given moment the determining factor, even at the expense of a book's accuracy? Was the child or was politics the primary consideration? A letter from Betty Bacon to Meridel Le Sueur concerning the book on tools that Le Sueur proposed to write for Young World in 1945 reveals how editor-author collaborations gave shape to particular texts as "socially symbolic projections" encompassing several individuals' vision of the child and balancing political ideals with the attempt to appeal to a child reader and the juvenile marketplace.[62]

Responding, apparently, to an outline or synopsis Le Sueur had sent, Bacon calls the material "wonderful" and suggests that the book would fill a real gap in children's book offerings. As Bacon notes, "[T]here is absolutely nothing [else] that even begins to touch on the question of labor." Bacon approves Le Sueur's organization as "good" and logical. "Beginning with the hand and the extension of the hand sets the tone very well indeed," she notes. Neither Bacon nor Le Sueur mentions him, but Engels makes the very same point about the hand as man's primary tool for "impressing his stamp on nature" in *The Dialectics of Nature*. He writes that "the specialization of the hand—this implies the *tool*, and the tool implies specific human activity, the transforming reaction of man on nature, production." Certainly Bacon was aware of Engels's writings (as was Le Sueur, whose library was stocked with Marxist classics).[63] Bacon may well have been interested in Le Sueur's proposal in the first place because it might have simply illustrated, through a discussion of tools, basic Marxist principles of social evolution.

Bacon suggests "working out" the book in a way that certainly implies a Marxist framework:

> Begin with man and his hand. Present the *idea* of extending the hand through simple tools, then the machine. Present the *idea* of man as inventor and master of the machine. Then go into the historical account, keeping it as strictly chronological as you can (the kids get confused if you jump around too much). Then labor, strikes, distribution of profits, etc. And finally the vision of the future. Bring in the songs and stories wherever they fit and as many as you need. Keep the writing simple, keep the basic structure simple.[64]

Despite the clear concern with politics, Bacon's letter seems to imply that her greater concern was the book's potential to interest, engage, and speak to the child—although doing so within a dialectical framework was, for her, even better. The strength of Le Sueur's outline, in Bacon's view, was that "it throws a new and wonderful light on the whole question of tools for kids and is the kind of thinking in terms of immediate experience that is most meaningful to them." Bacon's criticisms point to this same concern for young readers. Although Bacon approved of Le Sueur's plan to use songs and tall tales, she notes that "the tall-tale tone and the strong, rhythmic swing all the time is just too much. The kid needs pauses in which he can catch his breath. He needs simple statements of fact in terms of every-day [sic] experience that he can assimilate easily." She recommends that Le Sueur look at Il'in and Segal's *How Man Became a Giant*, noting that "kids like [Il'in's] simple, humorous approach." She cautions Le Sueur about using her proposed motif of "David and the Worker" to tell her story, noting that the form "inevitably carries an element of condescension" and "implies that he [the child] is not able to cope with the material itself."[65]

Though she may have philosophically rejected capitalism as a system, Bacon did have to think about how to create a book that would sell to a varied audience of children, parents, teachers, and librarians. But despite the extent to which Bacon was inescapably caught within the confines of what the market would bear, Young World is clearly distinguished from other trade publishers because of the entire enterprise's connection to the CP. Even so, moving away from the organizational bounds of the party and into the juvenile book field in general, we find similar thematic patterns within texts. We also find varying degrees of editorial and authorial allegiances to social and political principles, principles which clearly influenced the texts themselves.[66]

But more important than any party line, whether one wishes to call the children's books by writers on the Left "Marxist" or something else, one can still find a relatively coherent world view and set of values implicit in them. Both Young World's books relating to science subjects and trade books for children published in the postwar period by left-wing authors who did not necessarily have direct ties to the Communist Party treat science subjects in a way that embraces progressive, New Deal values of cooperation, democracy, empowerment for the worker, and antiracism; all promote children's questioning and experimentation; and all suggest that science is something accessible and available to all people, even children.

The Science of Trade Books

Young World Books was unique to the extent that it was a consciously political enterprise geared toward the trade children's market, but it never had the reach of many commercial publishers, for reasons both political and financial. The series set important precedents for subsequent work by left-wing authors, but it was by no means the primary outlet for Left-authored work. Overlapping personnel and themes suggest that the distinctions between Young World Books and the trade book marketplace should not be drawn too sharply, but both the parallels and the differences are worth further consideration. Le Sueur, though she did not pursue either her contract with International nor the subject of science did go on to publish trade children's books with Knopf.

Irving Adler, on the other hand, took up her subject of tools in several books, for instance, publishing *The Tools of Science* with John Day in 1958. This is a book whose style and address are very different from the one Le Sueur would have written. Adler's insistent refusal to "talk down to the child" manifests itself in a seriousness of tone that is in marked contrast to the folk songs and tales that Le Sueur planned to use to enliven her story.[67] On perhaps a more fundamental level, as the title indicates, Adler's book is about the tools of *science* in particular, rather than about tools or labor in general. Even so, there are important parallels between the books.

In a general way, Le Sueur's proposed book and Adler's completed book both attempt to communicate a basic understanding of tools as extensions of human motor and sensory organs, extensions that allow people to have greater control over the environment in which they live. This assumption about tools and human control operates for a hammer, a crane, a microscope, or a mass spectrometer, and it has a striking link to Engels's writings on science and dialectics (which Le Sueur, Bacon, and Adler would more than likely have read). Furthermore, both Adler and Le Sueur are historical in their approach and concerned with the ways in which various tools have developed within particular social and historical circumstances and have, in turn, altered those circumstances. As we might expect, given its later publication date (after McCarthy came on the scene) and the different circumstances of the books' intended and actual publication (International versus John Day), politics are less explicit in Adler's book than it seems they would have been in Le Sueur's: her book, as we have noted, was intended to connect the discussion of tools to "labor, strikes, distribution of profits, etc." But to say that Adler's book is apolitical would be inaccurate, as would be the suggestion that Richard Walsh, who ran the John Day Company, was naïve about Adler's politics. In fact, when Adler told Walsh he had been fired from the New York City schools for refusing to say whether he was or ever had been a member of the CP, Walsh (himself very liberal and married to progressive writer Pearl S. Buck) replied that this was none of his business.[68]

Looking at Adler's outline for *The Tools of Science*, we can see that, at least in part, he was writing about specific scientific tools as a way of defining a more general philosophy of science, a philosophy that, like Le Sueur's, was concerned with connecting science and technology to economics. In Adler's notes for the book, we find the central idea that informs the carefully charted and logically ordered sub-ideas: "purpose of science: 1. acquire facts. 2. acquire understanding. 3. acquire power to control economics." These points are not explicitly spelled out in the published text, but the book does demonstrate the ways in which human beings have, historically, gained greater control over all aspects of their lives by acquiring scientific knowledge and skills and by creating tools for scientifically observing, measuring, and analyzing phenomena. Moreover, by describing various tools and the way they work, in step-by-step detail, science in general is demystified and made accessible to the child.[69]

"Some of the tools of modern science look very complicated," Adler acknowledges in the book. "But when they are examined, they are found to consist of a few simple tools put together so that they can cooperate to do a special job." According to Adler, the scientist observes, measures, analyzes, theorizes, and tests his or her theories. Tools help with all of these. They make it possible for a person with "intelligent curiosity" to become a scientist, that is, a person who knows how to look for clues, how to form theories from a mass of seemingly unrelated facts, how, in sum, to approach the unknown. To illustrate intelligent curiosity, Adler uses the example of a boy who, almost instinctively, takes apart the watch he has just been given as a gift; we are reminded of the *New Pioneer*'s example of "the child who takes his velocipede apart or tears her doll to pieces." This child is not a bad kid but, rather, "an explorer."[70]

Suggesting that the complex mysteries of science are, in fact, simple enough to be understood by children—in an era when scientific knowledge was, increasingly, the property of an elite group of intellectuals and technocrats—was saying something essentially radical. At the very least, it was challenging a growing trend toward elitism in science education, despite the protests of progressive educators who insisted that "any tool as vital as science should be in control of all people." More pointedly, in a subtle but important way, Adler, echoing a number of progressive educators, rejects the idea that a scientist can be neutral or passive in any aspect of his or her work.[71]

So that we are encouraged to consider each tool and its use in this light, Adler emphasizes early in *The Tools of Science* that "observing is interfering." In the words of the book itself, "Observing nature is not like watching a show in a theater. The spectator who watches a play on a stage is a *passive* observer.... The scientist observes *actively*, consistently meddling with the thing he observes." Haldane, drawing upon Werner Heisenberg's "uncertainty principle," makes a remarkably similar point in his book *Marxist Philosophy and the Sciences*, noting:

> Our observation of any object is, among other things, a physical process which affects the object observed. It follows that there are no observers who are only observers and merely sit back and take no part in the processes of the universe. This is an extremely general principle of Marxism. Marx continually pointed out that observers of society are also active members of that society.[72]

Such general principles as these inform all of Adler's writings in the broadest sense. That said, instead of analyzing this particular book of Adler's in greater detail, I suggest that the larger concept that informs it is a useful umbrella category for books that focus broadly on the scientific method, or the tools of science. These books are, in turn, a logical jumping-off point for discussing other categories of science books, for they center on a kind of essence that unites almost all of the science books I consider. That essence embodies particular understandings of (a) "the scientific" as the basis for rationally understanding and controlling the environment; (b) "the scientific temper" as a quality of mind devoted to the quest for truth; and (c) "the scientific method" as the means to discovery. These understandings are implicit in books on nature (which tell children how to go about discovering nature's secrets); in books on human biology, anthropology, and archaeology (such books explain, through science, what factors unite us as human beings when we seem to be so different from one another); in books on how things work and on how materials and goods are produced and distributed; and in biographies of great scientists (which emphasize the attitude of mind that led the scientists to their great discoveries). Of course, they are also implicit in other categories of science books as well (books on astronomy, physics, and mathematics, for example), but I touch on books in the former categories because of the thematic parallels we can draw between books like those in the Young World series, published in the years following World War II, and Sputnik-era books which flourished in the market created by Cold War anxiety.

Books by writers on the Left focusing primarily on the tools and methods of science emphasize curiosity, questioning, observing, experimenting, analyzing, and comparing. In general, they attempt to communicate the excitement of scientific discovery. They show science to be something accessible to the child and, implicitly, offer children assurance that the mysterious workings of the world are, by and large, understandable. They suggest that the child's natural curiosity is a wonderful thing and that his or her questions, silly as they might sometimes seem, are always worth asking. They help the child to see himself or herself within a larger community in which all participants affect one another; that is, they give children, as Selsam put it in a 1958 article in *School Libraries*, "a sense of homeness in the world." Often, these books emphasize the process of development of scientific knowledge, whereby authority is continually supplanted by new ideas generated from questioning, observing, and experimenting. Further, they nearly always describe scientific achievements from an internationalist and cooperative perspective, and their authors try to cultivate "intelligent curiosity" in children. Books in this category treat science in a general way and seek not only to introduce children to scientific concepts and methods, but to show them the ways in which science, as an interconnected and unified (rather than as a fragmented and specialized) enterprise, is interesting, exciting, and fundamental to the world in which children live.[73]

Mary Elting's bestselling *Answer Book* (1959), for example, is entirely devoted to making children's funny questions into the serious business of science. "Why doesn't a spider get stuck in its own web?" "Why is a snake always sticking its tongue out?" "Why don't the planets bump into one another?" "How can ducks swim without having lessons?" "Why do people have different colored skins?" Elting breaks these questions, and their answers, into categories, such as "The Wonderful Animal World," "Information," "How Does It Work?" and "How Do We Know?" Culled from actual questions that children asked in school, the book not only validates children's inquisitiveness but also suggests that life's great unknowns have reasonable explanations. "Where would we be without questions?" Elting asks:

> Suppose nobody had ever said to himself, "I wonder why birds can
> fly and I can't." . . . A question is one of the most useful things in the

world. So is an answer. But no one ever needs to feel ashamed of saying, "I don't know." . . . The fun of answering really starts when you say,
"I'm not sure, but let's see if we can find out."

Though Elting's book does not directly take on political questions in the way
that, for instance, Riedman does (except in a few instances, like adding to her
explanation of why skin colors are different a note that "outside color does not
make people different inside"), she shares the fundamental premise that asking questions, even questions that are uncomfortable or that seem foolish, is
important and necessary to the growth of knowledge.[74]

Other books by writers on the Left, such as Rose Wyler's *First Book of Science Experiments* (1952), *Golden Picture Book of Science* (1957), and, with her
husband, Gerald Ames, *What Makes It Go?* (1958) and *Prove It!* (1963), and
many of Herman and Nina Schneider's books, encourage children to undertake simple science experiments for themselves with everyday materials from
around the house. Even this represents a conscious challenge to the trend
toward commercialization and packaged science "kits." A major toy maker,
impressed by Herman Schneider's *Everyday Weather and How It Works*, asked
him to design a plastic kit to work like the home weather bureau described in
the book. Herman indignantly refused, telling the toy maker that the whole
point of the book was to show children that the weather station—like many
scientific apparatuses—was something that could be made from "junk" that
children found themselves. The Schneiders, of course, did not stop the tide
of consumption, but in some small way they opted out of it themselves. To
writers like the Schneiders, who made a good living writing trade books and
school textbooks for children, book publishing must have seemed somehow
outside of an imagined commercial web that one enters by "selling out." One
could argue that books with educational value are geared more toward children's edification than toward producing profits; however, the latter tends to
be the primary concern for publishers, and rarely is making a living not a consideration of writers.[75]

To take this false commercial-educational dichotomy a step further, it bears
noting that science fiction books, which are generally classed in a more commercial realm, could be excellent educational tools, though they never achieved
enough status as such to win funding from the NDEA. Though it takes science
beyond the bounds of the real world, science fiction can also interest children
in science, introduce them to scientific methods and concepts, and suggest
something of the social implications of science. This certainly was the case for
the *Danny Dunn* books, written by left-wingers Jay Williams and Raymond
Abrashkin in the late 1950s and 1960s. In *Danny Dunn and the Anti-Gravity
Paint* (1956), for example, the daydreaming schoolboy who is more interested

in space travel than in his math class knows in his heart that his daydreams are the schemes of a scientist in the making. When disciplined for not paying attention in school, Danny says to his mother, "I can't help it. I want to find out how things work. She's [the teacher] just mad because I'm always experimenting or thinking about new things." When Danny goes off one day in a rocket ship, he is, of course, vindicated.[76]

The Nature of Science

Books about nature and biology by writers on the Left emphasize many of the same basic principles of science, especially the scientific process of observation, questioning, and experimentation. The books avoid anthropomorphism, and their authors generally reject explanations suggesting that nature works according to a divine plan. In *Caterpillars* (1961), Dorothy Sterling, perhaps building upon the success of her friend Millicent Selsam's *Nature Detective* (1958), plays further upon the lure of the detective, who figured prominently in postwar films, television programs, and comic books. "Detectives, at least in books, walk around with magnifying glasses looking for clues," Sterling writes:

> They notice little things other people overlook—the way a man ties his shoes, the glasses a lady wears, the ashes in the fireplace, the ink on a letter. . . . Catching caterpillars is a kind of detective work. You have to look for clues. You need sharp eyes to notice things most people never see. Even a magnifying glass helps.

The chewed leaf, for example, is, she says, a clue, a sign saying, "This way to the caterpillars." Sterling makes caterpillar hunting seem as exciting as the work of Sam Spade. She appeals to a child's curiosity and sense of adventure. She does not push the child toward becoming a scientist (or a caterpillar farmer) as a long-term career choice, but she does appeal to the scientist within the child and suggests ways to more scientifically observe caterpillars. "Most likely you won't be a caterpillar farmer when you grow up," she notes, but she tells readers that it is fun anyway to collect all kinds of insects and to watch them grow and change. "Besides collecting eggs and caterpillars, cocoons and chrysalises, you can also collect facts about them. It will make your work more interesting if you keep a notebook and write down where you found each caterpillar, the leaves it eats, and how often it sheds its skin." The child is encouraged to add something of his or her own to the caterpillar facts that Sterling has provided; she notes that "there is a great deal still to be learned about caterpillar lives, and boys and girls with sharp eyes may discover things that even scientists don't know!"[77]

For writers like Selsam and Sterling, the child interested in science is not a geek but a naturally curious kid, that is, a most kidlike kid. Defense imperatives may have created much of the new demand for juvenile science books, but the work of Selsam, Sterling, and others suggests that science study may create a person unwilling to blindly follow orders. Their works suggest that science study will help children to learn how to evaluate evidence and make intelligent decisions. As Selsam put it, "The better science books encourage a constant use of the methods of science; they encourage an ever-developing, expanding sense of inquiry and wonder about the world around them; they encourage a healthy skepticism with regard to prevailing superstitions and prejudices; and accustom young people to solving problems in a scientific way."[78]

Selsam's books, which deal primarily with the natural world but which sometimes involve child characters, strike a balance between appealing to the child's sensibilities, interests, and sense of wonder and teaching basic scientific principles. *Greg's Microscope* (1963), for instance, shows the excitement of scientific discovery and the intricate complexity of everyday substances. Joined by his friend Billy, Greg uses his microscope to look at salt, sugar, vegetables, pepper, wool, human hair, and dog hair. The illustrations by Arnold Lobel (figure 6.3) show the children's expressions of delight and wonder as they see everyday substances revealed in minute detail with the aid of the microscope. Through full-page (that is, magnified) drawings, Lobel shows us the images that Greg and Billy see through their microscope, including sugar crystals and onion cells. Greg models observant, resourceful, and questioning behavior for children, and the reader is invited to experience the wonders of science in ways that appeal to the child's own natural curiosity.

Books about nature can do several other things besides illustrating more general principles of science and encouraging children to explore the world around them. For one thing, discussions of biology almost by necessity involve discussions of development, evolution, and adaptation. Here is where the sense of dynamic movement that Bacon brought up becomes especially evident. Here, too, is where the qualities of the human world can be distinguished from the natural world, along the lines of Engels's discussions of that which distinguishes humans from animals: the brain, the hand, and the abilities to use tools, to learn, to adapt, to markedly change the environment. Here is where children can begin to understand their relationship to the world in which they live, as they connect plants to animals to humans.

In *See Up the Mountain* (1958), Betty Bacon (writing as Betty Morrow, with the editorial cooperation of Millicent Selsam) describes the adaptation of various species to different zones of a mountain environment. As we move through each zone, with the aid of illustrations by Winnie Lubell, we learn about the climate and the flora and fauna best suited to that area (the book is written in the

Figure 6.3. Illustration by Arnold Lobel from *Greg's Microscope* by Millicent Selsam. Billy and Greg use a microscope to look at everyday substances from salt crystals to human hair. Pictures copyright © 1963 by Arnold Lobel. Used by permission of HarperCollins Publishers.

second person, so we are asked to experience this journey as Bacon describes it). Beyond the introduction we are given to various plant and animal species, a larger lesson is presented: when we reach the top of the mountain, we are reminded that different life conditions operate in each zone. "The temperature, the amount of rain and wind, and the soil all changed. *We* were able to go through these changes by wearing sweaters and jackets and putting up a tent when it got too cold for sleeping bags in the open. But the other living things of the mountain have to stay where the conditions are just right for *them*." The quail can only live in the foothills, and "the mountain sheep are only at home on the crags." Humans, however, can go anywhere. The lesson is similar to that in Selsam's *Hidden Animals*: because they have the power to control the conditions of their existence, humans can adapt to any environment.[79]

That humans are the only creatures who can rationally think about their actions and plan their actions is a point made repeatedly. Sterling tells us in *Caterpillars* that the mother moth or butterfly always lays her eggs on the plant that caterpillars prefer: a good thing too, since caterpillars are fussy eaters. "Perhaps this doesn't surprise you," Sterling suggests. "After all, your mother buys you ice cream, and takes you to a candy store, and makes sure that you have plenty of vegetables and milk." But there's a big difference between the human mother and the butterfly or moth mother, Sterling emphasizes: "They can't think or plan for the future as people do. . . . When a Painted Lady Butterfly flies over a field, hunting for a thistle, she isn't thinking about flowers or leaves or eggs. She isn't thinking at all. Her actions are *instinctive*. She's doing exactly the same thing that her ancestors did fifty million years ago."[80]

Left-authored books on nature tend to emphasize dialectically evolving processes in their discussions of plants, animals, and environments. As Dorothy Sterling notes in *The Story of Mosses, Ferns and Mushrooms*, "The history of plants can't be told in a one-two-three-four succession. Neither can the history of animals or the history of man." Because of powerful opposition from the Christian Right, the word *evolution* was rarely used explicitly—it took Sputnik to finally supersede Scopes and make evolution a valid framework for teaching science. But left-wing writers very consciously injected ideas about evolution into their books, and schools in major markets like Texas and California still bought them. The science supervisor of Texas schools actually told Herman Schneider that his textbooks were adopted *because* they made no reference to evolution. "The funny thing is that the sixth-grade book had a big section called 'Changes in Living Things,'" Schneider remarked. "The key is to not hit directly." Mary Elting credits the success of her husband Franklin Folsom's book *Science and the Secret of Man's Past* to savvy marketing on the part of the book's publisher, Zola Harvey (Elting said, "You can guess something about him from his first name," which was evidently taken from the French novelist Emile Zola, known for his dark realism). Despite a "simple but frequent reference to evolution" in the book, Harvey managed to persuade the Los Angeles schools "to take a huge order" for *Science and the Secret of Man's Past*. Elting likewise gave credit to librarians and teachers for resisting pressure from creationists, pointing out that no teacher or librarian ever called attention to the book's emphasis on evolution, and thus it never got banned.[81]

Man Is a Giant: Harnessing Human Power, Naturalizing Sex, and Denaturalizing Racism

Like books about nature, books on human society or human bodies helped children to feel a sense of connection to human beings and to the world around them. Several books connect humans to a longer chain of beings, suggesting interdependence within the natural world and the connections and distinctions between animals and humans. In contrast to the Darwinian notion of "survival of the fittest," in *Life on Earth* (1953), Rose Wyler and Gerald Ames emphasize prehumans' ability to cooperate as the key to their survival. "The poor cooperators died out; the good cooperators lived," they assert. "Struggling jointly to master their world, the cooperators became men." It is this "intelligent cooperation," Wyler and Ames insist, that distinguishes the human from other animals. Setting out clearly their conviction (which may not have the scientific basis they claim for it) that human progress is more a factor of cooperation than of individual achievement, they note, "Men, through co-operation, have cultivated plants instead of gathering them, and have bred animals instead of hunting them. They have created systems of agriculture rich enough to support large populations and great cities. Men have gained control over vast sources of energy." Man can do what animals cannot do: "He speaks with his fellows; together they work, teach, and learn; by their cooperation they create things that no man could create alone." They argue that "work is so productive, or can be so productive, that men and women gain the leisure to learn and to become complete and creative human beings." And yet, like Engels, Wyler and Ames assert that man is not yet completely human, because "a portion of the materials and energies controlled by men is still used, not to foster life, but to destroy life through war."[82]

A few books, rather than discussing human beings in the longer context of evolution, focus more exclusively on the human body with the idea of demystifying human development, human functions, and, especially, human sexuality. These books are designed not only to make the child feel more comfortable with himself or herself as an individual; they also aim to make the child understand what it is that makes us human, no matter how different we might seem. "Everywhere, all over the world, right at this minute, children are eating green peas, chopped blubber, raw fish, shashlik, rice, pemmican, roast beef," the Schneiders write in *How Your Body Works*. "They eat so they can grow and be strong. . . . All of us have a brain and a stomach and a heart fixed in their places, and blood that moves in and out of all those places all over the body. No matter where we come from or where we go, we can grow, can feel, can think." Barbara Ivins's illustrations in the book show children of different races—in contrast to most children's books published before 1965—and thus the child sees himself or herself in relation to other children who look similar and who look different. Children are therefore encouraged to recognize the commonalties among human beings despite differences in race and in culture.[83]

Books on archaeology and anthropology were especially popular during and immediately after World War II, as their cultural relativism was an antidote to the "scientific" racism propounded by fascists. Books on archaeology by authors such as Anne Terry White, Franklin Folsom and Mary Elting, and Rose Wyler and Gerald Ames link natural history to human history and emphasize the importance of rational action in the development of civilization.

Books on anthropology by people on the Left—including Ruth Benedict and Gene Weltfish, May Edel, Eva Knox Evans, and Ralph and Adelin Linton—are devoted to illustrating the distinction between culture and biology. These texts emphasize the richness of human cultures and the fact that no one culture, or way of living, is superior. In *All about Us* (1947) and *People Are Important* (1951)—extremely popular books that were reprinted by Golden Press—Eva Knox Evans recalls the development of human beings over time, from primitive humankind to the present. Humans evolved as they learned better ways to grow and harvest crops, as they invented machines and medicines, and as they shared ideas, wrote books and music, created works of art. Now, she says, they need to learn how to get along with one another, how to appreciate people who eat different foods, speak different languages, have differently colored skins, live in different kinds of houses, wear different kinds of clothes, and believe in different religions.

Like the Schneiders, who emphasize humans' common biological needs in *How Your Body Works*, Evans notes that everyone gets hungry and needs to eat. Moreover, eating different kinds of foods does not make people different from one another in any fundamental way. She presses this example further than do the Schneiders, however, adding that what *does* make people different is that some people get enough healthy food to eat, while others do not. Some people have poor land and are unable to grow the food they need; some people, who do not have land to cultivate, do not have enough money to buy good food. "What happens to people who are hungry?" Evans asks. "They have colds most of the time. Their muscles are weak and their bones ache; they feel sleepy and tired. Are they dumb and lazy and good for nothing? No, they are hungry." By asking, "Are they dumb and lazy and good for nothing?" Evans takes a cultural myth and uses science to demystify it, just as in *All about Us*, she insists that color is only "skin deep" and that blood type has nothing to do with race (figure 6.4).[84]

The authors of books on anthropology were particularly concerned with racism; they sought to show that *race* is a physical characteristic which, unlike culture, is unchangeable, but that *racism* is culturally conditioned and invented to serve the needs of those in power. *The Story of People: Anthropology for Young People* (1953) by May Edel and *Man's Way from Cave to Skyscraper* (1947) by Ralph and Adelin Linton are intended for older children but deal with many of the same principles as Evans's books on anthropology. The Lintons' book is partly a historical account of the development of human culture (clearly conceived in terms of a dialectical progression, with new methods disturbing the old order and patterns of living, leading to a period of adjustment, new changes, etc.) and partly a geographical account, examining different regions of the world and varied cultural patterns. The latter is the focus of Edel's book, which allows

They all can have the same blood type

Figure 6.4. Illustration by Vana Earle from *All about Us* by Eva Knox Evans. Picture and text together illustrate the point that there are no inherent differences between children of different races and ethnicities: "they all can have the same blood type." Copyright 1947, 1968 by Random House, Inc. Used by permission of Golden Books, an imprint of Random House Children's Books, a division of Random House, Inc.

her to put forth a theory of cultural relativism, based on her own studies with Franz Boas. Questioning the idea that Western nations have achieved a higher state of "civilization" than more ostensibly "primitive" societies, Edel notes that "there are plenty of crude and savage parts to our own history. . . . Untold members of Africa died of hunger and thirst or suffocated in the slave ships that carried them to a life of bondage. And in Boas' own day, children were working up to 14 hours a day in mills and even in mines." She suggests that Americans' cruel treatment of children in the not-too-distant past "would horrify the Eskimos and Indians and many other 'savages' who somehow managed to bring up their children without taking such cruel measures."[85]

Man's Way is explicitly concerned with racism and colonialism and with the extent to which science has been used to rationalize the exploitation of one group of human beings by another group. The Lintons argue that Europeans only became race conscious when they rose to world domination: "When white explorers set forth with ships and guns and were able to conquer people of other races, they immediately reduced their victims to a position of social inferiority. Physical characteristics thus became a prompt and easy guide to the social status of the individual." The authors suggest that early Europeans, by calling science to their aid and describing physical characteristics as the markings of inferiority, could justify their domination by relying on racial generalizations. According to the Lintons, the only way in which race is significant is that it has become a symbol of "social discrimination and prejudices." They contend that "at the present time the so-called primitive people are becoming as impatient with the white man's condescension as they are with his exploitation and are getting ideas of how both can be removed." The revolutionary undertone of their words speaks to the brewing anticolonial sentiments in Algeria, India, Uganda, and other colonized nations by the late 1940s, when their book was published. Their ultimate call, like Wyler and Ames, like Engels, like Novikoff, is for applying the methods of science to society, insisting that such planning is not only possible but necessary, particularly in light of the ways in which atomic power has changed fundamentally humankind's existence.[86]

"Truth Which You Do Not Immediately See with Your Eyes": The Mechanics of the Everyday

As anthropological books used science to break down myths concerning the social order, books about material production and the mechanics of everyday life, or what Evgeny Steiner calls "production books," emphasized not only human ingenuity but also human labor. They appealed to children's natural curiosity about the world around them and encouraged children to seek a deeper understanding of what seemed to be apparent and simply part of the world. The child who, like Danny Dunn, "want[s] to find out how things work," who seeks to understand human bodies and human societies, would naturally be drawn to books that explain how machines operate and how everyday materials are made and distributed, as well as books that reveal the invisible processes that allow society to function. Some of these books illustrate the ways in which simple explanations about the material workings of society can hold rich "companion" messages about race, labor, and historical development. They also consciously appeal to the child's world and imagination.[87]

For example, *Your Breakfast and the People Who Made It* by Leone Adelson and Benjamin Gruenberg, is geared toward the urban child who believes that orange juice comes from a jar, eggs come from a carton, and milk comes from—where else?—the milkman. The book tells, as one would expect, the story of the different foods that make up a typical middle-class American breakfast meal—bread, milk, eggs, sugar, and oranges—and describes the processes and labor required for their creation and distribution. To make the hatchery for the eggs takes more than chickens, for example:

> It takes carpenters to build hen houses, and painters to keep them white-
> washed.
> It takes electricians to wire the brooders and hen houses for light and
> heat.

And it takes truck drivers to carry baby chicks or eggs from one place to
another.

With all the many kinds of workers who help us to get all the eggs we need,
the breakfast parade is getting longer and longer. It is a good thing that
all these people are not bringing your breakfast right into your kitchen.
Where would you put all those workers?[88]

The illustrations by Kurt Wiese are lively and serve the subject well: he periodically shows the growing parade of workers marching along the pages, workers
whose images call forth the labor aesthetic of the 1930s (figure 6.5). Gruenberg and Adelson end by encouraging children to extend the breakfast parade
themselves, by thinking even more about the labor that goes into their morning meal: "Who made the machines that squeeze the oranges? Where did the
cans come from? Who made them? And where did the steel for the cans come
from? . . . There is almost no end to the questions, and no end to the number of
workers who are the answers to your questions."[89]

In another twist on this theme, Harry Granick's *Underneath New York* (1947)
is a historically informed portrait of the networks, systems, and departments—
from the sewage system to the mail system, from gas and electric energy gener-
ators to the city's subway system—that allow New York to function as a city. The
book is dedicated to "the two thousand years of scientists, engineers and workers whose labor made possible the modern city, and to the scientists, engineers,
workers and good citizens of today and tomorrow who will make the cities of
the future centers of health, ease of living, beauty and peaceful activity." From
the very beginning, the book appeals to the exciting mystery of that which is
hidden below the surface. The photograph on the opening page shows a crowd
watching workers down below them amid a maze of pipes, ropes, and girders
(figure 6.6). The strange image is entitled "Anatomy of a City." "Gaze down it,"
Granick urges his child readers. "Look at the maze of timbers and steel beams;
the huge pipes, the narrow tubes, the cables, the tunnels that dive into mysterious dark. Look at the men digging, drilling, sawing, riveting, pouring concrete;
the monstrous power machines that grind, mix, load, unload, carry."[90]

Granick goes back to ancient civilizations and, in broad brush strokes,
traces improvements in infrastructure and sanitation as science and technology advanced and as people came to understand, through science, the relationship between sanitation and disease. Granick describes the transition from the
primitive tools of the ancients to the machine age, emphasizing the importance
of knowledge accumulated over the years, despite the errors, confusions, and
misconceptions of people in the past. "History is like an assembly belt in an
automobile factory," Granick notes. "Some of its parts travel a long time before
their significance becomes apparent in the machine of progress."[91]

Figure 6.5. Illustration by Kurt Wiese from *Your Breakfast and the People Who Made It* by Benjamin C. Gruenberg and Leone Adelson. This picture shows the parade of breakfast workers who produce and deliver a child's breakfast. Copyright 1954 by Benjamin C. Gruenberg. Used by permission of Doubleday, a division of Random House, Inc.

In all of this, we can make analogies to the discursive style and thematic emphases that have been loosely identified here as "Marxist." But at the end of the book, Granick's writing becomes explicitly political. He calls for urban planning on the model of the New Deal's Tennessee Valley Authority, a "success story" in which "government-owned cheap water power transformed the lives of poverty-stricken, hopeless people into a richly useful, productive, hopeful pattern." This transformation was made possible, Granick says, by common people's fight for democratic planning against "the most desperate kind of resistance by selfish interests." He condemns segregated housing, slums, and the use of science to produce weapons rather than to improve living conditions. Like Bert Grant in the *New Pioneer*, Granick calls on children to be activists, making sure that the "city of the future" is the wonderful place it could be. He notes, in an ominous reminder of the new, atomic age, "There will be no cities, there will not be many people left on this ancient planet if you and I and our parents and friends allow another war to be fought." He urges children to work as hard to prevent another war as their parents worked to make sure that World War II was won. Moreover, he insists:

Figure 6.6. Photograph from *Underneath New York* by Harry Granick. Text reads: "Few places are more fascinating than a hole in the ground. But a hole in a city street—that is in a class by itself!" New York: Rinehart, 1947. Permission courtesy of Granick family.

> We must live in friendship among ourselves. That means we must regard our neighbors of whatever color or creed as having equal rights with us by reason of science and human justice and the Constitution of the United States in all the duties and privileges of American citizenship. It means we cannot afford Harlem ghettos throughout the city. It means we must not allow our government to assist builders of new housing who dare exclude Negro families as was done in Stuyvesant Town.

After baring the city's arteries, intestines, and nervous system, Granick suggests not only its wonder, but also its fragility, and the role that children must play in making sure the city of the future is, in Whitman's words, "The City of Friends."[92]

Again, such calls for economic planning, arms reduction, and international cooperation were arguably radical by 1947. And, as it happened, the FBI took notice of *Underneath New York*—but not because of such socialist sentiments. According to an FBI memo submitted to the attorney general in May 1948, a representative of the State Department (who claimed that Granick was "an out and out Communist") had brought Granick's book to the attention of the FBI because its subject matter and Granick's apparent political affiliation seemed like a potentially dangerous combination. In the formula that equated Communists with spies and saboteurs, the memo notes, "The State Department is fearful such a book might make its way to the Soviet Union or satellite countries and that it would be a perfect instrument to be used in case of sabotage in the event of hostilities between this country and Russia." Although there were immediate and urgent discussions concerning Granick's citizenship, the FBI seemed to drop the matter of the book until six years later, in 1954, when an FBI agent finally obtained a copy of the book from the Library of Congress and, apparently, read it. Though acknowledging material such as a two-page diagram of Grand Central Station that showed where gas and electricity entered, the agent nonetheless concluded that the book, given its "generalized" information and "dated" photographs, would not "be of much use to a potential saboteur." The FBI is silent on how useful it might be to children. Unlike the incident involving Le Sueur's *River Road*, such discussions of the book's danger—in this case, not to children, but to the nation itself—were never made public. But it seems more than coincidental that around this time Granick found himself blacklisted from television and radio writing, which had been his chief source of income.[93]

Going against the Grain: Biographies and the Politics of Publishing

If books on production and distribution and those on technical, social, and economic processes show the manifestations of science in the modern world and provoke children to think about the invisible activity underlying everyday phenomena, biographies of scientific figures use the experience of historical (or contemporary) figures to illustrate qualities of the scientific mind. These books, which often spend considerable time focusing on the scientists' childhoods, were popular with children and librarians. The recommended booklists from which librarians drew to order books, such as *The AAAS Science Book List for Children*, included a large number of biographies.[94] Almost without exception, as it emerges in juvenile biographies by people on the Left, a person possessing the scientific mind is someone willing to go against the grain. The young scientist is almost always a bit different from other children; he (only rarely were scientific biographies about women) is often a misunderstood outcast; and the ideas he puts forth as he grows up are often a great challenge to accepted authority. He is also, often, shown to be very much engaged with the world and the political issues of his time. For example, in her biography of the chemist Antoine Lavoisier (1957)—subtitled *Scientist and Citizen*—Sarah Riedman makes note of his involvement with the French Revolution; in her biography of Charles Darwin (1959), she emphasizes his support of the American Revolution and his revulsion for slavery; and her biography of Benjamin Rush (written with Clarence Corleon Green) is subtitled *Physician, Patriot, Founding Father*. Again, such books teach questioning and nonconformity as attitudes of mind worth cultivating.

Biographies of scientists could do more than give their authors an opportunity to explore, through individual examples, the process of scientific development and the general qualities of the "scientific temperament." A number of people on the Left wrote biographies of African-American scientists partly in order to discuss racism and racial discrimination. Showing African-American successes in the field of science was also a way to focus on the historical achievements of the race and to provide role models. To use the most common example, several people on the Left—including Sam Epstein and Beryl Williams Epstein, Shirley Graham (herself African American), Harold Coy, and Anne Terry White—wrote biographies of George Washington Carver which were very popular (the Epsteins' and Graham's books were both bestsellers).[95]

A proposed biography of Charles Drew by Emma Gelders Sterne—which became another book altogether—points to the "companion messages" that writers tried to insert in scientific biographies and also vividly illustrates the politics of publishing juvenile books through trade presses as compared with a press like International. Without question, part of Sterne's desire to write about Drew was the opportunity that his story provided to discuss racial issues. Sterne's agent, Edith Margolis, assured her initially that editors at Knopf were interested in the Drew biography, and Sterne began intensively researching the subject in the spring of 1957, only to have the contract put on hold as Knopf waited to see how well her recently released book on Mary McLeod Bethune would sell. This delay came as something of a surprise to Sterne and her agent, given the demand in the late 1950s among librarians for biographies of "scientists, explorers, etc." that were tied into school curricula, especially for children in the eight-to-eleven age group.[96] Ultimately, Virginie Fowler, an editor at Knopf, rejected the Drew idea, maintaining, according to Sterne's agent, that "a juvenile biography should deal with someone whose name would be 'instantly recognizable' to children." Undeterred, Margolis made another suggestion to Sterne. "I have an idea that a lot of parents who wouldn't select for their children, or encourage their children to select a book about a Negro scientist, might well choose a book about blood for those same children, without realizing that the kids are learning lessons in tolerance at the same time." She added, "Of course anyone who was interested in the Negro question and Negro scientists would read the book in any event."[97] Sterne accepted this idea. *Blood Brothers: Four Men of Science*, as the proposed book was called, would include sections on William Harvey, Marcelo Malpighi, Karl Landsteiner, and Charles Drew. This new format, which Fowler approved, still allowed Sterne to make general points about the nature and the dialectical development of scientific understanding through international cooperation and the exchange of ideas. It also gave her a way—even if in an abbreviated fashion—to tell Drew's story.

"The story of blood is the story of many people working together and also of those rare individuals who appear from time to time and, with their special understanding, unlock new doors of knowledge for all the world to use," Sterne writes in the first pages of *Blood Brothers* (1959) as it was finally printed. She goes on to recount a historical trajectory of social evolution: the helplessness of early man, the recognition of his differentiation from other creatures by his ability to use his hands and his brain, man's dialectically developing control over the circumstances of his life. "[A]mong all the creatures of the earth, Man alone could talk and dream of a brighter future for himself and his kind. He used his new-model brain and his free hands to make his dreams come true," Sterne writes. "From seeing, touching, examining, from experience and reasoning, Man spun a slender thread of usable, practical knowledge concerning the world around him." Science developed, she writes, as people came to trust their own senses and powers of reason instead of relying on magic.[98]

Her discussion of Harvey is reminiscent of Riedman's discussions in *How Man Discovered His Body* and Novikoff's in *From Head to Foot* about the grave danger, historically, of questioning Galen's authority on the movement of blood in the human body. She notes that Harvey's book on blood circulation was banned almost immediately after it was published. "But truth was in the field," Sterne maintains. "Authorities could forbid, threaten, punish and denounce. . . . Forbidding scholars to read a little book about blood circulation did not change the structure of the human body; and denouncing the 'new learning' could not stop the threads of knowledge from being passed along from hand to hand." Harvey's relationship to established authority has obvious political lessons. Of Karl Landsteiner, in contrast, Sterne can say little of note about his relationship to established authority. Yet she mentions the assassination in 1914 of Archduke Ferdinand in the midst of Landsteiner's research on blood transfusion, an event, she says, that was ignored by scientists, who believed that they were above politics. "'The search for truth has no politics,' they said. 'Science must be above nationality.'" Implicitly condemning the scientists who feel they can exist outside of politics, Sterne notes, "They talked among themselves of the beauty of a brotherhood of man; but they did nothing to bring this brotherhood about, nor to curb the ambitions of their rulers for glory, or the munitions makers for wealth."[99]

The text that was ultimately published was certainly informed by Sterne's political outlook, but none of this material provoked any controversy among Sterne's editors at Knopf. Their objections focused almost exclusively on the Drew section, which they felt was too long and more concerned with the racial issue ("which is not a main consideration in this book") than with the theme of blood. Moreover, as Fowler pointed out, in her draft of the manuscript Sterne had made much of Drew's death, suggesting it could have been prevented had he been allowed to receive plasma, which, ironically, he devoted much of his career to collecting and preserving. Because Drew was African American, Sterne maintained, he was denied access to a segregated blood bank and therefore died earlier than he should have. Fowler said that Sterne might mention Drew's unnecessary death, "but written briefly and tautly with the understatement that is always more effective than pathos." Sterne's research seems to have been inconclusive on this point, which may be why she did not press the issue, and the story of Drew's death does not appear in the published book.[100]

Fowler recommended a series of major cuts in the manuscript, including an extended discussion of segregation and the race riots of 1919. She noted in a letter to Sterne that this material was unnecessary. "By this time, almost everyone in the United States is cognizant of the problems that have arisen over segregation and race riots," she remarked, pointing to more recent events in Clinton and Little Rock, of which a child could not have failed to learn in current events classes. Moreover, Fowler insisted, this extra material on race threw off the balance of the book, which does not have such extended discussions in other chapters. Not wishing to suggest that she does not agree with Sterne's abhorrence of segregation and racial violence, she wrote, "I'm trying to bring home to you the contrast between your first three parts and the fourth part— where you have let a very personal feeling enter into the approach to a subject. It is a feeling I can understand and agree with—but this is not the place as you do not have enough space to give balance." Her final word of advice (after recommending twenty-two pages of specific cuts) is this: "Keep your statistics to a minimum—and the interest to a *child interested in science*, at a maximum."[101] In this regard her advice was not far from that which Bacon offered Le Sueur.

There is one final piece of Fowler's letter that is intriguing. By the late 1950s, when Sterne was writing about Drew, Betty Bacon, like Sterne, was living in the San Francisco Bay Area, active in the CP, and working in the California library system as a juvenile librarian. Bacon and Sterne were close friends. Fowler's final caveat in the letter to Sterne displays an anxiety on Fowler's part about getting caught up in a battle over racial politics. Fowler expressed her hope that Sterne would not try to involve the California Library Association in a

matter rightfully the "very close concern of author and publisher." The California Library Association had been a national leader in the battle for intellectual
freedom, and it is possible that Sterne may have threatened to cry censorship to
her librarian friends.[102]

Sterne's ultimate desire to maintain her lucrative relations with Knopf
must have helped sway her decision to cooperate with her editors. The Drew
section, as ultimately written, actually makes a point about race by attempting to evade the issue until the very end. Despite enough references to give
the informed reader a hint of Drew's racial identity (we are told of his work
at Howard University and at Freedman's Hospital, for example, but it is not
mentioned that these are historically black institutions), Drew's race is not
mentioned explicitly until the last few pages of the book. The reader is thus
expected to judge his achievements not as a *black* scientist, but as a scientist. The irony of Drew's situation—a black man running a blood bank that
segregates plasma—therefore becomes even more apparent when we see how
much of his work was dedicated to surpassing the traditional barriers of race
by working for all humankind.

Drew, Sterne notes, initially was silent about the segregation of blood,
even as others began to protest. "As a Negro he had had to suffer many personal affronts," Sterne explains, though she has not mentioned any of those
affronts up to this point in the book. "He knew what it was like to live in
segregated neighborhoods, to go to segregated schools. . . . He knew what it
meant to be confronted every day of your life with the barriers of discrimination." All scientists must overcome barriers, Sterne points out; Drew had
been lucky enough as a scientist to encounter few obstacles: he had been given
many opportunities and had been very successful in his work. "And *almost*,"
she writes, "he had been able to surmount the extra obstacle of being a Negro
in America. But the segregation of blood was not an affront to himself alone,
or to the Negro people alone, but to humanity's progress. . . . To permit out-
worn superstitions, old prejudices, to enter the realm of science was to poison
the well of truth itself."[103]

Drew, eventually driven to action, made a public statement saying that race
makes no difference in blood type. Shortly thereafter, Sterne tells us, Drew lost
his job. She takes this as an ominous lesson: though not burned at the stake as
some unpopular scientists were in Galileo's time, scientists in twentieth-century America who said something unpopular still could lose their support. Furthermore, race prejudice remained a barrier, and at the time of *Blood Brothers'*
publication, blood was still segregated in parts of the country, particularly the
South. Sterne ends the Drew section with this point, which still allows her to
make a strong statement on racism in the United States without mentioning the
circumstances of Drew's death.[104]

Like Helen Hoke and Franklin Watts in their dealings with Langston Hughes, Sterne's editors were not unsympathetic to her commitment to civil rights nor to her desire to bring in discussions of racial discrimination, when relevant. Yet they were also concerned with being balanced and with making sure that the book would sell. Bacon, reflecting upon the postwar period years later, suggested that the major form of censorship was actually self-censorship among authors. As Bacon noted, most people knew, for example, that a "political tract" was inappropriate for children. The subtly political aspects of Sterne's book aroused no comments from her editors, but in her extended discussion of racial issues in the Drew section, she seems to have crossed some line. Even so, whether politics were at issue or whether the concern really was over balance and the child's interest level is not entirely clear.

Similarly, when an editor at Western Printing asked Alexander Crosby to take references to the Tennessee Valley Authority out of his book on rivers, was it because the material was controversial or because it was inappropriate? "What is the proper scope and breadth of interest of a little book about the usefulness of rivers to us all in our daily lives?" an editor asked Crosby. "How much can a child be expected to understand?" What the child can understand; what will produce a balanced, quality book; what will serve the child's interests; what will best fit with school curricula; what parents are likely to buy for children—these are all essential considerations for any children's book editor and for any publisher.[105]

As we have seen, editors or publishers might go out on a limb and give contracts to people they knew were in political trouble during the McCarthy period. But did this mean that the books themselves were political? Crosby's wife, Nancy Larrick, a Random House editor in charge of the popular *Landmark* series, speaks now of herself as someone who was "on the Left" (though probably her husband was more political than she); even so, she dismisses the idea that politics entered her work in any way. Pressed further, she admits to publishing people who may have been controversial figures, like Anne Terry White. But how radical were White's books, whatever her own politics? If we look to her biography of George Washington Carver, we might, of course, be struck by her choice of subject and by the extent to which White consistently refuses to minimize Carver's struggles against discrimination, segregation, and racial prejudice. On the other hand, in White's depiction of him, though young George is constantly asking questions, always out in the woods experimenting with plants, he is also apt to slip out of a scientific mode and into a religious one. "There was something in the woods that carried George out of and beyond himself," White writes. "There was a spirit there—something big, something he couldn't touch or name, something he could only feel." Though clearly Carver was a man who made his own history, against great odds, in White's biography we see the young George comforted by the idea that he has a predetermined destiny, like the plants he studies. Reading the Bible, he revels over the part which tells "how God had made them [the different plants] all for a purpose. He liked to think that God had made everything the way it was for a reason. It made him feel there was a plan for him too." Belief in a divine plan is not usually the mark of a scientific mind. Such "teleological explanations," Selsam would argue, "keep a young person from asking questions as to how things come about."[106]

The point is that political people did not always write political books; even when they consciously tried to do so, they were still products of the society in which they lived and thus their work inevitably carried overtones of the dominant culture's biases. Likewise, people who may have consciously tried to keep their politics and their work separate could not always do so. More-over, the degree and importance that politics assumed for writers, editors, and publishers—and for the buyers of books—was always variable and complex. The realities of the marketplace, the intricacies of education-related legislation, and the whims of those who were arbiters of quality and taste (from Virginia Kirkus, known for her book review service, to the American Association for the Advancement of Science) all dictated what was publishable, as did implicit, shared, or individualized assumptions about the child reader. By operating within the field of trade publishing, left-wing writers could reach a broad audi-ence of children, but there were real limits on what they could, or even tried to, say. On the other hand, some would argue that a basic level of Marxist logic, which, intentionally or unintentionally, informed many Left-authored science books, had radical implications.

Marxist Zeitgeist and the Struggle against Despair

What, in fact, is the place of Marxist theory or a general Marxist world view in these books? Some writers, like Bacon and Wyler, who were active in the party, would insist that aspects of Marxism—that is, dialectical materialism applied as a tool of scientific analysis and the world view which Marxism encompassed— were implicit or explicit in their books and in the books of many left-wing writ-ers. While Bacon emphasized certain radical implications of books that com-municated a dynamic view of nature and physical processes and the sense of a constantly changing universe, Wyler pointed to a materialist outlook and a democratic commitment to "science for the citizen." Take these visions of radi-calism with a grain of salt, however. Wyler qualified her claims about the radical aspects of many popular books by noting, "I can't think of anybody who wrote a book that you would call a 'Communist book.' And the reason why was because it was inappropriate for children."[107] What a "Communist book" would look like, she did not say. Her own friend Helen Kay had written the revolutionary *Battle in the Barnyard* for children in 1932, and presumably Wyler knew this. But what she probably meant was that authors would not write such a book in the postwar period, not simply because they could not publish it, but because it no longer seemed suitable for children. Both Bacon and Wyler understood "the political" in general and Marxism specifically in rather expansive terms; that is, they could see political value in books that teach children *how* to think, rather than *what* to think. Thus, they also could insist that the books they wrote and those that they helped to get written were not "ideological" in the common sense of the term.

Dorothy Sterling, Mary Elting, and other left-wing writers, in contrast, contended that to call their children's books—or those of most other left-wing writers—"Marxist" is absurd. Even so, when they talk about what they *were* trying to do, they express perspectives similar to those of Bacon and Wyler. "I don't think it was Marxism—that is, textbook Marxism—or any definable ideology that really drove the movers and shakers," Elting noted:

> The simplest, or I should say simplistic Marxist idea—that it is possible to organize society in such a way that everybody has a chance to develop their personalities—I think it was that feeling that everybody on the progressive side made part of their lives somehow. . . . I don't think it was what even my good Marxist husband [Franklin Folsom] would have cited as dialectical materialism that made good left books. . . . Herman and Nina [Schneider] would have giggled if anyone even mentioned the idea.[108]

Herman and Nina Schneider did indeed dismiss the idea with a giggle when I suggested it to them, but they did not challenge Elting's insistence that the Schneiders were "materialist in their thinking." In general, Elting maintained, "[I]t was zeitgeist rather than philosophy that guided us."[109]

Sterling, likewise, maintains that "at least on a conscious level, I did not write science books because I was a Marxist." Yet she acknowledges that part of her interest in science and her wish to teach children something practical came from the fact that she was "a materialist." Moreover, as someone who came of age during the depression as a "semi-skilled intellectual," she thought that children should gain practical knowledge and skills. Ultimately, she said that she always wrote not primarily to teach children but rather to feed her own curiosity. Wise to the vagaries of authorial intent, Sterling noted, "Of course my left-wing leanings influenced my choice of topics and the straightforward way I wrote about them. I certainly only wrote about the real world." Though she was not consciously writing as a Marxist, her books demonstrate certain Marxist principles; though she says she was not consciously writing for a child reader, the way in which her writing suggests a conscious address to a child reader is striking (think of the young detectives seeking out caterpillars). Just how much can we make of an author's retrospectively stated intent? When I spoke to Leone Adelson about *Your Breakfast and the People Who Made It*, commenting on its messages about labor, Adelson said she had never thought of the book in those terms, but wished she had, because then she and Gruenberg might have promoted the book through the labor movement. She also seemed not to know—or pretended not to know—that many of her friends, whom I had also interviewed, had been Communists.[110]

Philosophy or zeitgeist, might there be something unifying about the Left's outlook that made left-wing people interested in writing about science and in writing for children? Adler, noting the importance of scientific theory, suggests in *The Secret of Light* that "a mass of unconnected facts are bewildering, whereas theories help one see how the facts are connected." Sparks, more pointedly turning toward Marxism, claims that because few scientists have learned to think dialectically, "boundless confusion . . . now reigns in theoretical and natural science and reduces both teachers and students, writers and readers to despair." Might the coherence of Marxist philosophy have provided a holistic world view to counter what Tom Engelhardt calls the "triumphalist despair"—bewilderment, fear, sadness, dread—that affected many Americans in the aftermath of Hiroshima and Nagasaki? "What is it that draws scientists toward Communism, toward Marxism?" Sparks asks. "Is it the fact that Marxism is able to shape order out of the turmoil of new developments in science as in social life, which appear so chaotic to the bourgeois mind, and that Marxism is able to demonstrate man's capacity to dominate the gigantic forces of nature?"[111] Indeed, after man had unleashed the power of the atom, it was comforting to believe that humans still had the ultimate power of reason. Marxists' world view made science an appealing subject for them, but it also may have helped to distinguish their books from other offerings, providing a coherence that seemed to be lacking in other books.

Commentators on postwar books for children suggested that many science books were plagued by fragmentation, neglecting the unity of science and overemphasizing individual achievement and personal success. According to an article by science writer Alexander Marshack, which was published in the *Library Journal* in the late 1950s:

Our approach to science lacks either that naïve unity it had in the early days of the 17th–18th centuries, or the naïve unity it has within the official philosophy of Communist "dialectical materialism." Lacking a clear, working philosophy we are left with a multitude of facts and anecdotes and discoveries which are offered to the public piecemeal.

In words that suggest the value of an overarching theory of scientific processes, Millicent Selsam notes that "a good science book for children links many observable facts into fundamental concepts."[112]

Obviously, a scientist trying to fit all concepts into a Marxist framework would compromise his or her scientific integrity. However, Marxism per se was probably less important than a general orientation toward the Left, which corresponded to particular ways of understanding the relationships among science, society, and the child. Herman and Nina Schneider, writing for an elementary education journal in 1958 on "The Role of Science in Child Development," ask: "Is the 'age of science' inevitably accompanied by the age of anxiety?" The Schneiders contend that "the anonymous relationship to the things we make and use has converted us into little islands, unaware of the substructure that joins us." Perhaps they had this in mind when they wrote books such as *Let's Look under the City*, *How Big Is Big*, or *You among the Stars*, which give children a sense of perspective and a sense of the relationships between individuals and objects in the world (figure 6.7). The Schneiders contend that economic and military competition and "the increasing tempo of destructive warfare" have created a world that threatens children's psychological development. Science, they suggest, can give children a framework for making sense of the world; that is, it can help them to understand the processes by which their food, clothing, and shelter are created and can give them the opportunity, through experimentation and observation, to see these processes directly in action. Science can contribute to wholesome growth and development and can make children feel at home in the world. "As he gains insight into the world of plant and animal life, a child discovers many patterns of interdependence and friendship," they write. "In . . . simple experiences in conservation he learns that his acts have significance, that he is part of the world."[113]

Curiosity, questioning, experimenting, an attitude of independent thought, even, perhaps, a geeklike fascination with detail, are all necessary to scientific pursuit, itself viewed as necessary for national defense in postwar America. But what to do with the young scientist, possessing an elite education, paid for by the government, who thinks too independently, who, for example, questions the idea that scientific knowledge should be used to create ever more advanced weapons of mass destruction? As the writers I consider emphasize, there can be no scientific progress without questioning. But how, then, to serve the needs of national security? Where is the distinction between questioning irrational authority and being unpatriotic? This conundrum never really came up for people working with scientific books for children in the postwar era, because

As you stand there in the dark night, among the stars, you are looking far, far into distant space, beyond the most distant galaxies. You are looking at the whole universe.

Figure 6.7. Illustration by Simeon Shimin from *You among the Stars* by Herman and Nina Schneider. By placing the stargazing child on a street, in a city, in the United States, on the earth, in the solar system, among the Milky Way, and within the universe, children can imagine their places within a universe much larger than themselves and also feel at home in the world. New York: Scott, 1951. Permission courtesy of Nina Schneider.

the people selecting books for school libraries were, as a rule, not the same people who were setting national education policies to conform with national security concerns. Both groups, like the writers of science books and their editors, wanted simply—and naïvely, we see now—to teach children scientific "truths."

Along with science books of all kinds, many of those Sputnik-inspired books by radicals on rocket ships, space satellites, and astronomy were supported by the National Defense Education Act. But did they serve military purposes? Alexander Crosby and Nancy Larrick's *Rockets into Space* (1959) ends by noting that "the moon looks beautiful to us now. We would feel differently if it were loaded with hydrogen bombs that could be aimed at the earth." Is this subversion or is it common sense? Who should decide what truths, whose truths, we should tell children?[114]

7

Ballad for American Children

History, Folklore, and Leftist Civic Education

In Meridel Le Sueur's *River Road: A Story of Abraham Lincoln*, the young Lincoln wrestles with questions of slavery and the temptations of wealth, and these remain central emphases throughout the text. Le Sueur paints Lincoln as bitterly opposed to slavery, troubled by his own white-skin privilege, and mistrustful of those who try to "shift their share of the common labor to others." Abe is hostile to smooth talkers and those who do not work with their hands, but he is not anti-intellectual. Indeed, he tells his cousin Dennis Hanks that there are things in books he must find out about: "I got to figure out why some say, 'You toil and earn bread and I'll eat it.' We got this here now not from the mouth of a king but the same tyrannical principle, an excuse for one race enslaving another race. I got to think out what's the common right of humanity and what's the right of kings." A boat trip to New Orleans is portrayed as a life-altering event for Lincoln. There he sees human beings sold naked on the auction block, sees families torn apart, and sees wretched poverty alongside regal plantations with their great white pillars. To a friend who tells Abe that he has no slaves and thus bears no guilt for slavery, Abe responds by saying that "even if one man is a slave and one man sits by and says nothing—there is guilt."[1]

Lincoln's forthright opposition to capitalism and racism in *River Road* distinguishes *River Road* from many other Lincoln biographies. But the other, even more unusual aspect of Le Sueur's "story of Abraham Lincoln" is the prominence given to Abe Lincoln's mother, Nancy Hanks, "a woman not much sung about, but one whose long evening dreams and noonday work went into the makings of us all." Her role in Lincoln's life—and, by extension, in the building of the nation—is highlighted not only in *River Road*, but also in a prior book by Le Sueur, *Nancy Hanks of Wilderness Road: A Story of Abraham Lincoln's Mother*, which is devoted entirely to Hanks's chores, musings, and premonitions of something "yonder." As the narrator of that book notes in a strikingly early call for women's history: "My grandmother always said that there are many tales told of famous men but no one sings of the women. This made my grandmother very angry."[2] The memories that Le Sueur attributed to her feisty grandmother—especially the memory of a Lincoln who seemed to stand for the values of the Popular Front—would make the Right, for its part, very angry as well.

History may be in the past, but, unlike science, few believe it to be objective. Meridel Le Sueur's conspicuously anticapitalist and antiracist biography of Abraham Lincoln and an attack on the book by the right-wing *Milwaukee Sentinel* (discussed in an earlier chapter), point to a battle over American tradition and a struggle between Left and Right to define and speak for "the people." Left-authored children's books published in the postwar period rewrote popular myths and historical narratives—and celebrated "people's heroes" like Lincoln—in order to emphasize a version of the past that predicted a more egalitarian future. By the late 1950s, however, leftists looking to the past for models of resistance to present power structures and for visions of a more democratic future increasingly turned to African Americans in history who had challenged discrimination and racial hierarchies in the past. These figures spoke to a blossoming civil rights struggle that became core to the leftist project.

Left-authored books exploring both the Anglo-American and the African-American past offered a civic education that ran counter to the official curriculum in schools. Even so, these works found markets in part because of the very Cold War conditions that made the books potentially controversial. American tradition was called upon as a weapon in the Cold War, but this call also summoned works that challenged the Cold War common sense.

The Great Depression and Second World War had heightened popular interest in American tradition and had united Americans in the struggle against fascism. After the war, however, when outspoken antifascists became "subversives" rather than patriots, their vision of the past, likewise, became more marginal: their "twentieth-century Americanism" became, in many contexts, "un-American." But despite an apparent "cult of the American consensus" among professional historians (which, as Jesse Lemisch proclaimed at an address to the American Historical Association in 1969, amounted to "fighting communism through history"), a quiet battle was waged by a more marginal kind of historian, that is, the amateur historian who wrote for children. The amateur historian writing historical juveniles was not only "freer," as Howard Fast would put it, but also far more willing to embrace a utopian view of the past and, by extension, the future. Thus, a significant number of authors exploring history through children's literature attempted, on the one hand, to reframe hegemonic "master narratives" of the past (or to invest them with new meanings) and, on the other hand, to recover forgotten stories, particularly those of African Americans, the working class, and women of all races. By rewriting familiar narratives of history and recovering forgotten or repressed stories, leftists were able, with varying degrees of success, to project a vision of the future to children that challenged the Cold War consensus and what critic Nancy Larrick would call the "all-white world of children's literature."[3]

Civic Education and the Return of the Repressed

In the years following World War II, formal school curricula were increasingly geared toward supporting the national security state and the corporate order it upheld. Both of these, in turn, were stabilized by class, racial, and gender hierarchies that children were generally taught not to question. Part of the project of naturalizing the existing social order, which included racial segregation and black disfranchisement in the South, a Cold War with the Soviets, and a hegemony defined by corporate capitalism and consumerism, involved demonstrating the historical basis for the existing status quo. Thus, as education became more and more fundamentally geared toward "developing strong national loyalties," American history became a central element in American educators' Cold War arsenal. By 1948, thirty-nine states had made the study of American history a requirement for high school graduation, and in most cases that study was explicitly intended to further current national imperatives and to naturalize the existing social order.[4]

A 1949 report, *American Education and International Tensions*, published by the National Education Association, urged an emphasis upon "the elements in our national tradition that merit greatest devotion, of the qualities of our national greatness that are most worthy to be admired and fostered." That 1949 report may have been prescriptive, but at some level it was descriptive of programs already in place. A law passed in New Jersey in 1945, for instance, mandated that grade-school children be taught "the history of the origin and growth of the social, economic, and cultural development of the United States, of American family life, and of the high standard of living enjoyed by citizens of the United States as will tend to instill into every boy and girl a determination to preserve these principles and ideals."[5] Thus studying history became a lesson in patriotism, an attempt to validate the Cold War status quo.

Likewise, "citizenship education"—to which the study of history was central—became a fundamental priority of schools as school boards realized the need to distinguish the American way of life from Communism. As William F. Russell, president of Columbia University's Teachers College, noted in 1953 in regard to the ambitious new Citizenship Education Project, "There will obviously be far less need for teachers' oaths, Communist banning, and textbook inquiries when pupils are engaged in powerful programs of Americanism." Numerous states passed laws requiring citizenship or civic education programs, which in practice were little more than lessons in Americanism versus Communism (a "history" textbook used in Louisiana actually took this as its title). This approach to history was in marked contrast to the critical approach to history advocated by progressive educators in the 1920s and 1930s: those educators had argued that "education for citizenship" would emphasize critical thinking and human values rather than patriotism and would stress the value of public service over the mere attainment of wealth.[6]

If texts like progressive educator Harold Rugg's social studies series were criticized by right-wingers in the 1930s because the books "tried to give the child an unbiased viewpoint instead of teaching him real Americanism," by the 1950s the Right had clearly won the battle for control of American school textbooks, notwithstanding ongoing accusations of liberal bias in textbooks. Textbooks on U.S. history, under intense scrutiny from the Right, were, in effect, "changed to suit [the] Cold War" (as Ralph Ellison charged in an article for the *Daily Worker* in 1954). Tracking changes in school history textbooks over the course of the twentieth century, Frances FitzGerald found that although several of the 1930s texts she examined were "clearly the work of liberals," by the 1950s, all references to poverty in America were eliminated, and the emphasis was on the United States' global leadership in the "struggle for democracy." In postwar textbooks, the United States is portrayed "as playing an essentially benevolent role in the world," and by the middle of the decade, history in the texts becomes subordinated to the struggle against Communism; indeed, the emphasis shifted almost entirely from history per se to comparing "the Russian and the American way[s] of life." According to FitzGerald, in some texts, "the morbid fear of Communism becomes an overriding passion—to the point where . . . the whole of American history appears a mere prologue to the struggle with the 'Reds.'"[7]

Popular culture showed a similar trend, with television and movies endlessly replaying the American tradition of red-hunting through enormously popular westerns and through historical programming more generally. Pointing to "the wave of live-action history films that [Disney's] studio began churning out early in the 1950s," historian Steve Watts argues that the "turn to history" during this period "was itself a clear product of the Cold War, since respect for the past had begun to emerge as a crucial article of faith in the anti-Communist creed."[8]

But respect for the past was also an article of faith in the Left's creed, and leftists turned to the past to challenge the status quo rather than to uphold it. The Right did gain control of the textbook market, and blacklists erased much

of the Popular Front structure of feeling from mass culture. However, a significant proportion of trade children's books about American history and tradition, which escaped the kind of scrutiny paid to textbooks, represented a kind
of return of the repressed. While civic education programs and history courses
used textbooks glorifying America's heritage, supplementing these textbooks
were dozens of Left-authored trade books on American history and folklore
that drew upon American tradition in a very different way. Moreover, the very
factors that made history and civic education courses critical to the Cold War
struggle not only created markets for books like *Americanism versus Communism*, but also for books such as *River Road*, which, likewise, explored the
nature of American tradition.

We, the People

What is at stake, of course, in defining "tradition," are claims to power and
authority in the present. Tradition in general and history in particular were
an "arsenal for liberation" for the Popular Front Left, providing, as radical historian Herbert Aptheker put it, "sustenance, guidance, courage, dignity, [and]
maturity." Writing for *New Masses* in 1944, Henrietta Buckmaster insisted,
"History has no value whatsoever unless it becomes to us a living instrument
for explaining how and why and when and with what weapons the people of the
world have fought for progress, for enlargement of life, for defeat of whatever
would seek to rob man of his birthright."[9]

In challenging master narratives of American history, especially through
core figures of American history and myth, leftists attempted to challenge the
hegemony of those currently in power. They did so by tracing lines of connection between popular heroes like Lincoln and members of the contemporary working class (both of whom leftists tended to invest with more hostility toward racism than they actually possessed); by implicitly or explicitly
aligning American "revolutionary" struggles against a corrupt, undemocratic
power with contemporary struggles on the part of disfranchised and marginalized groups; and by aligning the battle for freedoms protected in the Bill
of Rights—e.g., freedom of speech and freedom of the press—with contemporary struggles for free expression and belief. In general, whether rewriting
master narratives or recovering buried, untold stories, their project was simply
to show what they believed to be the truth of history, on the assumption that
"truth is revolutionary."[10]

Early socialist and Communist publications for children reflect a desire
to draw lessons from the past and rather baldly express the ideological orientation of their authors. A series on the "History of Our Country" in the

Little Socialist Magazine for Boys and Girls (1909–1912) emphasized "truths" about American history not taught to children in schools and debunked the "myths" that were propagated as history: Thomas Paine was the real father of our country, not George Washington; George Washington could, and did, tell lies; and the American Revolution was inspired not by the masses but by those in power, since "the masses of any nation never made war on any other nation." In the 1930s the *New Pioneer*'s regular feature on "American History Retold in Pictures" would have a more revolutionary slant, emphasizing the consistent oppression of the working class at the hands of powerful elites and the common cause between white workers and people of color (see figure 2.4). When leftists turned their energies away from creating literature for "young revolutionists" and toward creating books for the masses of children, the nation's "immense revolutionary tradition" still seemed like the obvious place to begin. As Jean Simon put it in her 1935 call for accessible, progressive children's literature, "if we want Daniel Boone to belong to us, we must make him come to life for ourselves."[11]

Leo Huberman's *We, the People* is paradigmatic of the Left's attempts to reclaim a master narrative of the American national past in a way that draws upon Marxist principles but resists the kind of sectarian rhetoric that could drive away liberal and progressive readers. Originally published by Harper in 1932, the book was revised and reprinted in 1940, 1947, and 1952, after which Harper stopped reprinting the book (Huberman's "unfriendly" testimony before the McCarthy committee probably had something to do with that decision). Over the years, *We, the People* received praises from groups, institutions, and publications ranging from the Child Study Association, the Progressive Education Association, and the New York Public Library to the *New Masses*, making it a model of how to connect the radical agenda with that of progressives and liberals.[12] Still, if the book's explicit anticapitalism made it an unlikely text for the Cold War, its problematic racial and gender politics ultimately made it an unlikely text for the Left as well, predicting the shift away from sweeping master narratives and toward individual stories of minorities and women.

Accentuated by evocative illustrations by Thomas Hart Benton in what Denning would describe as a "proletarian grotesque style," *We, the People* recasts the whole of Euro-American history from the perspective of workers, pioneers, and farmers. Huberman's basic narrative framework echoes Frederick Jackson Turner's famous 1893 frontier thesis, which held that successive American frontiers offered continual rebirth and renewal for the American people, allowing virtuous men to escape the excesses and materialism of the East by heading west into the primitive wilderness, which they could tame and cultivate. Huberman glorifies the traits supposedly inherent to the pioneer and the frontiersman: his "hatred for pomp," his "belief in equality and freedom,"

FACTORY WORKERS

Figure 7.1. Illustration by Thomas Hart Benton from *We, the People* by Leo Huberman. Forlorn laborers trudge off to another day's work in the factory. New York: Harper, 1932, 1947, 1952; copyright resumed by Monthly Review Press. Reprinted by permission of Monthly Review Foundation.

his independence (Huberman says little about the pioneer woman).[13] In celebrating the pioneer, he displays a resigned attitude toward the unfortunate and unjust—though inevitable—displacement of the Indians, who ultimately stand in the way of progress.

Thomas Hart Benton's pen-and-ink illustrations support the populist, anti-capitalist tone of Huberman's text with images of raucous Mississippi boatmen; the rugged cowboy; Indians sorrowfully retreating from the frontiersmen's pointed guns; railroad workers; and factory laborers trudging wearily toward another day's work (figure 7.1). The image of forlorn laborers belies the power they assume in the book as they come to learn the value of "working-class organization," though it is clear throughout Huberman's tale that power and law have historically served to protect capital.[14]

Huberman builds upon a familiar narrative of democracy in the West triumphing over privilege in the East, and, in the tradition of progressive historians, economic explanations dominate the movement of Huberman's work. Huberman argues, for instance, that divisions in the antebellum South were based on class more than race (a few slave owners had power over a mass of common or poor whites, as well as over enslaved blacks, Huberman tells us). In the North there were "daring businessmen" and "canny schemers," "who would stop at nothing in their desire for more profits." These men had the power over a "larger group, . . . the army of labor, the men, women and children who did the actual work of digging, building, making." In later editions of the book, which included a discussion of the New Deal, Huberman praises Franklin Roosevelt's ambitious program but insists that it "did not change the system of private ownership or the means of production in which the primary object is the making of profit." According to Huberman, the real solution to the problems that the depression revealed would be "ultimately to abolish the profit system."[15]

Though Huberman's epic tale of the American working man never really gets past the myths of the "savage" and "vanishing" Indian, and though Huberman subordinates his discussion of racial oppression to that of poor and working-class whites, people of color, especially African Americans, and white ethnics are certainly part of his story. For instance, noting frequent slave uprisings that "American history books hardly ever mention," Huberman makes it clear that "Southern whites were quick to act whenever slaves declared a challenge to their supremacy." Likewise, he acknowledges the violence that accompanied Anglo-American "progress" and links American empire building to the European imperial project.[16]

Ultimately, Huberman makes working-class struggles central, rather than marginal, to American tradition. He not only reclaims Daniel Boone and Abe Lincoln, but also the millions of voiceless, forgotten working people who "built America." Even so, Huberman's reference to "savage Indians" suggests that pioneers like Daniel Boone are "heroes" in large part because they violently displaced native peoples occupying the land claimed as America's "manifest destiny." In other words, the master narrative, in any variation, is inherently racist and in other ways problematic. While the master narrative was bound to show evidence of repressed stories, it was also bound to reveal the power of capitalism and the ideologies that support it.[17]

Juvenile Biographies and the Left-Wing Lincoln

The conflict over Lincoln's legacy suggests the possibilities and limits of the leftist effort, at the height of the Cold War, to reclaim national, or master, narratives. Moreover, as an example of what I would call a "folk biography," combining elements of history, biography, and folklore, it points to the particular appeal of the biographical genre, as well as folklore, for juvenile authors seeking to elucidate a particular set of lessons from the past. Biography's appeal was partially tied to the opportunities in this area because of demand from the educational market. Similar to the effect of the NDEA and other initiatives on the demand for science trade books, the same imperatives that led to civic education programs generated demand for tales of "great" Americans from history and sent publishers scrambling to find writers. Another reason the genre was appealing to left-wing writers was that the conventions of juvenile biography (more so than adult biography) allowed considerable room for imaginatively reconstructing the past. The biographer for children is traditionally given license to recreate dialogue or scenes whose specific parameters are undocumented or to move beyond existing evidence to probe an individual's thoughts, motivations, and aspirations. Indeed, these speculative aspects of juvenile biography, or what might be called their literary elements, are thought to contribute to their truth value, rather than to reveal their authors' biases. Considered from another angle, the appeal of biography to children and to those mediating children's reading is obvious: individuals from the past offer powerful examples of human achievement and will, and children are encouraged to find role models in the figures they read about from the past.[18]

Largely in response to demand from the educational marketplace, many publishers inaugurated major series of juvenile biographies (or nonfiction series that included biographies) in the late 1940s and early 1950s. Several were edited by leftists or people open to working with left-wing writers.[19] Many of these series proved to be enormously popular (children would often read through an entire series on the library shelf, moving in alphabetical order), and the books were often of high quality.[20] Juvenile biographies of historical figures became a staple of the Left during the Cold War as progressive writers, illustrators, and editors learned to marry their agenda to market realities: their "historical" focus resisted "bumping into the controversial issues of the contemporary scene," while the focus upon individuals further couched lessons in the safety and innocuousness of the particular and the anecdotal.[21] Subjects of Left-authored biographies included a range of figures: George Washington, Thomas Jefferson, Ethan Allen, Daniel Boone, Ben Franklin, Johnny Appleseed, Andrew Jackson, Franklin Delano Roosevelt, Haym Solomon, Elizabeth Blackwell, Henry David Thoreau, Nellie Bly, and Emma Lazarus. By the mid-1950s, African-American figures such as Harriet Tubman, Phillis Wheatley, Benjamin Banneker, Jean Baptiste Point Du Sable, Frederick Douglass, Booker T. Washington, George Washington Carver, Paul Robeson, and Mary McLeod Bethune would increasingly stir the imagination of leftists interested in exploring and reinterpreting American tradition. For decades, however, Abraham Lincoln occupied a special position of his own in the leftist imagination. For this reason, we return to the "pink-tinged pages" of River Road.

Published in 1954, River Road arrived on the scene with McCarthy's shadow beside it and the Brown verdict in the wings, and Lincoln's significance to the contemporary scene is never far below the surface. Throughout the story are metaphors of saplings, trees, and wood: Abe is the young green sapling, challenging the ancient hickory and its set ways, its roots that resist the ways of the new. Thinking about the entrenched institution of slavery in the South, Abe asserts:

[A]n idea is like a tree—took a century to grow it—it's against change, conservative by nature, and the axe is the radical—it's got to bite deep and hold, strike into the cleft, hold the cranium open and pour in a new thought, a wedge, until the old knots and old woods accept it, and all the little minds are jolted apart and lie open to reason.[22]

The centrality of slavery in Le Sueur's narrative is key to the "reason" or truths she wished for young readers to glean from the book, deeper human truths that, technically, may not have been truths about Lincoln per se. Most important, the thrust of Le Sueur's Lincoln portrait can easily be extended beyond the historical context of Lincoln's era to condemn 1950s race relations in the South and economic inequality more generally and to celebrate those who voice just, if unpopular, views in repressive times.

Though never claiming to tell it all (*River Road* was "*a* story of Abraham Lincoln," not "*the* story of Abraham Lincoln"), Le Sueur's "selected tradition," particularly because of its contemporary relevance, was vulnerable to challenges. In condemning the book, the *Sentinel* acknowledged that "some people may wonder how a book about Abraham Lincoln could be criticized as subversive." However, the paper's editor explained, "there are others who realize that it has been a long-time tactic of American Communists to sanctify some of their projects by pasting Abraham Lincoln's name over them. The latter will look at this book and realize that Abe has been used again."[23]

Communists, of course, were not the only ones to "use" Lincoln; indeed, his power as myth comes partly from the fact that his memory can be put to so many, often contradictory uses. Lincoln was both a "self-made man" and a "son of the working class," a Republican and a republican, a great compromiser and a man of principle, a southerner, a midwesterner, and a northerner. He was hailed as a hero by Aaron Copland, Carl Sandburg, Dwight D. Eisenhower, Joseph McCarthy, and Martin Luther King. By the 1950s, one could purchase Abe Lincoln Bibles and Abe Lincoln insurance, visit the Lincoln Memorial, celebrate Lincoln's birthday, and read about Lincoln in one of the several thousand biographies, tributes, and other texts dedicated to preserving particular histories and memories of the man. Republicans, Democrats, and Communists claimed to be the rightful heirs of Lincoln's legacy: the Republican party held Lincoln Day dinners (which, according to the *Daily Worker*, were just another occasion to hold "an anti-Soviet, anti-Labor field day"), and Joseph McCarthy quoted Lincoln in 1954 "to support his contention that the mortal danger to the nation was from Communists operating within this country."[24]

Although Carl Sandburg inaugurated Lincoln as the homegrown hero of the Left in 1926 with *Abraham Lincoln: The Prairie Years*, Lincoln became a characteristic icon of the Communist Left in the 1930s. Under the Popular Front, Lincoln, Lenin, and Washington were hailed as the secular trinity of twentieth-century Americanism. Lincoln was the true "son of the working class," the "genuine revolutionary" whom Marx had praised long before CP leader Earl Browder. Communists sponsored the Abraham Lincoln Brigade in support of Spanish loyalists fighting the fascist dictator Francisco Franco, and the 1938 song by Alfred Hayes and Earl Robinson, "Abraham Lincoln," concludes with a verse that asserts, "every year the party [Lincoln] made [the Republicans] says Lincoln's theirs (No Sir)." Speaking in Springfield, Illinois, on Lincoln's birthday in 1936, CP leader Browder insisted that Communists were the only rightful heirs of "the traditions of Lincoln" and that "revolution is the essence of the teachings of Lincoln." Browder's remarks concluded with a Lincoln line that became a favorite among Communists and other radicals: "This country, with its institutions, belongs to the people who inhabit it. Whenever they shall grow weary of the existing government, they can exercise their constitutional right of amending it, or their revolutionary right to dismember or overthrow it."[25]

At least sixty juvenile books about Abraham Lincoln were published between 1945 and 1965 (which added to the 3,958 Lincoln-related titles cataloged in the *Lincoln Bibliography* as of 1945). Of those juvenile books on Lincoln published in the postwar period—arguably the "zenith" of Lincoln's popularity (according to Merrill Peterson)—at least ten of those books, or nearly 20 percent, were by left-wing authors. Le Sueur's is probably the most politically charged, but other Left-authored Lincoln biographies are also inflected with a subtle class-consciousness. For instance, Franklin Folsom's *Real Book about Abraham Lincoln* (written under the pseudonym Michael Gorham), gently plugs "the socialist way of living" by describing Lincoln's attraction to New Harmony in Indiana, "a huge farm where everybody was supposed to work together to help each other out. No one was going to make any profit from anyone else's labor." Like Le Sueur, Folsom highlights the New Orleans trip as a turning point in Abe's life, during which he is said to have told the two friends with him, "If I ever get a chance to hit slavery, I'll hit it hard." The text of *America's Abraham Lincoln* (1957) by May McNeer (illustrated by Lynd Ward) gives little attention to racial questions, but Ward's illustrations, which show the revolutionary John Brown in heroic and even prophetic dimensions, give another layer to the story (figure 7.2). Finally, *The Boy on Lincoln's Lap* (1955) by Jerrold Beim presents an apt metaphor for the struggle to maintain a particular memory of Lincoln. In this contemporary story, published just a year after McCarthy's censure, a

Figure 7.2. Illustration by Lynd Ward from *America's Abraham Lincoln* by May McNeer. This stirring image of the revolutionary figure John Brown adds a political dimension to May McNeer's biography of Abraham Lincoln. Copyright © 1957 by May McNeer Ward and Lynd Ward; renewed 1985 by May McNeer Ward. Reprinted by permission of Houghton Mifflin Company. All rights reserved.

group of boys who like to play around a statue of Lincoln stop a troublemaker from defacing the statue with graffiti.[26]

More conservative books, like Clara Ingram Judson's *Abraham Lincoln: Friend of the People* (1950) or Genevieve Foster's *Abraham Lincoln* (1950), downplay Lincoln's opposition to slavery, focusing on his primary commitment to saving the union, and they deemphasize an antiaristocratic outlook that is played up in Left-authored books. If Lincoln's strong opposition to slavery distinguishes Le Sueur's book from her literary father, Sandburg, whose antiracism is implicit rather than explicit, it is in pronounced contrast to Judson's portrait, in which the slavery question is barely raised. Though Judson does acknowledge that "Lincoln believed slavery was an evil," she emphasizes that "he did not favor abolition as the remedy." She mentions Lincoln's trip to New Orleans and comments upon how the sight of a slave auction affected the young Lincoln, but her discussion of the auction lasts only two pages, in contrast to approximately forty pages in Le Sueur's book. In Judson's book, Lincoln's main interest is saving the union; he expresses none of the hatred of southern aristocracy that is characteristic of Le Sueur's version, and Judson suggests that Lincoln's supposed poverty is a myth: "The Lincolns were comfortable enough according to the standards around Knob Creek."[27]

In the years following the Second World War, historians had begun to challenge the mythic portrait of Abraham Lincoln embraced not only by Communists, but also by progressive historians, who had characterized American history in terms of a conflict between "capital" and "the people." In terms that Clara Ingram Judson would echo in her juvenile biography of Lincoln, Richard Hofstadter noted in 1948 in his famous essay "Abraham Lincoln and the Self-Made Myth":

> Lincoln may have become involved in a gross inconsistency over slavery and the Negro, but this was incidental to his main concern. Never much troubled about the Negro, he had always been most deeply interested in the fate of free republicanism and its bearing upon the welfare of the common white man with whom he identified himself.

Le Sueur, not surprisingly, objected to Hofstadter's "terrible influence," writing in a letter to fellow midwesterner Jack Conroy, "Hofstadter is one of the most reactionary and poisonous historians."[28]

Le Sueur, whose own family had been part of an American radical tradition, deeply resented the idea that radicalism was somehow un-American. Le Sueur's mother and grandmother had been fiery suffragists, and her stepfather, Arthur Le Sueur (whom she identified as her father), was a close friend of socialist leaders Eugene Debs and Victor Berger, who had been elected as Milwaukee's mayor in 1912. As a child, she had known Carl Sandburg, whose writings on Lincoln directly inspired Le Sueur. Her attraction to Marxism and Communism grew out of an upbringing steeped in "indigenous traditions of protest," including the People's party, the Non-Partisan League, and the IWW, traditions which drew a number of antiauthoritarian midwesterners, Le Sueur among them, into the orbit of the CP.[29] Le Sueur's claim to a connection with her subject is bolstered by a device she uses in most of her children's books: she tells the stories as though they were reported by "my grandmother," an apparently age-defying figure who knew Abe Lincoln, Nancy Hanks, Davy Crockett, and Johnny Appleseed. This device emphasizes the oral, folk quality of the stories, but it also directly ties Le Sueur to that folk tradition.

It is understandable then that Le Sueur would reject the postwar trend toward consensus history, personified by Hofstadter, for in her mind his work was only a more moderate version of the right-wing extremism represented by the *Sentinel* exposé, which sought to deny radicals like Le Sueur a stake in the American tradition. Writing in her journal, she reflected upon the "conspiratorial" effort of the Right to make the work of people like her appear to be subversive and un-American; for instance, the *Sentinel*'s revelation that Le Sueur wrote for the Communist *Worker* was in reality no revelation at all. "[F]ar from being a conspiracy it is a public fact, widely advertized [*sic*], both here and abroad that I have written publicly and proudly for 29 years," Le Sueur noted.

Such innuendo about Le Sueur's secret past and affiliations produced in her a response not unlike the one she attributed to Lincoln in the face of watching a slave auction: a feeling of being a stranger in one's own country. "It is very hard living in this atmosphere of conspiracy not to at times feel its cold shadow," Le Sueur noted in her journal. "I even find myself peeking into river road [sic] half expecting to meet some dire language unknown and unseen even to myself. Such is the power of this blood and thunder, cops and robbers spillane [sic] doings." Her anger was not just about her own situation, her own reputation, or her own misconstrued motivation, however. "If it were only a question of the river road . . . ," her journal continues:

> but what about all the great books on the democratic heritage, from which my life and my books stem and which express the great stream of the american [sic] tradition of the common man. Of the whole great democratic struggle from Jefferson, jackson, lincoln, also bob la follette roosevelt [sic] and my father. . . . what about Sandburg my literary father, and his volumes on Lincoln which more eloquently than I bring forth the same democratic root of lincoln.

Indeed, she reflects, "what about . . . the great history of milwaukee [sic] itself . . . so rich in this struggle and so courageous in its collision with these same forces the sentinel [sic] represents."[30]

She sent a copy of the book to the mayor of Milwaukee, noting her family's association with that other history of Milwaukee, along with a letter asking him to judge the book on its own merits, rather than through *Sentinel* reporter Robert Riordan's "distorted view of it." Turning her guns on the *Sentinel*, she wrote an angry letter to the editor criticizing the paper's suggestion that "a book be judged by the political views or private lives or associations of its author" and its presumption that "the American child must be mentally goose stepped into making up his mind about the ideas he examines."[31]

Sentinel reporter Robert Riordan had argued that Le Sueur misused Lincoln's legacy by distorting it to serve the "Communist line," identifying passages which, in his mind, would give the impression that "religion is a myth" and "that Abe Lincoln's society was divided into two hostile classes; a minority of rich people and a vast mass of oppressed workers and farmers." Riordan seemed to be the only reviewer who found its pages to be dangerously "pink" (which makes it unlikely that children noticed the book's politics at all: as fourteen-year-old Elizabeth Allen of Boone, Iowa wrote of *Little Brother* and *Nancy Hanks*, "I liked the books very much. They have nice pictures to illustrate the story too. I liked them because they are easy to read and interesting."). However, if one was looking for politics in the book and knew where to look, it was not so hard to find them. Thus the right-wing Riordan was not the only one to emphasize the book's political message. A letter to the *Daily Worker* from Eloise MacAllister (who may have been a friend of Le Sueur's), which sang the praises of *River Road*, singled out many of the same passages that Riordan did. MacAllister, however, hailed the book for condemning the "rich leisure of the few" and for celebrating the "plain people in the long struggle." In other words, for people in the Communist movement, the book clearly spoke to some vision of a shared people's past; whether that vision was un-American was debatable.[32] Le Sueur herself apparently did not see the book as radical or subversive or even unusual in its outlook.[33]

Moreover, the positive reception that the book received just about everywhere but in the pages of the *Sentinel* would suggest that most readers were more struck by the poetics of the book than by the politics. They were deeply stirred by the imagery and the intensity of Le Sueur's portrait, and they did not question its fundamental truths. Opening a discussion of *River Road* for NBC's "Carnival of Books," recorded in 1954 (prior to the *Sentinel* exposé, which caused the program to be pulled from NBC's national schedule), the program's host, Ruth Harshaw, told Le Sueur, "I don't think I ever really understood the teenage Lincoln before." One of the St. Paul high school students taking part in the discussion agreed, noting that the book made her think of Lincoln as "more of a man, not just a character."[34] Perhaps the extent to which people were moved by Le Sueur's story is what people like Robert Riordan found so maddening. Did these naïve readers know they were learning about Lincoln from a red?

Mentioning how powerful she found the book, another student taking part in the "Carnival of Books" discussion asked Le Sueur whether all of the incidents in the book were true. Le Sueur responded by saying that she "wouldn't dare" make up anything about Abe Lincoln. Asked why she chose to write about Lincoln, Le Sueur responded by telling the children that her own family "came up the same trail" as Lincoln. "I always felt like I was part of the same country and the same experience."[35]

Keeping the Tune but Changing the Words

Le Sueur's use of Lincoln—as a figure bound as much to legend as to history— is suggestive of the way in which American folklore was refunctioned by leftists, who capitalized on the broad recognition of folk heroes like Lincoln and Davy Crockett. Folklore had appealing, archetypal qualities that spoke to children, and for teachers, folklore represented a patriotic way to talk about "the rank and file of the people" at a time when "class" had fallen out of the national vocabulary. Moreover, the same imperatives that created demand for supplemental works in American history created markets for material on American folklore and folk heroes.[36] Perhaps most important, folklore was also endlessly malleable. As folklorist B. A. Botkin maintained, "What makes a thing folklore is not only that you have heard it before, yet want to hear it again, because it is different, but also that you want to tell it again in your own way, because it's any body's [sic] property." Botkin's open-ended view of folklore and his interest in how elements of an oppressive social order could be reemployed to help create a very different society was a direct or indirect inspiration to a number of left-wing writers, including Le Sueur. Botkin headed a League of American Writers panel on the use of folk materials, which Le Sueur probably attended. There, composer Earl Robinson aptly encapsulated the strategy of refunctioning, suggesting that "if you choose a tune which is hallowed and sanctified by the people having sung it and loved it, then they will be interested in your words also."[37]

The popular association between the folk and the Left may be one of "the most important and lasting effect[s] of the Popular Front in the cultural realm," according to historian Robbie Lieberman. For all of their commitment to materialism and the "truth" of history, by the mid-1930s, Communists had upgraded folklore from the status of superstitious relic to storehouse of worker empowerment.[38] As the lore and lyrics of the common man, often depicting "the triumph of the laborer over his environment," the appeal of folklore and folksong to the Popular Front Left is easy to imagine. Thus Elie Siegmeister would proclaim of southern sharecroppers, whose songs he celebrated in *Work and Sing: A Collection of the Songs that Built America* (1944), "[O]ut of their drudgery, sweat, and toil, they come up smiling and singing, telling us of the great future of the common man." Books like *The Fast Sooner Hound* (1942) and *Slappy Hooper: The Wonderful Sign Painter* (1946) by Jack Conroy and Arna Bontemps show machines being outwitted and individuals struggling to maintain control over the conditions of their work, in tales adapted from the oral narratives of workers. Bontemps would later collaborate with Langston Hughes on *The Book of Negro Folklore* (1958), a compilation (intended primarily for adults) that repeatedly highlighted "weakness overcoming strength through cunning" at a time when, according to the left-wing *Masses and Mainstream*, the "fashion among folklorists is to rebuke those who find social meaning in such material."[39] Irwin Shapiro's stories of the pioneer Davy Crockett, the immigrant steel man Joe Magarac, and the mighty railroad worker John Henry can also be placed within this tradition of oppressed people triumphing over seemingly insurmountable odds.

Although the folk—along with history more generally—were certainly enlisted in the Cold War cause, the malleability of American legend made it an apt arena for competing attempts to speak of, and for, the people, among whom

Meridel Le Sueur certainly counted herself. Leftist tales of revolutionary general Francis Marion (the "Swamp Fox"), the Newbery Award–winning *Johnny Tremain*, and left-wing versions of the Davy Crockett story directly competed with Disney film and television versions of these stories and often benefited from their popularity.[40] Popular Front patriotism in texts like these was almost indistinguishable from the Cold War patriotism of the Disney movies: Francis Marion, for instance, in both the Disney and left-wing versions, is a populist hero who resists tyranny, though in one instance the tyranny is, implicitly, the totalitarianism of Communism, and in the other it is the oppressive capitalist state. Such confusion points to the limits of master narratives as vehicles for anticapitalist messages but does not negate their powerful potential.

In the same way that traditional Appalachian folksongs were made into union ballads and, conversely, blue bloods like Pete Seeger and Alan Lomax transformed themselves into banjo-twanging folk heroes, writers like Meridel Le Sueur and Irwin Shapiro attempted, for instance, to transform Davy Crockett, a figure alternately invoked as a crude, racist, and chauvinistic "mouthpiece for jingoistic expansion" or, more famously, as a "Cold war icon," into an antiracist, anticapitalist, and even feminist friend of the Indians and the workers. The central enemy in Crockett tales by Le Sueur and Shapiro is capitalism, personified in the shady figure of the Yankee peddler, Slickerty Sam. As Le Sueur puts it in *Chanticleer of Wilderness Road: A Story of Davy Crockett* (1951), this man of "many disguises" could "talk a mean fight, take candy from a baby, and my grandmother and all her neighbors of true grit and whole hearts, working from can't see to can't see, thought this fellow a most pestiferous, cantankerous old codger, who was against all work of any nature and wanted only to turn an easy coonskin."[41]

If Disney's Crockett is "huntin' the redskins down" in the popular made-for-television *Davy Crockett: King of the Wild Frontier*, in Shapiro's *Yankee Thunder: The Legendary Life of Davy Crockett* (1944), Davy calls himself "one o' the tribe" and makes peace between whites and Indians after a peddler "cheated the tribe" and convinced them that "a white man couldn't be trusted." And while the original Crockett almanacs have Crockett declare that he could "swallow a nigger whole without choking if you butter his head and pin his ears back," Le Sueur had *her* Crockett turn this boast into a jibe against the peddler: "You're a slick one," Crockett says to the peddler in Le Sueur's version. "Grease your head and pin down your ears, and I could swallow you at one bite." Crockett himself and the statements he purportedly made are here refunctioned with new meanings. Thus although historian Steve Watts makes an elegant argument for the ways in which Disney's Crockett "symbolized the American character in the death struggle with the Communist foe," Crockett could also represent "the people" against corrupt power. As Le Sueur's Crockett tells his son, "I am a great lover of

Figure 7.3. Slickerty Sam Patch, the peddler. Illustration by James Daugherty from *Yankee Thunder: The Legendary Life of Davy Crockett* by Irwin Shapiro. Through the figure of Slickerty Sam, capitalism becomes the villain in this version of the Crockett story, but the image (probably unintentionally) evokes Jewish stereotypes. New York: Messner, 1944. Used with permission (to the extent that they may own the rights) courtesy of Charles M. Daugherty Estate.

my country and my people . . . but not of its office holders, land grabbers, pork barrel plutocrats, psalm-singin' bigots." The power of such familiar tales with "new words" was evident in the quite spectacular sales of anything Crockett related, and both Le Sueur and Shapiro were direct beneficiaries of the Disney-inspired Crockett craze in 1955.[42]

The tricky maneuvers required to recuperate a figure like Crockett as an anticapitalist, antiracist, feminist friend of the Indians predicted the search for new heroes who were not as complicit in a male, Anglo-American narrative, with all of the contradictions this narrative embodied. Botkin acknowledged the contradictory aspects of folk heroes, noting the "essential viciousness" of many beloved American heroes, "especially in their treatment of minorities—Indians, Negroes, Mexicans, Chinese, etc." Le Sueur and Shapiro, undoubtedly aware of this issue, nonetheless capitalized on the popularity of Crockett and tried to recast his memory in new terms, for instance, making the peddler Slickerty Sam the villain rather than the Indians. But it is telling that James Daugherty's image of Slickerty Sam the peddler in Shapiro's *Yankee Thunder* clearly (if unintentionally) evokes the Jewish Shylock figure (figure 7.3). Daugherty's own Newbery Award–winning *Daniel Boone* (1939) similarly celebrated

Figure 7.4. Illustration by James Daugherty from *John Henry and His Double-Jointed Steam Drill* by Irwin Shapiro. This picture of John Henry's wife offered a powerful image of a strong black woman. New York: Messner, 1945. Used with permission (to the extent that they may own the rights) courtesy of Charles M. Daugherty Estate.

the pioneer in part by showing his bravery against savage Indians. Even the *New Masses*, which heartily recommended many of Daugherty's books, including *Daniel Boone*, seemed to miss this contradiction.[43] Daugherty's images of African Americans—for instance, his portrait of John Henry's powerful wife (figure 7.4)—were clearly intended to be sympathetic, but in some instances his representations of African Americans veer dangerously close to caricature.

Shapiro and, even more so, Le Sueur, made women powerful figures in their folk retellings: the women in their Crockett tales, for instance, who can "outrun, outjump, outfight, and outscream any critter in creation," make a sharp contrast to the demure, June Cleaver type who plays Crockett's wife in the Disney version. But even devoting a whole book to Nancy Hanks, as Le Sueur does, fails to counter the assumption that women can only enter national narratives as "republican mothers," supportive sisters, and dutiful daughters to the real historical actors. Perhaps tellingly, the stories that Le Sueur and Shapiro told about figures not part of an Anglo-American tradition—for example, Shapiro's book about the immigrant steel man Joe Magarac and Le Sueur's *Sparrow Hawk*—never managed to sustain the sales of the Crockett books.[44] However, they predicted a shifting focus of the Left, one that would eventually be supported by a somewhat ironic Cold War imperative to challenge racism, especially in schools.

By the mid-1950s, leftists had significantly shifted their attention toward minorities and women for a number of reasons. The "essential viciousness" of many traditional heroes, or what we might call their basic commitment to capitalism, was one thing. But a changing political and social climate and a corresponding change in the Communist movement's focus also spurred this shift. For one thing, direct critiques of capitalism became too self-evidently "subversive" in the postwar period. For another thing, the Left lost much of its labor movement base as many members of the white working class abandoned the remnants of the Popular Front and moved to the Right. Partly as a consequence of these developments, civil rights struggles and gender equity increasingly occupied the energy and imagination of a Cold War Left looking for revitalization.[45]

Le Sueur's *Sparrow Hawk* (1950), though written prior to *River Road*, was suggestive of the shift away from Anglo-American heroes toward figures less inextricably tied to the dominant culture. The book focused upon the friendship between Sparrow Hawk, an adopted son of the Sauk Indian leader Black Hawk, and Huck, whose very name conjures images of youthful independence, aversion to aristocracy, and interracial friendship (and, again, places Le Sueur squarely in an American literary tradition). In this tale, poor whites and Indians share a commitment to "corn democracy," that is, a communal ethic, which is threatened by land-grabbing capitalists. Offering a striking contrast to more popular images of screeching, savage Indians, *Sparrow Hawk*, perhaps not surprisingly, never achieved the sales of Le Sueur's books on Lincoln, Crockett, or even Nancy Hanks. It did, however, contain more revolutionary messages—which, incidentally, were apparently never challenged. In one scene, young Sparrow Hawk proclaims, "Corn is like land. . . . It belongs to all. . . . It belongs to the person who uses it and makes things grow. All red men have equal rights to land and corn." (Presumably, he means native people, rather than all of the "reds" who share this communal ethic.) Huck agrees, marveling with Sparrow Hawk about the corn they have cultivated together: "You see, both our nations got corn democracy. Some hogs want all the land and corn, they want to root everybody out of the trough. Sometimes you got to do away with a hog that makes the rest thin and wild."[46]

Several books by writers on the Left attempted to bring an American Indian point of view to U.S. history. Franklin Folsom's *Real Book about Indians* (1953)—published under the name Michael Gorham—opens with the story of Columbus's landing, told from the point of view of the Indians observing the ship's arrival on the shores of San Salvador. The Indians watch the explorers plant a stick with cloth fluttering from the top into the ground; they notice the pale creatures' hairy bodies, their guns, and their knives; and they wonder why the pale men do not offer gifts, a pipe, or some sign of friendship. "The naked people standing on the beach were looking at the first white men they had ever seen—at the first armor and swords and guns and sailing ships, at the first flag carried into their land by a conquering invader." Certainly it was unusual to call Columbus and his men "conquering invaders" in an age when American exceptionalism was a reigning paradigm in the academy and westerns typically perpetuated the idea that "the only good Indian is a dead Indian."

Other ethnic minorities, including Jews, received some attention from left-wing writers in trade books (e.g., in Howard Fast's biography of Haym Solomon, financier of the American Revolution, or in Eve Merriam's biography of Emma Lazarus), but especially in light of the growing civil rights struggle, African-American history in particular came to be seen as perhaps the primary "arsenal for liberation," to borrow Herbert Aptheker's formulation. Fortuitously, leftists' interest in recovering African-American history was served by Cold War pressure to eliminate segregation and demonstrate official commitment to racial equality.[47] As civil rights became a Cold War imperative, schools began to purchase books relating to African-American history and tradition as part of their programs in civic education. Thus there emerged a small but growing market for what was known as "interracial books." Even so, it would be at least another decade before the "all-white world of children's literature"—and school textbooks—would receive more widespread challenges. Leftists drew attention to civil rights issues, but their power was limited as opponents of civil rights drew attention to the Left.

"An Honest Interpretation of American History"

Leftists, for their part, believed that African-American history, told truthfully, would necessarily highlight the oppressive nature of capitalism and the continuing struggles of contemporary African Americans. But they found few schools willing to broach this history. At a 1951 Jefferson School forum on the Problems of Progressive Parents, one of the chief complaints voiced by parents was that "nowhere in school do their children get an honest interpretation of American history, and of the role played by Negro, Jewish, and other peoples in building our country." Though African Americans and other minorities were already underrepresented in school curricula, the gains in diversifying the curriculum made through the brief, World War II–inspired "intercultural education" movement fell by the wayside shortly after the war. Certainly it was difficult to discuss, for example, African Americans, without acknowledging the emptiness of American democratic rhetoric and the failure of the American dream when applied to blacks in the United States.[48]

Postwar school textbooks tended to uphold the racial status quo by making minorities invisible or by showing them in demeaning and stereotyped roles. In a 1947 study of 146 social studies textbooks undertaken by Aubrey Haan for the liberal journal *Common Ground*, of 75 illustrations showing

"Negroes"—out of 40,000 pages examined—"14 showed slaves performing personal services for white masters or mistresses; 12 portrayed cotton pickers; 10 were unclad primitive blacks in Africa, 6 were porters, 6 were banana, tobacco or sugar cane planters or harvesters, 3 were waiters; [and] 6 were laborers in South African mines."[49]

Many American history textbooks portrayed slaves as "happy" and "irresponsible, if not lazy," and slave owners as "kindly, humane men." The majority diminished or simply ignored the historic achievements of African Americans and other minority groups, and slave revolts almost never made it into history books. Mirroring the "lost cause" school of historiography, which valorized the Old South and painted its aftermath as a "tragic era," Reconstruction was typically described from the former slave holders' point of view. The *Common Ground* study found that highly respected social studies texts described black lawmakers elected during Reconstruction as having "had no idea of business." They "ran their states deeply into debt" and raised taxes to an unbearable level until "the Southerners [i.e., white southerners] could endure the situation no longer." "The Southerners" then proceeded to prevent African Americans from voting. Such treatment of Reconstruction was symptomatic of a larger pattern of bias and distortion, according to Haan:

> In the same way the texts omit the positive contributions of the Negro people to the physical upbuilding of the nation, their creation of an original music, their part in all the wars the United States has fought, their importance in labor and political history, and their development of educational institutions.

The treatment of Asian Americans, Jews, and recent immigrants, Haan found, was similarly characterized by omission, distortion, and stereotype. A discussion of textbook bias in *Jewish Life* likewise pointed to a prejudice against colonial people and certain "unwelcome" immigrants.[50]

The bias against African Americans was enforced by textbook publishers' fear of losing southern markets. Textbook adoptions were usually carried out state by state, with states' approval governing the purchase of all local school materials. Anything portraying African Americans in a positive light or seeming to advocate "interracialism" was unlikely to pass muster with southern school boards. Not surprisingly, anti-Communist hysteria also kept publishers from correcting racial bias in textbooks. Southern segregationists routinely argued that challenges to racial segregation were Communist-inspired; after the *Brown* decision in 1954, mandating school desegregation, for example, Governor Herman Talmadge of Georgia attributed the victory for integration to "vicious and dangerous brain-washing" by Communist propagandists. The FBI often equated racial mixing and white activism on behalf of African Americans with Communist subversion, and the Cold War atmosphere of repression may have reinforced this association.[51]

Dorothy Sterling's half-joking insistence that any pre-1965 book showing sympathy for the plight of African Americans was probably by a Communist shows the other side of this coin. Involvement in the Civil Rights movement, especially on the part of whites, was inseparable from Cold War politics. Although dissenters were often unfairly classified as "reds" or "agitators," it is also true that left-wingers were a significant bloc in the early Civil Rights movement, and this is especially true for whites who were involved. Given the repressive political climate, individuals not directly affected by racial oppression were likely to get involved with civil rights struggles only if they were activists who viewed racial discrimination as a more systemic problem. As we have seen, Jews were particularly outspoken on race issues. Mark Naison points out that many left-wing Jews "saw the struggle against racial discrimination as the harbinger of a revolution in ethnic relations that would allow them to assimilate into the American nation without feeling defensive about their background." *Jewish Life*, which began publication in November 1946 with an explicit goal of "strengthening the ties of the Jewish people with labor, the Negro people, and all oppressed groups," probably gave as much attention to African-American issues as to Jewish issues, and curricula in secular Yiddish schools run by the International Workers Order repeatedly linked the struggles of Jews to those of African Americans.[52]

Although leftists highlighted the suffering of children in general as part of their critique of the Cold War status quo, they paid special attention to the burdens suffered by African-American children, who experienced not only economic deprivation and the psychological effects of legal and de facto segregation, but also state-sanctioned violence in the South. In *The Game of Death: The Effects of the Cold War on Our Children*, Albert Kahn presented a long list of the "crimes, atrocities, and frightful violations of the individual being committed against Negro children and youth in the U.S."[53] Kahn pointed, for instance, to the slaying of Emmet Till by unchecked vigilantes and to the practice of trying black children of twelve, thirteen, and fourteen years of age as adults and imposing sentences far surpassing the weight of their crimes. Incidents like these seemed to show that black children were being denied their right to childhood.

At the core of black children's deprivation, according to many leftists, was "the calculated destruction of their heritage." As playwright and activist Lorraine Hansberry noted, "From the time he is born the Negro child is surrounded by a society organized to convince him that he belongs to a people with a past so worthless and shameful that it amounts to no past at all." How were African-

American children expected to grow up with any hope for the future, indeed, how could they possibly be inspired to struggle for equality themselves when history, for them, was "shorn of its power to enlighten or inspire"? This evisceration of history arguably began with teacher training, and it translated directly into classrooms.[54]

Leftists argued that denying African Americans "an inspiring past worthy of study weakens them and their allies in the present-day efforts for equality and freedom." Part of the effort to keep African Americans "in their place" involved perpetuating the myths that blacks had historically accepted their subordinate position and that they lacked the ability or the desire to participate fully in politics, business, and society, myths that any study of African-American history would quickly explode. Condemning the prejudice in Harlem's schools, former teacher and union activist Alice Citron—one of eight New York City teachers, all of whom were Jewish, who were suspended in 1950—pointed out that the children in these schools got a distorted view of African-American history and culture, or no view at all:

> They will never learn that their people fought for freedom. They will never learn in the public schools that Harriet Tubman, Sojourner Truth, Denmark Vesey, Nat Turner raised the torch of freedom high. They will never hear the name of Frederick Douglass. They will hear instead that the Civil War and the Emancipation Proclamation were a mistake.[55]

Certainly, African-American children were less likely to learn African-American history after teachers like Citron were forced out of the school system. From a poor Jewish family in East Harlem, Citron strongly identified with her black students and, according to Mark Naison:

> made it her personal mission to demonstrate their capabilities, both to themselves and to a skeptical school bureaucracy. She wrote plays for her classes dramatizing themes from black history, took them on field trips and invited them to her home, compiled bibliographies on black history for other teachers in the system, and joined black teachers in agitating for the celebration of Negro History Week.

With Citron as the standard bearer, "activity of this kind became something of a trademark of Communist teachers," says Naison.[56]

Though people on the Left placed special emphasis on the *suffering* of African-American children, activism on the part of people such as Citron suggests that leftists also, increasingly, directed their hopes for social transformation toward them. Aware of what was missing from school curricula, leftists sought other ways to teach history, especially African-American history, to children. As radical teachers like Citron were purged from schools, this became an ever more pressing imperative. Left-wing media began to emphasize African-American struggles, and material directed toward children often highlighted black history. The children's pages of left-wing periodicals like *Fraternal Outlook* and the *Daily Worker* frequently featured events or individuals from African-American history, and secular Yiddish school materials published by the Jewish People's Fraternal Order regularly linked the historic persecution of Jews to that of African Americans. The radical African-American newspaper *Freedom* carried a monthly series of stories for children about African-American figures from history. One month, for example, featured Josiah Henson, upon whose life *Uncle Tom's Cabin* was said to be based, though as writer Linda Lewis notes, "You can see from his real life he was no Uncle Tom at all. He was not meek and humble. He had no love or loyalty for the slave masters." Lewis adds, "Real-life heroes, like the brave Josiah Henson who fought for his people, are better models for us to follow than any old Uncle Toms."[57] Such stories not only provided the children of *Freedom's* left-wing, African-American readers with role models, they also made it clear, in contrast to the myth that Emancipation came only from the efforts of white abolitionists, that African Americans themselves had historically struggled to better their own lives and the lives of their children. However, as important as stories like these were, relatively few children had access to them as long as they circulated primarily in left-wing media.

But it was becoming more possible to tell these stories in children's trade books. If anti-Communist propaganda inhibited the Civil Rights movement and enforced segregation in textbooks well after schools themselves had been integrated, the Cold War also created pressure to stake a stand on civil rights, particularly in response to critiques of American racial practices voiced by Communist countries and leftists within the United States. The situation of African Americans in the United States grossly undermined official U.S. slogans of democracy and equality that were loudly trumpeted abroad, contributing to widespread support among northerners for the *Brown* decision in 1954 and grudging acceptance of it in most parts of the South. Thus, while textbooks remained, on the whole, "lily white," Langston Hughes's experience with Franklin Watts suggests that despite the pressure from southern markets, a number of trade book publishers recognized an untapped market and also a chance to make a statement in favor of civil rights.[58]

Because trade books were published in smaller quantities than textbooks and required a smaller investment of time and money, publishers could afford

Figure 7.5. Harriet Tubman. Illustration by Lynd Ward from *North Star Shining* by Hildegarde Hoyt Swift. Text reads, in part: "I was Harriet Tubman, who would not stay in bondage. . . . I was Harriet Tubman who could not stay in freedom, / While her brothers were enslaved." Permission courtesy of Robin Ward Savage and Nanda Ward.

to take greater risks on them. So while they were still a rarity, books with African-American characters and subject matter began to pop up more frequently starting around 1945. *Two Is a Team* (see figure 4.1), for instance, came out that year, and Hildegarde Hoyt Swift's *North Star Shining: A Pictorial History of the American Negro*, with illustrations by Lynd Ward (figure 7.5), came out in 1947. Despite initial hesitation among several publishers to take on the latter book when Swift proposed it in 1945, by that fall several firms were bidding for it, and one editor told Swift, "You don't seem to know what a good thing you have." The *Brown* decision in 1954 accelerated the trend toward "interracial books," most dealing with African-American history.[59] Once again, the interests of people in the Communist Left dovetailed with imperatives that created new markets for exactly the kinds of books they wanted to write.

By the mid-1950s, the Cold War trend toward history-related library purchases increasingly began to include black history and biography. Historical biographies were popular and less controversial than books dealing with contemporary race relations not only because they depicted a time in the past, but also because their focus on individuals could suggest that racial struggles and African-American achievement were more the exception than the norm. But for children, black and white, who were encouraged to identify with the black protagonists, these books were a source of pride and sympathetic understanding.

Black History and the "Woman Question"

Although African-American men like Frederick Douglass, Benjamin Banneker, George Washington Carver, Charles Drew, and even Booker T. Washington were celebrated by left-wing writers, in this project of recovering African-American history, the history of black *women* was increasingly given a prominent role as well. By the late 1940s, Communists considered the position of "the Negro woman" to be "a pivotal one in all democratic struggles," because of her "triple oppression" as African American, worker, and woman. Historian Kate Weigand maintains, "in the racist and sexist atmosphere of the 1950s, [white] Communists were probably the only white political activists who were thinking and writing so much about black women's particular social, economic, and political circumstances." In the same way that the abolitionist movement spurred women's rights activism in the nineteenth century, among Communists in the mid-twentieth century, sustained attention to the problem of "white chauvinism" created at least rhetorical acknowledgment of "male chauvinism" as another factor that inhibited unity on the Left and thus served capitalism.[60]

The "woman question" had itself remained relatively unexamined in Left-authored children's literature until the 1947 publication of Lorraine Beim's *Sugar and Spice*, a novel for adolescents (the *young adult* classification had not yet come into popular usage), which highlighted issues that Betty Friedan would claim to have discovered more than fifteen years later. Ann, the protagonist of *Sugar and Spice*, is discouraged by her family from going to college to become a psychologist so that her brother, an unenthusiastic student, can afford to go. The story centers on Ann's growing consciousness of her predicament as a woman with ambitions that include, but are not limited to, marrying and having a family. In one scene, her friend from the library, Charlotte, who recently earned her master's degree in psychology (she has no brothers), complains that she should have been made head of a survey but instead the post was given to a man who hadn't finished his degree, while she was sent to the field "to do what is called the leg work." Another young woman comments that although women have more opportunities than they used to, women professionals are still judged on the basis of their sex, not their merits. Ann, struck by the injustice of this situation, insists that something ought to be done. But her friends remind her that the problem goes very deep. "That's the kind of problem we are studying," Charlotte tells Ann. "Attitudes, prejudices, where people get them, where they come from, if possible how to alter or change them." Ann, amazed by all she is hearing, asks if this is part of their survey, to which Charlotte responds, "Not directly, no. But the field of psychology is very concerned with this question—the woman question! It's just as important as the racial question, or religious, national, abnormal, social or political behavior."[61]

What made *Sugar and Spice* so unusual as a children's book was its explicit concern with the "woman question." But the book's implicit agenda of empowering girls to imagine and construct a life beyond socially circumscribed gender expectations came to be a relatively common one in Left-authored children's literature and a conscious project of progressive writers and others in the field. Lilian Moore, for instance, recalled commissioning works for the Arrow Book Club, including a biography of Florence Nightingale called *The First Woman Doctor* and another on the life of Eleanor Roosevelt, books meant to "encourage girls" with models of "independence" and autonomy. Moreover, what Moore conceded was a "premature feminist" agenda often coincided with the desire to likewise challenge the racial status quo and to support the growing movement for African-American civil rights (which certainly received more attention from leftists than did gender issues).[62]

Dorothy Sterling's initial foray into black history is revealing in this respect. A secular Jew who became active in the Communist movement during the Popular Front era, Sterling chose Harriet Tubman as the subject of her first juvenile biography because she wanted to write a book about an African-American figure who would allow her to address civil rights issues and also empower girls. Someone suggested Tubman. "You can't believe what an unknown figure she was—in the white community, not in the black, of course," Sterling recalled. "I would have never heard of her if I hadn't been reading the left-wing press."[63] Sterling also wanted her book to be illustrated by an African American. Delicately suggesting this idea to the art editor at Doubleday, who happened to have drawings on file by the artist Ernest Crichlow (illustrator of Jerrold and Lorraine Beim's *Two Is a Team*), the editor agreed. Not coincidentally, Crichlow was close to the party as well.[64] Crichlow and Sterling became good friends, and Crichlow illustrated three more of Sterling's books after *Freedom Train: The Story of Harriet Tubman* (1954). Sterling and Crichlow were among the leftists, white and black, who worked to ensure that American history as portrayed in children's literature would include African Americans.

Civil Rights and Black Biographies

Biographies of African Americans such as Sterling's *Freedom Train* represent the logical culmination of the trends described in this chapter. African-American history and biography became a focus for left-wing juvenile book authors in part because of a growing leftist focus on the Civil Rights movement. But just as important, Cold War–inspired demand for books on American tradition increasingly made space for books exploring African-American tradition, especially as international attention to racial discrimination in the United States helped to make desegregation a Cold War imperative.[65] And women's history, particularly African-American women's history, also received attention from left-wing writers as the "woman question" became a priority in leftist circles.

Several themes that consistently arise in what I call "civil rights" biographies by writers on the Left illustrate how ideas circulating in leftist discourse entered the cultural mainstream through children's literature and offered a kind of alternative civic education. First, an implicit or explicit commentary in these books on the power of history and stories, and on education in general, encouraged children to connect what they were reading to the world in which they currently lived, that is, a social and political landscape dominated by Cold War repression and conformity, on the one hand, and an increasingly militant struggle for African-American civil rights, on the other. Second, by showing figures who challenged convention, the books implicitly encouraged children to think and act independently, positing this as a kind of civic duty. Finally, several of the books, by commenting on historical gender roles and by making models of independent, forthright girls and women, challenged the "feminine mystique" that was at its height when the books were published.

For the sake of coherence, I concentrate here on biographies, most for older children, by four writers: Dorothy Sterling, Emma Gelders Sterne, Shirley Graham, and Ann Lane Petry. The former two women were Jewish, the latter two were African American. All of these women were initially influenced by left-wing politics in the 1930s or 1940s, and all remained "committed" writers throughout their careers, even when committed writing was out of fashion. All were storytellers with an abiding interest in history. All could be called feminists, although they might not have applied this label to themselves.[66] All were moved, for one reason or another, to teach children about people and events absent from or glossed over in schools and in most media directed at children. Finally, all were groundbreaking: by and large, their biographies were the first (or the second) books to be written for children on their subjects, though a flood of similar books would come in the 1970s and after. Shirley Graham, who many people know only as the woman who married W. E. B. Du Bois very late in his life (when Graham was in her forties), began writing African-American biographies in 1944 with a book on George Washington Carver that became a bestseller. Graham went on to more controversial figures, including her contemporary Paul Robeson, and published the first full-length biography for children of Frederick Douglass (which won the 1947 Julian Messner Award for a book combating racial intolerance) and the first children's biography of Benjamin Banneker (which won the Anisfield-Wolf Award, given to books that further public understandings of racism and diversity, in 1950). Since then, at least fourteen biographies of Banneker have been published, and hundreds of books teaching children about Frederick Douglass have come out. When Dorothy Sterling published her book on Harriet Tubman in 1954 (and Petry published hers in 1955), the only other juvenile biography of Tubman to speak of was Hildegarde Hoyt Swift's *Railroad to Freedom*, published in 1932 (left-winger Earl Conrad had published a biography for adults in 1943); again, hundreds of Tubman-related sources for children have come out since.[67] At least fifteen books have been published on Robert Smalls since Sterling wrote the first children's biography in 1958, and at least as many books on Mary McLeod Bethune have been published for children since Sterne's book came out in 1957.

History and storytelling operate as significant themes in nearly all of the biographies by these writers, at different levels. Sterne's discussion of history, legacy, and memory in *Mary McLeod Bethune* (1957) is particularly politicized. As her agent Edith Margolis wrote upon first reading the manuscript: "I wonder whether any publisher today will allow some of the material you have to go into a book for young people . . . I think you've included in this material a lot of history which is never touched on in our accepted versions of the Reconstruction Era, and for that reason, I fervently hope the script will be left as it is." It was, apparently.[68]

The book opens by placing Bethune's story within a longer history of slavery and within a history of the conscious effort among whites to cut black Americans off from their African cultural roots. Moreover, Sterne comments upon the ways in which the maintenance of racial hierarchy under slavery (and, implicitly, after Emancipation) depended on the repression of African-American history and memory. "It was to the advantage of the slaveholders that the memories be blurred," Sterne writes:

> It was easier to keep people from rebelling against the conditions of slavery if they could be made to believe that their present way of life, however miserable, was better than they had known in "savage" Africa. And it was easier for gentlemen and ladies who lived off the work of the slaves to quiet their own consciences if they came to believe that all Africans were barbarians, something less than human.[69]

Keeping African-American history alive was thus a deliberate act of defiance. Bethune's great-grandmother kept the memory of Africa alive and passed that memory to her daughter Sophia; though sold away from her mother, Sophia passed that memory on to her daughter and to her granddaughter Mary. And Mary, the first in her family to have a formal education, became a teacher herself and ensured that all of her students—poor children in the Jim Crow South—learned something of African-American history and culture. As the central figure of the story, Bethune is never left completely out of sight, but she is not actually born until thirty-six pages into the book, precisely because readers must see her life in the context of slavery's legacy and the legacy of African-Americans' longing and ongoing struggles for freedom. These both inform the historical moment in which Mary was born in 1875: free from slavery but only, as her father points out sorrowfully, "part-way free."[70] By 1875, of course, the Klan and Jim Crow had begun to rob African Americans of nearly every gain they had made since Emancipation.

In *Harriet Tubman: Conductor on the Underground Railroad* (1955), Petry consciously uses history in another way, which ties the oral tradition of storytelling that frames Tubman's immediate experience to a wider historical context. As a child, Harriet is told stories by her elders about the Middle Passage and about Africa, about survival and about slaves' trickery and masters' foolishness. She is also taught songs: songs from the Bible, freedom songs. Both Petry and Sterling emphasize in their biographies of Tubman the importance of an oral network or grapevine among slaves, through which both stories and information about the world beyond the plantation were communicated. The slaves hear stories about Nat Turner and Denmark Vesey in Petry's version; in Sterling's a literate, elder slave named Cudjoe tells slaves about the Declaration of Independence and reads them excerpts of David Walker's *Appeal* and William Lloyd Garrison's antislavery paper. Sterling notes that Harriet is stirred by the talk of equality in the Declaration of Independence and that she is surprised to learn that there are white people interested in helping slaves. But when she asks Cudjoe if "maybe they'll get us free sometime," he warns, "Don't figure on angels of the Lord flying here waving fiery swords at Master. We got to do it ourselves. Then, with the help of the Lord and the Abolitionists, we're sure to make it."[71]

The message is a clear one, which comes up in many of the other books as well: slaves and free blacks were vital actors in the effort to end slavery, contrary to the popular myth, still prevalent in the mid-twentieth century, of the "passive slave" whose liberation from slavery was accomplished only through the efforts of white abolitionists.[72] Sterne makes an explicit point of noting that slaves and free blacks used every power they had to end slavery: speaking out where they could speak publicly, petitioning when a member of the community was literate enough to make up a petition (slaves were forbidden to learn to read or write), holding meetings, singing freedom songs, and, occasionally, forcefully rebelling. Tales of every success, every effort to challenge slavery, whatever the outcome, gave slaves strength, according to these writers. Especially in Petry's version of Tubman's story, Tubman is said to have become a storyteller herself, and all those who heard her stories, or tales of her bravery, were inspired.

Juxtaposed to the oral tradition that is highlighted in Petry's tale of Tubman, or parallel to it, Petry follows the specific episode in each chapter with one or several italicized paragraphs that point to other events in the same historical moment. These paragraphs are different in tone from the rest of the text: more impersonal, more "history" than story. Their inclusion invites readers to place Tubman's story within a longer and wider trajectory of history. For example, a chapter describing the first time that Harriet is hired out—in 1826, at the age of six—ends with a commentary on Thomas Jefferson's death in the same year. More important, it describes Jefferson's "vehement philippic against Negro slavery" that was in his original draft of the Declaration of Independence (the biographies of Banneker and Bethune, by Graham and Sterne, respectively, also mention Jefferson's statement). Removed to placate southern delegates at the Continental Congress, all that was left of Jefferson's original words was the proclamation that all men had the "inalienable right" to "Life, Liberty and the Pursuit of Happiness." Yet even these rights were utterly incompatible with the idea of slavery. According to Petry, "Many a slave carried the dream of freedom in his heart because of these words of Jefferson's. Not because the slave had read them, but because they were written down somewhere, and other people had read them, and ideas are contagious—particularly ideas that concern the rights of man."[73] This point was fundamental to the Left's vision of civic education: ideas are contagious. Cold Warriors promoted civic education as a way to inoculate children against Communism, but they may have unwittingly created a forum for leftists to spread their contagious ideas. Even so, upon close examination, these are not Communist ideas but, at a very basic level, American ones.

Frederick Douglass believed deeply in the Constitution, Graham tells us, insisting that the guarantee of liberty meant that by all logic there should have been no more slavery after the American Revolution. Douglass made it his mission to convince Americans to truly follow the Constitution, to recognize their own hypocrisy (a hypocrisy still underlying discriminatory practices in the Jim Crow South in 1947, when *There Was Once a Slave* was published). When Graham quotes Douglass speaking in 1847, she may as well be quoting Martin Luther King, Jr., in the 1960s:

Americans! Your republican politics, not less than your republican religion, are flagrantly inconsistent. You boast of your love of liberty, your superior civilization, and your pure Christianity, while the whole political power of the nation . . . is solemnly pledged to support and perpetuate the enslavement of three million of your countrymen. . . . You invite to your shores the fugitives of oppression from abroad . . . but the fugitives from your own land you advertise, hunt, arrest, shoot and kill. . . . your gallant sons are ready to fly to arms to vindicate her cause against the oppressor, but in regard to the ten thousand wrongs of the American slave, you would enforce the strictest silence. . . . You are all on fire at the mention of liberty for France or for Ireland; but are as cold as an iceberg at the thought of liberty for the enslaved of America![74]

The parallels between stories told about the past and the contemporary situation are often self-evident, but the past tense makes the messages far less confrontational. Indeed, Graham's 1946 biography of her contemporary Paul Robeson would get banned from U.S. overseas libraries in the 1950s, as would Sterling's 1959 *Tender Warriors*, a nonfiction portrait of school integration (written with Donald Gross), though by and large their historical works were accepted.[75] Petry's *Tituba of Salem Village* (1964), like Arthur Miller's *Crucible*, could be read as a comment on McCarthyism, but in Petry's case, one that added racism to the mix by focusing on the slave Tituba Indian. The distant context made the comment on "witch hunting," complete with a racist subtext, far less subject to controversy.

These authors exposed the contrast between proclamations of liberty and trade in human flesh; they commented upon the tragedy of privileging economics over human freedom and dignity in the name of national unity. In doing so, they inevitably raised the specter of continuing horrors in the South at the time of their books' publication. Sterne, for instance, asserted in the Bethune biography that the compromise on slavery—"in the name of 'unity'"—by Adams, Franklin, Jefferson, and all those who professed to hate the "peculiar" institution, "set a pattern at the expense of the enslaved Negro that was to lead the new nation into tragedy."[76]

Almost all of the subjects of the biographies are shown to consciously appropriate the language and values of the United States' founding principles and to act out of their perceived duty to make these principles apply to all Americans and especially to African Americans. Mary McLeod, impressed by what she learns in school about the American Revolution, "made the great language of American democracy her own." Consequently, she made a lifetime project out of civic education. Her school, as she envisioned it, would both prepare children for higher learning and give them practical skills; it also would be "a living part of the community." As Sterne puts it, "It would stir up people to do something about the Jim Crow laws and about the lynchings. It would keep men voting even if they risked their lives to do it. It would be a rallying place for the citizenship of the fathers—and yes, for the mothers too."[77]

A sense of civic duty is central to other books as well. Certainly it played into Robert Smalls's decision to run for Congress, as it inspired him during the Civil War to take over a Confederate ship and pilot it to the Union side. Benjamin Banneker, a free, educated African American who lived through the American Revolution, is moved by Thomas Paine's *Common Sense* and by the Declaration of Independence. But he does not feel compelled to act on behalf of his enslaved brethren until a poor sailor confronts him, asking him to talk about what the "liberty" that revolutionaries were preaching meant for slaves. "I knows ye sma't man," the sailor says to him. "Ye can tell da people 'bout dis liba'ty. No?" The poor sailor leaves Banneker feeling suddenly ashamed of his own taken-for-granted privileges as a free man and conscious of the responsibility that comes with freedom (and, implicitly, with education). Banneker realizes that "he was a free man—free to act!" He comes to see, with some prodding by the liberal physician Benjamin Rush, that the popular almanac he publishes can be a powerful source of antislavery and antiracist propaganda. He also writes directly to Thomas Jefferson, urging him "to eradicate that train of absurd and false ideas and oppinions [*sic*], which so generally prevails with respect to us [African Americans]." He condemns Jefferson's hypocrisy, calling him "guilty of that most criminal act which you professedly detested in others with respect to yourselves."[78]

If the principles of "Americanism" are adopted on behalf of the disfranchised, oppressed, and marginalized of this country, they are not invoked as the exclusive privilege of Americans, nor do the writers use the biographies to suggest a hierarchy of oppression. We learn about Douglass's insistence that attaining the vote for poor whites and for blacks and for women of all races was part of the same struggle. And Bethune, in true Popular Front rhetoric, insisted in her old age—as the Civil Rights movement was becoming a reality—that "white[s] and Negroes alike understand the current intensity of the Negro's fight for status as part of a world people's movement."[79] The commentaries on racialized injustice do not preclude a critique of economic injustice, colonialism, or gender constraints; indeed, the economics of racism are vividly exposed, and the struggles for the equality of black and white, male and female, are shown to be linked.

By reading these stories, children are taught something of bravery, individual initiative, and community responsibility. They learn that challenging what is wrong is a humanizing experience that empowers others as well as themselves. And they are taught that when there is no way to make needed changes from within the existing system, it is reasonable and right to challenge that system, possibly by force when absolutely necessary. For example, Tubman, in Sterling's version, is said to have supported John Brown. As Sterling puts it, she "came to believe his prediction that slaveholders will never give up slaves until they feel a big stick about their heads."[80] (In contrast, Petry shows Tubman to ultimately reject Brown's violent methods, and Graham likewise suggests that Douglass rejected them as well.)

Both Petry and Sterling describe Harriet's brave support of a fellow slave who runs away from the plantation where they are working. When Harriet stands between him and the overseer so that the slave can get away, a brick meant to halt the runaway lands squarely across Harriet's forehead and knocks her out. But surviving this battle is a great victory for Harriet. "Singlehandedly, she had fought against slavery and had survived," Sterling writes. "She was no longer only a piece of property, like the horses and cows who dumbly did the Master's bidding. While still a slave in form, she was in spirit a human being and a free woman." Harriet Tubman's powerful behavior is echoed by other men and women. After Frederick Douglass stands up to the slave breaker Covey, "his fellow workers looked up to him with something like awe," Graham asserts.[81] Mary McLeod Bethune defies the Ku Klux Klan. Lucretia Mott, whose work as an abolitionist Sterling highlights, defies Quaker convention by speaking out when only men should speak out, by inviting African Americans into her home, and by insisting upon the right of women as well as men, blacks as well as whites, to vote.

Each subject of these biographies acts bravely and boldly, but always does so on behalf of a larger community and always works to bring others into the struggle for justice. In that sense, education is a consistent subtext, either in the traditional sense of "book learning"—as Frederick Douglass teaches other slaves to read or Mary McLeod Bethune starts her own school—or in the less traditional sense of education for survival, as Harriet Tubman's father teaches her how to find her way in the woods. Along lines similar to the thinking promoted in Left-authored science books, education in these biographies involves separating truths from falsehoods, especially when young African Americans—under slavery and long after—were taught by whites to believe that they were worthless, less than human. Young Mary McLeod, singled out to receive an education, learns in school that Africans are heathen savages; this information conflicts, of course, with what she has learned from her grandmother, and she decides she must not take all that she learns in school as gospel.

Children reading these books thus learned that independent thinking and rebellion against injustice were traits and behaviors worth emulating; they learned this at a time when children and youth were being vilified for challenging adult authority, blamed for being angry at the hypocritical society into which they had been born. These authors focused attention on the conditions that had historically made rebellion necessary, just as other leftist commentators challenged the dominant explanation for contemporary juvenile delinquency that blamed children and mothers instead of poverty, racism, and adult hypocrisy. Graham, Sterling, and Petry emphasized that the conditions of slavery robbed young Frederick Douglass and young Harriet Tubman of their childhoods, their innocence. "Although Harriet had not yet passed her eighth birthday," Sterling writes of a sunny spring day in 1827, "there was no running and skipping for her, no rolling on the grass or climbing on the trees. For her there was only work, and sometimes a stolen minute to look through the window and watch the birds as they flew North."[82]

Although these biographies implicitly urge children to be brave, independent thinkers, readers are also made to understand that adults have the responsibility, along with the power, to make the world better for the children who will inherit it. Bethune, for instance, bravely anticipating harassment by the Klan, remembers words she heard somewhere: "If there be trouble, let it be in my time, that my children shall have peace." By "my children," Sterne says, Bethune did not just mean her own son, or the girls attending her school:

> These, surely, but also the others, in flimsy shanties, in the turpentine camps and in cotton fields, in tenements and in back streets, in Savannah and Atlanta and Chicago and New York. Black-skinned, brown-skinned—yes, and white-skinned—the children of the white-robed night riders, inheritors of hatred and ignorance. Let all children of God have peace.[83]

Not only do these books present models of young people's bravery and independence: they also present models of parenting. Just as consciousness of racial oppression was a chief factor eliciting a critique of gender oppression, so this attention to the "woman question" was closely tied to awareness of children's rights on the Left. As Kate Weigand notes, "Communist advice columnists argued [that] . . . the best way to respect children and to raise self-confident, political adults, was to allow them to question and challenge the status quo and to involve them in family decision making as often as possible." *Lucretia Mott: Gentle Warrior* (1964) makes an explicit commentary on childrearing. Sterling notes that "at a time when parents were household dictators and children were expected to obey orders without questioning, Lucretia believed that a child, like all human beings, had inalienable rights." Moreover, "recalling her own childhood, she encouraged her children to think for themselves." Raised a Quaker, Lucretia grew up believing in her value as a person. According to Sterling, Unlike Puritan children who left church each day with a belief in their own unworthiness, Quaker children "were introduced to a God of hope and love rather than a God of wrath. The 'inner voices' spoke of the here-and-now rather than the hereafter."[84] The Quaker philosophies of nonviolence and social activism are also convenient filters for teaching these practices to children, and it is worth thinking about the effects this book and others might have had. An eleven-year-old who read about Harriet Tubman or Frederick Douglass in the mid-1950s would go to college in time for the sit-ins and Freedom Summer. A twelve-year-old who read about Mott in 1964 would enter college in 1970, at the height of the rebellion against the Vietnam War and at the dawn of the women's movement.

Lucretia Mott: Gentle Warrior is perhaps most consciously prochild, but it is also the most self-consciously feminist, which, given its later publication date, is not surprising. Lucretia's father pulls her out of a school that denies a full and equal education to girls. Off at a Quaker institution where Lucretia teaches part time in addition to attending classes, she comes to learn that the male teachers have higher salaries than the female teachers. Sterling quotes Mott's later writing on the subject: "The injustice of the distinction was so apparent, that I resolved to claim for my sex all that an impartial creator had bestowed." Mott dedicates much of her life to activism, particularly for women's rights, but also against a litany of injustices, especially slavery. "She saw many wrongs that needed righting," Sterling notes. "Men were imprisoned for debt and hanged for minor crimes. Women were unjustly treated. Wages were low, working hours long, and thousands were jobless. . . . The greatest wrong of all was slavery."[85]

Clearly offering a commentary on what they saw as an unhealthy emphasis on girls' appearance, clothes, and popularity and success with boys, Sterling, Petry, and Sterne portrayed strong, unconventional women who were all described as *not* conventionally pretty or feminine and who were all shown to proudly develop traditionally unfeminine qualities. Mott, like both Tubman and Bethune, is said to be unattractive by prevailing ideals of femininity and beauty. Sterling says that her eyes were "too bright and knowing. Even her walk was wrong. Instead of taking mincing, dainty steps she strode . . . with a clatter of heel and toe that announced her strength and determination." Sterling explicitly makes a point of saying that Harriet Tubman at fifteen was not beautiful, but, she says, "there was a magnetic quality about Harriet. When she ran barefoot across the fields with her head erect and her firm muscles rippling under her dark, lustrous skin, men and women stopped to admire her grace and strength." The sexual undertones here betray something of white leftists' fetishizing of African Americans as icons of struggle; even so, Sterling proudly attests that many of her readers, both black and white, have mistakenly assumed that she is African American. Sterling and Petry both tell us that Harriet was as strong as any man, echoing the famous words attributed to Sojourner Truth. Tubman escaped from slavery alone, acting independently when neither her husband nor her brothers would go with her. Later in Tubman's life, Sterling tells us, John Brown was "so impressed . . . with her courage and leadership that he frequently spoke of her in masculine terms." Ernest Crichlow's illustrations of Sterling's story show Harriet as a proud "Moses," leading the masses of her people, much as Ward's image of a determined, gun-toting Tubman in *North Star Shining* (figure 7.5) shows a strength and energy that defy feminine convention. The overwhelming image of Tituba Indian, the protagonist of Petry's *Tituba of Salem Village* (1964) is one of strength and oppositional consciousness, traits that draw suspicion to her power to heal. And of Mary McLeod Bethune, Sterne writes, "[N]o one would have called the tall, big-boned woman pretty. But there was something about her that made even strangers feel more alive in her presence. 'Electric' was the word her friends used to describe her."[86] Such descriptions of black women were backhanded compliments to African-American girls growing up in the 1950s and early 1960s and confronting a white standard of feminine beauty, but they also may have foreshadowed the "black is beautiful" rhetoric of the late 1960s.

Mott especially, but also Bethune, Tubman, and Douglass, we learn, all became activists on behalf of women's rights, and each consciously linked the struggle for equality between men and women to the struggles to achieve justice for all oppressed groups, including African Americans, workers, and the poor. In addition to changing laws, they worked to change attitudes. Mott, for instance, wanted "to rid women of false notions of delicacy which hampered them in their daily lives."[87] But if women were hampered by "false notions of delicacy," they were also hampered by men who failed to see the value of their work. All of the women in these books struggle to find a balance between their activism and their roles as wives, mothers, and keepers of the home.

Both Sterling and Petry say that Harriet Tubman's husband, John, mocked her desire to be free. As Sterling puts it, "'There have always been masters and slaves,' he would tell her. 'You can't change those things.'"[88] Especially in Petry's version, Harriet has real remorse and sadness about leaving her husband to escape slavery, giving up her chance for love and a family. Though in Sterling's story Harriet hardly gives her husband a second thought after she has left him, in Petry's she actually returns to Maryland, two years after she had first left, to persuade John Tubman to come north with her. She arrives at their old cabin, wearing a man's suit covered with burrs and briars, a man's shoes, and a "battered old hat." Standing there with all traces of her femininity hidden for the sake of freedom, she finds John with another woman. And this lovely, properly submissive woman seems to belong there with John in this cabin on the master's plantation, as Tubman does not. Fleetingly, Harriet wishes that she could have both freedom and love, wishes she could possess once again John's love and attention, wishes she could be beautiful for him:

> She thought, If only she had been wearing fine clothes, silk or satin instead of the torn shabby suit. Not silk or velvet, just a simple calico dress, a dress that would have immediately revealed that she was a woman. Then she shook her head. How could she sleep on the ground in a dress, climb in and out of a potato hold in long skirts? Besides, clothes did not change a person, did not really matter. Love and devotion should not depend on the kind of clothes one wore. A man's suit or a woman's dress would not have made one whit of difference. Neither the one nor the other could change the kind of person she was. Her mind, her soul, would always wear freedom's clothes. John's never would.

Later in life, Petry tells us, Tubman would further challenge the norms of women's fashion, acquiring for herself a "bloomer" outfit because long, full skirts were impractical for an active woman and because, moreover, she believed in the movement for women's rights that the wearing of bloomers represented.[89]

Like Tubman, Bethune (with whom Sterne may have identified because of a similar struggle in her own life) found it impossible to integrate marriage and the kind of active and public life that she wanted to lead.[90] As Sterne depicts it, Bethune's husband seems somewhat jealous of her career aspirations and hints that she should give up teaching to raise a family. She wants a child, but worries about sacrificing the work that is so important to her. Talking it over with her mother, she is convinced that she cannot give up everything else to have children. As her mother tells her, "Childbearing, working, tryin' to move the world forward a little bit—they all got to go together, daughter." And they do all go together for Mary McLeod Bethune, but somehow her relationship with her husband falls out of the equation. Alburtus, her husband, was satisfied with the simple life they had together, but she wanted more; she wanted to make her mark on the world, to better the condition of African Americans in whatever way she could. Finally, she sets off on her own to start a school in Daytona, Florida. When Alburtus finally comes to join her for a few months one summer, he feels like there is no place for him, so he returns to Georgia, where he has been teaching. Thus they live apart until Alburtus's death, friendly but not as husband and wife. "Perhaps with a different type of man, Mrs. Bethune might have made a success in the role of wife as she did in other human relationships," Sterne speculates. "Perhaps not. She was surely capable of deep, warm emotion.

She had grown up in a household sunlit with love. But the very qualities that made her great made marriage difficult."[91]

Only Mott seems to have balanced marriage, family, and work. Though she works hard caring for her house and family, Sterling says of Mott that she is "determined not to become 'kitchenified.'" Her marriage appears to have been quite unusual, to the extent that her husband, James, though less outspoken and probably less radical than she, supported all of her work, sharing much with her but also allowing his wife her freedom and independence. Later in life, Mott would describe her prescription for success in marriage, which Sterling deems worthy of quoting: "In the true marriage relations the independence of husband and wife is equal, their dependence mutual and their obligations reciprocal."[92] Such a balance was and is hard to achieve; indeed, traditionally, fewer women than men became the subjects of biographies because their obligations to home and family make it more difficult to become distinguished in public life. Le Sueur's portrait of Nancy Hanks demonstrates this more than it does anything else.

In one sense, the fact that most of Shirley Graham's biographies were about men suggests that she believed that men had a more significant role in history than did women. The two biographies of women that Graham did publish have somewhat ambivalent messages, both in terms of gender expectations in general and in terms of women's civic duty in particular. Her story of Pocahontas (1953), for instance, describes the young Indian "princess" as brave, outspoken, independent-minded, and tomboyish. She does her brother's chores (much to her mother's consternation); she brags that she can "shoot an arrow as straight as any" of the ancient heroes described in tribal songs; and she runs as fast as the fastest boy in her village. But her feminine compassion compels her to stand up for Captain John Smith when he is to be executed by her tribe for the crimes of his men. Although she witnesses repeated incidents of the white settlers' treachery and sees how little respect they have for her people (Pocahontas hears herself and other Indians with her called "a jolly pack of naked little heathen," for instance), she still repeatedly reaches out to the white settlers, bringing them food and supplies in the hope of bringing peace between the two peoples. Pocahontas finally decides to learn "the white people's way," allowing herself to be "civilized" and Christianized so that she might become a link between her people and the white settlers. She agrees to marry a man she does not know or love to cement this peace. Graham exposes the manipulation, disingenuousness, and treachery of the white settlers, and yet she seems to suggest that Pocahontas is a hero, not a sellout or a dupe. "Though the lovely Pocahontas died while she was still young," Graham writes, "she had served her people faithfully. She had been the worthy daughter of a great chief. She had helped bring peace for a time between settlers from Europe and Indians in Virginia.

Her son was a tie between Old World and New World."[93] It is difficult to say whether Graham wants readers to question the cost of Pocahontas's decisions, given how openly critical she is of the whites.

The portrait that Shirley Graham Du Bois paints of Phillis Wheatley as a loyal servant in *The Story of Phillis Wheatley* (1949) is also striking, though Graham does include in the book antislavery poetry by Wheatley, thus showing her opposition to the conditions that made her success as a poet so remarkable. This enigmatic take on women may be partly explained by Graham's somewhat awkward position as a radical member of the black intelligentsia struggling for success on her own terms but partially riding on the coattails of larger-than-life heroes like Paul Robeson, W. E. B. Du Bois, and Kwame Nkrumah of Ghana, with whom Graham had close relationships. She achieved a level of professional status unusual for a woman of any race, but she never embraced a feminist politics as openly as Sterne, Sterling, and Petry ultimately would.[94] Even so, her biographies of figures like Paul Robeson, Frederick Douglass, and Julius K. Nyerere are among the most openly radical juvenile books (albeit for older children) that reached a popular audience in the postwar period. Le Sueur, likewise, wrote only one children's book focused on a female character, but she would openly embrace feminism in the 1970s.

• • •

As this limited set of examples suggests, the post–World War II civic education of the Left, in its sometimes ambivalent, but relatively consistent prolabor, antiracist, and anticolonial components and in its nascent feminist consciousness, challenged much of what was taught about the American past and present in schools, colleges, and the mass media. In general, it opposed the value system of the Cold War and the apparent consensus around it. As Helen Heffernan, a prominent progressive educator declared in 1951 (in a proposal for a social studies textbook series that Sterne fielded during her tenure as an editor for the American Book Company):

> Good citizenship implies more than an understanding of the world of men and affairs. It means active interest in and genuine concern for the welfare of human beings. It means active opposition to all forms of political, social, and economic injustice. It means faith in human nature, in democracy, in the ability of mankind to meet and to solve problems through the processes of intelligent cooperation.

While mainstream civic education taught children to revere the American way of life as it was, progressives and radicals made "active opposition" to injustice and "intelligent cooperation" hallmarks of good citizenship.[95]

271

For all of its limitations, the Left's venture into American tradition predicted the more sweeping challenges to historical inquiry that would be posed by the young activists of the 1960s and 1970s, who were the figurative and sometimes the literal descendants of the Old Left. Revisionist historians would remind the academy in the 1970s and 1980s that questioning capitalism only seemed to be subversive if one ignored the fact that most history serves as propaganda for capitalism, something W. E. B. Du Bois observed in a 1935 essay on "the propaganda of history." By the late 1960s and early 1970s, as a result of the same movements that challenged the status of history in the academy, authors of children's books would no longer need to shield their social criticism behind the cover of science or history or couch it in the more individualized terms of liberating one's own imagination. By this time, popular understandings of childhood itself had changed, and the ideas put forth by the Old Left in postwar children's literature had become fairly mainstream. This is why many of the children's books discussed here do not seem particularly radical to us today. However, their existence at the height of the Cold War helped to transform the field of children's literature.[96]

Epilogue

Transforming an "All-White World"

Members of the Council on Interracial Books for Children (CIBC) have different recollections about exactly how and when the group originated, but nearly everyone agrees that the idea for the group came at a meeting of the Loose Enders, probably at Herman and Nina Schneider's brownstone in Greenwich Village—which was, incidentally, across the street from the row house that Weather Underground radicals would blow up a decade later. Dorothy Sterling claimed that the meeting was on the night of John Kennedy's assassination, which would neatly date it at the moment that the Cold War consensus, such as it was, began unmistakably to unravel. Franklin Folsom, one of the main forces behind the organization, dated its origins nearly two years later. In any case, all agree that the spark galvanizing this group of Old Leftists at one of their regular gatherings of eating and kibbitzing was the Civil Rights movement.[1]

Lilian Moore's stepson, like many northern white college students, had gone to Mississippi to register voters and to work in the Freedom Schools. Keenly aware of all the challenges he and others faced, this young man complained to his stepmother that there weren't any good books available in the South for teaching black children, no books in which a black child could recognize himself or herself. Moore, as a juvenile editor, ought to have been in a position to change this situation. Hearing what her son had to say, Moore was "very moved and upset," and so she reported it to her friends at one of their dinner get-togethers. In Moore's remembrance of things, Franklin Folsom, whom Moore called "a man of action," heard her story and organized a meeting. What emerged was the Council on Interracial Books for Children, which, whenever its initial inspiration, was officially established in February 1965.[2]

People like Moore, Folsom, Sterling, and the Schneiders had been quietly winning small but notable victories in their efforts to challenge what editor and council board member Nancy Larrick would describe as "the all-white world of children's literature." Surveying publishers' offerings from 1962 to 1964, Larrick came up with some startling statistics, which she published in a groundbreaking article in the *Saturday Review* in September 1965. Of the thousands of books surveyed in Larrick's study, only 6.7 percent included "one or more Negroes." But even this low number actually made things seem better than they were, Larrick argued, because the figure encompassed books showing a single dark face in a crowd, as well as books with stereotypical and even negative representations. As Larrick noted, "Many children's books which include a Negro show him as a servant or slave, a sharecropper, migrant worker, or a menial." Most disturbing to Larrick was the lack of books—fewer than 1 percent—that "tell a story about American Negroes today." She was perhaps too dismissive of the biographies and histories that had been published in the previous decade, but she was right to insist that "to the child who has been involved in civil rights demonstrations in Harlem or Detroit, it is small comfort to read of the Negro slave who smilingly served his white master."[3] Still, she did single out Dorothy Sterling's *Forever Free: The Story of the Emancipation Proclamation* as among the recently published books with "outstanding literary merit" that included people of color.

That Larrick singled out Sterling's book was not coincidental. Indeed, among the few books she praised for their positive portrayal of African Americans, a striking number of them were by writers on the Left, including Dorothy Sterling, Langston Hughes, Millicent Selsam, Milton Meltzer, Arna Bontemps, and Lorenz Graham, the brother of Shirley Graham. As the clearest evidence of a change in the air, Larrick pointed to the Council on Interracial Books for Children, which, she said, "operates on the principles that, given encouragement, authors and artists will create good children's books that include nonwhites, and that given the manuscripts, publishers will produce and market them."[4]

Becoming more diverse each year in both its composition and its range of initiatives, the council raised consciousness about racism, sexism, militarism, class bias, and other issues in children's literature. Issues of the council's *Bulletin* focused on such subjects as Puerto Ricans in children's literature, the black experience in children's books, nonbiased testing, the Chicano movement, and the unmet needs of Mexican children. The organization sponsored writing contests for new minority writers, and it actively worked to empower minority publishers.[5] Its impact on children's literature was profound. Publishers, librarians, parents, educators, nonprofits, and government agencies turned to council members for their expertise as they sought children's books that were more representative of the nation's cultural diversity. New writers, including Sharon Bell Mathis, Walter Dean Myers, and Kristin Hunter, who became major figures in the field, established themselves through the council's writing contests. And many publishers expanded their lists in response to criticism from the council. Council members like Sterling suddenly became sought-after experts on "the treatment of minority groups in text and library books used in the nation's schools," and they were called to testify before educational groups and brought in as consultants by publishers.[6] If, as Sterling half-jokingly claimed, before 1965 only a Communist would to try to publish a book that was sympathetic to African Americans, by 1966 the few people who had been bold enough in the repressive postwar period to challenge the "all-white world of children's literature" now seemed to have important insights to offer to educators, publishers, and others trying to navigate a disorienting new social and cultural climate.

The establishment of the Council on Interracial Books for Children represented a pivotal moment for the children's book field, but its full significance went beyond what Larrick described. Larrick's references to books like Lorenz Graham's *South Town* and Dorothy Sterling's *Mary Jane* operated as a subtext or backstory to a narrative that could only tell half the story, for obvious reasons. Former activists in the Old Left had joined with prominent liberals and progressives to confront issues facing children, issues that young people like the Little Rock Nine, the students sitting-in at lunch counters, and Moore's stepson had propelled into the national spotlight.[7] Children's literature linked the Old Left radicals, who came of age in the 1930s, to the young people of the Civil Rights movement and the New Left, or the generation which became active on university and college campuses in the early to mid-1960s.

Many activists in the social movements of the 1960s had, as children in the 1940s and 1950s, read books by members of the Communist or post-Communist Left. Red-diaper baby Nancy Mikkelson, for instance, recalled receiving Jerrold and Lorraine Beim's *Two Is a Team* as a young child in the 1940s, and even at that time she recognized that this simple story of interracial friendship was a "radical" book.[8] The children of radicals may have been more sensitive to the political messages in widely marketed texts, but this does not mean the texts did not have a broad impact upon young people who may have only been subconsciously attuned to their politics. The young people who read (or had read to them) Little Golden books, *Danny and the Dinosaur*, and *Harold and the Purple Crayon*; who purchased paperbacks in school through the Arrow Book Club; who sat studiously in the public library reading *Landmark* books; who checked books by Irving Adler out of the school library as background to a science project; who fantasized about one day inventing a "homework machine" like Danny Dunn; or who encountered Eve Merriam's *Mommies at Work* (1961) (with its "bridge-building mommies," "atom-splitting mommies," and "assembly-line mommies building cars") two years before Friedan published *The Fem-*

inine Mystique were part of the generation that grew up to reject established authority and to challenge deeply entrenched institutions.[9]

It would be impossible (and far too reductive) to draw some kind of cause-and-effect link between childhood reading and the rebellions of the 1960s. Even so, the generational lines are not merely coincidental. The young people in their teens and twenties who joined the Civil Rights movement and called themselves the "New Left," who protested the Vietnam War, who formed con-sciousness-raising groups, and who imagined a kind of "liberation" for their own children through books like *Free to Be You and Me* (1974) had grown up in an age marked by conformity and the repression of dissent. Yet they also managed to find material promoting interracial friendship, critical thinking, "science for the citizen," and a "working-class Americanism."[10] Through trade books, many children learned a version of history that was left out of their textbooks, and they found stories that encouraged them to trust their imagina-tions and to believe that the impossible was possible. The books that members of the Communist Left wrote, edited, illustrated, and sold in these years were by no means revolutionary or even political, especially by today's standards. But the politics are nearly invisible today in part because these books, and the people who wrote, illustrated, edited, and disseminated them, helped to change the basic assumptions about what children ought to read.

And so, as E. L. Doctorow pointed out in his novel about the Rosenbergs' legacy, *The Book of Daniel*, it should have been no surprise when alienated, seemingly apolitical Holden Caulfield types joined the New Left. Although sociologists studying high school and college-age youth in the 1950s found them "alienated" and "uncommitted," many of these same alienated youth, or their younger brothers and sisters, would turn into "young radicals" only a few years later. As the Daniel character in Doctorow's novel observes, "The Trust-ees of Ohio State were right in 1956 when they canned the English instructor for assigning *Catcher in the Rye* to his freshman class. They knew there is no qualitative difference between the kid who thinks it's funny to fart in chapel and Che Guevara. They knew then that Holden Caulfield would found SDS."[11] This is not a claim for J. D. Salinger's radical impulses but, rather, a point about the fact that young people of Holden's generation grew up very aware of adults' hypocrisy. Many young people recognized a disconnect between what the world might be like and how it actually was, and this was, in part, due to their childhood reading.

Books provided more than indirect inspiration to young activists, however. To give one moving example, a student at the Greensboro, North Carolina, sit-in, when asked why he was there, told a reporter that he had been inspired by *A Pictorial History of the Negro*, a book cowritten by Old Leftists Milton Meltzer and Langston Hughes and first published in 1956. According to Meltzer:

In essence, the reporter was saying, "you guys have been oppressed for hundreds of years, how come at this moment you, students, decided to do something about it?" And the answer was that "we've been reading in our group *A Pictorial History of the Negro in America* and we saw example after example of the guts and determination and courage of our forebears to do something about discrimination, segregation, and oppression, so we felt we ought to get off our butts and do something too."[12]

Though it was originally intended for adults, as Larrick pointed out, many school libraries purchased *A Pictorial History* because it filled a gap in children's book offerings; certainly no textbook provided this kind of information. The book's popularity with young people helped to convince Meltzer to devote the latter half of his career to writing books for young readers about the "underdog."

The ties between the Old Left and the New Left went beyond reading material. In 1967, when Emma Gelders Sterne was in her mid-seventies, she spent ten days in prison with Joan Baez and other activists for sitting-in at the Oakland Induction Center in protest of the Vietnam War. Ernest Crichlow cofounded the Cinque Gallery in New York, which became a center for the Black Arts movement that blossomed in the late 1960s. Black Panther activist Stokely Carmichael referred to Shirley Graham Du Bois as "Grandma," and she herself spoke of Malcolm X as a "son" and Panther leader Elaine Brown as a "daughter."[13] Irving Adler organized a peace group in Vermont in the 1960s in protest against the Vietnam War and became outspoken against nuclear weapons and for environmental protection. Franklin Folsom, in his eighties, was the oldest participant in the peace march undertaken across the United States in 1986. Meridel Le Sueur was rediscovered in the early 1970s by a new generation of radicals seeking foremothers.

The sudden explosion of activism in the 1960s—the blossoming of the Civil Rights movement, the organizing of SDS and other New Left groups on college campuses across the nation, the growing protest against U.S. involvement in Vietnam—was like a breath of fresh air to Old Left radicals who had been forced to temper, or at least couch, their political views and to curtail their involvement with radical organizations. Children represented the last vestige of hope for Popular Front radicals wishing to maintain and express their vision in the midst of the Cold War. Thus many older radicals, whose hopes for Soviet socialism had been dashed and whose relation to the American establishment had been permanently altered by the experience of McCarthyism, looked hopefully to the activism of youth too brazen or naïve to fear the potential repercussions of their actions.

There is a kind of circular effect here. Many young people were ultimately radicalized in part by a stream of dissent that ran beneath the Cold War consensus, and these young people, in turn, helped to reinspire an older generation of leftists. Some writers of the Old Left generation, including Meltzer, Leo Lionni, William Steig, Alice Childress, Rosa Guy, and Jacob Lawrence, began writing for children in the 1960s as a kind of second career (Charlotte Pomerantz, younger than these folks but close to the Old Left milieu, also began writing for children in the mid-1960s); others, who were well established in the field, began to publish openly political work. Here, Anne Terry White's example is particularly striking. The books she wrote in the 1940s and 1950s are, at least on the surface, apolitical, including titles like *Lost Worlds: Adventures in Archeology* (1941), *All about Our Changing Rocks* (1955), and *The Golden Treasury of Myths and Legends* (1959). Even her 1953 biography of George Washington Carver shows little of the political conviction evident in biographies by Shirley Graham, Emma Gelders Sterne, and others. In contrast, in the late 1960s and early 1970s, White began to be openly critical of capitalism, race relations, and government policies in books like *False Treaty: The Removal of the Cherokees from Georgia* (1970), which ends with oblique references to the American Indian movement; *Human Cargo: The Story of the Atlantic Slave Trade* (1970); and *Eugene Debs: American Socialist* (1974). Likewise, by the early 1970s, Lilian Moore felt comfortable using her editorial credentials as the basis for civil rights activism, starting the Firebird Books series at Scholastic, with the editorial assistance of Dorothy Sterling and Milton Meltzer. This series of books, many of which were by Old Left authors, is sometimes strikingly political, concerning people and topics like Marcus Garvey, Malcolm X, Japanese-American internment, Mexican-American activism, John Brown, and Reconstruction. The Firebird books reflect the desire to recover and celebrate the historic struggles of not just African Americans but oppressed people of color more generally.[14] Even titles of books are suggestive of the new political climate: consider, for instance, Franklin Folsom's *Red Power on the Rio Grande: The Native American Revolution of 1680* (1973), which also went well beyond his *Real Book about Indians* (1953) in its political message. It is hard to imagine any talk of "red power" in the 1950s, given the status of the nation's "reds"—in both senses of the term—at that moment in history.

In general, while members of the Popular Front Left had concentrated their subtle social critiques on racism against African Americans, on labor relations, and, especially through books on science themes, on the need for critical evaluation of received authority, their books published in the late 1960s and 1970s contained more explicit critiques of contemporary relations between blacks and whites and also gave extended attention to other minorities. They also more explicitly tackled issues of gender and sexuality, confronted poverty in the inner city, engaged directly with contemporary social movements—from Black Power to Vietnam protests to the environmental movement—and challenged colonialism.[15] Shirley Graham's biography of African leader Julius K. Nyerere, *Teacher of Africa* (1975), offered a sharp critique of colonialism and Western domination of the Third World. Other books, like Eve Merriam's *Boys & Girls, Girls & Boys* (1972) and Jay Williams's feminist fairy tales, such as *Philbert the Fearful* (1966), about a knight who would rather use his powers of reasoning than his sword, and *The Practical Princess* (1969), explicitly challenged traditional gender roles. Alice Childress's *A Hero Ain't Nothin' but a Sandwich* (1973) was partly told from the point of view of a thirteen-year-old heroin addict living in Harlem, and *Ruby* (1976) by Rosa Guy was one of the first books for young people to frankly explore homosexuality (while simultaneously taking on urban poverty, racism, and violence). Alexander Crosby's *One Day for Peace* (1971) told the story of six children who formed a committee to end the Vietnam War. Charlotte Pomerantz's *The Day They Parachuted Cats on Borneo: A Drama of Ecology* (1971) offered an ecological allegory (in rhyme) involving DDT, mosquitoes, cats, and rats—and was one of ten American books chosen for the International Year of the Child in 1978. Even imaginative works like Leo Lionni's picture book for young children, *Swimmy* (1963), asserted the unmistakably political message that little fish can scare off the big fish if they organize and swim together.

But if the open politics in many of the books published in the 1960s and 1970s offer a striking contrast to most of the books that left-wingers published in the postwar period, Moore insists that by the 1970s everything was different, and "you didn't have to fight for it." It is true that children's literature had already begun to change quite dramatically by 1969, the year Julius Lester's *To Be a Slave* was named a Newbery Honor book and the multiracial children's television program "Sesame Street" began broadcasting, showing the inner city *as* America, rather than as the "other America." That year, publishers reported rising demand from bookstores as well as libraries for titles dealing with "race relations," and the Elementary and Secondary Education Act (passed in 1965) and Head Start (also launched in 1965) certainly fueled the demand from school libraries.[16] Books and other materials for children and young adults— Lester's *To Be a Slave*, Virginia Hamilton's *Planet of Junior Brown* (1971), both Newbery Honor books, Eve Merriam's *Project 1-2-3* (1971) (which normalizes life in an urban project), and the enormously influential *Free to Be You and Me* (which appeared as a television program, a record album, and a book)—began more consistently to confront racism, poverty, gender stereotypes, and environmental degradation and to address children with a frankness that clearly no longer assumed their innocence. Paul Zindel's *The Pigman* (1968) and Robert Cormier's *The Chocolate War* (1974) showed children's capacity for cruelty and evil, and the groundbreaking works of Judy Blume, beginning in 1970 with *Are You There God? It's Me, Margaret*, would frankly acknowledge adolescent sexuality.

Moore's insistence that she no longer needed to fight to publish a series like Firebird Books in the 1970s minimizes all of the time that people like her had spent fighting, during an intensely repressive period. For instance, in 1957, just after the incidents in Little Rock, Arkansas, Helen Kay tried to publish a story about interracial friendship and the Fresh Air Fund, a story she wanted to call *Summer to Share*. Two years later, her editor, Jean Colby, thought the climate would finally be more receptive, and she tentatively agreed to publish the book. However, after showing the galleys to book buyers, Colby did an about-face and forced Kay to change the book to a more conventional story of a white city kid visiting a country cousin. This was the book that was published in 1960, reflecting none of Kay's original intent. Ironically, several years later, Kay was asked if she would like to republish *Summer to Share* with a black protagonist, but she was so frustrated by the original response that she refused.[17] Nancy Larrick cited the whitening of *Summer to Share* as symptomatic of the control that southern markets had managed to exert over the publishing industry for decades, ensuring that white supremacy would continue in children's books even after it had been deemed to be unconstitutional in schools.

Dorothy Sterling had been more fortuitous with *Mary Jane* (1959), which she too fought to get published. That book, which sympathetically told a story of school integration from the point of view of a fictional black protagonist, was ultimately published throughout the world in several languages and went through multiple editions. As such, it was so unusual that Larrick devoted a whole section of her article to it, noting its successful distribution through the Arrow Book Club despite pressure from southern states. Not surprisingly Sterling had far less success with her nonfiction portrait of integration in the South, *Tender Warriors* (coauthored by Donald Gross), which was published in the same year as *Mary Jane*. *Mary Jane* had described the experiences of one fictional child, showing the cruelty she encountered from whites as well as the kindnesses that ultimately sustained her. In contrast, the nonfiction *Tender Warriors*, based on a trip that Sterling took with photographer Myron Ehrenberg to recently integrated schools in six southern states, offered a less prettified picture (it was about children, but probably written more for adults). That book was banned from overseas libraries, and its distribution in the United States was extremely limited. As Larrick's survey suggested, it remained difficult to publish work that critically examined contemporary race relations in the United States until well into the 1960s. If it was easier in the 1970s to publish books that tackled controversial subjects and realistically portrayed the experience of childhood for a diverse group of children, this was partly because of the ongoing efforts of individual leftists and because of groups, like the Council on Interracial Books for Children, that grew directly out of the Old Left.[18]

Left-wingers had been at the forefront of efforts, beginning in the early 1940s, to make children's books more realistic, racially diverse, and conducive to critical thinking, and they only became more radical in their expression when the times permitted it. Contrary to the prevailing liberal narrative, which suggests that after World War II members of the Old Left were either silenced or, in renunciation of their youthful radicalism, became part of the establishment and embraced Cold War values, the example of leftists in the children's book field suggests a very different trajectory and, indeed, shows that the concerns and output of these Old Leftists evolved to look very much like those of activists in their children's generation. Although their particular concerns evolved, quite a few members of the Popular Front Left continued as they aged to push for a culture that would reflect their lingering dreams of social justice and plenty for all. And they continued to hope that a new generation of young people would eventually make this dream a reality. When the Cold War consensus ultimately broke down, in the Cuban missile crisis, Kennedy's assassination, Birmingham, the shouting voices of Berkeley's Free Speech movement, the Watts riots, and the domestic civil war over U.S. involvement in Vietnam, the impulses that had operated as a subtle stream of resistance during the Cold War became relatively mainstream.[19]

Today, in the twenty-first century, the Right and the Left are still sparring over textbook content as well as children's books. Despite the flood of "multicultural" children's books, not all the gains in this realm from the 1960s and 1970s have been permanent (new variations on Don Freeman's 1968 classic, *Corduroy*, which eliminate the African-American characters, represent a striking example). But if it seems as though the religious Right often has a disproportionate influence over textbook publishers, who struggle to offend as few people as possible, school and public libraries continue to allow children access to material representing a range of viewpoints. Thus children who read in school textbooks that homosexuality is deviant can still check out from their school or public library *Heather Has Two Mommies* (1989) or *King & King* (2002)—children's books that normalize homosexuality—just as they can find many children's books that teach them about evolution, even in states that have tried to remove any reference to Darwin from school textbooks or science curricula.[20]

Children's literature, though always limited by obvious generic constraints, remains a surprisingly free avenue for expression, freer than textbooks, television, or most other media, despite ongoing (and publicity-producing) attempts to censor it.[21] The work of left-wingers in the children's book field throughout the most repressive years of the Cold War points to the counterhegemonic impulses that may thrive even during periods that seem to foreclose dissent. In that respect, children's literature is like Tony's "wonderful door," with which this book opened: it provides an unexpected glimpse into ongoing efforts to challenge the most oppressive elements of the status quo.

NOTES

Introduction

1. Howard Fast, *Tony and the Wonderful Door* (New York: Blue Heron, 1952), 62.

2. Ibid., 63.

3. Fast's *The American* was listed by the American Library Association as one of the fifty outstanding books of 1946, yet his *Citizen Tom Paine* was "segregated" by New York City school libraries in 1947. In 1952 he and his books were placed on a "red reading" list by a citizens' committee in San Antonio that called for special labeling of "pro-Communist" books, and at least seven of Fast's books were removed from American overseas libraries in 1953. On the "segregating" of his books from New York City school libraries, see Louise S. Robbins, *Censorship and the American Library: The American Library Association's Response to Threats to Intellectual Freedom, 1939–1969* (Westport, Conn.: Greenwood, 1996), 23. On the San Antonio list, see Mrs. Myrtle G. Hance, "Read [*sic*] Reading: A Report on Our San Antonio Public Libraries: Communist Front Authors and Their Books Therein" (San Antonio, Tex.: 1953?), 7–8. On the banning of Fast's books from overseas libraries, see Milton Bracker, "Books of 40 Authors Banned by U.S. in Overseas Libraries," *New York Times* (June 22, 1953): 1, 8.

4. Although my focus is on literature, other media that catered to children also provided a welcome home to leftists during the McCarthy period. See, for instance, Paul Buhle and Dave Wagner's *Hide in Plain Sight: The Hollywood Blacklistees in Film and Television, 1950–2002* (New York: Palgrave Macmillan, 2003). Folkways Records, the Children's Record Guild, and the Young People's Record Club, all operating in the 1940s and 1950s, included musical and spoken-word pieces by people on the Left, some blacklisted. For more on the Young People's Record Club and Children's Record Guild, see David Bonner, *Revolutionizing Children's Records: The Young People's Records and Children's Record Guild Series, 1946–1977* (Lanham, Md.: Scarecrow, 2005).

5. Almost all of the books discussed in this study, with the exception of those in chapter 2, were hailed by the critical establishment. For instance, most were listed in the *Library Journal*'s annual list of recommended children's books.

6. Fast comments in symposium on America in Books for Young People, November 25, 1947, speaking to the Child Study Association's Children's Book Committee, box 14, folder 133, CSA Papers.

7. Irving Adler, interview with author, October 11, 1997, North Bennington, Vermont.

8. Pete Seeger, interview with author, December 2, 1997, Cold Spring, New York.

9. Reflecting upon the book and the circumstances of its publication, Fast noted, "[S]ince it is my belief that most good writers are liberal and that most desire to pass on such a stance to their children, it is no surprise that writing a children's book, they would try, as innocuously as possible, to suggest some of their beliefs and positions—as indeed

I attempted in *Tony and the Wonderful Door*. That more or less sums it up." Fast, letter to author, February 15, 2002.

10. Ethel Rosenberg, *Death House Letters of Julius and Ethel Rosenberg* (New York: Jero, 1953), 114.

11. The Popular Front refers to a specific policy by the Communist party (CP), inaugurated in Moscow in 1935 to foster cooperation between Communists and all democratic and antifascist forces. However, in the United States, the Popular Front was successful in mobilizing a broad spectrum of the Left not because hordes of people suddenly joined the Communist party (they didn't), but rather because its rhetoric tapped into a broader democratic sentiment characterized by opposition to fascism, racism, and imperialism and by support of labor and popular democratic struggles. Thus the Popular Front may be best understood as a "structure of feeling," which was manifest culturally in the Dust Bowl ballads of Woody Guthrie, the photographic portraits of Dorothea Lange and Walker Evans, and much of the art, theater, and music produced in conjunction with the Works Progress Administration (WPA). The Popular Front strategy made it possible for the CP and many of its "front groups" to serve, in the words of Ellen Schrecker, as "the unofficial left wing of the New Deal," with supporters of the party active in labor organizations, artist groups, reform movements, and the New Deal administration itself. Michael Denning, *The Cultural Front: The Laboring of American Culture in the Twentieth Century* (New York: Verso, 1996); Ellen Schrecker, *Many Are the Crimes: McCarthyism in America* (Boston: Little, Brown, 1998), 15.

12. Denning, *The Cultural Front*, 9.

13. Fast, *Tony and the Wonderful Door*, 30.

14. The notion of "containment" as a metaphor for norms of belief and behavior during the Cold War (rather than simply as a basis for foreign policy) comes from Elaine Tyler May, *Homeward Bound: American Families in the Cold War Era* (New York: Basic, 1988). On "victory culture" see Tom Engelhardt, *The End of Victory Culture: Cold War America and the Disillusioning of a Generation* (New York: Basic, 1994).

15. David Riesman, *The Lonely Crowd* (New Haven, Conn.: Yale University Press, 1950), 107–11.

16. For more on this critique of children's literature, see Herbert Kohl, *Should We Burn Babar: Essays on Children's Literature and the Power of Stories* (New York: New Press, 1995). Jack Zipes has also argued that children's literature has traditionally served as an agent of "bourgeoisification." See Jack Zipes, "Second Thoughts on Socialization through Literature for Children," *Lion and the Unicorn* 5 (1981): 19–32. Books such as *Dr. Doolittle* and *Little Black Sambo* have been frequent targets of criticism for their racial stereotyping; see, for instance, Isabella Suhl, "The Real Dr. Doolittle," *Interracial Books for Children* 2, nos. 1–2 (Spring–Summer 1968): 1, 5, 6, 7. On the Stratemeyer series, see Meredith Wood, "Footprints from the Past: Passing Racial Stereotypes in the Hardy Boys," in *Re/collecting Early Asian America: Essays in Cultural History*, ed. Josephine Lee, Imogene L. Lim, and Yuko Matsukawa (Philadelphia: Temple University Press, 2002).

17. Alison Lurie, *Don't Tell the Grown-ups: Subversive Children's Literature* (Boston: Little, Brown, 1990), xi.

18. Information on Tibor Gergeley from Rose Wyler, interview with author, March 27, 1998, and from Tibor Gergeley Papers, Rare Book and Manuscript Library, Columbia University.

19. For a useful discussion of the "liberal narrative" see the introduction to Thomas Hill Schaub, *American Fiction in the Cold War* (Madison: University of Wisconsin Press, 1991). For discussions of the Old Left's influence in decades after the 1930s, see Alan Wald, *Writing from the Left: New Essays on Radical Culture and Politics* (New York: Verso, 1994); Denning, *The Cultural Front*; Kate Weigand, *Red Feminism: American Communism and the Making of Women's Liberation* (Baltimore, Md.: Johns Hopkins University Press, 2001); Daniel Horowitz, *Betty Friedan and the Making of the Feminine Mystique* (Amherst: University of Massachusetts Press, 1998); Bill V. Mullen and James Smethurst, eds., *Left of the Color Line: Race, Radicalism, and Twentieth-Century Literature of the United States* (Chapel Hill: University of North Carolina Press, 2003).

20. See Wald, *Writing from the Left*; and Buhle and Wagner, *Hide in Plain Sight*.

21. R. Gordon Kelly, "Literature and the Historian," *American Quarterly* 26 (May 1974): 141–59.

22. I include William Steig partly because of his activism with the Committee for the Defense of Public Education in the 1940s (see chapter 3). He also addressed the League of American Writers in 1941. Of his politics, his wife, Jeanne Steig, wrote (prior to his death), "Bill certainly was, and is, idealistic and progressive. His parents were ardent socialists, and he was raised to believe that the perfection of the world would be possible in his lifetime." She pointed to "his concern for children and whatever oppresses them," but she also insisted, "Bill is not a philosophical artist. He would not think of himself as progressive or radical as a writer. I think he works directly from his unconscious; and he strongly resists any attempts to describe the meaning of his work. I believe he would feel inhibited by such information." Jeanne Steig, e-mail to author, March 25, 2002.

23. John Patrick Diggins, *The Rise and Fall of the American Left* (New York: Norton, 1992), 40. According to Diggins, in contrast to the conservative Right, which has "generally stood for the primacy of family, religion, authority, and property," the radical Left "called for the liberation of the young, the demystification of religious beliefs, the destruction of traditional authority, and the abolition of private property"—although I would argue that only a small minority of the radical Left has ever believed in a total elimination of private property. They also tended to hold "unlimited visions of human possibility." Ibid.

24. Alan Wald, *Exiles from a Future Time: The Forging of the Mid-Twentieth-Century Literary Left* (Chapel Hill: University of North Carolina Press, 2002), 104. Locating my primary actors as products of 1930s-era struggles against poverty, fascism, racism, and imperialism provides a necessary historical specificity, but many of my readers will undoubtedly be frustrated by my terminology. Throughout this book, I will use the deliberately vague terms "leftist," "radical," and "progressive" (often interchangeably) to describe the people at the core of this study, although I do also refer to cultural workers in the "Communist milieu." On the Popular Front as a "structure of feeling," see Denning, *The Cultural Front*, 26. Denning borrows the idea of a structure of feeling from Raymond Williams. See Raymond Williams, *The Long Revolution* (New York: Harper and Row, 1966), 48–49.

25. On the importance of the Communist party to the Left in the mid-twentieth century see Wald, *Writing from the Left*, 71. Wald emphasizes that the party's influence stretched well beyond its actual membership, which was never large. While newly unearthed material in Soviet archives confirms the American Communist party's concrete ties to the

Soviet Union and even makes clear that there were American Communists who spied for the Soviets, these were exceptional cases. Most "fellow travelers" and actual party members showed far more independence of mind and acted far more autonomously than popular portraits of the Communist "ideologue" would suggest, using the organizational apparatus and support networks of the party to the extent that they served their needs. See, for instance, Robin D. G. Kelley, *Hammer and Hoe: Alabama Communists during the Great Depression* (Chapel Hill: University of North Carolina Press, 1990). My research suggests that those who wrote for children tended to embrace small-*c* communism for emotional rather than ideological reasons. See Vivian Gornick, *The Romance of American Communism* (New York: Basic, 1977). Numerous memoirs by former Communists, while often highly critical of party orthodoxy, also show that thoughtful, idealistic, and dedicated people were among those in the party's orbit. See, for instance, Howard Fast, *Being Red: A Memoir* (Armonk, N.Y.: Sharpe, 1994). For studies highly critical of the American Communist party that highlight ties to Moscow, see Harvey Klehr, John Earl Haynes, and Fridrikh Igorevich Firsov, *The Secret World of American Communism* (New Haven, Conn.: Yale University Press, 1995); John Earl Haynes, *Red Scare or Red Menace? American Communism and Anticommunism in the Cold War Era* (Chicago: Dee, 1996); Allen Weinstein and Alexander Vassiliev, *The Haunted Wood: Soviet Espionage in America: The Stalin Era* (New York: Random House, 1999).

26. Betty Bacon, interview with author, March 10, 1998. Berkeley, California.

27. Dorothy Sterling, telephone interview with author, June 20, 2002; interview with author, November 10, 1997, Wellfleet, Massachusetts.

28. Rose Wyler, interview with author, March 27, 1998, New York City.

29. Betty Bacon acknowledged:

> The people who were in the party usually knew each other. The other ones, I think they resented it, some of them, that there was a cohesive movement that they were not part of, who were really running things. . . . And also, I think we weren't always very tactful in how we ran things. We pushed through things that we thought needed to be done. Push push. Bossy. I'm right. . . . we weren't always very tactful.

Betty Bacon, interview with author, February 20, 1999, Berkeley, California.

30. Cultural historian Judy Kutulas maintains that "progressives" had many of the same aims as Communists (and even, in many cases, shared Communists' admiration for at least some aspects of the Soviet Union), and they consciously cooperated with Communists on certain issues. However, they wished to avoid the discipline, secrecy, and, indeed, the dogmatism that often went with party membership. Self-described "liberals," on the other hand, were committed to reforming the system rather than radically transforming it, and especially after World War II, liberals tended to be explicitly anti-Communist. See Judy Kutulas, *The Long War: The Intellectual People's Front and Anti-Stalinism, 1930–1940* (Durham, N.C.: Duke University Press, 1995). In deference to the wishes of those who cooperated with me on this study, I will use the term *Communist* only for individuals who openly used that label themselves. The legacy of McCarthyism has meant that many of those who were actually members of the Communist party are still, decades after cutting ties with that organization (and years after the end of the Cold War), unwilling to be identified as such. Moreover, I

see no real value in "outing" them, given that party membership was itself not the most meaningful measure of political commitment, especially as people moved in and out of the party for a variety of reasons, and many individuals never actually joined but very much considered themselves part of a movement. Moreover, no matter what an individual's relation to the party was, rejecting Communism was not the same as rejecting political commitment; or, to put that another way, awakening to the horrors of the Soviet regime and becoming frustrated with the antidemocratic practices of the American Communist party were not equivalent to accepting the status quo and abandoning the struggle for social justice. See for instance, Wald, *Writing from the Left*, 72–77; Gornick, *The Romance of American Communism*, 5; Denning, *The Cultural Front*, 9.

31. Dorothy Sterling, interview with author, Nov. 10, 1997, Wellfleet, Mass.

32. Dr. Spock subscribed to the Communist literary journal the *New Masses* and wrote for the prolabor and antifascist newspaper *PM*; Dr. Seuss was a cartoonist for *PM*. See Lynn Bloom, *Dr. Spock: Biography of a Conservative Radical* (Indianapolis, Ind.: Bobbs-Merrill, 1972), 59. On Seuss and his politics, see Richard H. Minear, *Dr. Seuss Goes to War: The World War II Editorial Cartoons of Theodor Seuss Geisel* (New York: New Press, 1999); Philip Nel, "'Said a Bird in the Midst of a Blitz . . .': How World War II Created Dr. Seuss," *Mosaic* 34, no. 2 (June 2001): 65–85; Henry Jenkins, "No Matter How Small: The Democratic Imagination of Doctor Seuss," in *Hop on Pop: The Politics and Pleasures of Popular Culture*, ed. Henry Jenkins, Tara McPherson, and Jane Shattuc (Durham, N.C.: Duke University Press, 2002), 187–208.

33. Milton Meltzer, letter to author, November 1, 1997.

34. Information on the Loose Enders from interviews with Irving Adler, October 11, 1997, Bennington, Vermont; and Mary Elting Folsom, January 22, 1998, as well as from extensive correspondence with Mary Elting Folsom (quotations from Mary Elting Folsom, letter to author, February 7, 1998). Leone Adelson was also kind enough to send me the gag "minutes" of several Loose Ender meetings.

35. Regular and semiregular members of the group included Mary Elting Folsom and Franklin Folsom, Rose Wyler, Gerald Ames, Herman Schneider and Nina Schneider, Millicent Selsam, Irving Adler, Lilian Moore, Leone Adelson, Helen Kay (Goldfrank), May Garelick, Ira Freeman and Mae Freeman, Sarah Riedman, Isabella Suhl (librarian at the Little Red Schoolhouse), Hy Ruchlis, Ann McGovern, Abraham Marcus and Rebecca Marcus, Beatrice de Regniers, and Eleanor Clymer. Others, including Eve Merriam, David Lieske (Crockett Johnson) and Ruth Krauss, Nancy Larrick and Alexander Crosby, and Dorothy Sterling and Philip Sterling joined the group on occasion. Information from interview with Mary Elting, January 22–25, 1998, Boulder, Colorado, and correspondence from Mary Elting, March 4, 1998. Among the authors treated in this study, Millicent Selsam, Rose Wyler and Gerald Ames, Shirley Graham, Henry Felsen, Herman and Nina Schneider, Mary Elting, Lilian Moore, Franklin Folsom, Jerrold Beim, Lynd Ward, Peggy Bacon (a *New Masses* artist), Syd Hoff, Crockett Johnson, Ruth Krauss, and William Steig all wrote bestselling children's books. Jean Spealman Kujoth, *Best-selling Children's Books* (Metuchen, N.J.: Scarecrow, 1973). The American Library Association listed *Dr. George Washington Carver, Scientist* by Shirley Graham Du Bois and George Liscomb; *The Biggest Bear* by Lynd Ward; *Mary McLeod Bethune* by Emma Gelders Sterne; *Lost Worlds: Adventures in Archeology* by Anne Terry White; and Ann Petry's biography of Harriet Tubman as among the most notable children's books pub-

lished between 1940 and 1959. List of notable books in papers of children's book editor and librarian Velma Varner.

36. Jewish authors included Howard Fast, Dorothy Sterling, Eve Merriam, Millicent Selsam, Syd Hoff, Jerrold and Lorraine Beim, Helen Goldfrank (a.k.a. Helen Kay), Anne Terry White, Jay Williams, Raymond Abrashkin, Sarah Riedman, Henry Gregor Felsen, Emma Gelders Sterne, Milton Meltzer, Irwin Shapiro, Lilian Moore, Harry Granick, Ben Appel, and Irving Adler. White and Granick were both immigrants from Russia. Most of the Jewish authors were children of immigrants. African-American authors or illustrators in the Popular Front milieu included Shirley Graham, Langston Hughes, Arna Bontemps, Ann Petry, Margaret G. Burroughs, Gwendolyn Brooks, and Ernest Crichlow.

37. Pierre Bourdieu, *The Field of Cultural Production* (New York: Columbia University Press, 1993), editor's introduction by Randal Johnson, 11.

38. Mary Lapsley, "Socially Constructive Literature for Children," LAW Papers, box 5. The timing of the congress, less than two weeks before Hitler invaded the Soviet Union, or during a period in which Communists and Communist sympathizers awkwardly resisted support for the war (because of the Nazi-Soviet pact of 1939), may also suggest a kind of desperate effort to extend progressive influence into popular culture by reaching into realms that were previously deemed insignificant.

39. They were also concerned with sexism but this concern tended to be muted until the late 1940s. For more on this see chapter 7.

40. Lapsley, "Socially Constructive Literature"; Ruth Kennell, "Introductory Remarks," Juvenile Craft Session (June 1941), LAW Papers, box 5.

41. Kennell, "Introductory Remarks"; Lapsley, "Socially Constructive Literature." Discussing the ideas of Bertolt Brecht, Walter Benjamin notes:

> [F]or the transformation of the forms and instruments of production in the way desired by a progressive intelligentsia—that is, one interested in freeing the means of production and serving the class struggle—Brecht coined the term *Umfunktionierung* [functional transformation]. He was the first to make of intellectuals the far-reaching demand not to supply the apparatus of production without, to the utmost extent possible, changing it in accordance with socialism.

Jack Zipes has translated *Umfunktionierung* as "refunction."

42. Bourdieu argues that beyond analyzing the text and its material production, one must take into account the "functions of artistic mediators (publishers, critics, agents, *marchands*, academics, and so forth) as producers of the meaning and value of the work." Bourdieu, *The Field of Cultural Production*, 11. The variety of occupations represented by those attending the LAW juvenile session points to Popular Front savviness about the larger "field of cultural production." Among the speakers were authors Ruth Epperson Kennell (chairing the panel), Wanda Gág (speaking, with comment from illustrator Howard Simon, on the relation of the artist to the juvenile writer), Mary Lapsley, Eva Knox Evans (speaking on realism in stories about contemporary America), Margaret Thomsen Raymond (speaking on "A World View in Writing for Children"), Marshall McClintock (speaking on the appeal of comics), and May McNeer (speaking on "The Socially Destructive Use of Thrillers"). Also on the program were Daniel Melcher of Viking Press; Miss Lingfelter, a librarian from Chicago; Ernestine Taggart, an editor at Scholastic; Helen Kingery, a representative from the Book and Magazine Union and an

editor at Random House; Maxine Wood of the International Workers Order; puppeteer and poet Alfred Kreymborg; musician Elie Siegmeister; and Maurice Foreman, a representative from the Federal Theater Project. Program advertisement in *New Masses*. June 3, 1941, 32; meeting minutes in LAW Papers.

43. Conceptually, I am drawing here upon Robert Darnton and Pierre Bourdieu. See Robert Darnton, "What Is the History of Books," *Daedalus* 111 (Summer 1982): 65–83; Bourdieu, *The Field of Cultural Production*.

44. On selling to the booksellers see "Selling Juveniles to the Booksellers," *Publishers Weekly* 155, no. 13 (March 26, 1949): 1397–98. On selling to schools see Nancy Larrick, "Schools Need Better Information from Trade Publishers," *Publishers Weekly* 158 (December 30, 1950): 2614–16. For a helpful overview of the children's book field in the mid-twentieth century, see Leo Lerman, "An Industry within an Industry," *Saturday Review of Literature* 24 (November 8, 1941): 3–7. For a more in-depth overview, see Jean Poindexter Colby, *The Children's Book Field* (New York: Pellegrini and Cudahy, 1952).

45. On the ease of obtaining community cooperation in promoting and selling children's books, see, for example, Ursula Nordstrom, "Perhaps Even Cheerful," *Retail Bookseller* 51, no. 639 (August 1948): 69–70. For further discussion of coalitions built around children's literature, see "Children's Book Council Established as a Year-Round Agency to Promote Children's Books," *Publishers Weekly* 147 (March 3, 1945): 1006–7. The safety of children's books from censorship—at any point in history—should obviously not be exaggerated, and I point throughout this study to self-censorship, general pressures imposed on children's book authors, and specific instances of actual censorship. On censorship, see Marjorie Heins, *Not in Front of the Children: "Indecency," Censorship and the Innocence of Youth* (New York: Hill and Wang, 2001). Heins's work suggests that most censorship has actually been on moral rather than political grounds. For instances of censorship based on politics, see Nicholas J. Karolides, *Literature Suppressed on Political Grounds* (New York: Facts on File, 1998).

46. The most famous expression of such fear vis-à-vis youth was Frederic Wertham's tirade against comic books, *Seduction of the Innocent*; the seduction discourse also rationalized the removal of Communist teachers from schools and the censorship of textbooks. See Frederic Wertham, *Seduction of the Innocent* (New York: Rinehart, 1954). Also see James Gilbert, *A Cycle of Outrage: America's Reaction to the Juvenile Delinquent* (New York: Oxford University Press, 1986).

47. According to Pierre Bourdieu:

The definition of the writer (or artist, etc.) is an issue at stake in struggles in every literary (or artistic, etc.) field. In other words, the field of cultural production is the site of struggles in which what is at stake is the power to impose the dominant definition of the writer and therefore to delimit the population of those entitled to take part in the struggle to define the writer. . . . In short, the fundamental stake in literary struggles is the monopoly of literary legitimacy, i.e. *inter alia*, the monopoly of the power to consecrate producers or products.

Bourdieu, *The Field of Cultural Production*, 42.

48. Figures on librarians from Christine Jenkins, "The Strength of the Inconspicuous: Youth Services Librarians, the American Library Association, and Intellectual Freedom for the Young, 1939–1955" (Ph.D. diss., University of Wisconsin, 1995), 23. On women in

publishing and in bookselling see John Tebbel, *History of Book Publishing in the United States* (New York: Bowker, 1978), 3:265–78.

49. See Jenkins, "The Strength of the Inconspicuous."

50. Elting, telephone interview with author, January 25, 2002.

51. Concerns about southern sales on the part of those in publishing made many liberal editors cautious on race-related issues, which were, of course, wrapped up in the Communist issue (as segregationists accused civil rights activists of being Communist agitators). For further discussion see chapter 7 and the epilogue.

52. Several of the people in this study worked, at various times, throughout the "communications circuit" (Darnton) traveled by children's books. Rose Wyler, Lilian Moore, and Emma Gelders Sterne, for instance, each worked as a teacher, editor, and writer; Betty Bacon worked as an editor, writer, and librarian.

53. For more on "progressive parenting," see Julia Mickenberg, "The Pedagogy of the Popular Front: Progressive Parenting for a New Generation, 1918–1945," in *The American Child: A Cultural Studies Reader*, ed. Caroline Levander and Carol Singley (New Brunswick, N.J.: Rutgers University Press, 2003). Also see Jenkins, "No Matter How Small." A useful discussion of Spock, especially vis-à-vis fascism, can be found in William Graebner, "The Unstable World of Benjamin Spock: Social Engineering in a Democratic Culture, 1917–1950," *Journal of American History* 67 (1980): 612–29.

54. On this trend toward nonfiction series see Lillian Hollowell, "Series in Children's Books," *Wilson Library Bulletin* 27 (May 1953), 736–38. Quotation from Betty Bacon, interview with author, March 10, 1998. Berkeley, California.

55. For more on this tradition, see Nick Salvatore, *Eugene V. Debs: Citizen and Socialist* (Urbana: University of Illinois Press, 1982); Sean Wilentz, *Chants Democratic: New York City and the Rise of the American Working Class, 1788–1850* (New York: Oxford University Press, 2004); Douglas Wixson, *Worker-Writer in America: Jack Conroy and the Tradition of Midwestern Literary Radicalism, 1898–1990* (Urbana and Chicago: University of Illinois Press, 1994).

56. This was a campaign slogan of Earl Browder when he ran for president in 1936 on the Communist ticket.

57. That liberal values taught to children in the 1950s had a formative influence on the 1960s radicals is not a new idea; see, for instance Richard Flacks, "The Liberated Generation: An Exploration of the Roots of Student Protest," *Journal of Social Issues* 23, no. 3 (1967): 52–75; Kenneth Keniston, "The Sources of Student Dissent," *Journal of Social Issues* 23, no. 3 (1967): 108–37. These studies point out that a significant number of student radicals were "red-diaper babies," but they do not consider the impact of left-wingers on culture more generally. The term "red diaper baby" refers to children of parents in the Communist Left. It was coined by the John Birch Society but reappropriated by the people it intended to mock. See Judy Kaplan and Linn Shapiro, eds., *Red Diapers: Growing Up in the Communist Left* (Urbana and Chicago: University of Illinois Press, 1998). The book's introduction describes the origins of the term.

58. Most surveys of children's literature point to this shift. See, for instance, John Rowe Townsend, *Written for Children: An Outline of English-Language Children's Literature* (London: Scarecrow, 1996); Marjorie Allen, *One Hundred Years of Children's Books in America* (New York: Facts on File, 1996); Sally Allen McNall, "American Children's Literature, 1880–Present," in *American Childhood: A Research Guide and Historical Handbook*, ed. Joseph M. Hawes and N. Ray Hiner (Westport, Conn.: Greenwood, 1985), 377–413. Also see Anne Scott MacLeod, *American Childhood: Children's*

Literature of the Nineteenth and Twentieth Centuries (Athens: University of Georgia Press, 1994).

Chapter 1

1. Alfred Kreymborg, *Funnybone Alley* (New York: Macaulay, 1927), 16–17.
2. Ibid., 25, 72.
3. Ibid., 85, 39.
4. Ibid., 167.
5. John Patrick Diggins, *The Rise and Fall of the American Left* (New York: Norton, 1992), 94–98.
6. Fishbein, introduction to Rebecca Zurier, *Art for the Masses: A Radical Magazine and Its Graphics, 1911–1917* (Philadelphia: Temple University Press, 1987), 3. Zurier notes that "diaries, letters and reminiscences reveal a self-aware '*Masses* crowd' (also known as 'Them Asses'), many of whom lived in Greenwich Village, frequented the same clubs and restaurants, and summered together in Provincetown, Gloucester, and Croton-on-Hudson" (xvi).
7. Fishbein, introduction to Zurier, *Art for the Masses*, 3; Frederick Lewis Allen, *Only Yesterday: An Informal History of the Nineteen-twenties* (New York: Blue Ribbon, 1931), 73; Malcolm Cowley, *Exile's Return: A Literary Odyssey of the 1920s* (New York: Viking, 1964), 69. Also see V. F. Calverton and Samuel D. Schmalhausen, eds., *The New Generation: The Intimate Problems of Modern Parents and Children* (New York: Macaulay, 1930).
8. Alfred Kreymborg, *Troubadour: An Autobiography* (New York: Boni and Liveright, 1925), 130; Franklin Folsom, *Days of Anger, Days of Hope: A Memoir of the League of American Writers, 1937–1942* (Niwot: University Press of Colorado, 1994), 299–300. The record was a collaboration between Alfred Kreymborg and Elie Siegmeister, with songs performed by Robert Penn, Margaret Tobias, and Tom Glazer, recorded by Asch Recording Studios (which eventually became Folkways Records).
9. See Joseph Wood Krutch, *The Modern Temper: A Study and a Confession* (New York: Harcourt Brace, 1929). For historical treatments see Lynn Dumenil, *The Modern Temper: American Culture and Society in the 1920s* (New York: Hill and Wang, 1995); Christine Stansell, *American Moderns: Bohemian New York and the Creation of a New Century* (New York: Metropolitan, 2000). On how these changes affected children in particular, see Paula Fass, *The Damned and the Beautiful: American Youth in the 1920s* (New York: Oxford University Press, 1977); Ellen Key, *The Century of the Child* (New York: Putnam, 1909). On the massive expansion of public education in the 1920s, see Fass, *The Damned and the Beautiful*, 46–49.
10. Carolyn Steedman, *Childhood, Culture and Class in Britain: Margaret Macmillan* (New Brunswick, N.J.: Rutgers University Press, 1990), 37. For a discussion of this shift in children's literature, see Gillian Avery, *Behold the Child: American Children and Their Books, 1621–1922* (London: Bodley Head, 1994).
11. See Robyn Muncy, *Creating a Female Dominion in American Reform, 1890–1935* (New York: Oxford University Press, 1991). On librarianship in particular, see Kay Vandergrift, "Female Advocacy and Harmonious Voices: A History of Public Library Services and Publishing for Children in the United States," *Library Trends* 44, no. 4 (Spring 1996): 683–718; Christine Jenkins, "The Strength of the Inconspicuous: Youth Services

Librarians, the American Library Association, and Intellectual Freedom for the Young, 1939–1955" (Ph.D. diss., University of Wisconsin, 1995), 58.

12. For further discussion of these lists and their power, see Jenkins, "The Strength of the Inconspicuous." Also see Margaret Bush, "New England Book Women: Their Increasing Influence," *Library Trends* 44, no. 4 (Spring 1996): 719–35; John Tebbel, *History of Book Publishing in the United States* (New York: Bowker, 1978), 3:266.

13. Tebbel, *History of Book Publishing* 3:266–67. Also see "The Beginnings of Children's Book Week," *Publishers Weekly* 110, no. 16 (October 16, 1926): 1592–93.

14. After Macmillan broke new ground in 1919 by hiring Louise Seaman, whose background was in teaching, playgrounds, and settlement house work, to head the first juvenile publishing division, other publishers quickly followed suit, most of them hiring former children's librarians to fill their posts. Tebbel, *History of Book Publishing* 3:276; "Three Librarians in the Publishing World," *Wilson Bulletin for Librarians* 5 (September 1930): 55–57. Also see Muriel Fuller's portraits of children's book editors in *Publishers Weekly*, beginning in the 1920s.

15. *Proceedings of the Sixth National Convention of the American Legion*, H.D. 517, 68th Cong., 2d sess. (Washington, D.C.: Government Printing Office, 1925), 126, 127, quoted in William Gellermann, *The American Legion as Educator* (New York: Bureau of Publications, Teachers College, Columbia University, 1938), 205. National essay contests were an early highlight of Education Week, with topics like "Why America Should Prohibit Education for Five Years" (1923) and "Why Communism Is a Menace to Americanism" (1924); the AL also gave awards, monitored school textbooks (as part of its program in "civic instruction"), and cooperated closely with the Boy Scouts. Gellermann, 216. The argument that progressive education reshaped schooling can be traced to Lawrence A. Cremin, *The Transformation of the School: Progressivism in American Education, 1876–1957* (New York: Knopf, 1961).

16. Kreymborg, *Funnybone Alley*, 205, 261.

17. Ibid., 207.

18. Ibid., 209.

19. For more in-depth discussions of progressive education, see Cremin, *Transformation of the School*; Patricia Graham, *Progressive Education: From Arcady to Academe: A History of the Progressive Education Association, 1919–1955* (New York: Columbia University, Teachers College, 1967); Stephen I. Brown and Mary E. Finn, eds., *Readings from Progressive Education: A Movement and Its Professional Journal* (Lanham, Md.: University Press of America, 1988).

20. Margaret V. Girdner, "School Library Visions," *Libraries* 34 (1929): 413–14.

21. Helen Butler noted in the *ALA* (American Library Association) *Bulletin* in 1934 that "school assignments are responsible for about 95 percent of the nonfiction circulation of children's reading rooms in public libraries." Helen L. Butler, "Correlation of the Library with the Social Sciences," *ALA Bulletin* 28 (1934): 403.

22. Cremin, *Transformation of the School*, 119–26.

23. Cremin, *Transformation of the School*, 119–26, 214–15; Dewey "Progressive," in Brown and Finn, eds., *Readings from Progressive Education*, 163; Norman Thomas, "Can Our Schools Face the Facts?" in *Children and Youth in America*, ed. Robert H. Bremner (Cambridge, Mass.: Harvard University Press, 1932), 1644–46.

24. The famous "Gary Plan," developed by William Wirt in Gary, Indiana, in which shop, laboratory, auditorium, and playground were used as fully as classrooms, presented a model of how a school—open twelve months a year—could be the true center

of artistic and intellectual life in the neighborhood and a model of innovations. While the plan earned the praise of many progressives, Wirt's plan also gained national attention and support because it was cost-effective: only half as many classrooms were needed if children did much of their learning elsewhere. Likewise, those progressives calling for a "science" of education fit in well with the new gospel of efficiency that served the interests of business. See Brown and Finn, eds., *Readings from Progressive Education*, 14–15. For more on the Gary Plan, see Cremin, *Transformation of the School*, 155. Also see John Dewey and Evelyn Dewey, *Schools of Tomorrow* (New York: Dutton, 1920).

25. Agnes De Lima, *Our Enemy, the Child* (New York: New Republic, 1925), 238.

26. For Freud's influence on theorists of progressive education, see Cremin, *Transformation of the School*, 206–14; Floyd Dell, *Were You Ever a Child?* (New York: Knopf, 1919), 179, 116.

27. Paul Goodman, *Growing Up Absurd: Problems of Youth in the Organized System* (New York: Random House, 1960); Dell, *Were You Ever a Child?* 90.

28. Avery, *Behold the Child*, 213. Reviewers at the time of the book's publication said that Sandburg had "developed a new field in American fairy-tale conception" and predicted that the stories "will clearly be the feature of the season." Review of *Rootabaga Stories* by Carl Sandburg, *New York Times* (November 19, 1922): 10; May Lamberton Becker, Review of *Rootabaga Stories* by Carl Sandburg, *Literary Review* (December 9, 1922): 208; "To Alice Corbin Henderson," May 10, 1920, in *The Letters of Carl Sandburg*, ed. Herbert Mitgang (New York: Harcourt, Brace and World, 1968), 187; Penelope Niven, *Carl Sandburg: A Biography* (New York: Scribner's, 1991), 136; Mitgang, ed., *The Letters of Carl Sandburg*, x–xii.

29. "To Paula Sandburg," in Mitgang, ed., *The Letters of Carl Sandburg*, 133.

30. Carl Sandburg, *Rootabaga Stories* (New York: Harcourt Brace, 1922), 3, 4, 6, 9.

31. Sandburg, *Rootabaga Stories*, 51, 111, 175–83; Carl Sandburg, *Rootabaga Pigeons* (New York: Harcourt, Brace and World, 1923), 116.

32. Sandburg, *Rootabaga Pigeons*, 146–47.

33. Sandburg, *Rootabaga Stories*, 134, 137.

34. Ibid., 137. For a useful discussion of the "new woman" of the 1910s and 1920s, see Stansell, *American Moderns*.

35. Sandburg told his publisher that he envisioned the book to be "for people from 5 to 105 years of age." "To Alfred Harcourt," July 29, 1922, in Mitgang, ed., *The Letters of Carl Sandburg*, 212.

36. "To Anne Carroll Moore," November 20, 1922, in Mitgang, ed., *The Letters of Carl Sandburg*, 220.

37. Sandburg, *Rootabaga Stories*, 10. "To Witter Bynner," September 5, 1922, in Mitgang, ed., *The Letters of Carl Sandburg*, 214. For Sandburg's influence on Hughes, see Arnold Rampersad, *The Life of Langston Hughes*, vol. 1: *1902–1941: I, Too, Sing America* (New York: Oxford University Press, 1986), 29. For his influence on Meltzer, see Milton Meltzer, *Starting from Home: A Writer's Beginnings* (New York: Viking Penguin, 1988), 111. For his influence on Le Sueur, see Le Sueur Papers, which contain references to Sandburg as a "spiritual father." Loose transcript, file folder "Miscellaneous Papers," 1930–1961, 144.I.19.5B10.

38. Richard W. Cox, "Wanda Gág: The Bite of the Picture Book," *Minnesota History* 44 (Fall 1975): 242, 247.

39. Ibid., 250–51; Wanda Gág, "I Like Fairy Tales," *Horn Book Magazine* 15, no. 2 (March–April 1939): 79. Leonard Marcus notes Moore's belief that childhood was "a

fixed state of innocence to be shielded from, rather than shaped by historical and environmental factors." Leonard S. Marcus, *Margaret Wise Brown: Awakened by the Moon* (Boston: Beacon, 1992), 57.

40. Ernestine Evans, "Russian Children and Their Books," *Asia* 31 (November 1931): 686–91. On Evans's career as a foreign correspondent and for a sense of her political outlook, see Ernestine Evans Papers.

41. Karen Nelson Hoyle, *Wanda Gág* (New York: Twayne, 1994), 31–39.

42. Ernestine Evans, "This Year's Crop," *Nation* 127 (November 21, 1928): 547–48.

43. Lynd Ward, "Wanda Gág, Fellow-Artist," *Horn Book Magazine* 23 (May 1947): 196.

44. Dell, *Were You Ever a Child?* 84–85.

45. Joyce Antler, *Lucy Sprague Mitchell: The Making of a Modern Woman* (New Haven, Conn.: Yale University Press, 1987), 238, 242.

46. Ibid., 314, 239. Franklin Folsom's FBI file notes that Mitchell "was listed as a sponsor of the United States Soviet Friendship Celebration at the Madison Square Garden in New York City on November 16, 1944." FBI file for Franklin Folsom, FOIPA No. 0990201–000.

47. Lucy Sprague Mitchell, "Making Real Teachers," *Educational Outlook* 20 (January 1946): 61; Antler, *Lucy Sprague Mitchell*, 311, 319, 413. All but Moore are mentioned by Antler; Moore herself told me about studying with Mitchell. Moore claimed that Mitchell's work and Bank Street's philosophy were political only "in the widest sense," or to the extent that "truth is political, or nurture is political," but she did concede that Mitchell had a "a big impact on people who were more political." Interview with Lilian Moore, November 22, 1998, Seattle.

48. Lucy Sprague Mitchell, *Here and Now Story Book: Two- to Seven-Year-Olds* (New York: Dutton, 1921), 20, 23.

49. Ibid., 22–23. Mitchell, *Another Here and Now Story Book* (New York: Dutton, 1937), xv. , xv.

50. Antler, *Lucy Sprague Mitchell*, 399. For information on the *Here and Now* stories' use in the Soviet Union, see Vera Fediaevsky, "'Here and Now' Stories in Russia: An Experiment," *Elementary School Journal* 26, no. 4 (December 1925): 278–89.

51. Rhoda Harris, "New Books for a Changing School," *Publishers Weekly* 118 (August 30, 1930): 816; Mitchell, *Here and Now Story Book*, 29. Antler cites the many glowing reviews of the *Here and Now Story Book*. See Antler, *Lucy Sprague Mitchell*, 252–54.

52. Lucy Sprague Mitchell, *Here and Now Primer: Home from the Country* (New York: Dutton, 1924), 58.

53. Mitchell, *Here and Now Story Book*, 231–35, 253–54.

54. The story's use of dialect and stereotypical depictions of African Americans also shows evidence of Mitchell's troubling racial politics, which were not unusual for her time (the only truly progressive group on race matters in the 1900s and 1910s were the Industrial Workers of the World). Leslie Fishbein argues that the *Masses* crowd embraced cultural pluralism but had a more ambivalent position toward African Americans. Typically, she says, they "appropriated blacks as a cultural symbol, an emblem of paganism free of the puritanical repression that plagued whites." Fishbein, introduction to Zurier, *Art for the Masses*, 15.

55. Virginia Burton, *Mike Mulligan and His Steam Shovel* (Boston: Houghton Mifflin, 1939).

56. Dell quoted in Antler, *Lucy Sprague Mitchell*, 399. Also see Harris, "New Books for a Changing School"; Nora Beust, "Books for Children: Reading: Some Methods and New Materials," Review of *Here and Now Story Book*, *Progressive Education* 2, no. 3 (July–September 1925): 196–99; Alfred Kreymborg, "The Decline of Mother Goose," in *The New Generation: The Intimate Problems of Modern Parents and Children*, ed. V. F. Calverton and Samuel D. Schmalhausen (New York: Macmillan, 1930), 623–32.

57. Gág, "I Like Fairy Tales," 76.

58. In *Diggers and Builders*, for instance, Tony the Steam Shovel Man, has "a hard job" but we learn that he is "very strong." And Pedro the Road Builder "is a good boss and his men work hard to please him." Henry Bolles Lent, *Diggers and Builders* (New York: Macmillan, 1931), 3, 54. The depiction of African-American laborers by progressives such as Mitchell is far more ambivalent, however. These laborers are not so much alienated as stripped of their ability to experience alienation. Review of *Funnybone Alley* by Alfred Kreymborg, *New York Times* (September 25, 1927): 5; Review of *Funnybone Alley* by Alfred Kreymborg, *New York Evening Post* (September 24, 1927): 10.

59. Frances Frisbie O'Donnell, "Educating for Peace," *Parents* 6, no. 7 (July 1931): 15; Valerie Watrous, "Books and the Child," *Progressive Education* 8, no. 7 (November 1931): 586–88; Diana Marcia Selig, "Cultural Gifts: American Liberals, Childhood, and the Origins of Multiculturalism, 1924–1939" (Ph.D. diss., University of California, 2001), 1–37.

60. Selig, "Cultural Gifts," 33.

61. Originally published in 1922, the book went through six editions and multiple printings, with an edition printed as late as 1968. Annie E. S. Beard, *Our Foreign-Born Citizens: What They Have Done for America* (New York: Crowell).

62. Hildegarde Hoyt Swift, *The Railroad to Freedom: A Story of the Civil War* (New York: Harcourt, Brace and World, 1932), 356, 352. Swift was clearly a liberal, as is particularly evident from her correspondence with radical artist Lynd Ward (with whom she collaborated on several books) praising him for his sensitivity to social issues. See letter from Hildegarde Hoyt Swift to Lynd Ward, July 3, 1945, Lynd Ward/May McNeer Papers, Georgetown University. Their *North Star Shining* is remarkably more enlightened as a work highlighting African-American freedom struggles, reflecting a growing awareness and more hospitable climate for such work.

63. Several other Newbery Medal or Honor books had black characters: *Glory of the Seas* by Agnes D. Hewes (1935) had a plot line concerning the Fugitive Slave Law and a family conflict over an escaped slave in which the slave was predictably stereotyped and in which both sides of the controversy over slavery were given equal play; and the *Dr. Doolittle* books by Hugh Lofting have in recent decades been condemned for their racist portraits of African natives. For more on the Newbery Medal and Honor books, see Linda Kauffman Peterson and Marilyn Leathers Solt, *Newbery and Caldecott Medal and Honor Books: An Annotated Bibliography* (Boston: Hall, 1982). Information (and inspiration) also drawn from Kenneth Kidd, "Newbery Gold: Children's Book Prizing in the United States." Unpublished paper presented at the University of Texas at Austin, March 11, 2005.

64. "Among the Books for Girls and Boys," *Progressive Education* 8, no. 8 (December 1931): 716–35.

65. Gillian Avery et al., "Children's Literature in America, 1870–1945," in *Children's Literature: An Illustrated History*, ed. Peter Hunt (New York: Oxford University Press, 1995), 225–51; Cornelia Meigs et al., *A Critical History of Children's Literature* (New York:

Macmillan, 1953), 383; Lucy Fitch Perkins, *The Pickaninny Twins* (Boston: Houghton Mifflin, 1931); Emma Gelders Sterne, *No Surrender* (New York: Duffield and Green, 1932); Review of *No Surrender* by Emma Gelders Sterne, *New York Times* (November 13, 1932): 9.

66. See, for example, "The Children's New Dresses" in Mitchell, *Here and Now Story Book: Two- to Seven-Year-Olds*, 234–35; Carl Sandburg, *Abe Lincoln Grows Up* (New York: Harcourt, Brace, 1954). For some of these racial representations in Sandburg, see 8–18, including the section on "Copper faces and white." Mary White Ovington, a white *Masses* contributor and founder of the NAACP, was an exceptional model in this regard: in 1913 she published *Hazel*, a sensitive account of a northern, middle-class, African-American girl living in Alabama, and in 1920 she compiled (with Myron T. Pritchard), *The Upward Path: A Reader for Colored Children*, which included classic and contemporary African-American authors such as Phillis Wheatley, Frederick Douglass, Paul Lawrence Dunbar, Booker T. Washington, W. E. B. Du Bois, and Fenton Johnson. In the late 1930s, Bank Street sponsored a special "Negro scholarship" for the Writers' Laboratory, suggesting a new awareness that African Americans were an integral part of the urban scene Mitchell wished to explicate. See Katharine Capshaw Smith, "From Bank Street to Harlem: A Conversation with Ellen Tarry," *Lion and the Unicorn* 23 (1999): 271–85.

67. Katharine Capshaw Smith, "Rendering the Red Summer of 1919 and The Scottsboro Boys: Representations of Violence in Black Children's Literature of the 1920s and 1930s," paper presented at the annual meeting of the American Studies Association, October 2003. Also see Katharine Capshaw Smith, *Children's Literature of the Harlem Renaissance* (Bloomington: Indiana University Press, 2004).

68. Diane Johnson-Feelings, ed., *The Best of the Brownies' Book* (New York: Oxford University Press, 1996), 12; Rampersad, *I, Too, Sing America*, 45; Langston Hughes, "Books and the Negro Child," *Children's Library Yearbook* 4 (1932): 109.

69. Cremin, *Transformation of the School*, 224; Upton Sinclair, *The Goose Step: A Study of American Education* (Pasadena, Calif.: Author, 1923). Also see Upton Sinclair, *The Goslings* (Pasadena, Calif.: Author, 1924). On schools as agents of social change see George Sylvester Counts, *Dare the School Build a New Social Order?* (New York: Day, 1932).

70. "Today's Children," *ALA Bulletin* 26 (1932): 628.

Chapter 2

1. In the book's preface, Kay introduces the story to her intended audience of Young Pioneers.

2. Helen Kay, *Battle in the Barnyard: Stories and Pictures for Workers' Children* (New York: Workers Library, 1932), 6, 28–29, 30.

3. The book's dissemination was apparently so limited that it did not even get mentioned in the otherwise extensive file the FBI compiled on Kay (Helen Colodny Goldfrank).

4. "For Young Revolutionists," Review of *Comrades for the Charter* by Geoffrey Trease, *Eddie and the Gypsy* by Alex Wedding, and *Martin's Annual*, ed. Joan Beauchamp, *New Masses* (August 20, 1935): 24.

5. E. A. Schachner, "Revolutionary Literature in the United States Today," *Windsor Quarterly* 2, no. 1 (Spring 1934): 58–61. Schachner distinguishes "proletarian" and "revo-

lutionary" literature, arguing that "the proletarian novel [in contrast to the "revolution-ary" one] is one which reflects the life of any typical cross section of the proletariat and need not be more revolutionary than the proletariat itself is at the time the novel is written." Other critics writing in the 1930s defined *proletarian literature* simply as lit-erature by poor or working-class authors. Some argued that any literature truthfully depicting the life of poor and oppressed people was ipso facto "revolutionary," for it would implicitly contrast "what is" with what "might be." For more on these debates, see Barbara Foley, *Radical Representations: Politics and Form in U.S. Proletarian Fiction, 1929–1941* (Durham, N.C.: Duke University Press, 1993), 86–128. I do not argue that all children's literature published by Communist publishers was proletarian, in any sense of the word.

6. On enduring (and often problematic) notions of childhood innocence that inform children's literature see Jacqueline Rose, *The Case of Peter Pan; or, The Impossibility of Children's Fiction* (Philadelphia: University of Pennsylvania Press, 1993). For scholarly discussions of proletarian literature, see, for instance, Daniel Aaron, *Writers on the Left: Episodes in American Literary Communism* (New York: Harcourt, Brace and World, 1961); Walter Rideout, *The Radical Novel in the United States: Some Interrelations of Literature and Society* (New York: Hill and Wang, 1956); Paula Rabinowitz, *Labor and Desire: Women's Revolutionary Fiction in Depression America* (Chapel Hill: University of North Carolina Press, 1991); Foley, *Radical Representations*. Alan Wald does note that leftists such as Myra Page wrote for children (stories by Page appear in the Communist magazine for children *New Pioneer*), but he does not discuss any specific writings for children. See Alan Wald, *Writing from the Left: New Essays on Radical Culture and Politics* (New York: Verso, 1994).

7. Paul C. Mishler provides one of the only existing substantive discussions of Com-munist children's literature in his book *Raising Reds: The Young Pioneers, Radical Sum-mer Camps, and Communist Political Culture in the United States* (New York: Colum-bia University Press, 1999). In discussing "Communist children's literature," Mishler, for the most part, limits his focus to explicitly political books used by Communist children's organizations; my discussion of this work is limited, in part because Mishler has already ably covered it. In contrast to Mishler's focus, I am on the whole less inter-ested in Communists' internal program of socializing young people than in the ways in which the broader Communist milieu affected American popular culture through children's books.

8. For specifics, see Mishler's chapter on Communist children's literature and his use-ful annotated bibliography; several of the books discussed by Mishler are also cited in my selected bibliography of children's books. A number of other children's books were published in foreign languages in conjunction with radical ethnic programs; particu-larly notable are Finnish and Yiddish children's books. For radical Jewish material (in Yiddish and English) see the Secular Yiddish Schools of America Collection at Stanford University. Finnish material can be found at the Immigration History Research Center, University of Minnesota, Twin Cities.

9. In the early 1930s the *New Masses* recommended several books by Wanda Gág; *Charlie Chaplin's Parade* by Mike Gold (a modernist fable that mocks the corporate order); and *The Teacup Whale* by Lydia Gibson (a story about a boy who brings home a "whale" he found in a puddle and his vindicated faith, against his mother's skepti-cism, that the "whale" would grow to full size). The *New Masses* also recommended Lucy Sprague Mitchell's books along with other here-and-now texts like Wilfred Jones's

How the Derrick Works and *A Steam Shovel for Me!* by Vera Edelstadt. These texts only seem political in terms of their visual aesthetic and their attention to labor. Still, until the 1940s the *New Masses* recommended few books by authors who were not aligned with the Left. See, for instance, *New Masses* (October 1929): 32; (June 30, 1930): 24; (July 1932): 31; Jean Simon, "Which Books for Your Children?" *New Masses* 17 (December 24, 1935): 23–25. Reviews and booklists published after 1935 tended to be much more expansive.

10. Van Gosse, "To Organize in Every Neighborhood, in Every Home: The Gender Politics of American Communists between the Wars," *Radical History Review* 50 (Spring 1991): 109–41.

11. Perhaps most notably, *The Working Woman*, a monthly newspaper that began publication in 1929, used a combination of eyewitness or personal testimony, reportage, and hard statistics from agencies like the Children's Bureau to paint a dire portrait of children's lives under capitalism.

12. Alice Withrow Field, "Happy Children in the Soviet Union," *Working Woman* (May 1933): 10. Also see Grace Hutchins, *Children under Capitalism*, vol. 33 (New York: International, 1933), 18; Ella Winter, "What Fascism Means to Mothers," *Working Woman* (August 1933): 6.

13. Michael Gold, "The Proletarian Child," in *The New Generation: The Intimate Problems of Modern Parents and Children*, ed. V. F. Calverton and Samuel D. Schmalhausen (New York: Macaulay, 1930), 675. For a general discussion of depression-era children, see Joseph M. Hawes, *Children between the Wars: American Childhood, 1920–1940* (New York: Twayne, 1997). For a more concrete discussion of depression-era schools from a Communist perspective, see Rex David, *Schools and the Crisis*, vol. 39 (New York: International, 1934). For figures on school closings David cites National Education Association, Joint Commission on the Emergency in Education, *The Schools and the Depression* (Washington, D.C.: Government Printing Office, 1933). Black students on the average spent, per year, 21 days fewer in school than did white students, who themselves spent an average of only 141 days a year in school (as compared to today's 180-day school year). U.S. Bureau of the Census, *Sixteenth Census of the United States* (Washington, D.C.: Government Printing Office, 1940), 108, 111. The actual number of child laborers was far higher, for census figures included only a fraction of those engaging in street trades, industrial housework, and various forms of agriculture. Also see T. Swann Harding, "What Price Parenthood?" in *The New Generation*, ed. Calverton and Schmalhausen, 330–56; Katharine DuPre Lumpkin and Dorothy Wolff Douglas, *Child Workers in America* (New York: McBride, 1937).

14. Hutchins, *Children under Capitalism*, 22; Martha Campion, *Who Are the Young Pioneers?* (New York: New Pioneer, 1934), 21. Communist organizations for children were concentrated in cities like New York, Los Angeles, and Chicago, but also existed in smaller cities. Summer camps, most often located in upstate New York, could also be found in Illinois, Michigan, Wisconsin, and other areas. Mishler, *Raising Reds*, 83–108; Young Communist League, *The Road to Mass Organization of Proletarian Children: Decisions of the Fourth International Conference of Leaders of Communist Children's Leagues, Moscow, September 1929* (New York: Young Communist League/Youth International, 1930), 29.

15. Mishler, *Raising Reds*, 46.

16. Campion, *Who Are the Young Pioneers?* 1; Michael Gold, Review of *Fairy Tales for Workers' Children* by Herminia [sic] Zur Mühlen, *Workers Monthly* 4, no. 12 (October 1925): 571.

17. See Carolyn Steedman, *Childhood, Culture and Class in Britain: Margaret Macmillan* (New Brunswick, N.J.: Rutgers University Press, 1990); John Spargo, *Bitter Cry of the Children* (New York: Macmillan, 1905); "'Mother' Jones Will Lead Textile Child Workers through Country to Win Sympathy: Army of 400 Boys and Girls in Living Appeal for Aid," in *Mother Jones Speaks: Collected Speeches and Writings*, ed. Phillip Foner (New York: Monad, 1983), 487–88. For a more optimistic view of childhood from a socialist perspective, see Horace Traubel, "Born Strikers," *Young Socialists Magazine* 12, no. 5 (May 1918): 7.

18. For example, in the story "Willie's Birthday," Willie, a well-cared-for child from a relatively affluent family, sees, while out shopping for his birthday present, ragged-looking children looking wistfully in shop windows. This moment becomes an occasion to teach Willie about the ideal of "STATE MAINTENANCE": as the story explains it, "the Socialists say that the nation should look after the children, and see they are properly brought up and properly educated." *The Child's Socialist Reader* (London: Twentieth Century, 1907), 102, 106–7.

19. Ibid., vii.

20. On their critique of the Boy Scouts, see "The American Boy Scout," *Little Socialist Magazine for Boys and Girls* 3, no. 8 (August 1910): 2.

21. William F. Kruse, "Socialist Education for Children," *Young Socialists Magazine* 11, no. 3 (March 1917): 9–10.

22. *The Child's Socialist Reader* provided a simple and clear explanation of why capitalism was wrong and socialism necessary:

> Socialists say that the land should belong to nobody, but should be for the use of the whole people—that no one can have a better right to it than the whole people. They also say that the workers should be free to work without giving the capitalists profit. Then we should not have poor people who have to go without proper food, while rich people have more of everything than they want.

The Child's Socialist Reader, 3. Nicholas Klein, *The Socialist Primer: A Book of First Lessons for the Little Ones in Words of One Syllable* (Girard, Kans.: 1908), 12. For the praises of London, see "A Wise Mother," *Little Socialist Magazine for Boys and Girls* 2, no. 12 (December 1909): 10. The magazine here reprinted a mother's request that they send her several of Jack London's books as a present for her son, and noted that "if every socialist mother did something like that for her children we would soon have a beautiful world full of happy people."

23. W. Gundlach, "Law of Gravitation," *Little Socialist Magazine for Boys and Girls* 3, no. 2 (March 1910): 4, 14.

24. "Happy Valley: A Fairy Tale," in *The Child's Socialist Reader* (London: Twentieth Century, 1907), 5–13.

25. Jack Zipes notes that the primary goal of these tales was "to compel young readers to think about their impoverished living conditions and the potential they had to change them through political action." Jack Zipes, ed., *Fairy Tales and Fables from Weimar Days* (Hanover, N.H.: University Press of New England, 1989), 20. Also see Lisa Tetzner, *Hans Sees the World* (New York: Covici, Friede, 1934).

26. Dailes, introduction to Hermynia Zur Mühlen, *Fairy Tales for Workers' Children*, trans. Ida Dailes (Chicago, Ill.: Daily Worker, 1925), n.p.

27. Zur Mühlen, *Fairy Tales for Workers' Children*, 64, 65.

28. Gold, Review of *Fairy Tales for Workers' Children*, 572.

29. Gold, "Notes of the Month," *New Masses* 5 (January 1930) 21, quoted in Foley, *Radical Representations*, 66. Ironically, Gold published his own fanciful children's book, *Charlie Chaplin's Parade*, the same year. Despite the popular practice of adapting traditional Russian folktales to fit contemporary Soviet circumstances, in general, on the subject of fairy tales, Soviet cultural policy makers took a line not unlike Mitchell's, arguing that "the proletarian child" had no need for fairy tales. Evgeny Steiner, *Stories for Little Comrades: Revolutionary Artists and the Making of Early Soviet Children's Books* (Seattle: University of Washington Press, 1999), 86, 197.

30. Foley, *Radical Representations*, 63–85. Foley suggests that while American proletarian literature certainly shows important parallels to Soviet literary developments, "there are many protracted time lags between Soviet and American developments, as well as many particularities in the American literary left's formulation of its goals, which indicate anything but a slavish desire on the Americans' part to 'follo[w] as closely as possible the current Soviet line'" (72). Foley's quotation comes from Eric Homberger, *American Writers and Radical Politics, 1900-1939: Equivocal Commitments* (New York: St. Martin's, 1986), 139–40. Foley summarizes debates around Soviet influence on 77. According to Foley, "[Mike] Gold's declaration that 'facts are the new poetry' echoed the contention of Russian writer Serge Tretiakov that writers 'must write facts, facts. . . . [N]othing must be made up out of the writer's head.'" Foley, *Radical Representations*, 66; Steiner, *Stories for Little Comrades*, 71.

31. This was actually the title of an American book published in the 1920s, but it suggested a general interest in the power of psychology to transform individuals, and some commentators looked to the Soviet example as evidence of, as Arthur Wallace Calhoun put it, "what might not life be if we would but give childhood a chance!" See Beatrice Hinkle, *The Recreating of the Individual* (New York: Harcourt, Brace, 1923); Arthur Wallace Calhoun, "The Child Mind as a Social Product," in *The New Generation*, ed. V. F. Calverton and Samuel D. Schmalhausen (New York: Macaulay, 1930), 86.

32. Betty Bacon, interview with author, November 14, 1998, Berkeley, California.

33. See, for an overview, Simon Doniger, "Instead of Baby Talk," *New Masses* (June 13, 1939): 21–23. For comments in non-Communist sources, see Thomas Woody, "Children's Literature in Soviet Russia," *Library Journal* 54 (1929): 915; "Children's Publishing House," *Kansas Library Bulletin* 3 (March 1934): 5–6; L. Haffkin Hamburger, "The Institute for Library Science at Moscow," *Library Journal* 50 (December 1, 1925): 991–93. On how Soviet state-printed books showed him the possibility of producing high-quality, inexpensive books for children, see Noel Carrington, "A New Deal in 'Juveniles,'" *Junior Bookshelf* 6, no. 2 (July 1942): 41–44.

34. Felicity Ann O'Dell, *Socialization through Children's Literature: The Soviet Example* (New York: Cambridge University Press, 1978), 59.

35. Ernestine Evans, "Russian Children and Their Books," *Asia* 31 (November 1931): 690–91.

36. Steiner, *Stories for Little Comrades*, 7. A 1924 resolution calling for the creation of children's literature under the close direction and supervision of the Communist Party "with a view to initiating children into the idea of the class struggle and thus promoting proletarian internationalism and collective work" is cited in Mary Orvig, "A Russian View of Childhood: The Contribution of Kornei I. Chukovsky (1882–1969)," *Horn Book* 50 (October 1974): 69–84. Felicity O'Dell maintains that "inventiveness and origi-

nality of approach" were accepted in children's literature because of the Soviet belief that books should amuse children as well as educate them and socialize them into the Soviet "world outlook." O'Dell, *Socialization through Children's Literature*, 56. Ronald Hingley likewise maintains that "children's literature has provided yet another refuge from political pressures." John McCannon, however, calls this claim "somewhat misleading," arguing that children's authors who failed to "balance their creative impulses and the need to stay within the cultural parameters set by the regime . . . faced dire consequences." Ronald Hingley, *Russian Writers and Soviet Society, 1917–1978* (London: Weidenfeld and Nicolson, 1979), 81; John McCannon, "Technological and Scientific Utopias in Soviet Children's Literature, 1921–1932," *Journal of Popular Culture* 34, no. 4 (Spring 2001): 165. Thanks to Peter Filardo for bringing the latter source to my attention. On the fate of the avant-garde constructivists under Stalin, see Steiner, *Stories for Little Comrades*, 169–76.

37. McCannon suggests that this utopianism went through three key stages as reflected in children's literature: first, in 1921–1928 under the New Economic Policy (NEP) utopia was envisioned as something in the distant future; second, under the first five-year plan, between 1928 and 1932, utopia was imagined as something in the very near future; and finally, after 1932, under Stalinization, Soviet society under Stalin was portrayed as a present-day utopia.

38. Peter J. Kuznick, *Beyond the Laboratory: Scientists as Political Activists in the 1930s* (Chicago: University of Chicago Press, 1987); Lucy L. W. Wilson, "Education in Soviet Russia," Review of *Education in Soviet Russia* by Scott Nearing, *Progressive Education* 3, no. 3 (July–September 1926): 270–71 (emphasis in original). Also see David C. Engerman, *Modernization from the Other Shore: American Intellectuals and the Romance of Russian Development* (Cambridge, Mass: Harvard University Press, 2003).

39. George S. Counts, *The Soviet Challenge to America* (New York: Day, 1931); John Dewey, *Impressions of Soviet Russia and the Revolutionary World: Mexico—China—Turkey* (New York: New Republic, 1929); Wilson, "Education in Soviet Russia"; Lucy L. W. Wilson, "The New Schools in the New Russia," *Progressive Education* 5, no. 3 (July–September 1928): 251–54; Gretchen M. Switzer, "The Red October School," *Progressive Education* 9, no. 5 (May 1932): 355–58. Also see introduction by Patty Smith Hill to Vera Fediaevsky and Patty Smith Hill, *Nursery School and Parent Education in Soviet Russia* (New York: Dutton, 1936); Anna Louise Strong, "Education in Modern Russia," *Progressive Education* 1, no. 3 (October–December 1924): 157–59. After a 1925 visit to "psychological laboratories, clinics, nurseries, kindergartens, and more than sixty schools" in the Soviet Union, Scott Nearing asserted that "the children seemed to have been freed from something that weighs them down in other parts of the world. They were eager, glad, optimistic." Scott Nearing, "The Child in Soviet Russia," in *The New Generation*, ed. V. F. Calverton and Samuel D. Schmalhausen (New York: Macaulay, 1930), 232–41.

40. Steiner, *Stories for Little Comrades*, 72.

41. McCannon, "Technological and Scientific Utopias," 161.

42. Nora Beust, "Books for Young America," *Progressive Education* 9, no. 7 (November 1932): 532–36. "The marvelous thing about it," said one reviewer of Il'in's work, "is that the many episodes, anecdotes, and little stories are not like the usual raisins in an otherwise dull cake, but they are the essence of the book." Review of *Black on White* by M. Il'in, *Publishers Weekly* 122 (August 6, 1932): 432.

43. M. Il'in, *What Time Is It? The Story of Clocks*, trans. Beatrice Kincead (Philadelphia: Lippincott, 1932), 92.

44. Review of *Black on White: The Story of Books*, by M. Il'in, *Times Literary Supplement* (November 24, 1932): 898; "No More Pencils, No More Books. No More Teachers' Dirty Looks," Review of *What Time Is It?* and *Black on White* by M. Ilin [*sic*], *New Pioneer* 2, no. 9 (September 1932): 20; Carol Drake, Review of *What Time Is It? The Story of Clocks* by M. Ilin [*sic*], *New Masses* 8 (September 1932), 25.

45. O'Dell says that "the didactic requirement" in socialist realism resulted in three requirements in Soviet literature for adults: first, all works must be "optimistic," or portray the triumph of good over evil (thus suggesting the inevitability of the good society); second, man must "be portrayed as being basically a social animal" (in contrast to Western individualism), and, by extension, literature must be accessible to the masses; and, finally, "every work of art should have 'ideological content.'" In children's literature, of course, the didactic imperative is even more pressing. O'Dell, *Socialization through Children's Literature*, 6–8.

46. *What Time Is It?* does note, for instance, that Galileo "came very near being burned at the stake because the earth revolves on its axis." However, the point is never dwelt upon, and children are left to condemn for themselves the ignorance of Galileo's fellow citizens who doubted the wisdom of his scientific thinking. Il'in, *What Time Is It? The Story of Clocks*, 90.

47. Considering the links between books like Jones's *How the Derrick Works* (which is full of rather dry descriptions of the technical means of operating derricks) and Soviet production books like those of Il'in, one is perhaps most struck by the aesthetic similarities in the illustrations, which, in each case, employ a modernist or "constructivist" style (see figure 1.2). For more on constructivism, see Steiner, *Stories for Little Comrades*, 30.

48. Mary Jossell, "Books," *New Pioneer* 4 (March 1934): 256; list of children's books sold through New Masses Book Service, *New Masses* (June 1930): 24; Simon, "Which Books for Your Children?"; Clara Ostrowsky, "Summer Reading for Children," *New Masses* 60–61 (July 9, 1946): 27–28.

49. M. Il'in, *New Russia's Primer*, trans. George S. Counts and Nucia P. Lodge (Cambridge, Mass.: Riverside, 1931), 12–13, 16, 158–59.

50. Beust, "Books for Young America," 536; Ernestine Evans, Review of *New Russia's Primer* by M. Il'in, *Books* (May 3, 1931): 5; Review of *New Russia's Primer* by M. Il'in, *New York Times* (May 17, 1931): 10; Review of *New Russia's Primer* by M. Il'in, *Saturday Review* 152 (July 11, 1931): 63; Review of *New Russia's Primer* by M. Il'in, *Yale Review* 20 (Summer 1931): 812. Several sources put the book at number 10 in the list of bestselling nonfiction of 1931.

51. Il'in, *New Russia's Primer*, ix; George S. Counts, "The Real Challenge of Soviet Education," *Educational Forum* 23, no. 3 (March 1959): 261–69. For evidence of teachers' radicalization see Committee on Social and Economic Problems, Progressive Education Association, *Call to Teachers of the Nation* (New York: Day, 1933). Also see *Frontiers of Democracy* and the *Social Frontier*, journals of the Frontier Thinkers, a radical arm of the Progressive Education Association.

52. Henry Storm, Review of *Dare the School Build a New Social Order?* by George Counts, *New Masses* (July 1932): 28. Also see Earl Browder, "Education: An Ally in the Workers' Struggle," *Social Frontier* 1, no. 4 (1935): 22–24. For an overview see Barry Rubin, "Marxism and Education: Radical Thought and Theory in the 1930s," *Science and Society* 36, no. 2 (Summer 1972): 171–201.

53. As noted earlier, Communist authors did not exclusively produce proletarian children's literature in the early 1930s. *Charlie Chaplin's Parade* by Mike Gold and *The Teacup Whale* by Lydia Gibson are some notable examples of Communist-authored children's books that were not openly ideological in their content.

54. A Moscow-published pamphlet, *The Road to Mass Organization of Proletarian Children*, suggests that "side by side with correspondence from children, [children's journals] should contain articles on current political issues, revolutionary stories and poems, articles on foreign countries, articles on natural science and technique, humorous stories, jokes, puzzles, etc. of interest to children." While the format of the *New Pioneer* would suggest that the magazine's editors followed this directive, all evidence seems to suggest that American children's books were never given the same attention as the children's papers. Children's literature is only mentioned as an afterthought in this thirty-two-page pamphlet on the revolutionary children's movement: "In addition to this press [for children] there is also to be mentioned the publication of special literature, which is now very poor. Interesting literature which is now skillfully used only by the bourgeoisie must be replaced by cheap but good revolutionary literature." Young Communist League, *The Road to Mass Organization of Proletarian Children*, 11, 30–32. This pamphlet, which was later seized upon by McCarthyites like J. B. Matthews, is the only clear indication I have found of Soviet attempts to influence American children's literature. Still, many left-wing writers in the United States continued to look to the Soviet Union for models.

55. Originally published (in 1939) in the *New Masses* and then published by the *New Masses* as a stand-alone text, *Mr. His* is clearly a parody of a children's book because by the time of *Mr. His* Communists had ceased publishing "revolutionary" children's literature, concentrating instead on instilling a democratic consciousness in the "broad masses" of children.

56. "Hello Fellers! Hello Girls!" *Pioneer* 1 (May 1931): 1.

57. Hazel Hakola, "The Work of Pioneers," *New Pioneer* 1–2 (August 1931): 17.

58. Foley, *Radical Representations*, 398–441.

59. "Bill Haywood, Pioneer," *Pioneer* 1–2 (May 1931): 8–9; Joseph Pass, "John Reed: A Hero of 1917," *New Pioneer* 1, no. 8 (November 1931): 8–9; Helen Kay, "Don't Let Them Burn!" *New Pioneer* 3 (October 1932): 10–11, 22; Mabel Worthington, "Free the Scottsboro Boys!" *New Pioneer* 3 (June 1933): 30–31, 46; "Listening In," *New Pioneer* 3 (April 1933): 16.

60. Sasha Small, "The Story of Sugar," *New Pioneer* (May 1935): 12–13.

61. Grace Hutchins, "Our Teacher Learned Something," *New Pioneer* (June 1933): 27, 28, 46. Hutchins was also the author of the pamphlet *Children under Capitalism* (New York: International, 1933).

62. Harry Alan Potamkin, "Mother Goose on the Breadline," *Pioneer* 1–2 (May 1931): 7; Sasha Small, "Alice in Hunger Land," *New Pioneer* 2, no. 11 (March 1933): 3–7, 20; Ned Donn, "Pioneer Mother Goose," *New Pioneer* (December 1934): 17–18.

63. Harrison George, "A Kitchen of Heroes," *New Pioneer* (February 1932): 12–13.

64. *New Pioneer* (August 1935): 1. This entire issue was devoted to the Boy Scouts.

65. The Nazi-Soviet Pact in 1939 also caused American Communists to leave the party in droves, so it may also be that the *New Pioneer* folded because it lost both staff and readers.

66. This is certainly suggested by letters to the editor, which tend to describe Pioneer activities and to offer critical views of American "bosses," political leaders, and practices in general, often in contrast to the Soviet Union.

67. For example, as a thirteen-year-old, Dahlov studied history and social studies with the socialist Leo Huberman. Dahlov Ipcar, interview with author, September 1997, Georgetown, Maine, and letter to author, November 28, 1997.

68. Ipcar, letter to author, January 7, 1998.

69. Dahlov Zorach, "The Miners," *New Pioneer* (July 1936): 21.

70. Of course, most writings for children published after 1935 by Communist authors were far more tempered in their revolutionary expressions, given the Popular Front policy of replacing calls for revolution with inclusive, democratic rhetoric in the service of antifascist unity.

71. Ipcar, letter to author, January 7, 1998. Ipcar noted, "I tried to show my feeling for working in books such as *One Horse Farm, Brown Cow Farm, The Cat in the Night,* [and] *Ten Big Farms. . . . Lobsterman* has that same feeling. I always felt like Emerson's intelligentsia of farmers that he envisioned for America."

72. On the historic racism of the white working class, see David Roediger, *The Wages of Whiteness: Race and the Making of the American Working Class* (New York: Verso, 1991); Alexander Saxton, *The Rise and Fall of the White Republic: Class Politics and Mass Culture in Nineteenth-Century America* (New York: Verso, 1990). Also see Lawrence Goodwyn, *The Populist Moment: A Short History of the Agrarian Revolt in America* (New York: Oxford University Press, 1978).

73. Paul Mishler argues that "although characters from European immigrant backgrounds are rare in this literature until the late 1930s, minority characters are present in greater numbers than in any other children's literature in the United States until the impact of the civil rights movement during the 1960s." Mishler, *Raising Reds,* 111. Although in Communist literature Africans and African Americans tend to merit special attention, other minorities are featured in proletarian stories as well: Trease's *Call to Arms* (1935) concerns Latin Americans; *Eddie and the Gipsey* positively portrays gypsies (although it bemoans their lack of class consciousness); and Japanese are heroes in "Reddening the Sky," a story in *Martin's Annual.* In the *New Pioneer Story Book,* "Siksika" concerns American Indians in the contemporary Northwest who learn to make alliances with whites from Workers' Aid against their "common enemy—the masters"; and "Julio Fights, Too" is about a Cuban boy who helps to turn soldiers working for the government (in support of the "Yanquis") to the side of the workers.

74. Mishler, *Raising Reds,* 37. On how this played out for Jews, see Paul Buhle, "Jews and American Communism: The Cultural Question," *Radical History Review* 23 (Spring 1980): 20–25.

75. *Workers' School* (New York: International Workers Order, 1933), 1. In Secular Yiddish Schools of America Collection, Stanford University, box 33, August Maymudes material. Very special thanks to Jerry Frakes for translating this material from Yiddish to English.

76. Ethnic identification was eventually encouraged under the Popular Front to the extent that ethnic (or religious) identification could be linked to the larger goal of international working-class solidarity. Jewish history, for instance, was taught in the Yiddish schools of the IWO's Jewish People's Fraternal Order to emphasize the historical struggle against oppression and for social justice, but black history was foregrounded in these schools as well. For instance, Benjamin Efron's *The Story of Passover* compares the story of the Hebrew exodus to the African-American struggle for freedom from slavery: the Jewish family in the story sings "Go Down Moses" at their seder and they drink to the

"hope that all people, black and white, all religions and races, will some day walk hand in hand, free and equal all over the world." Benjamin Efron, *The Story of Passover* (New York: Committee for Progressive Jewish Education, 1952), 14. Secular Yiddish Schools of America Collection, folder 4.

77. Steiner, *Stories for Little Comrades*, 99–109.

78. In the story, Sambo is given a basket of roast chickens to carry to his master, Judge Jackson, along with a piece of paper (which apparently notes the number of chickens Sambo was carrying). Sambo figures the judge will not notice if he eats one of the chickens on the way, but when he arrives, the judge glances at the piece of paper and somehow magically knows a chicken is missing, which earns Sambo a scolding. The next time he is sent on this mission, Sambo wises up. He senses that the paper has some special powers, so before he eats a chicken he hides the piece of paper under a stone so that the paper can't see what he is doing. "But the cursed paper was evidently possessed of some devil. For even when it was lying under the stone it had managed somehow to see everything and told the judge all about Sambo's little escapade!" Poor Sambo is never the wiser about what has happened, but the child reader can knowingly laugh at Sambo's ignorance even as he understands and opposes the illiterate Sambo's victimization by literate white oppressors. M. Il'in, *Black on White: The Story of Books*, trans. Beatrice Kincead (Philadelphia: Lippincott, 1932), 25–28.

79. Zur Mühlen, *Fairy Tales for Workers' Children*, 36–52.

80. "All Workers' Children Want to Read and to Know about 'Little Black Murzok,'" [*sic*] Review of *Red Corner Book for Children*, *New Pioneer* (June 1932): 20; *Red Corner Book for Children* (New York: International, 1932), 35–44.

81. *Red Corner Book for Children*, 35–44. The term *imperialist nostalgia*, meaning "a longing for what we have destroyed," is Renato Rosaldo's. See Renato Rosaldo, *Culture & Truth: The Remaking of Social Analysis* (Boston: Beacon, 1989).

82. Mark Naison, *Communists in Harlem during the Depression* (Urbana: University of Illinois Press, 1983), 11.

83. Ibid., 11–16. Resolution quoted on 18–19.

84. For more on the particular relationship between Jews and Communism, see Arthur Liebman, *Jews and the Left* (New York: Wiley, 1979); Robert Snyder, "The Paterson Jewish Folk Chorus: Politics, Ethnicity, and Musical Culture," *American Jewish History* 74 (September 1984): 27–44; Buhle, "Jews and American Communism: The Cultural Question"; Ezra Mendelsohn, ed., *Essential Papers on Jews and the Left* (New York: New York University Press, 1997). Naison suggests that for immigrant and second-generation immigrant Jews, work with blacks was tied to the "Communist version of an assimilationist dream. Participation in the affairs of the Party in a black community not only represented a highly valued political duty, but constituted an adventure in learning about American culture and values, albeit from a group whose experience was highly ambivalent." *Communists in Harlem*, 321–22.

85. On the international Scottsboro defense campaign, see James A. Miller, Susan D. Pennybacker, and Eve Rosenhaft, "Mother Ada Wright and the International Campaign to Free the Scottsboro Boys," *American Historical Review* 106, no. 2 (April 2001): 387–430.

86. Myra Page, "Pickets and Slippery Slicks," in *New Pioneer Story Book*, ed. Martha Campion (New York: New Pioneer, 1935), 91, 92, 93.

87. Ibid., 95.

88. Kay, *Battle in the Barnyard*, 46.

89. Arnold Rampersad, *The Life of Langston Hughes*, vol. 1: *1902–1941: I, Too, Sing America* (New York: Oxford University Press, 1986), 228.

90. Donald C. Dickinson, *A Bio-Bibliography of Langston Hughes, 1902–1967* (New York: Archon, 1967), 62.

91. Arna Bontemps and Langston Hughes, *Popo and Fifina: Children of Haiti* (New York: Macmillan, 1932), 35.

92. Ibid., 43.

93. Rampersad describes the book as "universally praised." Rampersad, *I, Too, Sing America*, 254.

94. Bontemps and Hughes, *Popo and Fifina: Children of Haiti*, 59.

95. Charles H. Nichols, ed., *Arna Bontemps–Langston Hughes Letters, 1925–1967* (New York: Dodd, Mead, 1980), 99, 410, 35, 51. The *New York Times Book Review* called *Popo* "a model of its kind that tempted one to think that all children's books should be written by poets." Quoted in Rampersad, *I, Too, Sing America*, 254.

96. On radical animators, see Paul Buhle and Dave Wagner, *Hide in Plain Sight: The Hollywood Blacklistees in Film and Television, 1950–2002* (New York: Palgrave Macmillan, 2003), 90–96.

Chapter 3

1. Marion Armstrong, "Child's Saga," Review of *Run, Run! An Adventure in New York* by Harry Granick, *New Masses* 42 (February 10, 1942): 26.

2. Harry Granick, *Run, Run! An Adventure in New York* (New York: Simon and Schuster, 1941), 49–50.

3. Ibid., 107.

4. Ibid., 90–91.

5. Ibid., 121.

6. Granick's membership in the League of American Writers is documented in Franklin Folsom, *Days of Anger, Days of Hope: A Memoir of the League of American Writers, 1937–1942* (Niwot: University Press of Colorado, 1994), 291. Folsom also notes that Granick taught at the New York Writers School, which was affiliated with the league. Granick told children's stories over WMAC, New York, "for a year of Sunday mornings" in 1934–1935 and authored the award-winning "Great Adventure" series, which aired over the radio between 1934 and 1954. At this point Granick was blacklisted and made his living primarily as a playwright. See inventory to Harry Granick Collection, American Heritage Center, University of Wyoming; and *Contemporary Authors*. Granick's FBI file claims that he is the brother of writer Mike Gold, which is inaccurate. Information on Granick's blacklisting and correction to FBI information from Barbara Granick (Harry's granddaughter), telephone interview with author, October 11, 2004.

7. Surveillance also confirmed that he spent most of his days in front of a typewriter, although nothing interesting turned up in his trash, which seemed "rather unusual." Memo dated September 26, 1944, Harry Granick FBI file, FOIPA #0990204–000.

8. See discussion later in this chapter of Granick's writing for the *New Masses* (as Harry Taylor) on children's literature; his radio and television writing for children also would suggest his sensitivity to the workings of the culture industry.

9. Jean Simon, "Which Books for Your Children?" *New Masses* 17 (December 24, 1935): 24. Mary Lapsley, "Socially Constructive Literature for Children," address at the

Juvenile Writers Craft session of the Fourth Congress of the League of American Writers, June 6–8, 1941, LAW Papers, box 5.

10. Simon, "Which Books for Your Children," 23. Emphasis in original.

11. On calls for progressive writers and books, see Harry Taylor, "What Shall My Child Read?" *New Masses* 44 (August 11, 1942): 24; Jay Williams, "What Do Kids Read?" *New Masses* 63 (June 10, 1947): 11.

12. Simon, "Which Books for Your Children," 23, 24.

13. Simon complained about

> books on the "old South," reeking with nostalgic sentimentality, books on our heroes of industry[,] . . . condescending books about Negroes, books with anti-Semitism lurking in the background, books of whimsy, all ballyhooed to the skies by the vested interests of the children's book-world who would have us believe that children are somehow insulated from the hardships that surround the rest of us.

Ibid., 23.

14. Ibid., 25; Kennell, introductory remarks at juvenile session, records of 1941 Writers Congress in LAW Papers.

15. Louis Lerman, *Winter Soldiers: The Story of a Conspiracy against the Schools* (New York: Committee for Defense of Public Education, 1941), n.p.

16. Quoted in Elmina R. Lucke, "The Social-Studies Curriculum in Lincoln School of Teachers College," in *Fourth Yearbook: The Social Studies Curriculum*, ed. National Council for the Social Studies (Philadelphia: McKinley, 1934), 139.

17. For more on the relationship between antifascism and adult-child relations, especially vis-à-vis progressive education, see William Tuttle, *Daddy's Gone to War: The Second World War in the Lives of America's Children* (New York: Oxford University Press, 1993), 186–88; William Graebner, "The Unstable World of Benjamin Spock: Social Engineering in a Democratic Culture, 1917–1950," *Journal of American History* 67 (1980): 612–29; Julia Mickenberg, "The Pedagogy of the Popular Front: Progressive Parenting for a New Generation, 1918–1945," in *The American Child: A Cultural Studies Reader*, ed. Caroline Levander and Carol Singley (New Brunswick, N.J.: Rutgers University Press, 2003).

18. Michael Denning, *The Cultural Front: The Laboring of American Culture in the Twentieth Century* (New York: Verso, 1996); Theodore Brameld, "Karl Marx and the American Teacher," *Social Frontier* (November 1935): 55–56. Also see Merle Curti, "Our Revolutionary Tradition," *Social Frontier* 1, no. 3 (1935): 10–13; J. S. Woodsworth, "Public Education and Social Change," *Social Frontier* 4, no. 34 (1938): 216–18. An editorial in the *New York Teacher*, the organ of the New York City Teachers Union, asserted in November 1935 that membership in the American Federation of Teachers had more than doubled in the past two years; as the editorial put it, "[T]here are thriving locals in all parts of the country which show that school-teachers do have the will and courage to unite with labor." *New York Teacher* 1, no. 4 (November 1935): 3. Also see Marjorie Murphy, *Blackboard Unions: The AFT and the NEA, 1900–1980* (Ithaca, N.Y.: Cornell University Press, 1990). Charles J. Hendley, "The Union's Stand," *New York Teacher* 1, no. 1 (November 1935): 6–7, 12.

19. For more on Communist educational programs, see, for instance, Marvin Gettleman, "'No Varsity Teams': New York's Jefferson School of Social Science, 1943–1956,"

Science and Society 66, no. 3 (Fall 2002): 336–59. On children in particular, see Paul C. Mishler, *Raising Reds: The Young Pioneers, Radical Summer Camps, and Communist Political Culture in the United States* (New York: Columbia University Press, 1999).

20. See Diana Marcia Selig, "Cultural Gifts: American Liberals, Childhood, and the Origins of Multiculturalism, 1924–1939" (Ph.D. diss., University of California, 2001). Also see issues of the magazine *Common Ground* and discussion of the journal in William Charles Beyer, "Searching for Common Ground, 1940–49: An American Literary Magazine and Its Related Movements in Education and Politics" (Ph.D. diss., University of Minnesota, 1988).

21. For books adopting a liberal, integrationist approach, see, for example, Ethel M. Duncan, *Democracy's Children* (New York: Hinds, Hayden and Eldredge, 1945).

22. Marion Cuthbert, *We Sing America* (New York: Friendship, 1936), 39, 46–48, 52–53, 64.

23. Kenneth D. Benne, "The Wartime Job of Teachers," *Frontiers of Democracy* 9 (April 15, 1942): 209–12; James L. Hymes, Jr., "The War Education of Young Children: More Quantity, More Quality," *Frontiers of Democracy* 9 (December 15, 1942): 71–72; Harold Rugg, "Educational Planning for Post-War Reconstruction," *Frontiers of Democracy* 10 (April 15, 1943): 217–21. The greatest exponents of such practices described their work in *Common Ground*, a journal inaugurated in 1940 and devoted to "explor[ing] gradually, from various angles, the racial-cultural situation and its problems which—perhaps especially acute at this time—have developed in the U.S." The magazine's editors believed that the "crisis" created by the war was an "opportunity" for mass reeducation. Louis Adamic, "This Crisis an Opportunity," *Common Ground* (Autumn 1940): 66–67. Tuttle, *Daddy's Gone to War*, 117. Fears about the damaging effects of prejudice on the development of personality were fueled by various psychological studies of the "authoritarian personality," studies that ultimately proved critical in the 1954 *Brown* decision. Theodor W. Adorno, *The Authoritarian Personality* (New York: Harper, 1950).

24. Robert Shaffer, "Multicultural Education in New York City during World War II," *New York History* 77 (July 1996): 305, 304.

25. Ibid., 318–20. Testimony of Walter S. Steele, chairman of the National Security Committee of the American Coalition of Patriotic, Civic, and Fraternal Societies, Hearings of the House Committee on Un-American Activities, July 21, 1947, 80th Cong., 40. See Ethel Rosenberg, *Death House Letters of Julius and Ethel Rosenberg* (New York: Jero, 1953), 114.

26. Shaffer, "Multicultural Education in New York City," 24–25. Daryl Michael Scott, "Postwar Pluralism, *Brown v. Board of Education*, and the Origins of Multicultural Education," *Journal of American History* (June 2004), http://www.historycooperative.org .content.lib.utexas.edu:2048/journals/jah/91.1/scott.html (8 May 2005). Also see Clarence I. Chatto and Alice L. Halligan, *The Story of the Springfield Plan* (New York: Barnes and Noble, 1945). For a discussion of wartime racial conflicts as they affected children, see Tuttle, *Daddy's Gone to War*, 162–89.

27. Shaffer, "Multicultural Education in New York City," 327. Also see U.S. Office of Education, *Handbook on Education and the War* (Washington, D.C.: Government Printing Office, 1942).

28. Quoted in M. B. Schnapper, "Legionnaires and Teachers," *Social Frontier* 4, no. 31 (January 1938): 123.

29. The Board of Education of Los Angeles voted early in 1936 to fingerprint every employee in the school system, and a bill introduced in New Jersey would have com-

pelled schoolchildren to salute the flag upon penalty of arrest. "Editorial Paragraphs," *New York Teacher* 1, no. 6 (April 1936): 101–2; "Editorial Paragraphs," *New York Teacher* 1, no. 4 (February 1936): 53. What became known as the "Little Red Rider," tacked onto a bill in the District of Columbia, proclaimed in 1936 that "hereafter no part of any appropriation for the public schools shall be available for the payment of the salary of any person teaching or advocating Communism." "Little Red Rider," *NEA Journal* 25, no. 5 (May 1936): 135. The law was later revised to disallow only the *advocating* of Communism, but the line between teaching and advocating could be fuzzy, as many teachers learned. By the 1950s, teachers could be fired just for belonging to any organization deemed to be subversive by the attorney general.

30. Quoted. in W. C. R., "School Textbooks and the NAM," *Frontiers of Democracy* (January 15, 1941): 101; Herbert M. Kliebard, *The Struggle for an American Curriculum, 1893–1958* (New York: Routledge, 1995), 175, 177; Alonzo F. Myers, "The Attacks on the Rugg Books," *Frontiers of Democracy* 7 (October 15, 1940): 18.

31. Arthur Foshay notes that "a school textbook carries with it the assumption that it contains the uncontroverted truth. . . . A textbook, accordingly, should never contain anything subject to controversy." Arthur W. Foshay, "Textbooks and the Curriculum during the Progressive Era: 1930–1950," in *Textbooks and Schooling in the United States: Eighty-ninth Yearbook of the National Society for the Study of Education*, ed. David Elliott and Arthur Woodward (Chicago: University of Chicago Press, 1990), 23–41. Talmadge quoted in John William Tebbel, *A History of Book Publishing in the United States* (New York: Bowker, 1981), 4:86. On attacks against intercultural education, see Shaffer, "Multicultural Education in New York City," 330–31. On the association of progressive education with Communism, see Kitty Jones and Robert L. Olivier, *Progressive Education in REDucation* (Boston: Meador, 1956).

32. Franz Boas, introduction to Lerman, *Winter Soldiers*.

33. Lerman, *Winter Soldiers*.

34. A number of prominent leftist authors of children's books, among them Irving Adler, Rose Wyler, Lilian Moore, Hy Ruchlis, Millicent Selsam, Sarah Riedman, Emma Gelders Sterne, and Alex Novikoff, had been teachers.

35. Kennell, introductory remarks, Juvenile Craft session, Fourth American Writers Congress (June 1941), LAW Papers, box 5.

36. Dagliesh quoted in Mildred R. Voelkel, "Children's Forum," *Library Occurrent* 13 1941): 257. It is worth noting, incidentally, that Dagliesh still assumed that young children (though never defined in terms of age) were still entitled to a "carefree" childhood. As she noted in the same discussion, "[O]f course this does not apply to the little ones. They still need protection in life and in their books." Julia Sauer, "Making the World Safe for the Janey Larkins," *Library Journal* 66, no. 22 (December 15, 1941): 49–53.

37. Helen Hoke, Leo Lerman, and Evelyn Hamilton, "The Problem Book," *Publishers Weekly* (October 18, 1941): 1550.

38. "Sing Me a Song with Social Significance" was a popular song in the hit musical sponsored and performed by the International Ladies' Garment Workers Union (ILGWU) *Pins and Needles*, a show that typified the cultural front's true popularity by crossing from the ILGWU's labor state to Broadway. For more on *Pins and Needles*, see Denning, *The Cultural Front*, 295–309.

39. Denning, *The Cultural Front*, 261. Elizabeth Morrow (Betty Bacon) quoted in Hoke, Lerman, and Hamilton, "The Problem Book," 1551.

40. The 1942 conference of the American Library Association focused on the war and how libraries could help foster free inquiry, international friendship, and intercultural understanding. Quotation from Christine Jenkins, "The Strength of the Inconspicuous: Youth Services Librarians, the American Library Association, and Intellectual Freedom for the Young, 1939–1955" (Ph.D. diss., University of Wisconsin, 1995), 210.

41. Louise S. Robbins, *Censorship and the American Library: The American Library Association's Response to Threats to Intellectual Freedom, 1939–1969* (Westport, Conn.: Greenwood, 1996), 3. On children's librarians' response to fascism in particular see Jenkins, "The Strength of the Inconspicuous," 157–260. On the Library Bill of Rights and intellectual freedom in the 1940s and 1950s, see Louise S. Robbins, "Champions of a Cause: American Librarians and the Library Bill of Rights in the 1950s," *Library Trends* 45 (Summer 1996): 28–49; Chris Schladweiler, "The Library Bill of Rights and Intellectual Freedom: A Selective Bibliography," *Library Trends* 45, no. 1 (Summer 1996): 97–125; Holly Crawford, "Freedom through Books: Helen Haines and Her Role in the Library Press, Library Education and the Intellectual Freedom Movement" (Ph.D. diss., University of Illinois, 1997).

42. This is one of the key arguments of Jenkins, "The Strength of the Inconspicuous."

43. See Sharon Hartman Strom, "'We're No Kitty Foyles': Organizing Office Workers for the Congress of Industrial Organizations, 1937–50," in *Women, Work & Protest: A Century of U.S. Women's Labor History*, ed. Ruth Milkman (London and New York: Routledge and Kegan Paul, 1987), 206–34; Murphy, *Blackboard Unions*.

44. Rose Wyler, interview with author, March 27, 1998, New York City.

45. Betty Bacon, interview with author, February 20, 1999.

46. "Librarians Form a Progressive Council," *Government Guide* (August–September 1939): 10–11 (PLC Papers, folder 1); William P. Tucker, "Progressive Librarians Council Formed," *Wilson Library Bulletin* 14, no. 29 (September 1939); Philip and Mary Jane Keeney, "Social Content in Library Training," *Wilson Library Bulletin* 14 (February–March 1940): 429–34, 497–503. Also see PLC Constitution, 1939, PLC Papers. On PLC efforts against racial discrimination see Bertha Schuman, "In Defense of Equality," *Wilson Library Bulletin* 14, no. 7 (March 1940). On cooperation with labor, see, in addition to PLC resolutions in the Tamiment Collection, Ida Goshkin, "Public Library Cooperation with Labor Organizations," *Wilson Library Bulletin* 17 (December 1942): 306–9. Also see William P. Tucker, "Where the Library Fails as a Social Force," *ALA Bulletin* (October 15, 1938): 883; Ellen Forsyth, "A New Note for Libraries," *Wilson Library Bulletin* (September 1938): 52; Bernard Berelson, "The Myth of Library Impartiality: An Interpretation for Democracy," *Wilson Library Bulletin* (October 1938): 87. For more on Rollins, see Nancy Tolsen, "Making Books Available: The Role of Early Libraries, Librarians, and Booksellers in the Promotion of African American Children's Literature," *African American Review* 32, no. 1 (Spring 1998): 9–22. Thanks to David Roediger for bringing this source to my attention. Rollins is listed on the 1942 roster of PLC members; there is also a photograph of her in the PLC papers promoting *We Build Together*. Margaret G. Burroughs dedicated one of her children's books, *Did You Feed My Cow?* to Rollins. Other children's librarians involved with the PLC included Clara Ostrowsky, David Cohen (a school librarian), and Bertha Schuman, the secretary and treasurer of the PLC, who was a children's librarian at the Chicago Public Library.

47. See 1941 speech by Theodore Norton, librarian at Lafayette College in Pennsylvania, given at Columbia University, "The Defense of Culture and Democracy in the Present Crisis," PLC Collection, filed under "Norton." David Cohen sat on the PLC Civil

Rights Committee in the 1940s; in the 1960s he would become involved in the Council on Interracial Books for Children and in the ALA's Social Responsibility Roundtable. Rose Agree, a former school librarian in Valley Stream, New York, mentioned Cohen's involvement with the CIBC and the Social Responsibility Roundtable. Agree, telephone interview with author, September 27, 1999.

48. *Adventures in Steel* was published by Modern Age Books, which aimed to bring to "American readers new books of a progressive character at prices they can afford to pay." Quoted in advertisement in the *Bulletin of the League of American Writers*, May 1938. The fall 1938 issue of the *Bulletin* mentions Davis as a league member. Materials in Genevieve Taggard Papers. Elie Siegmeister, *Work and Sing: A Collection of the Songs That Built America* (New York: Scott, 1944), 79.

49. Henry Vicar, *The Company Owns the Tools* (Philadelphia: Westminster, 1942), 109-10.

50. Using a formulation like Denning's, these writers can certainly be seen as part of the Popular Front structure of feeling, and several had concrete links to left-wing organizations at one point or another. Tunis, for instance, was on the advisory board for the Popular Front magazine *Champion of Youth*, which was geared toward the "young worker employed at miserable wages and under indecent conditions." See *Champion of Youth* (January 1937). Pearl Buck, Harry Granick, Eric Lucas, and others who wrote for children were also contributors to the newspaper.

51. *Bayou Suzette* (1943), for instance, tells the story of a Cajun girl from an extremely poor Louisiana family; *Strawberry Girl* (1945) focuses on members of a poor but industrious Florida "cracker" family; *Indian Captive: The Story of Mary Jemison* (a Newbery Honor book published in 1941) told the story of a young girl who, having been captured by Indians at an early age, rejected the chance to return to "civilized" society, choosing instead to remain with her communalist, "savage" Indian captors. Lenski consciously rejected the idea that authors should be "protecting" children with their books. See Jenkins, "The Strength of the Inconspicuous," 281.

52. Any flirtation with radical politics on Tunis's part (suggested by his work with *Champion of Youth*) seems to have been very brief, but he remained a strong advocate for labor and for minority rights. For further discussion of Tunis, see Richard Shereikis, "How You Play the Game: The Novels of John R. Tunis," *Horn Book* (December 1977): 642-48.

53. Like these works of realistic fiction, Dr. Seuss's fanciful books can also be seen as products of the Popular Front structure of feeling. An antifascist cartoonist for the labor newspaper *PM*, Dr. Seuss (Theodore Geisel) brought these same progressive, antiauthoritarian politics to his children's books—which he initially published with the leftist Vanguard Press. Indeed, Philip Nel has also drawn convincing links between Seuss's work and the radical artistic experimentation of the pre–World War I avant garde, that is, the Lyrical Left. On the parallels between Seuss's *PM* cartoons and his children's books, see Philip Nel, "'Said a Bird in the Midst of a Blitz . . .': How World War II Created Dr. Seuss," *Mosaic* 34, no. 2 (June 2001): 65-85. Also see Henry Jenkins, "No Matter How Small: The Democratic Imagination of Doctor Seuss," in *Hop on Pop: The Politics and Pleasures of Popular Culture*, ed. Henry Jenkins, Tara McPherson, and Jane Shattuc (Durham, N.C.: Duke University Press, 2002), 187-208. Philip Nel, "Dada Knows Best: Growing up 'Surreal' with Doctor Seuss," *Children's Literature* 27 (1999): 150-84. Vanguard, which was established in 1926 by the wealthy progressive Charles Garland to provide inexpensive books to the working class, was described by HUAC as a "Communist enterprise." On

the mission of Vanguard, see John Tebbel, *History of Book Publishing in the United States* (New York: Bowker, 1978), 3:181. The 1944 HUAC report is cited in the FBI file of Helen Colodny Goldfrank (Helen Kay), FOIPA No. 0990202–000.

54. Bacon, interview with the author, November 14, 1998, Berkeley, California.

55. This, like "for pleasure," was a category in a booklist compiled by Clara Ostrowsky for the Jefferson School of Social Science entitled "Books to Grow On: A Planned Library for Boys and Girls," Jefferson School Papers, folder: "Bibliographies," Tamiment Library, NYU.

56. Betty Bacon, interview with author, February 20, 1999, Berkeley, California.

57. Hoke et al., "The Problem Book," 1550. Both Tunis's *Keystone Kids* and Means's *Moved Outers* were selected for the CSA award. Form letter to publishers from Mrs. Hugh Grant Straus, chair, Children's Book Committee, June 16, 1943, CSA Papers.

58. Letter from Willard Johnson to Mrs. Hugh Grant Straus, February 15, 1943, and list of Juvenile Good Will Books; Vernon Ives, letter to Mrs. Hugh Grant Straus, CSA Papers, box 11, F104. Responses to the award included letters from Muriel Fuller of Thomas Nelson and Sons; Alice Dagliesh of Scribner's; J. Kendrick Noble of Noble and Noble Publishers; Helen Ferris of the Junior Literary Guild; Mrs. Frank Trager of the Bureau for Intercultural Education; E. Harvey at J. B. Lippincott; Vernon Ives of Holiday House; Bertha Gunterman of Longmans Green; Dorothy Bryan of Dodd, Mead; Elizabeth Bevier Hamilton of Harcourt, Brace; Lee Kingman of Houghton Mifflin; Marguerite Vance of Dutton; and others (box 5, folder 40, and box 11, folder 104).

59. Lapsley, "Socially Constructive Literature for Children." *Contemporary Authors* notes that Granick used the name Harry Taylor in theater reviews he wrote for radical periodicals like *Masses and Mainstream*. "Harry Granick," *Contemporary Authors Online* (Gale,2002), http://galenet.galegroup.com.content.lib.utexas.edu:2048/servlet/GLD/hits ?r=d&origSearch=true&o=DataType&n=10&l=d&c=1&locID=txshracd2598&secondary =false&u=CA&t=KW&s=2&NA=Granick%2C+Harry. Harold Taylor, president of Sarah Lawrence College, was also associated with a number of liberal causes, but given Granick's work in children's literature it is most likely that he authored this *New Masses* piece. Taylor, "What Shall My Child Read," 24.

60. Taylor, "What Shall My Child Read?" 22.

61. Ibid., 23.

62. Ibid., 24. A short-lived Children's Book Club, inaugurated in the mid-1940s and advertised in the *New Masses*, was the juvenile equivalent of left-wing book clubs like Book Find and the Labor Book Club. Left-run record clubs for children were more successful. See David Bonner, *Revolutionizing Children's Records: The Young People's Records and Children's Record Guild Series* (Lanham, Md.: Scarecrow, 2004). Also see Denning, *The Cultural Front*, 93.

63. Kennell, introductory remarks.

64. Bacon, interview with author, March 10, 1998, Berkeley, California.

65. Bacon, interview with author, February 20, 1999, Berkeley, California.

66. Another CSA Children's Book Committee member, Katie Hart, was married to League of American Writers member and chronicler of several congresses, Henry Hart. Sidonie Gruenberg, director of the Child Study Association, worked with the Rand School of Social Science and had ties with other socialist organizations; she was also active on the Women's Committee of the National Council of American Soviet Friendship (NCASF). See meeting minutes, May 9 and October 30, 1944, NCASF Papers, box 5.

67. Bacon, interview with author, November 14, 1998, Berkeley, California.

68. "BMC Sets Up Sub-Committee on Children's Books," *Daily Worker* (February 2, 1943): 7.

69. A juvenile literature committee of the Writers' War Board sponsored a forum in 1945 on detecting prejudice in children's books, and it planned to issue a pamphlet for editors on "proofreading without prejudice." CSA Papers, box 10. At another Writers' War Board discussion, December 27, 1945, on "Children's Books: Which Way for the Future?" Jerrold Beim, speaking from the audience, challenged the idea that reading does not necessarily form children's attitudes. He insisted that negative stereotypes "unconsciously . . . indoctrinate with the status quo. It is up to us to break down these stereotypes with a conscious literature." CSA Papers, box 14, folder 133.

70. The committee objected, for instance, to the negative image of Jews in *A Life of Our Lord for Children* (1945); on another occasion the Children's Book Committee chair, Flora Straus, conferred with Frances Clarke Sayers of the New York Public Library on the problem of "the villainous Indian" as a stereotype in many children's books. Letter to Sheed and Ward from Mrs. Straus, May 23, 1945, box 5, folder 40; letter from Mrs. Straus to Frances Clark Sayers, April 28, 1949, box 5, folder 42, both in CSA Papers; Josette Frank, letter to Miss Barbara Brown at Vassar College, March 31, 1948; Children's Book Committee of the Child Study Association, "Children's Books: Can Reading Educate for Peace?" *Child Study* (May 1938): 250. The book recommended in this instance was Leo Huberman's *Man's Worldly Goods*. Letter from Josette Frank to Lavinia Davis, May 19, 1948, box 5, folder 41, CSA Papers.

71. Howard Pease, address at the 1939 Sayers Institute in Berkeley, quoted in Jenkins, "The Strength of the Inconspicuous," 175.

72. Between 1943 and 1945 the CSA's Children's Book Committee received the National Conference of Christians and Jews "Books for Brotherhood" list (box 5, folder 44), and list of juvenile "goodwill" books (box 11, folder 104); the Conference's Chicago Roundtable sent their "Reading for Democracy" list (Box 5, folder 40). On August 17, 1944, Muriel Fuller from Thomas Nelson and Sons sent to the committee a review copy of a book "that should promote inter-racial and international understanding," which was fairly typical editorial packaging. Clara Ostrowsky and Elizabeth Morrow, "Children's Books Grow Up," *New Masses* 53 (December 12, 1944): 23–25.

73. Marshall McClintock, *Here Is a Book* (New York: Vanguard, 1939), 52.

74. In this spoof on the classic Gulliver tale, Betty Boop rescues the "book readers" and their allies—who have been imprisoned to squelch their calls for more schools and hospitals—from the authoritarian rule of a dictator and former circus clown, the Great Mohokus. Wallace West, *Betty Boop in Miss Gulliver's Travels* (Racine, Wis.: Whitman, 1935). A summary of McClintock's remarks at the Writers Congress are in LAW Papers.

75. See Noel Carrington, "A New Deal in 'Juveniles,'" *Junior Bookshelf* 6, no. 2 (July 1942): 42–43. Carrington says Russian state-printed books inspired him to launch Puffin Picture Books: "Here were beautifully coloured books by good artists, all for a penny or less."

76. Among the leftists who did work for Little Golden Books in one capacity or another were Anne Terry White, Emma Gelders Sterne, Rose Wyler, Lilian Moore, Alexander Crosby, Irving Adler, Irwin Shapiro, Priscilla Hiss, and Tibor Gergeley. Wyler contended that "the whole concept of mass-market books was a leftist idea," supporting the socialist notion that "nothing's too good for the masses." Wyler also argued that even the earliest Little Golden Books showed a commitment to racial diversity and rejected

racism. Rose Wyler, interview with author, March 28, 1998, New York City. Mary Reed, Ph.D., whose name can be found on the inside cover of every Little Golden book in the *Bank Street* series (supposedly verifying the books' educational value), was head of the kindergarten division at Columbia's Teachers College and had traveled to the Soviet Union in 1929 with a delegation of nursery school teachers. On Reed's trip, see Vera Fediaevsky and Patty Smith Hill, *Nursery School and Parent Education in Soviet Russia* (New York: Dutton, 1936), xviii. Thanks to Molly Arboleda for this reference. The papers of Lucille Ogle, who supervised Golden Books, have several files on "interracial" issues and record Ogle's support of organizations such as the Council on Interracial Books for Children.

77. Simon Doniger, "Instead of Baby Talk," *New Masses* (June 13, 1939): 21–23.

78. Similarly, in Shapiro's introduction to *Yankee Thunder: The Legendary Life of Davy Crockett* (1944), the villain of this story, the peddler Slickerty Sam Patch, "a compound of the traditional slyness of the backwoods peddler, the chicanery of the professional gambler, and the brutality of those who seek personal gain at any cost," is said to possess "the same traits of character" as "his cousins in Germany, Italy and Japan." Shapiro suggests, moreover, that a "basic American pattern," revealed in tales like Crockett's, is "in our times, and especially since Pearl Harbor, assuming greater importance each day." Irwin Shapiro, *Yankee Thunder: The Legendary Life of Davy Crockett* (New York: Messner, 1944), 9.

79. See *Tender Comrades* for an oral history of radical filmmakers who were blacklisted and a list of their films. Paul Buhle and Patrick McGilligan, eds., *Tender Comrades: A Backhistory of the Hollywood Blacklist* (New York: St. Martin's, 1999). Also see Todd Bennett, "Culture, Power, and *Mission to Moscow*: Film and Soviet-American Relations during World War II," *Journal of American History* 88, no. 2 (September 2001): 489–518.

80. Vernon Ives, "Children's Books and the War," *Publishers Weekly* 144 (October 23, 1943): 1592–93; Elizabeth Morrow, "Children's Books in a Wartime Year," *Retail Bookseller* 46, no. 579 (1943): 65–67.

81. Tuttle, *Daddy's Gone to War*, 156.

82. Morrow, "Children's Books in a Wartime Year"; Ives, "Children's Books and the War."

83. Mary Elting Folsom, letter to author, February 2003. On Planned Books see Mary Elting, "Building a Book," *Publishers Weekly* 144 (October 23, 1943): 1598–1602. Also letter from Mary Elting to author, December 8, 1999.

84. Mary Elting and Robert T. Weaver, *Battles: How They Are Won* (Garden City, N.Y.: Doubleday, Doran, 1944), 39, 44.

85. Ives, "Children's Books and the War," 1593.

86. Henry Gregor Felsen, *Struggle Is Our Brother* (New York: Dutton, 1943), 184.

87. A number of critically acclaimed children's books published during the war likewise praise the bravery of Soviet soldiers and/or civilians. These include, in addition to *Struggle*, Lorraine Beim and Jerrold Beim, *Sasha and the Samovar* (New York: Harcourt Brace, 1944); Ruth Epperson Kennell and Russian War Relief, Inc., *That Boy Nikolka and Other Tales of Soviet Children* (New York: Russian War Relief, 1945); William C. White, *Made in the USSR* (New York: Knopf, 1944); Arkady Gaidar, *Timur and His Gang*, trans. Zina Voynow (New York: Scribner's, 1943); Joseph Gollomb and Alice Taylor, *Young Heroes of the War* (New York: Vanguard, 1943). Also see May Lamberton Becker, ed., *Youth Replies, I Can: Stories of Resistance* (New York: Knopf, 1945).

88. Felsen, *Struggle Is Our Brother*, 166.

89. Henry Gregor Felsen, *Submarine Sailor* (New York: Dutton 1943), 31–32, 43.

90. Ostrowsky and Morrow, "Children's Books Grow Up," 23; Felsen, *Submarine Sailor*, 25.

91. Vicar, *The Company Owns the Tools*, 168, 178.

92. Henry Gregor Felsen, "Henry Gregor Felsen," in *Something about the Author Autobiography Series*, vol. 2 (Detroit, Mich.: Gale, 1986), 85–88; Mary Elting, letter to author, November 18, 1998.

93. Unsigned eulogy in Emma Gelders Sterne Collection, 1972 addition, box 2; *Twentieth Century Authors* quoted in introduction to the inventory of the Papers of Emma Gelders Sterne, June 1968; telephone interview with Marge Frantz, November 20, 1998.

94. Emma Gelders Sterne, *Incident in Yorkville* (New York: Farrar and Rinehart, 1943), 87.

95. Lyrics quoted in Denning, *The Cultural Front*, 128.

96. Sterne, *Incident in Yorkville*, 44–46.

97. Ibid., 149, 117.

98. Ibid.,166.

99. Ibid., 205.

100. Sterne's FBI file notes that she was on the Executive Board of the Joint Anti-Fascist Refugee Committee's Boston chapter and cites a mimeographed newsletter entitled "Good News for Anti-Fascists" (reportedly from September 1943), which briefly described *Incident in Yorkville* and noted that "Mrs. Sterne is generously contributing to this chapter her share of each copy of the book that we sell." FBI file for Emma Gelders Sterne, FOIPA No. 0990208–000.

Chapter 4

1. "New Lincoln Book Has Pink-Tinged Pages," Review of *River Road*, *Sentinel* (November 28, 1954): 1, 6. Special thanks to my cousin David Mickenberg for spooling through microfilms at the University of Wisconsin to find this material for me.

2. On McCarthyism see David Caute, *The Great Fear: The Anti-Communist Purge under Truman and Eisenhower* (London: Secker and Warburg, 1978); Ellen Schrecker, *Many Are the Crimes: McCarthyism in America* (Boston: Little, Brown, 1998); John Earl Haynes, *Red Scare or Red Menace? American Communism and Anticommunism in the Cold War Era* (Chicago: Dee, 1996). Also see Joel Kovel, *Red Hunting in the Promised Land: Anticommunism and the Making of America* (New York: Basic, 1994).

3. The heads of some of the nation's most prestigious publishing houses, magazines, and newspapers had turned out to celebrate the tenth anniversary of International Publishers in 1934. Sender Garlin, "Publisher on Trial: the Lifework of Alexander Trachtenberg," *Masses and Mainstream* 5, no. 10 (October 1952): 17–27. Publishing houses were singled out as cultural institutions particularly vulnerable to Communism in testimony before HUAC by Walter S. Steele. Committee on Un-American Activities, *Testimony of Walter S. Steele*, 80th Cong. (July 21, 1947), 117. See Clem Hodges, "Crisis in Publishing: Burning Books, Banning Authors," *Masses and Mainstream* 4, no. 11 (November 1951): 1–6. Also see *Counterattack* (August 31, 1951) (reprint in Alfred A. Knopf Collection, box 567, folder 3). Information on Hughes from Arnold Rampersad, *The Life of Langston Hughes*, vol. 2: *1941–1967: I Dream a World* (New York: Oxford University Press, 1988), 230.

4. Statement on *Yankee Doodle* quoted in Herbert Mitgang, *Dangerous Dossiers: Exposing the Secret War against America's Greatest Authors* (New York: Fine, 1988), 208; Hodges, "Crisis in Publishing: Burning Books, Banning Authors." Also see Louise S. Robbins, *The Dismissal of Miss Ruth Brown: Civil Rights, Censorship, and the American Library* (Norman: University of Oklahoma Press, 2000); "Further Censorship Efforts Reported from Many Localities," *Publishers Weekly* 163 (May 30, 1953): 2206–8; Mrs. Myrtle G. Hance, "Read [sic] Reading: A Report on Our San Antonio Public Libraries: Communist Front Authors and Their Books Therein" (San Antonio, Tex.: 1953?).

5. "Young Readers," Review of *River Road*, *Sentinel* (November 28, 1954): 2. "Child guardians" phrase from Kennell, "Introductory Remarks," LAW papers. Review of *Sparrow Hawk* by Meridel Le Sueur, *New York Times* (November 12, 1950): 30; Review of *Little Brother of the Wilderness* by Meridel Le Sueur, *New York Times* (May 25, 1947): 35; Louise Seaman Bechtel, Review of *Nancy Hanks of Wilderness Road* by Meridel Le Sueur, *New York Herald Tribune Book Review* (November 5, 1949): 16; Nell McCalla, Review of *Nancy Hanks of Wilderness Road* by Meridel Le Sueur, *Library Journal* (November 1, 1949): 1681.

6. Norma Rathburn, head of children's work at the Milwaukee Public Library, sent a letter to Le Sueur the day after the *Sentinel* article came out, telling Le Sueur how much they all enjoyed her program and how much positive feedback they had received. Given the fact that Le Sueur's visit to Milwaukee had been nearly a month earlier, the timing of Rathburn's letter shows she was responding to the *Sentinel* piece. Meridel Le Sueur Papers, 152.K.18.1B, box 1. A copy of a letter from Le Sueur to Sig [Eisenscher], December 5, 1954, notes that Rathburn "assured her that she wouldn't consider removing a book from the public library." However, Rathburn had apparently chastised Le Sueur for appearing at a *Worker* party, "even though saying they had no desire to curtail the personal or political life of authors, or in any way subscribe to 'guilt by association.'" Copy of letter to Sig, December 5, 1954, Le Sueur Papers, 152.K.18.1B, box 1.

7. Royalty statements in Le Sueur's papers, though incomplete, show sales numbers for various six-month periods. Sales of the books appear to have spiked in the early 1960s with the increase in educational funds that came available during the Johnson administration, but they sold reasonably well before that as well. *River Road* is not mentioned in royalty statements after the mid-1950s, suggesting that the book was allowed to go out of print. Le Sueur Papers, 144.I.195B 10, folder labeled "publication records: agreements, contracts, 1927–1986."

8. Ruth Harshaw, host of NBC's "Carnival of Books," informed Marjorie Thayer, a publicity person at Knopf, of the cancellation, which was because of the publicity around Le Sueur's appearance in Milwaukee, noting that the program had been in a similar situation once before, in which "supervisors of libraries were called before boards of education to explain why they were giving publicity to this author, and there was so much pressure on the local NBC stations that several of them informed us that they would not broadcast that particular show." Harshaw maintained that "it seems wise not to let this Le Sueur issue reach these proportions" and suggested that the publicity would "be as bad for her as for the show." Harshaw, who sent a copy of the same letter to Le Sueur, expressed her deep regret about the whole thing, noting how much she liked Le Sueur and *River Road*. "I cannot see the 'communist line' dangling anywhere," she said, "but then, perhaps I'm just not keen on that sort of thing. I have such a great respect for truth myself that it never occurs to me that others may want to tamper with it!" Letter from Ruth Harshaw to Marjorie Thayer, December 31, 1954; note to Le Sueur undated. In Meridel Le Sueur Papers, 152.K.18.1B, box 1, folder 15.

9. Editor Ruth Shair, notifying Le Sueur of the book's reprint with a new cover that played up the "Davy Crockett" subtitle, noted, "[T]he fad will die down eventually but while it is [sic] still lives we will make the most out of it." Ruth Shair, letter to Meridel Le Sueur, July 11, 1955, Meridel Le Sueur Papers, 144.I.195B 10.

10. In 1955 Le Sueur published *Crusaders*, a tribute to her parents, Marion and Arthur Le Sueur, with Howard Fast's Blue Heron Press, which was expressly created as an outlet for books that could not be published "by any other means." Howard Fast, letter to Meridel Le Sueur, December 20, 1954, Meridel Le Sueur Papers, 144.I.195B 10. Le Sueur may have published work using a pseudonym, but it is difficult to tell from her records.

11. Although Knopf was a longtime Republican, his files contain numerous copies of letters to senators and congressmen opposing McCarthy and urging his censure. Alfred A. Knopf Papers, box 587, folder 2. Knopf's papers also contain materials defending free speech. After Angus Cameron's dismissal from Little Brown, Knopf immediately asked Cameron to join his firm. John Tebbel notes of Knopf's action: "When he was congratulated for [hiring Cameron], Knopf is supposed to have said: 'It's a lot of nonsense. I don't believe any of it. And it's not brave of me when everyone knows that politically I'm right of the right-field foul line. As for Cameron, he's simply one of the best editors around. I'd be a fool not to take him.'" John William Tebbel, *A History of Book Publishing in the United States* (New York: Bowker, 1981), 4:708. Quote from Knopf taken from Hiram Hayden, *Words and Faces* (New York: Harcourt Brace Jovanovich, 1974), 355. Claims for the liberal predilections of people like Knopf can be taken too far, of course: in my original examination of Le Sueur's papers, I mistook correspondence about Le Sueur's children's books from an "Al K" as being from Knopf. Later examination of Knopf's handwriting and a closer look at the letters from "Al K" made it clear that this correspondent was not Knopf but a North Dakota Communist named Alfred Knutson, who probably was using Le Sueur's children's books for educational purposes. I regret the original error.

12. Mary Lapsley, "Socially Constructive Literature for Children," address at the Juvenile Writers Craft session of the Fourth Congress of the League of American Writers, June 6–8, 1941, LAW Papers, box 5; Jean Van Evera, "They're Not What They Used To Be!" *Parents* 21, no. 10 (October 1946): 28, 165.

13. Jay Williams, "What Do Kids Read?" *New Masses* 63 (June 10, 1947): 11.

14. Clara Ostrowsky, "Books for Children," *New Masses* 65, no. 10 (December 2, 1947): 18–21. One finds a similar pattern in the children's record offerings available from Folkways, the Children's Record Guild, the Young People's Record Club, and other outlets that had a relatively strong influence from the Left. For more on the Young People's Record Club and the Children's Record Guild, see David Bonner, *Revolutionizing Children's Records: The Young People's Records and Children's Record Guild Series, 1946–1977* (Lanham, Md.: Scarecrow, 2005). On Folkways and especially its founder, Moses Asch, see Peter D. Goldsmith, *Making People's Music: Moe Asch and Folkways Records* (Washington, D.C.: Smithsonian Institution Press, 1998).

15. Howard Fast, *Being Red: A Memoir* (Armonk, N.Y.: Sharpe, 1994). *Citizen Tom Paine* and several other books by Fast had already, at this point, been banned from New York City school libraries. His books would be banned widely throughout the United States and the world. Statements made by Fast in symposium on "America in Books for Young People," November 25, 1947, in conjunction with the opening of the Children's Book Committee's exhibit of children's books for 1947, box 14, folder 133, CSA Papers.

16. Fast, "America in Books for Young People."

17. Ernest Crichlow, interview with author, November 20, 1997, Brooklyn, New York.

18. On the liberal narrative, see Thomas Hill Schaub, *American Fiction in the Cold War* (Madison: University of Wisconsin Press, 1991). On Cold War integrationism, see Christina Klein, *Cold War Orientalism: Asia in the Middlebrow Imagination, 1945–1961* (Berkeley: University of California Press, 2003). Fast, "America in Books for Young People." Works by lesser-known authors like the Beims were occasionally banned as well.

19. Howard Pease, address at the 1939 Sayers Institute in Berkeley, quoted in Christine Jenkins, "The Strength of the Inconspicuous: Youth Services Librarians, the American Library Association, and Intellectual Freedom for the Young, 1939–1955" (Ph.D. diss., University of Wisconsin, 1995), 175.

20. The New York Public Library's January 1946 list of "Books for Young People" (part of the *Branch Library News*) also included a number of books on "America": Leo Huberman's Marxist history of the United States, *We, the People*; Mary Elting's *We Are the Government*; five books by Howard Fast; and *Deep River* by Henrietta Buckmaster—all books by authors with very committed left-wing politics. Other lists—like the "Reading for Democracy" list published by the Chicago Roundtable of the National Conference of Christians and Jews in 1945; the National Conference of Christians and Jews' "Books for Brotherhood" list, published in the 1950s (for which Josette Frank was a consultant); or the "Recommended Reading" lists for eight- to fourteen-year-olds published in the mid-1940s in *Common Ground*, a journal of the intercultural education movement—showed a similar pattern. CSA, box 5, folders 42 and 44. Also see Beatrice De Lima Meyers, "On Common Ground with Children's Books," *Common Ground* 1, no. 1 (Autumn 1940): 101–2.

21. Nancy Mikkelson, telephone interview with author, December 4, 1997; Mary Elting Folsom, interview with author, January 22–25, 1998, Boulder, Colorado. Josette Frank also nominated books for the Nancy Bloch award; official judges included Isabelle Suhl, librarian at the Elizabeth Irwin High School, and Eve Merriam, poet and author, who were both active on the Left and members of the Loose Enders. "The Nancy Bloch Award" (description), box 5, folder 47. Also see lists recommended for award from Josette Frank, box 12, folder 112. Brochures on the award in the same folder, CSA Papers. Mary Elting Folsom was a judge for the Jane Addams Award for many years.

22. On hearings relating to youth and popular culture in the 1950s, see Lynn Spigel, "Seducing the Innocent: Childhood and Television in Postwar America," in *Ruthless Criticism: New Perspectives in U.S. Communication History*, ed. William S. Solomon and Robert N. McChesney (Minneapolis: University of Minnesota Press, 1993), 259–83; James Gilbert, *A Cycle of Outrage: America's Reaction to the Juvenile Delinquent* (New York: Oxford University Press, 1986). For criticisms of comic books contemporary to the time, see Frederic Wertham, *Seduction of the Innocent* (New York: Rinehart, 1954).

23. See Benjamin Spock, "Will Our Children Meet the World Challenge?" in Benjamin Spock, *Problems of Parents* (1955; reprint, Boston: Houghton Mifflin, 1962), 277. Also see J. J. Haggerty, "The Communist Indoctrination Program: An Illustration and a Possible Answer," *Social Studies* 50 (April 1959): 129–35. For metaphors of disease and infection, see, for instance, Purnell Benson, "A 'Boys' Club' for Errants from Democracy," *Journal of Higher Education* 25, no. 1 (January 1954): 27–31.

24. On threats to the family (and fears of an "'international sit-down strike' against motherhood"), see "The Family: In Western Civilization It Is Seriously Threatened and Needs Material and Moral Help," *Life* (March 24, 1947): 36. The notion that Communists

advocated the abolition of the family was drawn from readings of the *Communist Manifesto*; see Clare Booth Luce, "The Communist Challenge to a Christian World," *New York Herald Tribune* (November 24, 1946): 7. On the family as the first line of defense, see Elaine Tyler May, *Homeward Bound: American Families in the Cold War Era* (New York: Basic, 1988); Laura McEnaney, *Civil Defense Begins at Home: Militarization Meets Everyday Life in the Fifties* (Princeton, N.J.: Princeton University Press, 2000). The judge sentencing both Julius and Ethel Rosenberg to death acknowledged that Julius was "the prime mover in this conspiracy," but condemned both of them as parents, insisting that "love for their cause dominated their lives—it was even stronger than their love for their children." Quoted in Ellen Schrecker, *The Age of McCarthyism: A Brief History with Documents* (Boston: Bedford, 1994), 145. Also see Kovel, *Red Hunting in the Promised Land*, 101, 277.

25. "The Family: In Western Civilization It Is Seriously Threatened," 36; Gilbert, *Cycle of Outrage*, 72–75. See, for instance J. B. Matthews, *The Commies Go after the Kids* (New York: National Council for American Education, 1949).

26. Albert Kahn, "School for Crime," *Masses and Mainstream* 7, no. 8 (August 1954): 46–51; Mike Newberry, "The Delinquent Society: Causes and Cures," *Worker* (September 7, 1958): 6. Also see Lorraine Hansberry, "Juvenile Delinquency? Child Labor Is Society's Crime against Youth," *Freedom* 5, no. 2 (February 1955): 2; "How Dense Is the Blackboard Jungle," *National Guardian* (November 8, 1954): 11. On the Rosenbergs and familialist rhetoric, see "In Sing Sing Death House, an 8-Year-Old Cold-War Victim Asks: 'Daddy, When Are You and Mommy Coming Home?'" *National Guardian* (August 8, 1951): 1. See, for instance, Albert E. Kahn, *Vengeance on the Young: The Story of the Smith Act Children* (New York: Hour, 1952). Also see Deborah Gerson, "Is Family Devotion Now Subversive? Familialism against McCarthyism," in *Not June Cleaver*, ed. Joanne Meyerowitz (Philadelphia: Temple University Press, 1994), 51–76.

27. Albert Kahn, "Comics, TV and Your Child," *Masses and Mainstream* 6, no. 6 (June 1953): 36–43; "Parents Stress Ideological Needs of Children at Jefferson School Conference," flyer dated February 1, 1951, in papers of the Jefferson School of Social Science, box 1, folder: "miscellaneous."

28. Haggerty, "The Communist Indoctrination Program: An Illustration and a Possible Answer," 13; U.S. House of Representatives, Committee on Un-American Activities, *100 Things You Should Know about Communism and Education* (Washington, D.C.: Government Printing Office, 1948), 9. Lora notes that thousands of copies of this publication were distributed to schools across the country, and several schools used the pamphlet as a textbook in sociology. Ronald Lora, "Education: Schools as Crucible in Cold War America," in *Reshaping America: Society and Institutions, 1945–1960*, ed. Robert H. Bremner and Gary W. Reichard (Columbus: Ohio State University Press, 1982), 228.

29. Lora, "Education," 230, 228. Carey McWilliams created a collection of materials relating to the New York Teachers Union and its response to investigations; the collection can be found at the Millbank Memorial Library, Teachers College, Columbia University. Also see Marjorie Murphy, *Blackboard Unions: The AFT and the NEA, 1900–1980* (Ithaca, N.Y.: Cornell University Press, 1990). Lucille Cardin Crain, who edited the *Educational Reviewer*, insisted that "unless the poisoning of the minds of our children is stopped—and unless they are taught while young to know about the benefits of our private enterprise system—the future managers and employees of American industry will not believe in the economic system in which these enterprises were created and in

which they have prospered." "What Is Taught to Your Children: Excerpts from Broadcast Recently Made on Americans, Speak Up! Program with Bill Slater, Master of Ceremonies," *Educational Reviewer* 2, no. 2 (October 15, 1950): 1.

30. Lora notes that Allen Zoll, who served as executive vice president of the National Council for American Education was a fascist propagandist and head of the American Patriots. Lora, "Education," 229.

31. "Texas Bill Proposes Author Anti-Red Oath," *Publishers Weekly* (May 2, 1953): 1843–44. For more on the politics surrounding textbook publishing, see Caroline Cody, "The Politics of Textbook Publishing, Adoption, and Use," in *Textbooks and Schooling in the United States: Eighty-ninth Yearbook of the National Society for the Study of Education*, ed. David L. Elliott and Arthur Woodward (Chicago: University of Chicago Press, 1990), 127–45. The importance of the Texas and California markets is discussed in Ian Westbury, "Textbooks, Textbook Publishers, and the Quality of Schooling," in Elliott and Woodward, eds., *Textbooks and Schooling in the United States*, 12.

32. The National Education Association (NEA) echoed a national consensus when its Educational Policies Commission unequivocally declared in 1949, "Members of the Communist Party of the United States should not be employed as teachers." The reasoning behind this decree was that "such membership . . . involves adherence to doctrines and discipline completely inconsistent with the principles of freedom on which American education depends." The NEA and other liberal groups were careful to make clear that finding Communists was tricky business and that the danger of lumping "progressives and liberals" together with "Communists" was a serious threat to civil liberties, but it was difficult to maintain a stance of liberal free inquiry and simultaneously forbid the employment of teachers who allegedly had political affiliations or beliefs that were difficult to prove. National Education Association Educational Policies Commission, *American Education and International Tensions* (Washington, D.C.: National Education Association, 1949), 39; National Council for American Education, *How Red Are the Schools? AND HOW YOU CAN HELP Eradicate Socialism and Communism from the Schools and Colleges of America* (New York: National Council for American Education, 1950). In April 1953 a New York City English teacher who had participated in an intercultural education course for teachers was called before HUAC based upon evidence of his promotion of "the new inter-cultural theory," and he was cited for making such statements as "Let us break down the idea that this is an Anglo-Saxon nation." A letter written in his defense noted a 1947 statement by the *Brooklyn Tablet*, organ of the Catholic diocese in Brooklyn: "there are certain words, which, after years of respectability, suddenly fall into disrepute because of questionable associations. The word 'intercultural' is one of these. It has now generally come to be associated with the propagation of the Communist Party line." Form letter from Abraham Lederman (of New York Teachers Union), May 4, 1953, in Carey McWilliams Papers, Millbank Library, Columbia University Teachers College, MG13, folder 1. The *Senior Scholastic* banning is noted in Louise S. Robbins, *Censorship and the American Library: The American Library Association's Response to Threats to Intellectual Freedom, 1939–1969* (Westport, Conn.: Greenwood, 1996).

33. Lester Levy, "Fascism Invades the School," *Jewish Life* (September 1949): 6–7. Also see Albert E. Kahn, *The Game of Death: The Effects of the Cold War on Our Children* (New York: Cameron and Kahn, 1953); "School Authorities Commit Crime against Our Children," *Freedom* 2, no. 5 (May 1952): 8; Kenneth B. Clark, "Are Jim Crow Schools Confined to the South?" *Freedom* (February 1954): 3–4; Elmer Bendiner, "The Shame

and Scandal of New York City Schools," *National Guardian* (January 17, 1951); Virginia Harnett, "Whitewash on the Blackboard," *New Masses* 58 (April 9, 1946): 10, 12–13. As a general rule, when mainstream attention was given to children's fears resulting from preparing for an atomic attack, the emphasis was on helping them to cope with "Cold War anxiety" rather than on changing the situation that had generated the anxiety in the first place. Dr. Benjamin Spock, for instance, advised parents, "[I]f our children press the question of what happens if an attack comes, we should be able to show some of the serenity and courage that the early Christians, pioneers, good soldiers have always demonstrated when they were sure their cause was right." Spock, *Problems of Parents*, 274.

34. Matthews, *The Commies Go after the Kids*, n.p. As this book was going to press I learned of a discussion of children's literature in Fred Schwartz, *You Can Trust the Communists (to Be Communists)* (Englewood Cliffs, N.J.: Prentice Hall, 1960). Schwartz, in contrast to Matthews, does point to children's literature as part of a Communist program of "brainwashing," mentioning "books printed in Moscow and Peking in English," but he seems unaware of books by American authors printed right here in the United States. Moreover, he seems confused by the fact that the books appear to be quite run-of-the-mill. He notes, "An examination of some of the children's literature produced by the Communists induces bewilderment in most loyal Americans, for they can discover nothing wrong with these books" (111–12). Cited in Elizabeth Parsons, "The Appeal of the Underdog: Mr. Lunch and Left Politics as Entertainment," unpublished paper submitted to author, 3.

35. Ibid.

36. The article makes several references to the pamphlet *The Road to Mass Organization of Proletarian Children* (discussed briefly in chapter 2 of this book), as evidence of Communists' "comprehensive program," not mentioning that the document was twenty years old (it was printed in 1930).

37. This argument is made in Arthur Liebman, "The Ties That Bind: The Jewish Support for the Left in the United States," in *Essential Papers on Jews and the Left*, ed. Ezra Mendelsohn (New York: New York University Press, 1997), 322–52.

38. Liebman interviewed former students of the Little Red Schoolhouse and Elizabeth Irwin High School, who testified to the schools' importance to their political development. Former students recalled the unconventional curriculum, where students "read about strikes, trade unions among the garment and subway workers, and union leaders such as Eugene V. Debs and John L. Lewis. They were taught about prejudice, and the drive for the emancipation of Negroes, of women, of labor." Liebman, "The Ties That Bind," 345.

39. The fall 1951 course booklet for the Jefferson School describes a new program in the children's division designed

> to satisfy the special needs of children from progressive and working-class families—Negro, Puerto Rican, and white. The Department seeks to develop in its pupils wholesome social attitudes toward each other and toward laboring people everywhere in the world, with love for and interest in work, and a deep sense of human dignity.

The same booklet describes a course on "Problems of Progressive Parents and Children," which was designed to help parents of school-age children meet some of the problems they face today. Your child's school experiences: national chauvinism, war hysteria and bomb scares, anti-Soviet indoctrination, white chauvinism and anti-Semitism. Combating prejudices and irrational fears; instilling an orientation towards peace and democracy, towards the working class and the Negro people. Special problems of the child in his relation to his fellows.

Jefferson School of Social Sciences program, fall 1951, 11, 21, in papers of Hugo Gellert, Archives of American Art, Smithsonian Institution, Washington, D.C. A course on "Child Development" taught at the Jefferson School also included a section on "Problems of Progressive Parents." Papers of the Jefferson School of Social Science, box 1, folder: "Psychology." Betty Bacon, Mary Elting, and Millicent Selsam gave lectures or taught classes on children's book writing at the Jefferson School.

40. For instance, the Jewish People's Fraternal Order put out the children's magazine *Jungvarg* (in Yiddish and English), with stories about Jewish pioneers, poets, laborers, and agitators. Groups such as the Committee for Progressive Jewish Education published books like *The Story of Passover* and *The Story of Purim*, both of which emphasized progressive Jewish traditions. See the Secular Yiddish Schools of America Collection, which contains numerous publications and curricular materials used by the Jewish Left. Unions sometimes published stories for the children of union members (see, for instance, Amalgamated Clothing Workers of America, *Mary Stays After School: or—What This Union's About* (New York: Amalgamated Clothing Workers of America, 1939). Left-wing newspapers and magazines like the *Worker* and *Fraternal Outlook* often had children's pages.

41. Matthews, *The Commies Go after the Kids*, n.p.

42. Elting, telephone interview with author, November 26, 2003; Mary Elting, *We Are the Government* (Garden City, N.Y.: Doubleday, Doran, 1946), 77–79.

43. Elting, *We Are the Government*, 22–23.

44. Mary Elting, letter to author, November 20, 2003; also telephone interview with author, November 26, 2003. Elting said in our phone conversation that there were very liberal people at Doubleday.

45. Helen Colodny Goldfrank's FBI file, FOIPA No. 0990202–000, entry dated February 8, 1952. Eve Merriam's shorter FBI file likewise monitors her comings and goings, mentions meetings and protests she attended and articles she published in radical journals (through 1959) but makes no mention at all of any children's books. Granick's *Underneath New York* did attract the FBI's attention (see chapter 6), but this was unusual. While it does not seem to have affected sales of the book, it may have helped to get Granick blacklisted from jobs in television and radio. Franklin Folsom's lengthy FBI file does mention that he wrote for children, but only has one more specific note: that Folsom was traveling to the Soviet Union to do research for a children's book; the book itself was never examined. Likewise, Betty Bacon's file notes that she was editing a series of juvenile books that were "favorable to the Soviet Union," but specific books are not mentioned nor are any of the books Bacon herself authored. Emma Gelders Sterne's file, quoting a newsletter of the Joint Anti-Fascist Refugee Committee, does note that *Incident in Yorkville* "is a story of a German-American youth, educated by the Nazis, who learned about democracy when he comes home to the U.S.," and picks up on the claim in the newsletter (apparently edited by Sterne herself), that "Mrs. Sterne is generously contributing to this Chapter her share of each copy of the book that we sell." The file also

noted that Sterne was working on editing condensed versions of *King Arthur* and *Little Women* for Golden Books. Again, in all of these instances, the books themselves were never examined or questioned. And while the bulk of Sterne's hefty file is devoted to reporting on her civil rights activity, the only mention of her civil rights–oriented children's books is a quote from a San José newspaper praising her books' contributions to the cause of "brotherhood." Henry Felsen's file makes indirect reference to several books but they are never treated as significant; Jay Williams's file shows the same pattern.

I have found record of congressional testimony for Helen Goldfrank, Leo Huberman, Langston Hughes, Howard Fast, Irving Adler, and Franklin Folsom, the former three in conjunction with investigations of overseas libraries. Fast was questioned about the "Voice of America," Adler about education, and Folsom about his involvement in the TASS news service. In all instances, the questions had almost nothing to do with the individuals' writing for children. Searching cumulative indexes for HUAC hearings, I found that quite a few people in this study were cited in testimony of others but not called to testify themselves. See especially U.S. Congress, House Committee on Un-American Activities, *Testimony of Walter S. Steele regarding Communist Activities in the United States* (Washington, D.C.: Government Printing Office, 1947).

46. C. P. Trussell, "Dashiell Hammett Silent at Inquiry," *New York Times* (March 27, 1953): 9; Henry Giniger, "Paris Follows Rule," *New York Times* (June 22, 1953): 8. The *New York Times* contained a lengthy article, beginning on the front page, on June 22, 1953, detailing responses in various countries to directives issued to remove books by suspicious authors, sixteen of whom (Goldfrank among them) were named specifically; authors who had pleaded the Fifth Amendment to questions about their Communist affiliations or activities were among those specifically named. Several books were actually "burned" before the State Department could hastily clarify that the books should "*not be destroyed but stored pending further instructions.*" Milton Bracker, "Books of 40 Authors Banned by U.S. in Overseas Libraries," *New York Times* (June 22, 1953): 1, 8. Later, the directive, which had originally called for the banning of books by certain authors regardless of their content, called for "scrutiniz[ing]" all of the books "to determine whether they could serve the interests of democracy and the United States." Walter H. Waggoner, "Johnson Deplores Program's Critics," *New York Times* (July 16, 1953): 11.

47. In the hearings Huberman was asked whether he had ever been a member of the Communist party; Huberman replied that he had not. Asked whether he had ever been a Communist, Huberman asked, "What does that mean?" Roy Cohn responded by asking, "What does it mean to you, sir?" "Well, if you mean by a Communist one who believes in socialism, I do believe in socialism," Huberman responded. When pressed, he clarified that he did not believe in abolishing private property, only private ownership of "means of production." When Roy Cohn asked, "Do you think works written by you should be used, purchased with the taxpayers' money and used in overseas information centers, the purpose of which is to give a true picture of our form of government to the people in Europe?" Huberman answered, "I say frankly, yes. I think that my responsibility as an author means that before I submit the final draft of a manuscript to a publisher, I must be content that it is true; that it is accurate; that it is sound scholarship and still is right. Once I have done that I stand behind the book, and at the risk of being immodest, if I can say that about a book, it is a good book." Testimony of Leo Huberman (July 14, 1953), *Executive Sessions of the Senate Permanent Subcommittee on Investigations, Investigations of the Committee on Government Operations*, vol. 2, 83rd Cong., 1st sess. (Washington, D.C.: U.S. Government Printing Office, 1953), 1223–30.

48. John J. Simon, "Leo Huberman: Radical Agitator, Socialist Teacher," *Monthly Review* 55, no. 5 (October 2003): 28–31. It does not seem to be coincidence that *We, the People*, published in 1932 and reprinted several times, had its final printing by Harper in 1952 (although the book was reprinted in 1964 by Huberman's own *Monthly Review*). The articles in the *New York Times* that mention Kay's book and several works by Howard Fast make no specific mention of Huberman, although the articles do note that their listings of banned books are only partial.

49. Along with Goldfrank/Kay's apolitical *Apple Pie for Lewis*, several books by Howard Fast—including *Haym Solomon*, which was for middle-school children—as well as *Paul Robeson: Citizen of the World* by Shirley Graham, were among the few juveniles removed from library shelves. Bracker, "Books of 40 Authors Banned by U.S. in Overseas Libraries."

50. Charles E. Merrill Co. was affiliated with American Education Press, suggesting the book was geared toward an educational marketplace. The only copy of *Insects* that I was able to obtain came from the Baldwin Library at the University of Florida; thanks to Trena Houp for making a copy of it for me. The difficulty of obtaining the book suggests its lack of wide distribution, or at least its ephemeral nature. Kay's FBI file, which I obtained shortly before sending in this manuscript, also makes reference to an entry in the *Cumulative Book Index, 1943–1948* (Minneapolis, Minn.: Wilson, 1950), citing Kay as the author of a Young World Book called *Land of the Golden Fleece: The Story of the Caucasus*. Kay's book is indeed listed in the index (with illustrations by Ernest Crichlow), but I have found no other record of it. It may be that the book was scheduled for publication but never actually published.

51. Lewis Goldfrank, telephone interview with author, December 16, 2003.

52. Joan Goldfrank, telephone interview with author, December 22, 2003; Helen Colodny Goldfrank FBI file. The file also attempts to prove that Kay attended the Lenin School in Moscow, as part of the FBI's case that she was a Soviet agent. What is fairly conclusive is that she was very active in the Communist party until the mid-1940s or so.

53. Helen Goldfrank testimony before the Senate Permanent Investigating Subcommittee, headed by Joseph R. McCarthy (March 26, 1953), *Executive Sessions of the Senate Permanent Subcommittee on Investigations, Investigations of the Committee on Government Operations*, vol. 2, 949–58. The autobiographical novel by Lillian Hellman, *Pentimento*, which was later made into the feature film *Julia*, may have been at least partially based on Hellman's friendship with Goldfrank, or at least this is what Helen Goldfrank told her children. Joan Goldfrank, telephone interview with author, December 22, 2003.

54. At least not in the memory of her children, who were old enough to be aware of something like this.

55. Lewis Goldfrank says his mother believed that editors were very reluctant to accept her work following her testimony, but he later read over editorial comments himself and believes the rejections may have been genuine. Both Lewis and Joan Goldfrank mentioned the Schwartzes, sympathetic editors who worked at Abelard-Schuman, as important to their mother's career. Joan Goldfrank told me that *One Mitten Lewis* (New York: Lothrop, Lee and Shepard, 1955) and *Picasso's World of Children* (Garden City, N.Y.: Doubleday, 1965)—the latter written for adults—each sold more than a million copies. Lewis Goldfrank, telephone interview with author, December 16, 2003; Joan Goldfrank, telephone interview with author, December 22, 2003.

56. The McCarthy hearing transcript as well as all articles about Goldfrank in the *New York Times* mention her use of "Helen Kay" as a pseudonym. On Hollywood radicals' work during the Cold War, see Paul Buhle and Patrick McGilligan, eds., *Tender Comrades: A Backhistory of the Hollywood Blacklist* (New York: St. Martin's, 1999); Paul Buhle and Dave Wagner, *Hide in Plain Sight: The Hollywood Blacklistees in Film and Television, 1950–2002* (New York: Palgrave Macmillan, 2003).

57. Information on Selsam from Rose Wyler, interview with author, March 27, 1998. Irving Adler mentioned Walsh's continued support despite Adler's political trouble; interview with author, October 11, 1997, North Bennington, Vermont; Nancy Larrick, interview with author, December 3, 1998. Other liberal editors, such as Helen Hoke Watts, took similar positions. See discussion of Langston Hughes in the next chapter.

58. Information on Hiss from telephone conversations with Tony Hiss, November 10, 2003, and July 16, 2004. Hiss reminded me that the Hiss affair immediately predated McCarthy, so to say that his father was a victim of "McCarthyism" is not really accurate. Hiss also wished to make clear to me that his parents, though targeted by the Right, were not "leftists" but "New Deal Democrats." The particulars of the Hisses' politics are, for my purposes, less important than the fact that children's literature offered a sympathetic home for Priscilla Hiss when most other avenues became closed to her. Following her dismissal from Dalton, after a few years of not working, Priscilla Hiss was employed for several years at a Doubleday bookstore (as the "notorious Mrs. Hiss," she was forced to work in the basement rather than on the sales floor, her son told me), and then at the Weyhe art gallery on Lexington Avenue, before landing at Golden Books in the late 1950s, by which time the red scare had lost much of its steam Still, the progressive politics of people at places like Golden Books should not be underestimated as a factor contributing to the field's relative immunity to right-wing attacks. Of the general political climate in children's literature Wyler asserted: "In those days, there were so few writers who were not progressive. It was hard to accept this McCarthy crap. Those who named names, got scared, they were progressive too." Wyler, interview with author, March 27, 1998.

59. Constance Coiner notes: "During this 'dark time' Alfred Knopf informed Le Sueur that she had been blacklisted but that he would continue to publish her children's books." Constance Coiner, *Better Red: The Writing and Resistance of Meridel Le Sueur and Tillie Olsen* (New York: Oxford University Press, 1995), 83. Coiner provides no documentation for this statement.

60. American Association of School Librarians Discussion Group, "Book Selection in Defense of Liberty in Schools in a Democracy," *ALA Bulletin* (November 1953): 484; Westchester Conference of the American Library Association and the American Book Publishers Council, "The Freedom to Read," *ALA Bulletin* (November 1953): 481–83.

61. Dorothy Broderick, "Children's Book Selection for a World in Ferment," *Wilson Library Bulletin* 36 (January 1962): 375–76, 386; Rose Agree, "The Freedom to Read on Long Island," *Top of the News* 23 (April 1966): 285–87. For an excellent overview of liberal advocacy for intellectual freedom among children's librarians, see Jenkins, "The Strength of the Inconspicuous." Edwin Castagna, "Courage and Cowardice: The Influence of Pressure Groups on Library Collections," *Library Journal* 88 (February 1, 1963): 501–10. Also see Sara Krentzman Srygley, "Schools under Fire," *Library Journal* 76 (1951): 2049–50. Many librarians probably agreed in principle with Castagna and Srygley, but librarians were themselves victims of McCarthyism, and, even more often, they practiced self-censorship to avoid precisely the kind of situation in which librarians in Mil-

waukee found themselves when Le Sueur's book was attacked. See Robbins, *Censorship and the American Library*, 55.

62. On the 1951 award, see CSA Papers, box 11, folder 105. On changing criteria, see 1954 statement describing the Children's Book Award, CSA Papers, box 11, folder 106. A draft description of the award-winning book for 1952, Miriam Powell's *Jareb*, notes that "the tender story of a boy and his dog presents a realistic and profound picture of family relationships, of birth, death, and survival in an impoverished area of our land." In the final draft the words "in an impoverished area of our land" were eliminated. CSA Papers, box 11, folder 105.

63. Ruth Krauss, *A Very Special House* (New York: Harper, 1953), n.p.

64. Williams, "What Do Kids Read," 13.

Chapter 5

1. Clara Ostrowsky, "Young World Books," *New Masses* (November 27, 1945): 24–27. Quotation within original text not attributed.

2. Information from Irving Adler, interview with author, October 11, 1997, North Bennington, Vermont.

3. Mary Elting, telephone interview with author, January 25, 2001. Millicent Selsam FBI file, FOIPA No. 0990206-000. Joyce Antler, *Lucy Sprague Mitchell: The Making of a Modern Woman* (New Haven: Yale, 1987), 413.

4. Helen Dean Fish, "What Is This Association of Children's Book Editors," *Library Journal* 71 (April 15, 1946): 544–46.

5. Elizabeth M. Bacon, "Children's Books about Labor," *Worker* (November 10, 1946): 10; Elizabeth Morrow Bacon, "How to Pick a Picture Book," *Worker* (May 5, 1946): 11; Elizabeth M. Bacon, "Growing Up on Books," *Worker* (June 9, 1946): 8. I became aware of these articles because of citations in Bacon's FBI file, which show the government was also interested in Bacon's tips for choosing books—or at least in the fact that such tips were being offered. The articles are cited but not actually discussed in the file.

6. Bacon, "Growing Up on Books."

7. Bacon, "Children's Books about Labor."

8. See letters to Meridel Le Sueur from Betty at Young World Books, December 12, 1945, and June 22, 1946, Meridel Le Sueur Papers, 144.I.195B 10. Helen Kay's FBI also claims to have found notice of a Young World Book authored by Kay on the Caucasus, called *Land of the Golden Fleece*. The title is listed in the *Cumulative Book Index, 1943–1948* (Minneapolis, Minn.: Wilson, 1950), but I have not found any other record of this book.

9. Julian Brazelton, who illustrated several Young World books, had illustrated Elie Siegmeister's *Work and Sing*, which he did in cooperation with Bacon while she was working for W. R. Scott. Herbert Kruckman, who illustrated three Young World books, would author or illustrate books distributed within the Jewish Left, as well as Edith Segal's 1964 collection of poems, *Be My Friend*. Kruckman also gave "chalk talks" on art for children, which were advertised in the *New Masses*. Ida Scheib illustrated several other books after her work with Young World. Ward, who was already well established, would go on to win a Caldecott Medal in 1953 for *The Biggest Bear*. Kirkus, *Library Journal*, the *New York Times*, and the *Weekly Book Review* gave laudatory reviews of *Egg to Chick*. A reviewer for *Book Week* insisted that "Ilin [*sic*] can make the world of science more interesting

to children than almost any writer today" (quoted in *Book Review Digest* [1945]: 472). Other reviewing outlets offered similar praises. The books were also included on several recommended booklists. For instance, the Play Schools Association booklist, prepared by the Children's Book Committee of the Child Study Association, recommended Clara Hollos's *Story of Your Bread* (Child Study Association Papers, box 12, folder 112). *The Library Journal's Recommended Children's Books of 1952* recommended Irving Adler's *The Secret of Light*; and a New York Public Library list of recommended books singled out Novikoff's works for praise. For more on the critical reception of these books, see the next chapter. Betty Smith, current president of International Publishers, told me that International was never able to devote much publicity to Young World Books; she also told me that International was also taken to court by the publishers of the *World Book Encyclopedia*, who did not want to tarnish the "World Book" name.

10. See discussion in chapter 6 of Alexander Trachtenberg's attempts to make Novikoff follow the "party line" in his book on evolution. Unlike many librarians, red-hunters did make the connection between Young World and the CP: for instance, in his testimony before HUAC, Walter S. Steele mentioned Young World as "another outfit designed to propagandize among the youth" and noted that "it distributes books on evolution and Soviet and pro-Communist themes." See *Testimony of Walter S. Steele* (chair of the National Security Committee of the American Coalition of Patriotic, Civic, and Fraternal Societies and managing editor of *National Republic* magazine), 80th Cong. (July 21, 1947), 107. It is difficult to determine what effect such testimony had on sales. The books kept being published for several more years after Steele's testimony and kept being well received. FBI files for Bacon and Kay likewise mentions the series. On Trachtenberg's imprisonment and on his background more generally, see Sender Garlin, "Publisher on Trial: The Lifework of Alexander Trachtenberg," *Masses and Mainstream* 5, no. 10 (October 1952): 17–27.

11. Jay Williams, "What Do Kids Read?" *New Masses* (June 10, 1947): 11.

12. Rose Wyler, interview with author, March 27, 1998, New York City.

13. May Garelick overlapped with Bacon at William R. Scott Publishers and stayed there for quite some time. Algernon Black was a "very progressive" editor at Doubleday, according to Mary Elting. Elting, telephone conversation with the author, November 26, 2003. Marshall McClintock, who spoke at the League of American Writers' juvenile session, worked at various points at Whitman, Vanguard, and Messner and was married to writer and editor May Garelick. Daniel Melcher, whose father, Frederic, was the chief editor of *Publishers Weekly*, worked at several publishing houses and then became general director of the *Library Journal*. Daniel Melcher is listed among the juvenile session participants in the League of American Writers Papers. On Daniel Melcher's later career see John William Tebbel, *A History of Book Publishing in the United States* (New York: Bowker, 1981), 4:553. Gertrude Blumenthal, editor at Messner (and later vice president at Simon and Schuster) began the Messner series of biographies in the mid-1940s and made a conscious effort to include biographies of African Americans. She published a number of books by leftists. Interview with Rose Wyler, March 27, 1998. Emma Gelders Sterne worked as an editor at Aladdin Books in the early 1950s. Marjorie Groves, a close friend of Betty Bacon, was an editor for Henry Schuman, a liberal who published people on the Left; liberal editors there were especially supportive of Helen Kay after her run-in with McCarthy. Lilian Moore and Rose Wyler were both on the staff at Scholastic in the 1950s, and Scholastic had a history of employing progressive people (Leo Huberman worked there in the 1930s, and Ernestine Taggart was listed on the program for the League of

American Writers' juvenile session in 1941 as an editor at Scholastic). Moore eventually became editor of the Arrow Book Club. Millicent Selsam worked as an editor at Walker later in her career, and Hy Ruchlis, another Loose Ender, ran the Science Materials Center, which published books and records; Ruchlis also worked for Houghton Mifflin and Basic Books. Irwin Shapiro and Ann McGovern worked as editors for Golden Books, which published quite a few radicals. Bradford Chambers, who would later run the Council on Interracial Books for Children, worked for Parents Press. Elizabeth Hamilton was a progressive editor who worked at Harcourt Brace and then at William Morrow, publishing the controversial work of Jerrold and Lorraine Beim as well as Hildegarde Hoyt Swift and Lynd Ward's *North Star Shining*. There are undoubtedly other examples.

14. Maxim Lieber was an agent for Langston Hughes, Meridel Le Sueur, and Jack Conroy; Edith Margolis was an agent for Emma Gelders Sterne. Rose Wyler mentioned Bart Bok as an agent who helped a number of leftists, and Mary Elting mentioned Margaret Gossett, with whom she worked on Planned Books. Nettie King was an agent for Lynd Ward, May McNeer Ward, Nancy Larrick (Crosby), and Alexander Crosby.

15. William R. Scott was involved with the progressive Downtown Community School and was known especially for showcasing the work of experimental, modern artists as well as the Here and Now books that attempted to put progressive educational theories into practice. Further discussion of Scott can be found in Barbara Bader, *American Picturebooks from Noah's Ark to the Beast Within* (New York: Macmillan, 1976), 214–37. Also Rose Wyler interview with author, November 27, 1998, New York City; and Mary Folsom, telephone interview with author, July 19, 2004. Scott published Herman and Nina Schneider's first science books, Dahlov Ipcar's first children's book (Ipcar, recall, was the daughter of left-wing artists William and Marguerite Zorach), and work by Lucienne Bloch, Millicent Selsam, Ruth Krauss, and other progressive and radical writers and artists. Vanguard was established in 1926 by Charles Garland, who used a large inheritance to support progressive causes. The purpose of the press was "to bring education to the working class with books sold as close to cost as possible." John Tebbel, *History of Book Publishing in the United States* (New York: Bowker, 1978), 3:181. Capitol is cited in Franklin Folsom's FBI file for its supposed left-wing connections. References to Messner, Golden, Schuman, and Simon and Schuster from Rose Wyler, interview with author, November 27, 1998. References to Random House from telephone interview with Rose Agree, September 27, 1999. Day published a number of radical books in the 1930s; its head, Richard Walsh, was married to the progressive Pearl S. Buck and was supportive of Adler after he was dismissed from the New York City schools. The papers of Lucille Ogle, who was head of Golden Press, contain friendly correspondence and holiday cards from Lilian Moore, Irving Adler, Rose Wyler, Irwin Shapiro, Emma Gelders Sterne, Lynd Ward, and others.

16. See discussion concerning Emma Gelders Sterne and Louis Hartman later in this chapter. Mary Elting, Franklin Folsom, and/or Peg Gossett helped Henry Felsen, Langston Hughes, and Jane Sherman to get contracts with Watts. In regard to Watts authors handled by Gossett and referred through Mary Elting and/or Franklin Folsom, see letter from Franklin Folsom to Louise Silcox of the Authors Guild, March 25, 1954, in Folsom-Elting Papers (MS 246), box 5, Authors Guild Correspondence 1952–1956. Also Mary Elting, letters to author, November 18, 1998, and May 7, 1999. Rose Wyler told me that Millicent Selsam's husband, Howard, wrote several books using her name. Wyler interview, November 27, 1998. Wyler mentioned writers helping each other to secure contracts but did not mention names. As mentioned earlier, Franklin Folsom often wrote

books using names of *Mayflower* passengers. Herman and Nina Schneider, never black-listed themselves, fronted for Nina's brother, a Hollywood screenwriter. See Paul Buhle and Patrick McGilligan, eds., *Tender Comrades: A Backhistory of the Hollywood Blacklist* (New York: St. Martin's, 1999), 722.

17. Betty Bacon, interview with author, February 20, 1999, Berkeley. On leftists at Golden Books, see chapter 3. Josette Frank of the CSA was on the Children's Book Club advisory committee. See advertisement in April 2, 1946, issue of the *New Masses*, on the back cover.

18. Mary K. Smith, *Meridel Le Sueur: A Bio-Bibliography* (M.A. thesis, University of Minnesota, 1973); letter from William N. Hall to Meridel Le Sueur, September 18, 1953, folder: correspondence 1950, 1951, 1953, box 144.I.195B 10, Le Sueur Papers; letter from Rachel D'Angelou to Meridel Le Sueur, May 21, 1954, in Le Sueur Papers, box 144.I.195B 10. D'Angelou later was an important mentor to Rose Agree, a children's librarian who had been a union organizer before going to library school. Rose Agree, telephone interview with author, September 27, 1999.

19. Letter from Genieve Fox to Meridel Le Sueur, January 16, 1955, box 152.K.18.1, folder 19, Le Sueur Papers.

20. Recall that Henry Holt summarily fired nearly every employee who had helped to publish work by Hughes, and Hughes's contracts there had been canceled. Arnold Rampersad, *The Life of Langston Hughes*, vol. 2: *1941–1967: I Dream a World* (New York: Oxford University Press, 1988), 230.

21. Herman and Nina Schneider, whose science textbooks were major sellers in the 1950s, were able to require their publishers to illustrate the textbooks with both black and white faces, a major victory, which the Schneiders and others mentioned to me. The inclusion of black faces in Elting and Bendick's *The Lollipop Factory* was also the result of battles with the publisher. Members of the Child Study Association likewise pressed for more black characters in children's literature: Josette Frank, for instance, asked writer Doris Gates if she would be willing to make the protagonist of her story in the Child Study Association's *Read to Me Story Book* an African American. Frank, letter to Gates, Child Study Association Papers, box 88, folder 68.

22. Hoke, letter to James Daugherty, October 20, 1944, James Daugherty Papers, University of Oregon.

23. Rampersad, *I Dream a World*, 181. See letter from Walter E. Cooper, councilor at law, to Common Council for American Unity, November 14, 1944, justifying the cancellation of Hughes's talk at Cranford High School in Jersey City, New Jersey, box 186, folder: "Common Ground," Langston Hughes Papers. Also see letter from Maxim Lieber to Langston Hughes, December 20, 1950. Of the contract Lieber noted, "[T]he only reason I'd accept it is because their record of exceptional sales leads me to believe one might make as much as a thousand or more in royalties for about a week's work or less." Hughes Papers, box 103, folder 1946.

24. Rampersad, *I Dream a World*, 191.

25. New York, incidentally, still winds up seeming like a pretty rosy place, though Terry's mother does tell a young cousin of Terry's who is visiting from the South that "in New York colored people find it hard to rent a house except in streets where Negroes live. And there are some fashionable restaurants that do not like to serve us. But most of them do." Langston Hughes, *The First Book of Negroes* (New York: Franklin Watts, 1952), 57. Elting also suggested that the southern cousin whom Terry visits be a girl instead of a boy. Helen Hoke Watts agreed that this would help girls to identify with the book

but said the matter was not "too important." Letter from Helen Hoke Watts of Franklin Watts, Inc. (with addenda from Franklin Watts and including comments from Mary Elting) to Langston Hughes, March 3, 1952, in General correspondence, box 163, folder: "Franklin Watts," Hughes Papers.

26. Hughes, *The First Book of Negroes*, 21, 40.

27. Information on the Baker reference from Rampersad, *I Dream a World*, 230. At the same time, editors at Dodd, Mead demanded a series of major cuts in Hughes's *Famous American Negroes*, which he was working on in the summer of 1953, basically amounting to the "excision" of all "references to racial discrimination." Rampersad, *I Dream a World*, 229–30.

28. Letter from H.H.W. to Langston Hughes, March 3, 1952, General correspondence, box 163, folder: "Franklin Watts," Hughes Papers. Emphasis in original.

29. Hughes, *The First Book of Negroes*, 65–66. Emphasis in original.

30. The books listed were *Story of the Negro* by Arna Bontemps; *Booker T. Washington: Educator of Hand, Head, and Heart* by Shirley Graham; *Dr. George Washington Carver, Scientist*, also by Graham (and George Liscomb); Dorothy Sterling's *Freedom Train: The Story of Harriet Tubman*; and *North Star Shining*, written by Hildegarde Hoyt Swift and illustrated by Lynd Ward. The other book listed was *Amos Fortune: Free Man* by Elizabeth Yates (1950), which was part of a series edited by Emma Gelders Sterne.

31. For Hughes's publicity suggestions, see letters from Hughes to Helen Hoke Watts, box 163, Hughes Papers. Hughes wrote to Helen Hoke Watts on April 3, 1953, expressing his "very deep gratitude" to her and Franklin "for all your help and kindness and worry and consideration in all this time-taking business," noting further plans to clear his name, in box 163, folder "Watts," Hughes Papers. Hughes was barred from several speaking engagements in 1952, as discussed in Rampersad, *I Dream a World*, 197–99.

32. Virginia Stumbough, letter to Franklin Watts (copy), March 10, 1953, Hughes Papers, box 187, folder "Good-bye Christ." Note her name is spelled Stumbough and also Stumbaugh in the copied letter; the proper spelling is unclear, but Stumbough is used more frequently.

33. Copy of letter from William Harris to Virginia Stumbough, March 6, 1953, Hughes Papers, box 187, folder "Good-bye Christ." On Harris's list, passed on by Watts to Hughes, Hughes noted "wrong" to Harris's claim, taken from appendix IX of the House Un-American Activities Committee, that Hughes "was for a period of approximately twenty years a professed card-holding member of the Communist Party, USA," as well as to the claim that he had been associated with the American Peace Mobilization and had, in 1934, been president of the National Negro Congress ("a C.P. front"). He put question marks next to documentation that he had from 1925 to 1933 been a member of the "All America Anti-Imperialist League"; that in 1932 he had been a member of the League of Professional Groups organized to support the candidacy of William Z. Foster for presidency on the CP ticket; that he had been on the editorial board of *Soviet Russia Today* in 1937; that he had signed a public statement in 1938 supporting Stalin's purges; and that he'd been involved with seven other "front" organizations. That left thirty-three other affiliations on Harris's list that Hughes did not dispute.

34. Being a cooperative witness meant that he answered the committee's questions fully and honestly, and in doing so cleared his name. Thus his books published after 1950, when Hughes said he broke all ties with Communism, *were* allowed in American libraries overseas. When asked, for instance, if he had ever been a Communist, Hughes responded, in terms not unlike Huberman, "It depends what you mean by your defi-

nition of Communism." When asked about specific pieces that the committee considered incendiary or subversive, Hughes responded, "[T]o give a full interpretation of any piece of literary work one has to consider not only when and how it was written, but what brought it into being. The emotional and physical background that brought it into being." He proceeded to tell the committee about his childhood, his family, and encounters with prejudice throughout his life. Citing the early and important influence of Eugene Debs, Hughes explained to the committee:

> I never read the theoretical books of socialism or communism or the Democratic or Republican party for that matter, and so my interest in whatever may be considered political has been non-theoretical, non-sectarian, and largely really emotional and born out of my own need to find some kind of way of thinking about this whole problem of myself, segregated, poor, colored, and how I can adjust to this whole problem of helping to build America when sometimes I can not even get into a school or a lecture or a concert or in the south go to the library and get a book out. So that has been a very large portion of the emotional background of my work, which I think is essential to one's understanding.

Langston Hughes, testimony, March 26, 1953, before Executive Sessions of the Senate Permanent Subcommittee on Investigations of the Committee on Government Operations, vol. 2, 83d Cong., 1st sess. (Washington, D.C.: Government Printing Office, 1953; made public January 2003), 976, 988. For further discussion of Hughes's testimony before the McCarthy committee, see Rampersad, *I Dream a World*, 215–19. Also see Victor Navasky, *Naming Names* (1980; reprint, New York: Penguin, 1991), 191–92.

35. Quoted in Rampersad, *I Dream a World*, 191.

36. For instance, *The First Book of Negroes* was deliberately omitted from the National Conference of Christians and Jews' Books for Brotherhood bibliography in 1953 (and possibly from other lists as well) "in view of the temper of the times." See letter from Louis Radelet to Josette Frank, September 21, 1953, explaining his decision to omit *The First Book of Negroes* from the Books for Brotherhood list, box 5, folder 44, CSA Papers. Hughes wrote to his agent, Maxim Lieber, on July 10, 1953: "THE FIRST BOOK OF NEGROES, so Watts reports, is doing right well [in] spite of the Los Angeles anti-U.N. lady Red Baiting it like mad—which I countered by reading from it at the McCarthy hearing, thus achieving bigger coverage than she did—national TV!" Hughes Papers, box 103, folder 1946.

37. Adler, interview with author, October 11, 1997, North Bennington, Vermont.

38. Rosemont added that "kids' series mysteries *always* involve the kids outwitting the bad adults—it's always a matter of being smarter, never of physical force or violence." Rosemont also emphasized the radicalizing aspects of many science fiction series. Franklin Rosemont, letter to author, January 24, 1998. Also see Franklin Rosemont, "'From Indianapolis to Rangoon': Walter Gibson and the Biff Brewster Series," *Mystery & Adventure Series Review* 18 (Spring 1987): 18–32.

39. Marge Frantz, telephone interview with author, November 20, 1998. Faith Lindsay more recently explained to me that Hartman was a relative of Sterne's by marriage.

40. Caroline Lynch, letters to Emma Gelders Sterne, August 11, 1964, and January 5, 1965, Sterne Papers, main collection, box 2; Carrie Lynch, letter to Emma and Barbara, September 10, 1963, Sterne Papers, 1972 addenda, box 1; Sterne, letter to Lucille

Ogle, May 28, 1963, Sterne Papers, main collection, box 2. Marge Frantz mentioned a Bay Area children's book writers group; Bacon and Sterne also saw each other socially. Marge Frantz, telephone interview with author, November 20, 1998; Bacon, interview with author, February 20, 1999. Hartman was also helped out by Angus Cameron, while Cameron was an editor for Knopf. Cameron encouraged Hartman to write an account of his experiences, to be called *The Harmful Truth*; the book was, most likely, never completed. In correspondence with Cameron, Hartman mentions his indictments before federal investigating committees and his work on the *Kathy Martin* books. He thanks Cameron for his encouragement and also sends regards from Betty Bacon (with whom Hartman would collaborate on a children's book about Chanukah). Letters from Louis Hartman to Angus Cameron in Alfred A. Knopf Papers, box 382, folder 11.

41. Letter from Carrie Lynch to Lou Hartman, July 6, 1965, Sterne Papers, main collection, box 2.

42. Josephine James, *Search for an Island* (New York: Golden, 1963).

43. "Borden's thoughts on prospective for Kathy Martin VII, IN SEARCH OF AN ISLAND (working title)," February 1, 1962, Sterne Papers, 1972 addenda.

44. Letter to Pete Borden from Barbara and Emma, February 5, 1962, Sterne Papers, main collection, box 2.

45. Letter to Emma and Barbara from Carrie, September 16, 1963, in 1972 addenda, box 1, Sterne Papers. Emphasis in original.

46. Ibid.

47. The idea of a "communications circuit" comes from Robert Darnton, "What Is the History of Books," *Daedalus* (Summer 1982): 65–83. Mary Lapsley, "Socially Constructive Literature for Children," June 1941, LAW Papers, box 5.

48. The Young People's Record Club was cited by HUAC, along with other groups, as an example of a "Communist front." See U.S. House of Representatives, Committee on Un-American Activities, *100 Things You Should Know about Communism and Education* (Washington, D.C.: Government Printing Office, 1948). Also see J. B. Matthews, *The Commies Go after the Kids* (New York: National Council for American Education, 1949); Miriam Sherman, interview with author, October 7, 1999, Los Angeles; Jennifer Charnofsky, interview with author, September 9, 1999, Los Angeles.

49. Although teachers could and did come to the store themselves, Genieve and Sid Fox, as well as the store's manager, Miriam Sherman, also brought materials directly to schools, teacher workshops, and library conferences, where they demonstrated how to integrate records, books, and filmstrips with school curricula. The Children's Music Center's 1960 catalog of "Recommended Records, Filmstrips, Books for the School Curriculum," for instance, features "Brotherhood Materials," including Paul Robeson's rendition of Earl Robinson's "Ballad for Americans" (as well as Robinson's "The House I Live In," "Free and Equal Blues," and "Black and White"); Dorothy Sterling's *Freedom Train*; Hughes's *First Book of Negroes*; Eva Knox Evans's *People Are Important*; and Edith Segal's openly political book of poetry for children, *Be My Friend*. Pete Seeger testified to Moses Asch's willingness to record whatever Seeger had to sing, even when he was blacklisted from most other outlets. Pete Seeger, interview with author, December 2, 1997, Beacon, New York. Information on the store comes from interviews with Miriam Sherman, October 7, 1999; and Jennifer Charnofsky, September 9, 1999, as well as from catalogs and other materials they provided.

50. Dr. Fitzhugh Dodson even specifically noted the center in his guidebook, *How to Parent*, which spoke of the store in glowing terms and helped to bring business from all

over the country, according to Sherman. Of the store Dodson wrote, "Children's Music Center, as far as I know, is practically one of a kind. You can demand that your local music store carry a better stock of children's records. . . . You mothers really have the unused power to get your local store to resemble the Children's Music Center!" But just in case his readers couldn't transform their local store, he noted that the center published a free catalog. Fitzhugh Dodson, *How to Parent* (New York: Signet, 1970), 404.

51. Sherman, interview with author, October 7, 1999, Los Angeles.

52. The John Birch Society, whose concerted anti-Communist campaigns began well after McCarthy had been censured, publicized the fact that Young People's Records had been cited as a "Communist front organization" in 1948 by the California Committee on Un-American Activities and made the argument that Young People's records (and those of their subsidiary, the Children's Record Guild) "had a harmful effect on the nervous system of children" and should be removed from schools. The records were said to be "subtly contrived hypnotic inductions [that] would be extremely detrimental to the health and welfare of children conditioned by repeated playing of the records." Two records cited as "particularly harmful" were "Tom's Hiccups," which was said to potentially "induce psychogenic allergy by causing children to identify with Tom, who goes through a series of ailments starting with hiccups and continuing through lisping, stammering, sneezing, drowsiness and wakeful snoring," and "The Little Puppet," which, "by repetitive playing convinces children they are unable to function of their own accord unless someone else pulls the string." See the Riverside County (California) *Daily Enterprise*, May 1, 1964, clipping provided by Miriam Sherman; David A. Noebel, *The Marxist Minstrels: A Handbook on Communist Subversion of Music* (Tulsa, Okla.: American Christian College Press, 1974). The records were actually removed from several school districts, including the Torrance Unified School District, though experts later determined there was, in fact, nothing subversive about them. The records were put back into the Torrance schools, to the dismay of some parents. See (Torrance) *Daily Breeze*, June 25, 1965, clipping courtesy of Miriam Sherman.

53. School librarian Rose Agree mentioned some people she got to know through her work, such as Leo Lionni, Arna Bontemps, and Hy Ruchlis (Agree, telephone interview with author, September 27, 1999).

54. Bacon, interview with author, February 20, 1999, Berkeley; Agree, telephone interview with author, September 27, 1999; Motz, interview with author, November 9, 1997, New York City.

55. On the growing demand for trade paperbacks, see, for example, Robert T. Jordan, "Wanted: Paperback Juveniles," *Publishers Weekly* 180 (November 13, 1961): 18–19; Moore, interview with the author, November 22, 1998, Seattle.

56. Moore, interview with the author, November 22, 1998, Seattle.

57. Ibid.

58. Moore, interview with author, November 22, 1998.

59. Lilian Moore, *Little Raccoon and the Thing in the Pool* (New York: McGraw-Hill, 1963); Moore, letter to author (dictated to Kim Casper), May 25, 2004. Moore apparently realized that by insisting that her work was not political, she had actually diminished the unconscious social vision that she brought to her work. This clearly tormented her enough that she dictated this letter to her caretaker just a month before she died, also sending me a copy of *Little Raccoon*. The term "political unconscious" comes from Frederic Jameson, *The Political Unconscious: Narrative as a Socially Symbolic Act* (Ithaca, N.Y.: Cornell University Press, 1981).

60. This report, entitled "You and I and Mother Goose; or, The Economics of Writing for Children," was completed May 6, 1957. It can be found with the papers of Franklin Folsom, University of Colorado, Boulder. (I viewed this report when it was still in the possession of Mary Folsom, but it has since been donated to the University of Colorado.)

61. Franklin Folsom wrote to Authors Guild president Pearl Buck on February 23, 1959, noting that the guild's representation of juvenile authors had decreased even as the number of authors had increased. Also see letter from Franklin Folsom to Louise Silcox, March 25, 1954; and letter to William R. Shirer, October 30, 1954, all in Folsom-Elting Papers (CU), box 5, Authors Guild materials. Also see "Report on Meeting of Children's Book Writers of the Authors Guild, February 26, 1964" and "A PROPOSAL FOR A NEW PROGRAM FOR THE AUTHORS GUILD" (n.d.), in Papers of Mary Elting Folsom, University of Colorado. Further information from Herman and Nina Schneider, interview with author, June 23, 1999, West Tisbury, Massachusetts.

62. Materials on conference, held in the spring of 1967, in Mary Elting Folsom Papers; Folsom, letter to Ruth Tooze, December 10, 1956, Folsom-Elting Papers (CU), Authors Guild materials, 1952–1956. Milton Meltzer also mentioned his involvement with the Authors Guild study to determine significant subjects about which more children's books were needed. Meltzer, interview with author, October 15, 1997, New York City.

63. "Children's Book Contracts," Children's Book Committee News Letter 2, no. 1 (Winter 1961): 1–3; "What Writers Should Know about Libraries for Children," News Letter 2, no. 1 (Winter 1961): 4–6; Catherine Urell, "Writing Textbooks for Children," News Letter 3, no. 3 (Summer 1962): 1–4; Mary K. Harmon, "Federal Funds," News Letter 7 (Spring 1966): 1–2; Eleanor Clymer, "For Children of Minority Groups," News Letter 6 (Spring 1965): 7–8; "Loyalty Oath," News Letter 4, no. 2 (Fall 1963): 4. The latter article was suggested by Franklin Folsom. Letter from Franklin Folsom to Eleanor Clymer, October 14, 1963, and draft of article, in Franklin Folsom papers in the possession of Mary Elting Folsom. Folsom's original draft article invited other authors to discuss their feelings about the loyalty oath issue, offering to print all responses in the newsletter, but the printed article omits this invitation, indicating some reluctance to open this issue up for discussion. Eleanor Clymer, "The Junior Feminine Mystique," News Letter 5 (Summer 1964): 6–7. Copies of News Letter in Folsom Papers, CU.

64. Mitgang notes FBI files on the Authors' Guild and the placement of informers; Folsom's papers also note some of the battles over leadership. See Herbert Mitgang, Dangerous Dossiers: Exposing the Secret War against America's Greatest Authors (New York: Fine, 1988), 231. Irving Adler described the Loose Enders as a "left-wing caucus of the Authors Guild." Irving Adler, interview with author, October 11, 1997, North Bennington, Vermont; Lilian Moore, telephone interview with author, February 15, 1998. Moore got both Milton Meltzer and Eve Merriam into writing children's books; Moore and Leone Adelson collaborated as did Moore and Mary Elting, and Elting and Rose Wyler. Wyler had advocated on behalf of Adler when he was fired from the New York City schools; the group also spoke out in favor of Ben Appel when he was asked to take a loyalty oath, as cited earlier from the newsletter of the Authors Guild's Children's Book Committee. For a list of the Loose Enders, see notes to the introduction.

65. Wyler, interview with author, March 27, 1998, New York City. In our interviews, Lilian Moore mentioned Wyler's success at getting royalties from Golden Books. Herman and Nina Schneider, interview with author, June 23, 1999, West Tisbury, Massachusetts; Lilian Moore, telephone interview with author, February 15, 1998.

66. Nancy Larrick, "The All-White World of Children's Books," *Saturday Review* (September 11, 1965): 63–65, 84–85. For further discussion, see the epilogue.

Chapter 6

1. For books on rockets, space, satellites, and so on published around this time, see Rose Wyler, *Exploring Space* (1958); Rose Wyler and Gerald Ames, *The Golden Book of Astronomy* (1955); Alexander Crosby and Nancy Larrick, *Rockets into Space* (1959); Irving Adler, *Man-Made Moons: The Earth Satellites and What They Tell Us* (1957); Irving Adler, *Seeing the Earth from Space: What the Man-Made Moons Tell Us* (1959); Beryl Williams Epstein and Sam Epstein, *The Rocket Pioneers on the Road to Space* (1955; reprint, 1958); Hyman Ruchlis and Alice Hirsh, *Orbit: A Picture Story of Force and Motion* (1958); and Mary Elting, *The Answer Book* (1959), of which the first chapter deals with space. Irving Adler, interview with author, October 11, 1997, North Bennington, Vermont. The NDEA created and supported a variety of programs affecting all grade levels, from elementary to graduate. It provided funding not only for teaching and scholarship but also for "additional materials" to enhance instruction and learning, including audiovisual supplies and, significantly, library books.

2. I am making this claim based on listings in Hillary J. Deason, ed., *The AAAS Science Book List for Children* (Washington, D.C.: American Association for the Advancement of Science, 1963), and Jean Spealman Kujoth, *Best-selling Children's Books* (Metchuen, N.J.: Scarecrow, 1973).

3. Philip J. Pauly, "The Development of High School Biology: New York City, 1900–1925," *ISIS* 82 (1991): 662–88. On the ways in which a deep belief in science and technology entered into mid-twentieth-century perfectionist impulses, see Warren Susman, *Culture as History: The Transformation of Tradition in the Twentieth Century* (New York: Pantheon, 1984), xxvi–xxvii. On the postwar faith in experts, see Elaine Tyler May, *Homeward Bound: American Families in the Cold War Era* (New York: Basic, 1988), 26. Also see Ellen Herman, *The Romance of American Psychology: Political Culture in the Age of Experts, 1940–1970* (Berkeley: University of California Press, 1995). Benjamin Spock's *Common Sense Book of Infant and Child Care* was first published in 1946 (in an inexpensive and readily available Pocket Books edition). *Them!* a movie about giant ants created by mutations caused by radioactive fallout, is notable among the science fiction films. The movie is framed at either end by children. The opening scene shows a terrorized little girl walking through the desert in shock after giant ants have destroyed her family; the end focuses on two young boys trapped in the Los Angeles drainage system and cornered by the ants. Instead of filling the drainage system with high-power ant poison, the city is put at risk so that the two young boys might be saved. On science fiction and mutant movies, see Paul Boyer, *By the Bomb's Early Light: American Thought and Culture at the Dawn of the Atomic Age* (New York: Pantheon, 1985), 270. On the ICBM toy, see Tom Engelhardt, *The End of Victory Culture: Cold War America and the Disillusioning of a Generation* (New York: Basic, 1994), 81. On the atomic submarine drinking cup, see N. W. Ayer Collection of American Advertising, box 356, Archives Center, National Museum of American History, Smithsonian Institution.

4. On the trials of academic scientists, see Robert Iversen, *The Communists and the Schools* (New York: Harcourt Brace, 1959), 299; Jessica Wang, *American Science in an Age of Anxiety: Scientists, Anticommunism, and the Cold War* (Chapel Hill: University

of North Carolina Press, 1999). Also see Ellen Schrecker, *No Ivory Tower: McCarthyism and the Universities* (New York: Oxford University Press, 1986); David R. Holmes, *Stalking the Academic Communist: Intellectual Freedom and the Firing of Alex Novikoff* (Hanover, N.H.: University Press of New England, 1989). On the extent to which scientists and science curricula came to be understood as weapons in the Cold War, see for example, Peter J. Kuznick, *Beyond the Laboratory: Scientists as Political Activists in the 1930s* (Chicago: University of Chicago Press, 1987), 2; Pauly, "Development of High School Biology," 662; David M. Donahue, "Serving Students, Science, or Society? The Secondary School Physics Curriculum in the United States, 1930–65," *History of Education Quarterly* 33, no. 3 (Fall 1993): 321–52; Scott L. Montgomery, *Minds for the Making: The Role of Science in American Education, 1750–1990* (New York: Guilford, 1994), 188–218.

5. Paul O'Neil, "U.S. Change of Mind," *Life* 44, no. 3 (March 1958): 91. For an overview of the politics surrounding the NDEA, see Barbara Barksdale Clowse, *Brainpower for the Cold War: The Sputnik Crisis and the National Defense Education Act of 1958* (Westport, Conn.: Greenwood, 1981). Also see discussions in Donahue, "Serving Students, Science, or Society?"

6. Louis McKernan, "The New Religion of Science," *Catholic World* 186 (January 1958).

7. On the manpower crisis, see Lora, "Education"; Clowse, *Brain Power for the Cold War*. Some examples of sources from the period include Alfred F. Nixon, "Are Our Schools Preparing for the Scientific Age?" *Science Education* 36, no. 1 (February 1952): 23–24; Charles A. Quattelbaum, "Development of Scientific, Engineering, and Other Professional Manpower," U.S. Congress, House Committee on Education and Labor, 85th Cong., 1st sess. (Washington, D.C.: Government Printing Office, 1957); Joseph Gallant, "Literature, Science, and the Manpower Crisis," *Science* 125, no. 3252 (April 26, 1957): 787–91; Robert J. Havighurst, "Is Russia Really Out-Producing Us in Scientists?" *School and Society* 86, no. 2131 (April 26, 1958): 187–91; Earl J. McGrath, "Sputnik and American Education," *Teachers College Record* 59, no. 7 (April 1958): 379–95.

8. Howland H. Sargeant, "Soviet Challenge in Education," *Commonweal* 66 (April 26, 1957): 81–83.

9. Havighurst, "Is Russia Really Out-Producing Us in Scientists?"; Kenneth Holland, "The Current Challenge of Soviet Education," *School and Society* 86, no. 2134 (June 7, 1958): 261–63; Sargeant, "Soviet Challenge in Education"; "Education in the USSR," *School Life* 40, no. 3 (December 1957): 6–7; Lawrence G. Derthick, "The Russian Race for Knowledge," *School Life* 40, no. 9 (June 1958): 3–4; George S. Counts, "The Real Challenge of Soviet Education," *Educational Forum* 23, no. 3 (March 1959): 261–69.

10. Actually, reports on the Soviet system began being published much earlier, but they were reports of a different character, often describing the Soviet system with great admiration. After the Second World War commentators in the United States became much more critical of the extent to which "indoctrination" into the Communist world view was a central component of Soviet education. Even so, such criticisms were mixed with a kind of awe and admiration of Soviet achievements and a universal acknowledgment of the Soviets' commitment to education. See "The Cold War Comes to the Classroom," *Senior Scholastic* 71 (December 6, 1957): 16–18; Gerald S. Craig, "Science in Russian Elementary Schools," *Science Education* 16, no. 1 (October 1931): 3–5.

11. Charles W. White, "Our Young People Haven't Been Told the Romance of Science," *Saturday Evening Post* (August 3, 1957): 10.

12. Margaret Mead and Rhoda Metraux, "Image of the Scientist among High-School Students," *Science* 126 (1957): 384–90.

13. Messages from the corporate world were even worse: during the 1950s, for example, Bell Telephone placed ads in magazines like *Boys' Life* and *American Boy* highlighting the wonders of new technology, while ads in *Girls' Life* and *Seventeen* showed young women longingly waiting by the telephone and musing, "Wonder if he'll call." On science courses for girls, see Donahue, "Serving Students, Science, or Society?" 329–33. For examples from the Bell Telephone advertising campaign, see N. W. Ayer Collection of American Advertising, box 32, Archives Center, National Museum of American History.

14. The full employment of men and women in the Soviet Union and talk of socialized housework and childcare made it more imperative to showcase American "family values" in which women were primarily devoted to serving their homes, husbands, and children. The American press consistently showed Soviet women as "mannish" in contrast to feminine American women. See, for instance, May, *Homeward Bound*, 13. On the ways in which the discourse of "civilization" has been used to uphold traditional gender roles, see Gail Bederman, *Manliness & Civilization: A Cultural History of Gender and Race in the United States, 1880–1917* (Chicago: University of Chicago Press, 1995).

15. *Industry on Parade: Youth and Science* (audiovisual), National Association of Manufacturers, ca. 1958, Archives Center, National Museum of American History, Smithsonian Institution. On the values of American parents, see McGrath, "Sputnik and American Education."

16. Rickover quoted in Donahue, "Serving Students, Science, or Society?" 344. National Defense Education Act, HR 2688, August 21, 1958, p. 3, title I, sec. 101. The fact that the Soviet Union sacrificed humanities for the sake of science and math was a refrain consistently replayed in the American press, as was the idea that American students received a more balanced education, one that prepared them not only for technical careers but also for living well. However, books like *What Ivan Knows That Johnny Doesn't* (a kind of follow-up to the bestseller *Why Johnny Can't Read*) suggested that Soviet students had far superior training not only in math and science, but in the humanities as well. See Arthur S. Trace, *What Ivan Knows That Johnny Doesn't* (New York: Random House, 1961).

17. "The Cold War Comes to the Classroom," 16. Of course, there were commentators on the Left arguing just the opposite, suggesting that the United States supported science for military purposes and for the benefit of a wealthy elite, while the Soviet Union supported "science for the citizen." See, for example Mildred Burk, "Science under Socialism," *Soviet Russia Today* (November 1938): 42–43; *Science in Soviet Russia: Papers Presented at Congress of American-Soviet Friendship, New York City, November 7, 1943* (Lancaster, Pa.: Cattell, 1944); William Rudd, "Planned Science, Free Scientists," *New Masses* (December 21, 1943): 19–20.

18. On American history textbooks, see Frances FitzGerald, *America Revised: History Schoolbooks in the Twentieth Century* (Boston: Little, Brown, 1979). On the enduring notion of American innocence, see Patricia Nelson Limerick, *Legacy of Conquest: The Unbroken Past of the American West* (New York: Norton, 1987). On the concept of a virtuous New World in contrast to the corrupt Old World, see David W. Noble, *The End of American History: Democracy, Capitalism, and the Metaphor of Two Worlds in Anglo-American Historical Writing, 1880–1980* (Minneapolis: University of Minnesota Press, 1989).

19. Raymond Williams, *Marxism and Literature* (Oxford: Oxford University Press, 1977), 64. On this earlier vision of science for the citizen, see Kuznick, *Beyond the Laboratory*. On attempts to maintain a progressive Left vision after the war and the repression of these efforts, see Wang, *American Science in an Age of Anxiety*.

20. Haldane, introduction to Friedrich Engels, *Dialectics of Nature*, ed. J. B. S. Haldane (New York: International, 1940), vii, xv; Patrick Murray, *Marx's Theory of Scientific Knowledge* (Atlantic Highlands, N.J.: Humanities Press International, 1988), 225; Charles W. Merrifield, "Science and Society: Intellectual and Social Implications of Science and Technology for Democracy," *Science and the Social Studies: National Council for the Social Studies Yearbook* 27 (1956–1957): 163–86; N. Sparks, "Marxism and Science," *Political Affairs* (December 1948): 1114–28. Four key principles, outlined by Engels and subsequently reinterpreted by twentieth-century Marxists, illustrate the basic tenets of dialectical materialism, the core of Marxist philosophy. First, matter is the substance of all objective reality (the basic idea of materialism). Second, matter and motion are inseparable. Third, phenomena do not exist in isolation but in interconnection and interdependence. And, finally, development proceeds through the struggle and interpenetration of opposites. See J. B. S. Haldane, *Marxist Philosophy and the Sciences* (New York: Random House, 1939), 23; Engels, *Dialectics of Nature*, 26.

21. Kuznick, *Beyond the Laboratory*.

22. Paul E. Kambly, "The Elementary School Science Library," *School Science and Mathematics* 44, no. 388 (November 1944): 756–67. The books mentioned are by, respectively, Marjorie Flack (1934), Kurt Wiese (1930), Dorothy Lothrop Brown and Marguerite Antoinette Butterfield (1933), José F. Nonidez (1932), Hallam Hawksworth (1924). On nature study, see Pamela M. Henson, "'Through Books to Nature': Anna Botsford Comstock and the Nature Study Movement," in *Natural Eloquence: Women Reinscribe Science*, ed. Barbara T. Gates and Ann B. Shteir (Madison: University of Wisconsin Press, 1997), 116–43.

23. Montgomery, *Minds for the Making*, 109–10. On Spencer's popularity and particularly on the conservative nature of his philosophy, see Richard Hofstadter, *Social Darwinism in American Thought* (Boston: Beacon, 1955). For sources connecting science education and democracy in the 1930s, see Ernest E. Bayles, "A Philosophy for Science Teaching," *School Science and Mathematics* 39 (December 1939): 805–11; Samuel Ralph Powers, "Educational Values of Science Teaching," *Teachers College Record* 32, no. 1 (October 1930): 17–33; S. R. Slavson, "Science as Experience and Attitude," *Progressive Education* 8 (October 8, 1931): 458–60; Lallah Blanpied, "Preparing the Child for Science," *Progressive Education* 8 (October 1931): 501–7; John G. Pilley, "Scientific Method," *Teachers College Record* 40 (January 1939): 317–28; J. McKeen Cattell, "Science, Education and Democracy," *School and Society* 50, no. 1287 (August 26, 1939): 284–85.

24. Montgomery, *Minds for the Making*, 116.

25. Slavson, "Science as Experience and Attitude," 459; Lillian Putnam, "Exploring Our Environment," *Progressive Education* 8, no. 6 (October 1931): 437.

26. On early biology education in particular and the development of science education more generally, see Pauly, "Development of High School Biology"; Montgomery, *Minds for the Making*.

27. Many scientists, believing that the devastation caused by the depression might have been avoidable if scientific expertise had been more uniformly applied, were politicized by what they saw as an egregious failure of scientific planning. Marxism, or some variant, appealed to a number of scientists as a rational science of society. The Soviet

commitment to science also attracted the attention and admiration of many American scientists who were interested in finding models for planned science programs developed in response to the needs of society and particular communities. Other scientists joined political ranks as they learned of the Nazis' abuse of science. See Kuznick, *Beyond the Laboratory*; David C. Engerman, *Modernization from the Other Shore: American Intellectuals and the Romance of Russian Development* (Cambridge, Mass.: Harvard University Press, 2003); Wang, *American Science in an Age of Anxiety*.

28. Craig, "Science in Russian Elementary Schools," 3.

29. Mary Elting spoke particularly of Il'in's impact on her. Elting, interview with author, January 22–25, 1998, Boulder, Colorado. On Soviet science textbooks translated into English and used in the United States, see advertisement for the Workers Book Shop in New York City, noting a list of Soviet school books available in English, in *New Masses* (May 7, 1935). Also see discussion of Soviet books in chapter 2.

30. Rose Wyler, interview with author, November 27, 1998. On Reed's trip to the Soviet Union, see Vera Fediaevsky and Patty Smith Hill, *Nursery School and Parent Education in Soviet Russia* (New York: Dutton, 1936), xviii.

31. Donahue, "Serving Students, Science, or Society?" 334.

32. Like Marx and Engels themselves, socialist writers of children's books were strongly influenced by Lewis Morgan's *Ancient Society* (first published in 1877), which was thought to offer a materialist theory of human evolution from savagery to civilization, exposing the relationship between economic stages of production and social or cultural phenomena, such as marriage customs, family life, and the idea of private property. See the introduction by Leslie A. White to Lewis Henry Morgan, *Ancient Society* (Cambridge, Mass.: Belknap Press of Harvard University Press, 1964). Also see Franklin Rosemont, *Karl Marx and the Iroquois* (Brooklyn, N.Y.: Red Balloon Collective, n.d.); William F. Kruse, "How to Teach History in the Primary Grades," *Young Socialists Magazine* 13, no. 11 (January 1920): 7. Books about primitive peoples included *Rhymes of the Early Jungle Folk* (1922) and *Stories of the Cave People* (1917), published by Charles H. Kerr, the socialist publishing house, and written by Mary Marcy, who edited the *International Socialist Review*. Other examples are Katharine Dopp's series, *The Tree Dwellers* (1903), *The Early Cave-Men* (1904), *The Later Cave-Men* (1906), and *The Early Sea People* (1912); Jack London's *Before Adam* (1907); G. H. Lockwood's *The Giants and Their Tools* (1922); and Harry Hall's *Days before History* (1908). See the list of recommended books in "Socialist Education for Children," *Young Socialist Magazine* (June 1918): 1. Paul Mishler also has some discussion of socialist children's books in *Raising Reds*, 112–15. On socialist schooling, including a discussion of texts used with the curriculum, see Kenneth Teitelbaum, *Schooling for Good Rebels: Socialist Education for Children in the United States 1900–1920* (Philadelphia: Temple University Press, 1993).

33. Henson, "Through Books to Nature," 111–21; Caroline Nelson, *Nature Talks on Economics* (Chicago: Kerr, 1912), 12–13.

34. Henson, "Through Books to Nature," 122; Nelson, *Nature Talks on Economics*, 27.

35. William Montgomery Brown, *Science and History for Girls and Boys* (Galion, Ohio: Bradford-Brown, 1932), 278, 36.

36. Ibid., 21, 6, 33, 67, 71–72, 256–58; Richard Levins, "A Science of Our Own: Marxism and Nature," *Monthly Review* 38 (July–August 1986): 3.

37. Bert Grant, "Science and Nature for Johnny Rebel," *New Pioneer* (July 1933): 67; Bert Grant, "The Powder of Empire," *New Pioneer* (April 1932): 15.

38. Bert Grant, "Can Girls Be Scientists?" *New Pioneer* (April 1936): 18–19; Bert Grant, "The Fascination of Science," *New Pioneer* (October 1938): 2.

39. See Nolan Lushington, "Science Books: An Analysis of Selection Aids," *Library Journal* 83 (February 15, 1958): 616–19; Millicent E. Selsam, "Scientific and Non-Scientific," *School Libraries* 7, no. 2 (January 1958): 13–15; Kambly, "The Elementary School Science Library." Also see Betty Bacon, "The Art of Nonfiction," *Children's Literature in Education* 12, no. 1 (1981): 3–14. In our conversations, Mary Elting also noted the lack of good nonfiction for children before the 1940s.

40. Betty Bacon, interview with author, February 20, 1999, Berkeley, California.

41. Betty Bacon, interview with author, November 14, 1998, Berkeley.

42. In 1946, Lela Rogers testified before HUAC that her daughter, Ginger Rogers, had been forced to recite Communist propaganda in Dalton Trumbo's 1943 film *Tender Comrade*, with the offensive line being "Share and share alike, that's democracy." Victor Navasky, *Naming Names* (1980; reprint, New York: Penguin, 1991), 79. The Taft-Hartley Act, reversing many of labor's gains under the New Deal's Wagner Act, was passed in 1947. U.S. Congress, House Committee on Un-American Activities, *Testimony of Walter S. Steele regarding Communist Activities in the United States* (Washington, D.C.: Government Printing Office, 1947), 101. Bacon's FBI file also mentions Young World Books.

43. Review of *Climbing Our Family Tree* by Alex Novikoff, illustrations by John English, *Scientific Book Club Review* 16 (November 1945): 4; May Lamberton Becker, Review of *Egg to Chick*, by Millicent Selsam, pictures by Frances Wells, *Weekly Book Review* (August 18, 1946): 5. These and other reviews are excerpted in *Book Review Digest*.

44. See Jean Spealman Kujoth, *Best-selling Children's Books*; Zena Sutherland and May Hill Arbuthnot, *Children and Books* (New York: HarperCollins, 1991), 537–45. For Peter Hunt and Dennis Butts, science writing and Millicent Selsam are almost synonymous. See Peter Hunt and Dennis Butts, *Children's Literature: An Illustrated History* (New York: Oxford University Press, 1995), xiii. Novikoff's other offers from publishers were noted by Betty Bacon, telephone interview with author, May 12, 1999. On Novikoff, see Holmes, *Stalking the Academic Communist*. Also note that Ida Scheib, who illustrated Adler's *Secret of Light* went on to illustrate a number of children's books, including one by Adler and one by Sarah Riedman. Bacon claimed Novikoff wrote no more books for children because he was more interested in science than in children. Bacon, interview with author, February 20, 1999, Berkeley. Holmes suggests that writing children's books brought limited financial rewards and, more pointedly, Novikoff's academic career depended upon his devoting his energies to more scholarly works. Holmes, *Stalking the Academic Communist*, 92.

45. L. M. P., Review of *Egg to Chick*, by Millicent Selsam, pictures by Frances Wells, *New York Times* (May 19, 1946): 28.

46. Millicent Selsam, *Egg to Chick* (New York: International, 1946), n.p.; Engels, *Dialectics of Nature*, 17. Engels writes:

> When, after thousands of years of struggle the differentiation of hand from foot, and erect gait, were finally established, man became distinct from the monkey and the basis was laid for the development of articulate speech and the mighty development of the brain that has since made the gulf between man and monkey an unbridgeable one. . . . With men we enter *history*. . . . the more that human beings become removed from animals in the narrower sense of the word, the more they make their own history consciously, the less

becomes the influence of unforeseen effects and uncontrolled forces on this history, and the more accurately does the historical result correspond to the aim laid down in advance.

He adds that because of a lack of planning and because individual material gain is often valued over general human betterment, as a race humans are in fact far behind where they ought to be. See *Dialectics of Nature*, 17–19.

47. Lois Palmer, Review of *Hidden Animals* by Millicent Ellis Selsam, *New York Times* (August 10, 1947): 25.

48. Millicent Selsam, *Hidden Animals* (New York: International, 1947), n.p. Emphases in original.

49. On the scientific principles guiding Selsam's literary choices, see Selsam, "Scientific and Non-Scientific."

50. Clara Hollos, *The Story of Your Coat* (New York: International, 1946), 46. For a simplified version of Marx's discussion of linen, coats, and the labor theory of value, see Hugo Gellert, *Karl Marx's "Capital" in Lithographs* (New York: Long and Smith, 1934), 23–31. The frontispiece to *The Story of Your Bread* discusses Roth's efforts to represent changing artistic styles.

51. Brown, *Science and History for Girls and Boys*, 280. For further discussion of the middle-class norm in children's literature, see Herbert Kohl, *Should We Burn Babar: Essays on Children's Literature and the Power of Stories* (New York: New Press, 1995).

52. Sarah Riedman, *How Man Discovered His Body* (New York: International, 1947), 17.

53. Alex Novikoff, *From Head to Foot: Our Bodies and How They Grow* (New York: International, 1946), 44.

54. Ibid. Riedman makes a similar statement, noting that "science makes strides when questioning and experimenting are freely permitted. When people think science is a sin, darkness and ignorance are sure to follow." She also notes that "at all times, even today, scientists are opposed by those who refuse to learn new facts." Riedman, *How Man Discovered His Body*, 23–24, 119.

55. Pauly, "Development of High School Biology," 675; Novikoff, *From Head to Foot*, 76, 59–60. Nydorf's wife said Trachtenberg was actually resistant at first to having an illustration that showed the penis, but Nydorf was persistent and Trachtenberg finally agreed. Elsie Nydorf, telephone interview with author, May 16, 2002.

56. Haldane, introduction, Engels, *Dialectics of Nature*, 7; Riedman, *How Man Discovered His Body*, 14.

57. Karl Marx, *The Eighteenth Brumaire of Louis Bonaparte* (1852; reprint, New York: International, 1994), 15; Irving Adler, *The Secret of Light* (New York: International, 1952), 92; Riedman, *How Man Discovered His Body*, 118.

58. Novikoff, *From Head to Foot*, 8; Alex Novikoff, *Climbing Our Family Tree* (New York: International, 1945), 69; Sparks, "Marxism and Science," 1127.

59. Adler, *The Secret of Light*, 93; Riedman, *How Man Discovered His Body*; Sarah Riedman, *Food for People* (New York: Abelard-Schuman, 1954), 33.

60. Novikoff, *Climbing Our Family Tree*, 21; Haldane, *Marxist Philosophy and the Sciences*, 43. Also see Murray, *Marx's Theory*, 225, where Murray notes:

Insofar as Marxian science identifies actual contradictions, it offers leverage points, first, for recognizing the possibility of altering the existing world, and, second, for developing strategies for social and political practices based on more than subjective "oughts." But these actions are not derived from science, like lemmata from a mathematical theorem; Marxian science is not a cookbook for revolutionaries.

61. Elting, letter to author, May 7, 1999.

62. The notion of the text as a "socially symbolic projection" comes from Frederic Jameson, *The Political Unconscious: Narrative as a Socially Symbolic Act* (Ithaca, N.Y.: Cornell University Press, 1981). See also Jack Zipes, "Second Thoughts on Socialization through Literature for Children," *Lion and the Unicorn* 5 (1981): 19–32.

63. Betty Bacon, letter to Meridel Le Sueur, December 12, 1945, Meridel Le Sueur Papers; Engels, *Dialectics of Nature*, 17–18. Le Sueur donated her library to Augsburg College in Minneapolis, where researchers may take note of the range of her reading (and, also, consult her books).

64. Bacon letter to Le Sueur, December 12, 1945, Le Sueur Papers. Emphases in original.

65. Ibid. For a more general (and recent) discussion on Bacon's part of what makes nonfiction good, see Bacon, "The Art of Nonfiction."

66. On Bacon's ideas about "appropriate" material for children, see Betty Bacon, ed., *How Much Truth Do We Tell the Children* (Minneapolis, Minn.: MEP Publications, 1988).

67. In a discussion of the principles guiding Adler in his writing for children, Adler cautioned others:

> Don't talk down to the child. Talk to him seriously about serious subjects. The stuff of science is interesting by itself; there is no need to motivate enthusiasm artificially by providing a so-called "human interest" setting. I squirm with embarrassment whenever I read a science book that begins with conversations between Ned and his uncle as they take a walk. I am sure that the child reader squirms, too, because he is not interested in Ned or his uncle or their inane conversation. He is interested in science, and he wishes they would hurry and get to it.

Irving Adler, "On Writing Science Books for Children," *Horn Book Magazine* 41, no. 5 (October 1965): 528.

68. Interview with Irving Adler, October 11, 1997, North Bennington, Vermont.

69. For notes and manuscripts see Irving Adler Papers, Kerlan Collection of Children's Literature and Manuscripts, University of Minnesota.

70. Irving Adler, *The Tools of Science* (New York: Day, 1958), 23.

71. Quotation from Gerald Craig, "Using Science to Make Democracies Strong," *Childhood Education* 34, no. 7 (March 1958): 300. On the issue of scientific neutrality, see, for example, James R. Newman, "The Scientific Attitude," *New Republic* 121 (September 26, 1949): 16–19.

72. Adler, *The Tools of Science*, 12 (emphases in original); Haldane, *Marxist Philosophy*, 85.

73. Selsam, "Scientific and Non-Scientific."

74. Elting, *The Answer Book*, 130.

75. Herman and Nina Schneider, interview with author, June 23, 1999, West Tisbury, Massachusetts.

76. Jay Williams and Raymond Abrashkin, *Danny Dunn and the Anti-Gravity Paint* (New York: Whittlesey House, McGraw-Hill, 1956), 19. The first *Danny Dunn* book was conceived of by Abrashkin, who had been an elementary school teacher, a playwright with the Provincetown Players, a journalist for *PM*, an agent for Bank Street Books, and one of the main forces behind the Young People's Record Club. He also created the film *The Little Fugitive*, which received an Academy Award nomination. The idea behind the *Danny Dunn* books was to make the stories as scientifically accurate as possible, but also entertaining and commercially viable. Although the main protagonist of the books is Danny Dunn, his friend Irene is a strong and feisty character, who predicts Jay Williams's later efforts writing feminist fairy tales. Hank Abrashkin, interview with author, June 19, 2002, Northampton, Massachusetts. Abrashkin also provided me with correspondence between Williams and Abrashkin and from publishers relating to the *Danny Dunn* books.

77. Dorothy Sterling, *Caterpillars* (Garden City, N.Y.: Doubleday, 1961), 39, 61.

78. Selsam, "Scientific and Non-Scientific," 15.

79. Betty Morrow, with the editorial cooperation of Millicent E. Selsam, *See Up the Mountain* (New York: Harper and Row, 1958), 45.

80. Sterling, *Caterpillars*, 34.

81. Dorothy Sterling, *The Story of Mosses, Ferns and Mushrooms* (Garden City, N.Y.: Doubleday, 1955), 41–42. Several writers with whom I spoke, including Rose Wyler, Mary Elting, and Herman Schneider, noted the taboo on explicit discussions of evolution. See Gary Wills, *Under God: Religion and American Politics* (New York: Simon and Schuster, 1996), 113. Herman and Nina Schneider, interview with author, June 23, 1999; Elting, letter to author, April 11, 1998. *Science and the Secret of Man's Past* is notable for more than its references to evolution: it also subtly questions the authority of the Christian church, whose teachings contradict the findings of science, and it implicitly calls all received authority into question. Franklin Folsom, *Science and the Secret of Man's Past* (Irvington-on-Hudson, N.Y.: Harvey House, 1966).

82. Rose Wyler and Gerald Ames, *Life on Earth* (New York: Schuman, 1953), 138–40.

83. Herman Schneider and Nina Schneider, *How Your Body Works* (New York: Scott, 1949), 11–12. The Schneiders were groundbreaking in the world of science textbooks for insisting that the second edition of their immensely popular D. C. Heath science textbook series (published in 1954—just in time to meet new standards established in the wake of the *Brown* decision) be integrated. On what Herman Schneider called the "lily white" nature of children's books published prior to the 1960s, see Nancy Larrick, "The All-White World of Children's Books," *Saturday Review* (September 11, 1965): 63–65, 84–85.

84. Eva Knox Evans, *People Are Important* (Irvington-on-Hudson, N.Y.: Capitol, 1951), 47; Eva Knox Evans, *All about Us* (New York: Capitol, 1947), 27–29, 38.

85. May Edel, *The Story of People: Anthropology for Young People* (Boston: Little, Brown, 1953), 6–7.

86. Ralph Linton and Adelin Linton, *Man's Way from Cave to Skyscraper* (New York: Harper and Brothers, 1947), 17–18, 179.

87. On "companion" meanings in science books, see Douglas A. Roberts, "Analyzing School Science Courses: The Concept of Companion Meaning," in *Problems of Meaning*

in Science Curriculum, ed. Douglas A. Roberts and Leif Ostman (New York: Teachers College Press, 1998), 5–12.

88. Leone Adelson and Benjamin Gruenberg, *Your Breakfast and the People Who Made It* (Garden City, N.Y.: Doubleday, 1954), 41.

89. Ibid., 57.

90. Harry Granick, *Underneath New York* (New York: Rinehart, 1947), 3.

91. Ibid., 10, 18.

92. Ibid., 209–10.

93. Memos dated May 1 and May 13, 1948; one internal and one from the director of the FBI to the attorney general repeat the same material. Harry Granick FBI file, FOIPA No. 0990204–000. A series of "urgent" memos circulated in June 1948 between the director of the FBI and the attorney general on the question of whether Granick, who was born in Russia and had immigrated to the United States as a young boy, had been naturalized as a citizen. Ultimately they concluded that he had been naturalized, which presumably limited their authority to act against him. Memorandum from M. A. Jones to Mr. Nichols, June 15, 1954, Harry Granick FBI file. Even after being blacklisted, Granick was able to continue as a playwright and to achieve considerable success at this. Information on Granick's blacklisting from Barbara Granick (Harry's granddaughter), telephone interview with author, October 11, 2004. *Underneath New York*, incidentally, was reprinted by Fordham University Press in 1991.

94. See Deason, ed., *The AAAS Science Book List for Children*.

95. Anne Terry White, *George Washington Carver: The Story of a Great American* (New York: Random House, 1953); Harold Coy, *The Real Book about George Washington Carver* (New York, Watts, 1951); Shirley Graham and George D. Liscomb, *Dr. George Washington Carver, Scientist* (New York: Messner, 1944); Beryl Williams Epstein and Sam Epstein, *George Washington Carver: Negro Scientist* (New York: Garrard, 1960). The latter two books are cited in Kujoth, *Best-selling Children's Books*.

96. Edith Margolis, letter to Emma Gelders Sterne, May 13, 1957; Edith Margolis, letter to Emma Gelders Sterne, July 2, 1957 (in which she notes Margaret Martignoni's report from the American Library Association convention). Sterne wrote to her original editor at Knopf, Martignoni, expressing her disappointment about the hold on the Drew contract, meanwhile offering suggestions for selling and publicizing the Bethune book; for example, she offered to share with publicists at Knopf her "personal list of about two hundred and fifty names associated with Southerners for Civil Rights, a small organization of liberal Southerners living in New York." Sterne noted that she was chair of this group and said its members "are keenly aware of the need for reaching young people with books on Negro leaders." Her suggestions for publicizing the Bethune book were implicitly an entreaty to push forward on the Drew project; she noted that "Knopf, and you personally, have done so much to advance the cause of the Negro in America that I need not belabor the question." Though it is doubtful that Sterne's editors knew she was active in the Communist party, this and other correspondence indicates that they certainly were well aware of her involvement in the Civil Rights movement. Emma Sterne, letter to Margaret Martignoni, July 19, 1957. All correspondence in Emma Gelders Sterne Papers, box 2, Special Collections, University of Oregon, Eugene.

97. Edith Margolis, letter to Emma Gelders Sterne, January 10, 1958, Sterne Collection, box 2.

98. Emma Gelders Sterne, *Blood Brothers: Four Men of Science* (New York: Knopf, 1959), 3–7.

99. Ibid., 42–43, 114–15.

100. Virginie Fowler, letter to Emma Gelders Sterne, April 9, 1959 (cc. Edith Margolis), Sterne Papers, box 2. Drafts of the book and research notes are also in the Sterne Papers.

101. Ibid. Emphasis in original.

102. Ibid. On the California Library Association, see Cindy Mediavilla, "The War on Books and Ideas: The California Library Association and Anti-Communist Censorship in the 1940s and 1950s," *Library Trends* 46, no. 2 (Fall 1997): 331–47.

103. Sterne, *Blood Brothers: Four Men of Science*, 168–69.

104. On the muddy circumstances of Drew's death, see, for example, Emma Gelders Sterne, letter to Asa G. Yancey, M.D., October 9, 1959, Sterne Papers, box 2.

105. Lloyd E. Smith, assistant secretary, Western Printing and Lithography, letter to Alexander Crosby, May 20, 1964, Alexander Crosby Papers, Special Collections, University of Oregon, Eugene. See related correspondence, February–June 1964, in the same collection.

106. Nancy Larrick, telephone interview with author, December 3, 1998. White, *George Washington Carver: The Story of a Great American*, 19–20; Selsam, "Scientific and Non-Scientific," 14.

107. Rose Wyler, interview with author, March 27, 1998, New York City.

108. Mary Elting Folsom, letter to author, May 7, 1999.

109. Ibid.

110. Dorothy Sterling, e-mail correspondence with the author, November 27, 1997, and April 20, 1999; Leone Adelson, interview with author, June 25, 1998, New York City.

111. Adler, *The Secret of Light*, 77; Sparks, "Marxism and Science," 1127, 1114.

112. Alexander Marshack, "How Kids Get Interested in Science," *Library Journal* (April 15, 1958): 13–15; Selsam, quoted in Bacon, "The Art of Nonfiction," 6.

113. Herman Schneider and Nina Schneider, "The Role of Science in Child Development," *National Elementary Principal* 37, no. 6 (April 1958): 11–14.

114. Crosby and Larrick, *Rockets into Space*, 73.

Chapter 7

1. Meridel Le Sueur, *River Road: A Story of Abraham Lincoln* (New York: Knopf, 1954), 5, 165.

2. Meridel Le Sueur, *Nancy Hanks of Wilderness Road: A Story of Abraham Lincoln's Mother* (New York: Knopf, 1949), 4.

3. John Higham, "The Cult of the 'American Consensus': Homogenizing Our History," *Commentary* (February 1959): 93, 95. The "fighting communism through history" comment comes from Jesse Lemisch, *On Active Service in War and Peace: Politics and Ideology in the American Historical Profession* (Toronto: New Hogtown, 1975), 56. Nancy Larrick, "The All-White World of Children's Books," *Saturday Review* (September 11, 1965): 63–65, 84–85.

4. National Education Association Educational Policies Commission, *American Education and International Tensions* (Washington, D.C.: National Education Association, 1949), 36. For instance, the National Council for American Education campaigned vigorously for making American history a required subject in the schools of all states. National Council for American Education, *How Red Are the Schools? AND HOW YOU*

CAN HELP Eradicate Socialism and Communism from the Schools and Colleges of America (New York: National Council for American Education, 1950); Ronald Lora, "Education: Schools as Crucible in Cold War America," in *Reshaping America: Society and Institutions, 1945–1960*, ed. Robert H. Bremner and Gary W. Reichard (Columbus: Ohio State University Press, 1982), 252.

5. National Education Association Educational Policies Commission, *American Education and International Tensions*, 36. History requirement information in William Tuttle, *Daddy's Gone to War: The Second World War in the Lives of America's Children* (New York: Oxford University Press, 1993), 113.

6. William F. Russell, "Communism and Education: American vs. European Policies," *Vital Speeches of the Day* 19, no. 6 (June 1, 1953): 185–89. See, for examples of civic education texts, Department of Public Instruction, *A Comparative Study of Democracy and Communism*, Curriculum Services Series No. 2 (Harrisburg, Pa.: 1960); Kenneth Colegrove, *Teacher's Guide to Democracy versus Communism* (New York: Institute of Fiscal and Political Education, 1958); George G. Dawson, *Communism, Menace to Freedom* (Pleasantville, N.Y.: Readers Digest, 1962); Shelby M. Jackson, State Department of Education of Louisiana, *Americanism versus Communism: A Unit of Work in American History*, Bulletin No. 928 (Baton Rouge, La.: 1961). All in Civic Education and Citizenship Education materials, American Legion Collection, Division of Community Life, National Museum of American History, Smithsonian Institution. Also see Sylvester B. Butler, "What Is Education for Citizenship," *Progressive Education* 2, no. 4 (October–December 1925): 210–16.

7. Herbert M. Kliebard, *The Struggle for An American Curriculum, 1893–1958* (New York: Routledge, 1995), 177. Kliebard is quoting an official from the Daughters of Colonial Wars. For accusations of liberal bias, see, for instance, Merrill Root, *Brainwashing in the High Schools: An Examination of Eleven American History Textbooks* (New York: Devin-Adair, 1958). Ralph Ellison, "School Books Changed to Suit 'Cold War,'" *Daily Worker* (December 13, 1954): 8; Frances FitzGerald, *America Revised: History Schoolbooks in the Twentieth Century* (Boston: Little, Brown, 1979), 115–21, 56.

8. On westerns as ritual enactments of anti-Communist red-hunting, see Tom Engelhardt, *The End of Victory Culture: Cold War America and the Disillusioning of a Generation* (New York: Basic, 1994). Also see Steven Watts, *The Magic Kingdom: Walt Disney and the American Way of Life* (Boston: Houghton Mifflin, 1997), 289.

9. Herbert Aptheker, "Negro History: Arsenal for Liberation," *New Masses* 62–63 (1947): 8–12; Henrietta Buckmaster, William Blake, and Howard Fast, "History in Fiction," *New Masses* 50 (January 18, 1944): 7–9.

10. Emma Gelders Sterne's *Printer's Devil*, a fictionalized account of a boy in revolutionary times (probably modeled on Forbes's *Johnny Tremain*), highlights the efforts to establish a bill of rights in terms that have striking resonance for the anti-Communist witch hunts taking place when the book was published. In books like this, the spirit of the American Revolution is clearly aligned with "the people" rather than with "men of property." "Truth is revolutionary" quotation from Michael Gold, "Daniel Boone Belongs to Us," *New Masses* (August 28, 1934): 26. Gold is quoting Barbusse here.

11. Frederick Krafft, "History of Our Country for Boys and Girls: Twelfth Chapter," *Little Socialist Magazine for Boys and Girls* 3, no. 2 (February 1910): 5–6; Frederick Krafft, "History of Our Country for Boys and Girls: Eleventh Chapter," *Little Socialist Magazine for Boys and Girls* 3, no. 1 (January 1910): 5–6; Frederick Krafft, "History of Our Country for Boys and Girls: Thirteenth Chapter," *Little Socialist Magazine*

for Boys and Girls 3, no. 3 (March 1910): 5–6. Despite this class consciousness, there is almost no discussion of slavery; chapter 10 of Frederick Krafft's "History of Our Country for Boys and Girls" notes, for instance, that "in the South there was the greatest freedom in social life." Frederick Krafft, "History of Our Country for Boys and Girls," *Little Socialist Magazine for Boys and Girls* 2, no. 12 (1909): 5. Also see Jean Simon, "Which Books for Your Children?" *New Masses* 17 (December 24, 1935): 23–25.

12. As a text intended for children as well as less literate adults (Huberman used it in his own worker-education programs), the book highlights the leftist tendency to link concern for children and concern for poor and working-class adults, which was the left-wing version of the tendency of reformers and policymakers to infantilize the poor and wage laborers. See John J. Simon, "Leo Huberman: Radical Agitator, Socialist Teacher," *Monthly Review* 55, no. 5 (October 2003): 28–31; The Editors, "Cooperation on the Left," *Monthly Review* 1, no. 11 (March 1950): 334–44. The New York Public Library included *We, the People* on its January 1946 list of "Books for Young People" on America, in the *Branch Library News*. For reviews of *We, the People*, see Nora Beust, "Books for Boys and Girls," *Progressive Education* 10, no. 7 (November 1933): 497–502. Also see Children's Book Committee of the Child Study Association, "Children's Books: Can Reading Educate for Peace?" *Child Study* (May 1938): 250. Simon recommends *We, the People* in Simon, "Which Books for Your Children?"

13. Denning argues that "the arts of the cultural front are better characterized as a 'proletarian grotesque' than as any kind of social realism," defining *proletarian grotesque* as a kind of plebeian modernism. He suggests that "proletarian grotesque is a plebian appropriation of the avant-garde hostility to 'art,' the anti-aesthetic of dada and surrealism." Michael Denning, *The Cultural Front: The Laboring of American Culture in the Twentieth Century* (New York: Verso, 1996), 123. On Turner's centrality to progressive historians, see David W. Noble, *The End of American History: Democracy, Capitalism, and the Metaphor of Two Worlds in Anglo-American Historical Writing, 1880–1980* (Minneapolis: University of Minnesota Press, 1989). Paul Buhle argues that American Communists' debt to progressive historians accounts for the fundamental limitation of their historical vision. See Paul Buhle, *Marxism in the United States: Remapping the History of the American Left* (New York: Verso, 1991), 146–85. Leo Huberman, *We, the People* (New York: Harper, 1947), 106, 42–43.

14. Art historian Erika Doss notes of Benton's art in the 1930s, "Benton promoted a revival of a worker-determined economy in the wake of what he perceived (and the Depression made clear) was the failure of corporate leadership. Much of Benton's Depression art was largely an attack against the consequences of a dehumanized organization of American life." Erika Doss, "The Art of Cultural Politics: From Regionalism to Abstract Expressionism," in *Recasting America: Culture and Politics in the Age of Cold War*, ed. Lary May (Chicago: University of Chicago Press, 1989), 195–220. Huberman notes, for instance, that laws designed to protect the growth of trusts were used to prevent the growth of organized labor. Huberman, *We, the People*, 239.

15. Huberman, *We, the People*, 171, 188, 298.

16. Ibid., 171. Noting the long list of countries and regions controlled by the United States ("Nicaragua, Cuba, the Philippines, Puerto Rico, and Guam," as well as "Hawaii, Samoa, Panama, Santo Domingo, Haiti, Alaska, and the Virgin Islands"), Huberman also points to "spheres of influence" that the United States controls "through the quiet but highly effective penetration of surplus capital." Huberman, *We, the People*, 253.

17. Jack Zipes argues that "*all* culture in Western industrialized nations—folklore and so-called 'high art'—is infused by capitalist ideology and patriarchalism." Jack Zipes, "Folklore Research and Western Marxism: A Critical Reply," *Journal of American Folklore* 97, no. 385 (1984): 329–37. Emphasis in original. By this logic, almost any text published in the United States would contain elements of capitalist ideology.

18. Ralph Brown and Marion Brown, "The Teacher and the Social Studies: The Social Studies Teacher and American Biography," *Social Studies* 43, no. 1 (January 1952): 10–20, 11; Ralph Brown and Marion Brown, "Biography in the Social Studies: The Values of Biography," *Social Education* 18 (1954): 67–70. The secondary literature on the nature of biography is immense; see, in particular, Leon Edel, *Writing Lives* (1959; reprint, New York: Norton, 1984). On biography and children, see, for example, Stuart Hannabuss and Rita Marcella, *Biography and Children: A Study of Biography for Children and Childhood in Biography* (London: Library Association, 1993).

19. Examples of series include Random House's *Landmark* series of biographies, edited by Nancy Larrick (who was married to labor journalist and juvenile author Alexander Crosby); Julian Messner's young adult biographies, edited by Gertrude Blumenthal; Aladdin Books' *American Heritage* series, edited by Emma Gelders Sterne; and Franklin Watts's *Real Books* series, edited by Helen Hoke Watts. Blumenthal published a number of left-wing writers in her biography series, including Howard Fast, Shirley Graham, and Irwin Shapiro; Larrick's series included several books by Anne Terry White, the wife of Harry Dexter White, and a biography of Napoleon by Frances Winwar, who had been a member of the League of American Writers. Franklin Folsom, Mary Elting, Harold Coy, Eve Merriam, Sam and Beryl Epstein, William Cunningham, and Jane Sherman were among the left-wing writers published in the *Real Book* series. Other biographical series that developed during the postwar period included the *Childhood of Famous Americans* series (Bobbs-Merrill), the *American Adventures* series (Wheeler), the *Real People* series (Row, Peterson), and the *Makers of America* series (Abington). Houghton Mifflin, Holt, and Wilcox and Follett also published a number of outstanding biographies for children during this time. See Brown and Brown, "Biography in the Social Studies." On the more general trend toward nonfiction series, see Lillian Hollowell, "Series in Children's Books," *Wilson Library Bulletin* 27 (May 1953): 736–38.

20. Dorothy Sterling described her daughter reading in this fashion, and English professor Paula Rabinowitz recalled reading this way as a child.

21. Lapsley, "Socially Constructive Literature for Children," June 1941, LAW Papers, box 5.

22. Le Sueur, *River Road*, 122–24.

23. Raymond Williams, *Marxism and Literature* (Oxford: Oxford University Press, 1977), 115–16; "Young Readers," Review of *River Road, Sentinel* (November 28, 1954): 2.

24. Merrill D. Peterson, *Lincoln in American Memory* (New York: Oxford University Press, 1994), 324–25, 353–57; Sam Sillen, "McCarthy Quotes Lincoln," *Masses and Mainstream* (January 1954): 1–2; "G.O.P. Dishonors Lincoln Day," *Daily Worker* (February 13, 1946): 7.

25. Arguing for the radicalism of the Popular Front, Michael Denning insists that John Brown was a more popular icon than Lincoln; this was not true for children's literature, for which John Brown was too radical a figure to be made into a hero in the 1950s, other than obliquely as in Ward's illustrations (see figure 7.2). Denning, *The Cultural Front*, 131; Peterson, *Lincoln in American Memory*, 319; Waldemar Hille, *The People's*

Songbook (New York: Boni and Gaer, 1948), 51; Earl Browder, *Lincoln and the Communists* (New York: Workers Library, 1936), 13–14.

26. Jay Monaghan, comp., *Lincoln Bibliography, 1838–1939* (Springfield: Illinois State Historical Library, 1943–1945); Peterson, *Lincoln in American Memory*, 312. Figures on the *Lincoln Biography* and comment on Lincoln's fame from Peterson, *Lincoln in American Memory*, 312. Peterson says Lincoln's fame reached its "zenith" with the sesquicentennial of his birth in 1959. In addition to Le Sueur's *River Road*, Left-authored juveniles on Lincoln published in the postwar period included Michael Gorham, *The Real Book about Abraham Lincoln: Behind-the-Scenes Incidents and Lively Anecdotes in the Story of a Great American* (Garden City, N.Y.: Garden City Books, in arrangement with Franklin Watts, 1951); Irwin Shapiro, *The Golden Stamp Book of Abraham Lincoln* (New York: Simon and Schuster, 1954); Carl Sandburg, *Abe Lincoln Grows Up* (New York: Harcourt, Brace, 1954); Jerrold Beim, *The Boy on Lincoln's Lap* (New York: Morrow, 1955); Helen Kay, *Lincoln: A Big Man* (New York: Hastings, 1957); May Yonge McNeer, *America's Abraham Lincoln* (Boston: Houghton Mifflin, 1957); Manuel Komroff and Charles Beck, *Abraham Lincoln* (New York: Putnam, 1959); Helen Kay, *Abe Lincoln's Hobby* (Chicago: Reilly and Lee, 1961); Ann McGovern, *If You Grew Up with Abraham Lincoln* (New York: Four Winds, 1966). Quotes from Gorham, *The Real Book about Abraham Lincoln*, 50–51, 65; Beim, *The Boy on Lincoln's Lap*.

27. Clara Ingram Judson, *Abraham Lincoln: Friend of the People* (Chicago: Wilcox and Follett, 1950), 117, 25. Sandburg has Lincoln noticing the signs posted by slave traders that turn human beings into commodities, but in Sandburg's rendering of him Lincoln offers no comment on what he sees. James Daugherty's drawing of the "slave market" shows finely dressed white gentlemen bidding on a proud, haughty African-American woman who is attempting to cover her body with a cloth she has draped over herself; in the foreground several black men, also scantily clad, huddle and look to the ground mournfully; another woman tries to comfort a naked child. Sandburg, *Abe Lincoln Grows Up*, 218–21.

28. On progressive historians' version of history, see Noble, *The End of American History*; Richard Hofstadter, "Abraham Lincoln and the Self-Made Myth," in *The American Political Tradition* (New York: Vintage, 1961), 118. Lincoln stated publicly that he was opposed to "bringing about in anyway the social and political equality of the white and black races," as well as intermarriage. See Fourth Debate with Stephen A. Douglas at Charleston, Illinois, September 18, 1858, in *The Collected Works of Abraham Lincoln*, ed. Roy P. Basler (New Brunswick, N.J.: Rutgers University Press, 1953–1955), 3:145–46. Also see Meridel Le Sueur, letter to Jack Conroy, n.d., Meridel Le Sueur Papers, 152.K.18.2.

29. Douglas Wixson, *Worker-Writer in America: Jack Conroy and the Tradition of Midwestern Literary Radicalism, 1898–1990* (Urbana and Chicago: University of Illinois Press, 1994), 149.

30. Meridel Le Sueur, loose typescript in Le Sueur Papers, 144.I.19.5B10.

31. Copy of letter from Le Sueur to "the Honorable Mayor of Milwaukee," December 5, 1954, Le Sueur Papers, 144.I.19.5B10; Le Sueur, draft of letter to *Milwaukee Sentinel*, Le Sueur Papers, 144.I.19.5B10, folder 15.

32. Robert J. Riordan, "Red Party Line Is 'Catch Line' in New Abe Lincoln Book," Review of *River Road*, *Sentinel* (1954): 6. Elizabeth Allen, letter to Le Sueur, February 3, 1954, Le Sueur Papers, 152.K.18.1, folder 16. Eloise MacAllister, letter to Joseph North, Le Sueur Papers, 152.K.18.1B, folder 14. In addition to MacAllister's letter, there are a number of letters in Le Sueur's papers from other leftists praising her portrait of Lincoln.

33. In her letter to the *Sentinel*, which condemned its dangerous attack on the "right to publish" and the "freedom to read" any books that "do not conform to the present or popular concepts," Le Sueur quickly added, "and my book even today is not one of these." Le Sueur, draft of letter to *Milwaukee Sentinel*, Le Sueur Papers, 144.I.195B, folder 15.

34. The *New York Times* said of *River Road*: "This book is beautifully done. The writing approaches the level of prose poetry. Moods of fervor for justice to all men, an intense yearning for accomplishment and even a brooding sadness prevail. Lincoln's road to greatness began on such paths as this book traces." G. A. Woods, Review of *River Road*, *New York Times* (September 5, 1954): 12. The *New York Herald Tribune* recommended that librarians and teachers "try reading this aloud" (May 16, 1954: 21), and a reviewer for the *Library Journal* maintained that "the author has admirably told, with interesting quality of frontier vernacular, Abe's reactions to what he saw and their effect on his character and later achievements" (May 1, 1954: 864). All quoted in Mary K. Smith, *Meridel Le Sueur: A Bio-Bibliography* (M.A. thesis, University of Minnesota, 1973), 20–21. Smith also cites reviews in *Booklist* and *Horn Book*. "Carnival of Books" recording (includes a reading from Le Sueur's *River Road* and Le Sueur's discussion of the book with students from St. Paul schools in 1954). Reel-to-reel tape in Le Sueur Collection, 152.K.19.13B, box 42, tape 96.

35. "Carnival of Books" recording.

36. In her letter to the *Worker* praising Le Sueur's *River Road*, Eloise MacAllister noted, "as we read the story, we remember much of it out of legend—the priceless legend of 'old Abe Lincoln who believed he could read from darkness and build from shadows.'" MacAllister, letter to Joseph North. Many people viewed folklore as especially suited to children, a colorful adjunct to "hard" history that "sheds new light upon the intricate pattern of native experience." Philip D. Jordan, "Folklore for the School," *Social Education* 15 (February 1951): 59–63.

37. B. A. Botkin, ed., *Treasury of American Folklore: Stories, Ballads and Traditions* (New York: Crown, 1944), xxi; Jerrold Hirsch, "Folklore in the Making: B. A. Botkin," *Journal of American Folklore* 100, no. 395 (January–March 1987): 3–38. Also see B. A. Botkin, "Paul Bunyan Was OK in His Time," *New Masses* 62 (April 23, 1946): 12–14; B. A. Botkin, "The Folk-say of Freedom Songs," *New Masses* 64 (1947): 14–16. Information on the panel is in Le Sueur's papers, 152.K.18.1. Robinson is quoted in Robbie Lieberman, *My Song Is My Weapon: Song, American Communism, and the Politics of Culture, 1930–1950* (Urbana: University of Illinois Press, 1989), 39.

38. Lieberman, *My Song Is My Weapon*, 46. The shift in folklore's status came with the move toward "socialist realism" as a Soviet cultural policy in 1934. According to Richard Reuss:

> Hitherto folk traditions had been regarded as an important cultural product of the masses but too corrupt or nonmilitant in themselves to be of use to the proletariat. Now it was emphasized that songs, legends, and other lore offered a realistic reflection of the people's historical and social experiences and that folk art portrayed the people's genuine feelings for reality. Folklore provided emotional solace for the folk and helped ease their burdens of toil and misery. Frequently, if not always, it recounted the democratic aspirations and revolutionary traditions of the past and present, lending a sense of hope and communal spirit.

Richard Reuss, *American Folk Music and Left-Wing Politics, 1927–1957* (Lanham, Md.: Scarecrow, 2000), 60–61. Also see R. Serge Denisoff, *Great Day Coming: Folk Music and the American Left* (Urbana: University of Illinois Press, 1965). The League of American Writers had panels devoted to folklore at its 1939 and 1941 conferences.

39. Carl Carmer, "Stranglers of the Thunder," *New Masses* 27 (April 12, 1938): 81; Elie Siegmeister, *Work and Sing: A Collection of the Songs That Built America* (New York: Scott, 1944), 39. Russell Ames, "More Than Just Folks," Review of *The Book of Negro Folklore*, ed. Langston Hughes and Arna Bontemps, *Masses and Mainstream* 12, no. 2 (February 1959): 48. Conroy was likewise inspired by Botkin. "Industrial folklore" that Conroy collected for Botkin while he and Bontemps worked on the Illinois Writers Project would become the basis for their children's stories. For more on this highly unusual collaboration between a white "worker-writer" and an erudite African-American scholar, see Douglas Wixson, "'Black Writers and White!' Jack Conroy, Arna Bontemps, and Interracial Collaboration in the 1930s," *Prospects* 23 (1998): 401–30.

40. See Eric Lucas, *Swamp Fox Brigade: Adventures with General Francis Marion's Guerillas* (New York: International, 1945); Esther Forbes, *Johnny Tremain: A Novel for Old & Young* (Boston: Houghton Mifflin, 1943). On Disney versions of these tales, see Watts, *The Magic Kingdom*, 290–93.

41. Andrew Hutton, introduction to *A Narrative in the Life of David Crockett, by Himself*, ed. David Crockett (Lincoln: University of Nebraska Press, 1987), xxxix; Richard Dorson, *American Folklore* (Chicago: University of Chicago Press, 1977), 208; Watts, *The Magic Kingdom*, 317; Meridel Le Sueur, *Chanticleer of Wilderness Road: A Story of Davy Crockett* (New York: Knopf, 1951), 11.

42. Irwin Shapiro, *Yankee Thunder: The Legendary Life of Davy Crockett* (New York: Messner, 1944), 66, 69–70. Perhaps ironically, Shapiro also scripted *Davy Crockett: King of the Wild Frontier*. However, the music, casting, costumes, and other elements of the film, which are out of the writer's control, effectively minimize any progressive message the script might have originally contained. The script for the program is copyrighted under Shapiro's name in the U.S. Copyright Office. Dorson, *American Folklore*, 211; Le Sueur, *Chanticleer of Wilderness Road*, 53, 77; Watts, *The Magic Kingdom*, 317. A letter to Le Sueur from an editor at Knopf noted the positive impact of the "Crockett craze" on sales of *Chanticleer*, not only in the United States but abroad as well. Ruth Shair, letter to Le Sueur, July 11, 1955, Le Sueur Papers, 152.K.18.1, folder 20. Likewise, a 1955 letter from Gertrude Blumenthal to illustrator James Daugherty mentions the "hubbub over Davy Crockett" and notes that "the sales have gone up considerably, and this makes me happy for both you and Mr. Shapiro." Letter from Gertrude Blumenthal, children's book editor at Julian Messner, June 17, 1955, James Daugherty Papers, University of Oregon.

43. Botkin, ed., *Treasury of American Folklore*, xxvi. Alexander Saxton made this observation more recently and in more complex terms. See Alexander Saxton, *The Rise and Fall of the White Republic: Class Politics and Mass Culture in Nineteenth-Century America* (New York: Verso, 1990), 183–203. Daugherty was clearly an artist of "social conscience" and was included in an exhibit of such artists and in the catalog put together by Frances Pohl. See Frances K. Pohl and Terra Museum of American Art., *In the Eye of the Storm: An Art of Conscience, 1930–1970: Selections from the Collection of Philip J. & Suzanne Schiller* (San Francisco, Calif.: Pomegranate, 1995). He spoke in a New York Public Library program in 1941 on "backgrounds in the struggle for freedom" along with a group of children singing John La Touche's "Ballad for Americans" (Daugherty Papers, Archives of American Art); he was an outspoken critic of McCarthy and a supporter of

Spanish loyalists (see letter to Peyton Boswell, June 17 [no year] in Daugherty Papers, Archives of American Art); and radical artist Lynd Ward was a great admirer of Daugherty's work (see statement in Lynd Ward Papers, supplemental materials, folder 117).

44. Le Sueur, *Chanticleer of Wilderness Road*, 58–59. On the ideology of "republican motherhood," see Linda K. Kerber, *Women of the Republic: Intellect and Ideology in Revolutionary America* (New York: Norton, 1986). Royalty statements in Le Sueur's papers show *Sparrow Hawk* consistently trailing the other books in terms of sales, and a 1961 letter from Gertrude Blumenthal in Daugherty's papers noted that *Joe Magarac* was out of print though *Yankee Thunder*, published five years earlier, was still selling quite well. Letter from Blumenthal to Shapiro, December 7, 1961, James Daugherty Papers, University of Oregon.

45. Kate Weigand, *Red Feminism: American Communism and the Making of Women's Liberation* (Baltimore, Md.: Johns Hopkins University Press, 2001), 102–3. Weigand here draws upon Gerald Zahavi, "Passionate Commitments: Race, Sex, and Communism at Schenectady General Electric, 1932–1954," *Journal of American History* 83 (September 1996): 514–48.

46. Meridel Le Sueur, *Sparrow Hawk* (Duluth, Minn.: Holy Cow!, 1987 [orig. Knopf, 1950]), 37.

47. Aptheker, "Negro History: Arsenal for Liberation." For books about Indians, see, for instance, Shirley Graham, *The Story of Pocahontas* (New York: Grosset and Dunlap, 1953); May McNeer, *War Chief of the Seminoles* (New York: Random House, 1954); Michael Gorham, *The Real Book about Indians* (Garden City, N.Y.: Garden City Books, in arrangement with Franklin Watts, 1953), 3. Joseph Starobin suggests that among Communists in the late 1940s, "the view developed that [the African-American] struggle was replacing the struggle of the working class as a whole *as the true revolutionary force.*" Joseph Starobin, *American Communism in Crisis, 1943–1957* (Cambridge, Mass.: Harvard University Press, 1972), 201; emphasis in original. Also see Mary L. Dudziak, *Cold War Civil Rights: Race and the Image of American Democracy* (Princeton, N.J.: Princeton University Press, 2000).

48. "Parents Stress the Ideological Needs of Children," 2, flyer in papers of Jefferson School of Social Science, box 1, folder labeled "miscellaneous." For more on the intercultural education movement, see running commentary in the journal *Common Ground*. Also see Robert Shaffer, "Multicultural Education in New York City during World War II," *New York History* 77 (July 1996): 301–32.

49. Aubrey Haan, "Books Make Bigots," *Common Ground* 7, no. 3 (Spring 1947): 3–12.

50. David Alison, "Racism in School Textbooks," *Jewish Life* (March 1951): 16–19. The discussion of textbooks' portrayals of slavery are from quotations in this article taken from Edna McGuire, *America Then and Now* (New York: Macmillan, 1940), 247; Ralph V. Harlow, *Story of America* (New York: Holt, 1949), 195; and Herbert Townsend, *Our America* (New York: Allyn and Bacon, 1949), 131. For important scholarly challenges to this view, see Eric Foner, *Reconstruction: America's Unfinished Revolution, 1863–1877* (New York: Harper and Row, 1988); W. E. B. Du Bois, *Black Reconstruction* (New York: Harcourt Brace, 1935). Haan, "Books Make Bigots," 5; also see Maxwell S. Stewart, *Prejudice in Textbooks* (Washington, D.C.: Public Affairs Committee). A series of textbooks written by William Jansen, superintendent of the New York City schools in the early 1950s, was the subject of pointed criticism for its "unscholarly and prejudiced treatment of the people of Africa and the various colonial countries." Alison, "Racism in School Textbooks," 17.

51. Mary Dudziak, "Desegregation as a Cold War Imperative," *Stanford Law Review* 41 (November 1988): 61–120, 75, 117. Reading his FBI file, red-diaper baby David Wellman notes, for instance, that "the Detroit Red Squad was absolutely obsessed with race." Memos in the file repeatedly pointed to "interracial dancing," mixed-race gatherings, and protests against segregation and racial discrimination. David Wellman, "Mistaken Identities," in *Red Diapers: Growing Up in the Communist Left*, ed. Judy Kaplan and Linn Shapiro (Urbana and Chicago: University of Illinois Press, 1998), 173.

52. Dorothy Sterling, interview with author, November 10, 1997; Mark Naison, *Communists in Harlem during the Depression* (Urbana: University of Illinois Press, 1983), 49. "From Month to Month: Jewish Life," *Jewish Life* (November 1946): 3. For examples of antiracist material, see Alice Citron, "The Jews and Negro Rights," *Jewish Life* (July 1954): 8–9; W. E. B. Du Bois, "200 Years of Segregated Schools," *Jewish Life* (February 1955): 7–9; Louis Harap, "Why Jews Fight Segregation," *Jewish Life* (February 1955): 10–12; Doxey A. Wilkerson, "Fight Ahead on Desegregation," *Jewish Life* (March 1955): 10–12. Also see Frances Lym, "Brotherhood in Boyle Heights: Intercultural Activity of Mexican Americans with Other Groups in a Section of Los Angeles Furthers Local Democratic Unity," *Jewish Life* (September 1955): 21–1. For antiracist material used in secular Yiddish schools, see, for instance, Benjamin Efron, *The Story of Passover* (New York: Committee for Progressive Jewish Education, 1952). Alan Wald has recently challenged the portrait, popularized in Harold Cruse's *Crisis of the Negro Intellectual* (New York: Morrow, 1967), of Jews manipulating African Americans in Communist circles. See Alan Wald, "Narrating Nationalisms: Black Marxism and Jewish Communism through the Eyes of Harold Cruse," in *Left of the Color Line: Race, Radicalism, and Twentieth-Century Literature of the United States*, ed. Bill Mullen and James Smethurst (Chapel Hill: University of North Carolina Press, 2003), 141–61

53. Albert E. Kahn, *The Game of Death: The Effects of the Cold War on Our Children* (New York: Cameron and Kahn, 1953), 213.

54. Lorraine Hansberry, "Life Challenges Negro Youth," *Freedom* 5, no. 3 (March 1955): 7. Also see Jules Koslow, "The Right to the Three R's: An Open Letter to American Educators," *New Masses* (December 4, 1945): 15–17; Virginia Harnett, "Whitewash on the Blackboard," *New Masses* 58 (April 9, 1946): 10, 12–13; Alice Citron, "Are Harlem Schools 'a Place to Learn'?" *Freedom* 1, no. 9 (September 1951): 8; Jean Bolton, "A Harlem Mother Writes," *Freedom* (November 1952): 3; Harold Collins, "Teaching Teachers," *Worker* (April 13, 1958): 7.

55. Aptheker, "Negro History: Arsenal for Liberation"; W. H. King, "How the Freedmen Fought for Land," *New Masses* 63 (February 18, 1947): 18–21; Citron, "Are Harlem Schools 'a Place to Learn'?"

56. Naison, *Communists in Harlem*, 216.

57. Linda Lewis, "Josiah Henson: Kept Right on Traveling to Freedom," *Freedom* 1, no. 5 (May 1951): 7.

58. Dorothy Sterling testified at hearings on textbook bias held by Adam Clayton Powell in 1966, and at several national conferences for educators. See Dorothy Sterling, "What's Black and White and Read All Over," *English Journal* 58, no. 6 (September 1969), 817–32. On "Cold War civil rights," see Dudziak, *Cold War Civil Rights*. See the editorial discussion surrounding Langston Hughes's *First Book of Negroes* in chapter 5. On the fact that publishers of trade juveniles led the trend toward diversifying textbooks, see "Better Late than Never: Books about Urban Crisis," *Publishers Weekly* 198 (July 13,

1970): 125. "Lily white" descriptor from Herman and Nina Schneider, interview with author, June 23, 1999, West Tisbury, Mass.

59. Dorothy Sterling outlines developments in the field of African-American literature for children, beginning with Arna Bontemps's *You Can't Bet a Possum* and his collaboration with Langston Hughes on *Popo and Fifina*, both published in the 1930s. She points to Jerrold and Lorraine Beim's *Two Is a Team* (1945) as the first "integrated" picture book and notes other books that came out in the 1940s and 1950s that focused on black subjects. See Dorothy Sterling, "The Soul of Learning," *English Journal* 57 (February 1968): 166–80; Swift, quoting publisher in letter to Lynd Ward, October 24, 1945, Ward Papers, Georgetown University.

60. Herbert Aptheker, "The Negro Woman," *Masses and Mainstream* 2 (February 1949): 17; Weigand, *Red Feminism*, 111. Weigand's claims are somewhat controversial; scholars such as (red-diaper baby) Rosalyn Baxandall argue that the CP never gave serious attention to women's issues. See Rosalyn Baxandall, "The Question Seldom Asked: Women and the CPUSA," in *New Studies in the Politics and Culture of U.S. Communism*, ed. Michael Brown (New York: Monthly Review, 1993), 141–61.

61. Lorraine Levey Beim, *Sugar and Spice* (New York: Harcourt, Brace, 1947), 53–56.

62. Lilian Moore, telephone interview with author, March 24, 1999.

63. Dorothy Sterling, interview with author, November 10, 1997, Wellfleet, Massachusetts.

64. Crichlow was vague about how he happened to place his work in the *New Pioneer*, but he did mention his involvement with the International Workers Order. Ernest Crichlow, interview with author, November 20, 1997, Brooklyn, New York.

65. Dudziak, *Cold War Civil Rights*.

66. Because the term was employed by middle-class women pressing for the Equal Rights Amendment, which did not include special protections for women workers, women in the labor movement usually rejected it. Leftists also tended to believe that gender issues should be subordinate to economic issues, in contrast to professed feminists, who made gender issues a priority.

67. Leftist Henrietta Buckmaster's *Let My People Go* (1944), which was later adapted for children, also discusses Tubman.

68. Edith Margolis, letter to Emma Gelders Sterne, January 14, 1957, Sterne Papers. A week later Margolis informed Sterne that the editor at Knopf, Margaret Martignoni, was "delighted with the Bethune script." Ibid., dated January 22, 1957.

69. Emma Sterne, *Mary McLeod Bethune* (New York: Knopf, 1957), 8.

70. Ibid., 37.

71. Dorothy Sterling, *Freedom Train: The Story of Harriet Tubman* (Garden City, N.Y.: Doubleday, 1954), 35.

72. For a challenge to this myth in the left-wing press, see King, "How the Freedmen Fought for Land."

73. Ann Lane Petry, *Harriet Tubman: Conductor on the Underground Railroad* (New York: Crowell, 1955), 29. Sterne, drawing readers' attention to the contemporary struggles in the South in the late 1950s, says "this compromise in the name of 'unity' set a pattern at the expense of the enslaved Negro that was to lead the new nation into tragedy." Sterne, *Mary McLeod Bethune*, 12.

74. Shirley Graham, *There Was Once a Slave: The Heroic Story of Frederick Douglass* (New York: Messner, 1947), 171.

75. There certainly was banning of historical works, Graham's among them (her work, along with the work of Howard Fast, was subject to banning in the New York City schools, for instance). However, Graham's books on Benjamin Banneker and Frederick Douglass won national awards, and her (co-authored) book on George Washington Carver was a bestseller.

76. Sterne, *Mary McLeod Bethune*, 10–11.

77. Ibid., 110.

78. Shirley Graham, *Your Most Humble Servant* (New York: Messner, 1949), 117, 125, 220–22.

79. Sterne, *Mary McLeod Bethune*, 245.

80. Sterling, *Freedom Train*, 130–31.

81. Ibid., 48–49; Graham, *There Was Once a Slave: The Heroic Story of Frederick Douglass*, 30.

82. For commentary from the Left on juvenile delinquency, see chapter 4, note 26. Sterling, *Freedom Train*, 12–13.

83. Sterne, *Mary McLeod Bethune*, 183.

84. Weigand, *Red Feminism*, 131. Also see Julia Mickenberg, "The Pedagogy of the Popular Front: Progressive Parenting for a New Generation, 1918–1945," in *The American Child: A Cultural Studies Reader*, ed. Caroline Levander and Carol Singley (New Brunswick, N.J.: Rutgers University Press, 2003); Dorothy Sterling, *Lucretia Mott: Gentle Warrior* (Garden City, N.Y.: Doubleday, 1964), 162–63, 29.

85. Sterling, *Lucretia Mott*, 53, 73–74.

86. Ibid., 55; Sterling, *Freedom Train*, 130–31; Steriing, interview with author, November 10, 1997; Sterne, *Mary McLeod Bethune*, 89.

87. Sterling, *Lucretia Mott*, 162–63.

88. Ibid., 55.

89. Petry, *Harriet Tubman*, 227. For commentary by Petry that predicts the feminist position she communicates in her children's books, see Ann Petry, "What's Wrong with Negro Men?" *Negro Digest* 5 (March 1947): 4–7.

90. Faith Lindsay, interview with author, February 21, 1999, San Jose, California.

91. Sterne, *Mary McLeod Bethune*, 175–76.

92. Sterling, *Lucretia Mott*, 53, 191.

93. Graham, *The Story of Pocahontas*, 177–78.

94. Gerald Horne suggests that Graham "was able to resist anti-communism more successfully than she resisted male supremacy." Even so, he argues, "it would be a mistake to fail to view Graham Du Bois as a feminist," noting that "the texture of her life resonated with the idea of women's self-assertion and independence." Gerald Horne, *Race Woman: The Lives of Shirley Graham* (New York: New York University Press, 2000), 25, 122, 159.

95. Helen Heffernan, "A Comprehensive Program of Social Studies Textbooks, Grades One to Nine" (typescript, October 1951), 2. Sterne papers. Heffernan was head of elementary and rural education for the California Department of Education from 1926 to 1965.

96. Du Bois, *Black Reconstruction*, 711–29. On the changing character of children's literature (and the blossoming of young adult literature), particularly beginning in the 1960s, see John Rowe Townsend, *Written for Children: An Outline of English-Language Children's Literature* (London: Scarecrow, 1996), 258–82.

Epilogue

1. Dorothy Sterling, interview with author, November 10, 1997, Wellfleet, Massachusetts; Franklin Folsom, "The Beginning of the Council on Interracial Books for Children," typescript, in private papers of Mary Elting.

2. Lilian Moore, telephone interview with author, February 15, 1998. Organizational documents in the private collection of Stanley Faulkner date the council's official incorporation in February 1965.

3. Nancy Larrick, "The All-White World of Children's Books," *Saturday Review* (September 11, 1965): 65.

4. Ibid., 64.

5. The council sponsored conferences on Racism and Sexism in Children's Literature; it offered guidance to teachers and school boards on textbook and trade book evaluations; and it offered reviews of current literature. Its Racism and Sexism Resource Center for Educators put out filmstrips (such as "Unlearning 'Indian' Stereotypes" and "Understanding Institutional Racism"), curriculum units, and publications such as *Chronicles of American Indian Protest* (1971); *Stereotypes, Distortions, and Omissions in U.S. History Textbooks* (1977); and *Human and Anti-Human Values in Children's Books: A Content Rating Instrument for Educators and Concerned Parents* (1976). The council's writing contest for unpublished minority writers, which originally focused on African-American writers, later expanded to include any minority writer. On efforts to encourage minorities in publishing and minority-run publishing houses, see, for instance, Bradford Chambers, "Book Publishing: A Racist Club?" *Publishers Weekly* 199 (February 1, 1971): 40–44; Bradford Chambers, "Why Minority Publishing? New Voices Are Heard," *Publishers Weekly* 199 (March 15, 1971): 35–50; Bradford Chambers, "Interracial Books: Background of a Challenge," *Publishers Weekly* 200 (October 11, 1971): 23–29; James Fraser, "Black Publishing for Black Children: The Experience of the Sixties and Seventies," *Library Journal* 98 (November 15, 1973): 3421–26; Joel A. Roth, "Dick and Jane Make Some New Friends: Traditional Textbook Illustrations Are Giving Way before the Insistent Demands of an Integrated Society: Here's How Publishers Are Meeting the Challenge and Shifting from Fantasy to Reality," *Book Production Industry* (June 1965): 42–45; Dharathula H. Millender, "Through a Glass, Darkly," *Library Journal* 92 (December 15, 1967): 4571–76; Augusta Baker, "Guidelines for Black Books: An Open Letter to Juvenile Editors," *Publishers Weekly* 196 (July 14, 1969): 131–33; "Bookstore Demand for Race Relations Titles," *Publishers Weekly* 196 (July 14, 1969): 94; Paul Cornelius, "Interracial Children's Books: Problems and Progress," *Library Quarterly* 4 (April 1971): 106–27.

6. See, for instance, Dorothy Sterling, "The Soul of Learning," *English Journal* 57 (February 1968): 166–80. The article is the text of a speech given at the NDEA Institute in English held at the University of Wisconsin, Milwaukee. Also see correspondence in Sterling's papers at the University of Oregon, Special Collections, Eugene.

7. The council's initial list of contributors reads like a who's who of formerly red (or pink) authors of children's books, although many are invisible on the organization's letterhead, which showcases a respectable, interracial, liberal coalition. The council's advisory board included Albert Bronson, coordinator of curriculum materials for the human relations unit of the New York City Board of Education; poet Gwendolyn Brooks; the artists Ben Shahn and Bernarda Bryson Shahn; Mamie Phipps Clark, executive director of the Northside Center for Child Development in New York City (and a director

of the famous doll experiments that were used as crucial evidence in the *Brown* case); Josette Frank and Sidonie Gruenberg of the Child Study Association; authors Langston Hughes, John O. Killens, Milton Meltzer, Herman and Nina Schneider, and Ruth Tooze; Nancy Larrick, former president of the International Reading Association; Daniel Melcher, president of R. R. Bowker Company; retired librarian Charlamae Rollins; Benjamin Spock; Randolph B. Smith, principal of the progressive Elizabeth Irwin High School; Norman Studer, director of the Downtown Community School; and Whitney M. Young, executive director of the National Urban League. Contributors to the council included Franklin and Mary Folsom, Syd Hoff, Nancy Larrick Crosby and Alexander Crosby, Dorothy and Philip Sterling, Irving Adler, Anne Terry White, Helen Goldfrank, Hy Ruchlis, Ruth Tooze, Abraham and Rebecca Marcus, Jeanne Bendick, along with many of those on the advisory board. Contributor lists in the private collection of Stanley Faulkner, a prominent civil rights lawyer, who was one of the council's original founders and who served as treasurer.

8. Nancy Mikkelson, telephone interview with author, December 4, 1997.

9. Eve Merriam, *Mommies at Work* (New York: Knopf, 1961), n.p.

10. The latter term is from Gary Gerstle's book of that title. See Gary Gerstle, *Working Class Americanism: The Politics of Labor in a Textile City, 1914–1960* (Cambridge: Cambridge University Press, 1989).

11. E. L. Doctorow, *The Book of Daniel* (1971; reprint, New York: Ballantine, 1990), 118; Kenneth Keniston, *The Uncommitted: Alienated Youth in American Society* (New York: Harcourt, Brace and World, 1965); Kenneth Keniston, *Young Radicals: Notes on a Committed Young* (New York: Harcourt, Brace and World, 1968).

12. Meltzer interview with author, October 1997, New York City.

13. Gerald Horne, *Race Woman: The Lives of Shirley Graham* (New York: New York University Press, 2000), 260, 25.

14. Titles included White's *False Treaty*; *The Defenders: Osceola, Tecumseh, Cochise* (1970) by Ann McGovern; *John Brown's Raid: A Picture History of the Civil Rights Movement* (1972) by Lorenz Graham; *The Fighting Congressmen: Thaddeus Stephens, Hiram Revels, James Rapier, Blanche K. Bruce* (1971) by Henrietta Buckmaster; *To Change the World: A Picture History of Reconstruction* (1971) by Milton Meltzer; *It Started in Montgomery: A Picture History of the Civil Rights Movement* (1972) by Dorothy Sterling; *Three against Slavery: Denmark Vesey, William Lloyd Garrison, Frederick Douglass* (1972) by Philip Spencer; *Justice Denied: A History of Japanese in the United States* (1972) by Jennifer Cross; *Voices from the Southwest: Antonio Jose Martinez, Elfego Baca, Rejea Lopez Tijerina* (1973) by Jacqueline Bernard; and *The Question of Color: Marcus Garvey, Malcolm X* (1973) by Philip Sterling.

15. Some of these books are Council on Interracial Books for Children, *Chronicles of American Indian Protest* (Greenwich, Conn.: Fawcett, 1971); Bradford Chambers, *Chronicles of Negro Protest: A Background Book for Young People, Documenting the History of Black Power* (New York: Parents' Magazine Press, 1968); Philip Sterling, M. M. Brau, and Tracy Sugarman, *The Quiet Rebels: Four Puerto Rican Leaders: Josâe Celso Barbosa, Luis Muänoz Rivera, Josâe de Diego, Luiz Muänoz Marâin* (Garden City, N.Y.: Doubleday, 1968); Philip Sterling, *Sea and Earth: The Life of Rachel Carson* (New York: Crowell, 1970).

16. Interview with Lilian Moore, November 22, 1998; "Bookstore Demand for Race Relations Titles." There are discussions to this effect in the Authors Guild *Newsletter* and in Lucille Ogle's papers at the University of Oregon.

17. On the original incident see Helen Kay, "Blackout of a Negro Child," *Top of the News* 22 (November 1965): 58–61; Jean Poindexter Colby, "How to Present the Negro in Children's Books: An Editor Sweats Out the Problem," *Top of the News* 21 (April 1965): 191–96. Information on the editor's later change of heart as the climate became more hospitable to interracial books is from Joan Goldfrank, telephone interview with author, December 22, 2003.

18. Dorothy Sterling, interview with author, November 10, 1997, Wellfleet. When Moore retired from publishing in the 1970s she hand-picked her replacement, Barbara Walker, one of the first African-American juvenile editors. Thus through the council itself, in books she helped to bring out, and in her own hiring decisions, Moore did her part to challenge the "all-white world" of children's literature and the "racist club" of American book publishing. See Larrick, "The All-White World of Children's Books"; Chambers, "Book Publishing: A Racist Club?"

19. So much so that the Council on Interracial Books would be accused of enforcing a restrictive "political correctness" in children's literature.

20. The Texas Board of Education insisted in 2004 that middle school and high school textbooks must explicitly discuss marriage in terms of a union "between a man and a woman" rather than in the more dangerously vague terms of "two people who are in love," a decision that affects not only textbooks read by children in Texas, but also nationally, given that Texas is the second-largest textbook buyer in the country. As far as editing out racial content, in today's racial climate, the editing is not usually for openly racist reasons, but the effects are the same as they were in the 1950s. *Corduroy* (1968) by Old Left writer and artist Don Freeman, originally told a story of a teddy bear living in a department store who no one would buy until an African-American girl falls in love with him (despite a missing button) and buys him with all of her savings. The book became a classic—perhaps because children were taken with Corduroy's late-night excursion through the department store in search of his missing button—and it is still in print. However, some time after Freeman's death in 1978, the Corduroy character was licensed, and now you can buy books such as *Corduroy Makes a Cake* (2001), *Corduroy's Hike* (2001), *Corduroy Goes to School* (2002), or *Corduroy at the Zoo* (2000), which depict Corduroy with no owner at all. That part of the story must have simply seemed less interesting, or too complicated to deal with. Now we have a series of stories about a cute bear, with no racial subtext. Finally, in terms of conscious attempts by groups pushing a political agenda to influence children's books, there are some interesting recent examples. According to its jacket, *The National Review Treasury of Classic Children's Literature* "promotes those virtues and lessons that are increasingly at a premium in our current culture." Aside from a story by Buckley himself (about a boy off at boarding school), in this edited collection of "classic children's literature," nearly all of the selections, from people like imperialist Rudyard Kipling and business promoter Charles Lummis, are from the nineteenth century. The implication seems to be that there were few twentieth-century stories wholesome enough to include. William F. Buckley, Jr., *The National Review Treasury of Classic Children's Literature* (New York: National Review Books, 2002). More recently, right-wing television personality Bill O'Reilly published *The O'Reilly Factor for Kids* (2004), with advice on how to become rich and successful (and how to avoid turning into a liberal "pinhead"). Michael Newman, "The Pinhead Factor": Review of *The O'Reilly Factor for Kids* by Bill O'Reilly and Charles Flowers, *New York Times Book Review* (November 7, 2004): 22.

21. Just as school textbooks are subject to close scrutiny by school boards, television programs risk losing advertising revenue if they offend viewers (or advertisers). Films are more expensive to produce than books, and more cutting-edge films for children are less likely to generate enough revenue to make them profitable. Children's books, if they earn praises from the critical establishment, can still be guaranteed a certain number of sales to school and public libraries.

SELECTED BIBLIOGRAPHY

Archival and Special Collections Consulted

Raymond Abrashkin Papers. Private collection of William Abrashkin

Irving Adler Papers. Kerlan Collection of Children's Literature and Manuscripts, University of Minnesota

Irving Adler Papers. Tamiment Library, New York University

American Legion Collection. National Museum of American History, Smithsonian Institution

N. W. Ayer Collection of American Advertising. Archives Center, National Museum of American History, Smithsonian Institution

Peggy Bacon Papers, Archives of American Art, Smithsonian Institution

Arna Bontemps Papers. Beinecke Rare Book Library, Yale University

Brandon Films Collection. Museum of Modern Art, New York City

Thomas Brandon Papers. Pacific Film Archive, Berkeley, California

Children's Book and Music Center materials. Private collections of Jennifer Charnofsky and Miriam Sherman

Children's Literature Collections. Library of Congress

Child Study Association Papers. Social Welfare History Archives, University of Minnesota

Council on Interracial Books for Children/Bradford Chambers Papers. Schomburg Center for Research in Black Culture, New York Public Library. Also material in private collection of Stanley Faulkner, private collection of Franklin Folsom and Mary Elting Folsom, and Folsom Papers in University of Colorado Special Collections

Ernest Crichlow Papers. Archives of American Art, Smithsonian Institution

Alexander Crosby Papers. University of Oregon Special Collections, Eugene

James Daugherty Papers. Kerlan Collection of Children's Literature and Manuscripts, University of Minnesota

James Daugherty Papers. University of Oregon Special Collections

James Daugherty Papers, Archives of American Art, Smithsonian Institution

Encyclopedia Brittanica educational films. American Archives of the Factual Film, Iowa State University, Ames

Ernestine Evans Papers. Rare Book and Manuscript Library, Columbia University

FBI files for Betty Bacon, Henry Gregor Felsen, Franklin Folsom, Harry Granick, Helen Kay, Meridel Le Sueur, Eve Merriam, Millicent Selsam, Emma Gelders Sterne, and Jay Williams

Folkways Records Collections. Center for American Folklife and Cultural Studies, Smithsonian Institution

Franklin Folsom and Mary Elting Folsom Papers. University of Colorado, Boulder

Hugo Gellert Papers. Archives of American Art, Smithsonian Institution

Tibor Gergeley Papers. Rare Book and Manuscript Library, Columbia University

Harry Granick Papers, American Heritage Center, University of Wyoming

William Gropper Papers. Archives of American Art, Smithsonian Institution
John and Faith Hubley Papers. Pacific Film Archive, Berkeley, California
Langston Hughes Papers. Beinecke Rare Book Library, Yale University
Immigration History Research Center, Rare Book Collection. University of Minnesota
Industry on Parade series. Archives Center, National Museum of American History
International Publishers material. Tamiment Library, New York University
International Workers Order material. Tamiment Library, New York University
Jefferson School of Social Science Papers. Tamiment Library, New York University
Ruth Epperson Kennell Papers, University of Orgeon
Rockwell Kent Papers. Archives of American Art, Smithsonian Institution
Kerlan Collection of Children's Literature and Manuscripts. University of Minnesota
Alfred A. Knopf Papers. Harry Ransom Humanities Center, University of Texas, Austin
Herbert Kruckman Papers. Archives of American Art, Smithsonian Institution
Labor History Collection. Division of Political History, National Museum of American History, Smithsonian Institution
League of American Writers Papers. Bancroft Library, University of California, Berkeley
Meridel Le Sueur Papers. Minnesota Historical Society, St. Paul
Jack London Papers. Huntington Library, San Marino, California
Carey McWilliams Papers (relating to New York Teachers Union). Columbia University's Teachers College, Millbank Library
Milton Meltzer Papers. University of Oregon Special Collections
Eve Merriam Papers. Kerlan Collection of Children's Literature and Manuscripts, University of Minnesota
Eve Merriam Papers. Schlesinger Library, Radcliffe College
Lilian Moore Papers. University of Oregon Special Collections
Motion Picture Collections. Library of Congress, Motion Picture Reading Room
National Council on American Soviet Friendship Papers. Tamiment Library, New York University
Lucille Ogle Papers. University of Oregon Special Collections
Elizabeth Olds Papers. Archives of American Art, Smithsonian Institution
Political campaign materials. National Museum of American History, Smithsonian Institution
Progressive Librarians Council Papers. Tamiment Library 064, New York University
Radical Periodical Collections. New York Public Library; Tamiment Library, New York University
Secular Yiddish Schools of America Collection. Rare Book and Manuscript Library, Stanford University
Richard Simon Collection. Rare Book and Manuscript Library, Columbia University
Dorothy Sterling Papers. University of Oregon Special Collections
Emma Gelders Sterne Papers. University of Oregon Special Collections
Genevieve Taggard Papers. New York Public Library
Alexander Trachtenberg Papers. University of Wisconsin, Madison
Vanguard Press Papers. Rare Book and Manuscript Library, Columbia University
Velma Varner Papers. Rare Book and Manuscript Library, Columbia University
Lynd Ward Collection. Children's Literature Collection, University of Minnesota
Lynd Ward and May McNeer Papers. Georgetown University

Warshaw Collection of American Advertising and Americana. Archives Center, National Museum of American History, Smithsonian Institution

Interviews

Hank Abrashkin	Joan Goldfrank	Jonathan Moore
Leone Adelson	Lewis Goldfrank	Lilian Moore
Irving Adler	Tony Hiss	Minne Motz
Rose Agree	Ed Hoke	Elsie Nydorf
Betty Bacon	Dahlov Ipcar	Herman and Nina
Sanford Berman	Nancy Larrick	Schneider
Jennifer Charnofsky	Meridel Le Sueur	Pete Seeger
Ernest Crichlow	Faith Lindsay	Miriam Sherman
Stanley Faulkner	Ann McGovern	Dorothy Sterling
Mary Elting Folsom	Milton Meltzer	Vicky Williams
Marge Frantz	Nancy Mikkelson	Rose Wyler

Selected Bibliography of Children's Books

Adelson, Leone, and Benjamin Gruenberg. *Your Breakfast and the People Who Made It.* Illustrated by Kurt Wiese. Garden City, N.Y.: Doubleday, 1954.

Adler, Irving. *The Secret of Light.* Illustrated by Ida Weisburd. New York: International, 1952.

———. *Man-Made Moons: The Earth Satellites and What They Tell Us.* Edited by Ruth Adler. New York: Day, 1957.

———. *The Tools of Science.* New York: Day, 1958.

Amalgamated Clothing Workers of America. *Mary Stays After School; or, What This Union's About.* New York: Amalgamated Clothing Workers of America, 1939.

Baker, Nina Brown. *Lenin.* Illustrated by Louis Slobodkin. New York: Vanguard, 1945.

Beauchamp, Joan. *Martin's Annual.* New York: International, 1935.

Becker, May Lamberton, ed. *Youth Replies I Can: Stories of Resistance.* New York: Knopf, 1945.

Beim, Jerrold. *Swimming Hole.* Illustrated by Louis Darling. New York: Morrow, 1950.

———. *The Boy on Lincoln's Lap.* Illustrated by Tracy Sugarman. New York: Morrow, 1955.

Beim, Lorraine Levey. *Sugar and Spice.* New York: Harcourt Brace, 1947.

Beim, Lorraine, and Jerrold Beim. *Sasha and the Samovar.* Illustrated by Rafaello Busoni. New York: Harcourt Brace, 1944.

———. *Two Is a Team.* Illustrated by Ernest Crichlow. New York: Harcourt Brace, 1945.

Benedict, Ruth, and Gene Weltfish. *In Henry's Backyard: The Races of Mankind.* New York: Schuman, 1948.

Bontemps, Arna Wendell. *We Have Tomorrow.* Boston: Houghton Mifflin, 1945.

———. *Story of the Negro.* Illustrated by Raymond Lufkin. New York: Knopf, 1955.

———. *Frederick Douglass: Slave, Fighter, Freeman.* Illustrated by Harper Johnson. New York: Knopf, 1959.

Bontemps, Arna Wendell, and Jack Conroy. *The Fast Sooner Hound*. Illustrated by Virginia Lee Burton. Boston: Houghton Mifflin, 1942.
———. *Slappy Hooper: The Wonderful Sign Painter*. Illustrated by Ursula Koering. New York: Houghton Mifflin, 1946.
Bontemps, Arna, and Langston Hughes. *Popo and Fifina: Children of Haiti*. New York: Macmillan, 1932.
Brooks, Gwendolyn. *Bronzeville Boys and Girls*. New York: Harper, 1956.
Brown, William Montgomery. *Science and History for Girls and Boys*. Galion, Ohio: Bradford-Brown, 1932.
———. *Teachings of Marx for Girls and Boys*. Galion, Ohio: Bradford-Brown Educational, 1935.
Buckmaster, Henrietta. *Flight to Freedom: The Story of the Underground Railroad*. New York: Crowell, 1958.
Campion, Martha, ed. *New Pioneer Story Book*. New York: New Pioneer, 1935.
Childress, Alice. *A Hero Ain't Nothin' but a Sandwich*. New York: Coward, McCann & Geoghegan, 1973.
The Child's Socialist Reader. Illustrated by Walter Crane. London: Twentieth Century, 1907.
Cohn, Norma. *Little People in a Big Country*. New York: Oxford University Press, 1945.
Coy, Harold. *The Real Book about George Washington Carver*. New York: Franklin Watts, 1951.
———. *Real Book about Andrew Jackson*. Illustrated by Frank Nicholas. Garden City, N.Y.: Garden City Books, in arrangement with Franklin Watts, 1952.
Crampton, Gertrude. *Tootle*. Illustrated by Tibor Gergeley. Racine, Wis.: Golden, 1945.
Crosby, Alexander L. *One Day for Peace*. Boston: Little, Brown, 1971.
Crosby, Alexander, and Nancy Larrick. *Rockets into Space*. Illustrated by Denny McMains New York: Random House, 1959.
———. *Rivers: What They Do*. Racine, Wis.: Whitman, 1961.
Cunningham, William. *The Real Book about Daniel Boone*. Garden City, N.Y.: Garden City Books, in arrangement with Franklin Watts, 1952.
Cuthbert, Marion. *We Sing America*. Illustrated by Louise E. Jefferson. New York: Friendship, 1936.
Davis, Lavinia R. *Adventures in Steel*. Illustrated by Frank Dobias. New York: Modern Age, 1938.
———. *Americans Every One*. Illustrated by Leonard Weisgard. Garden City, N.Y.: Doubleday, Doran, 1942.
Dopp, Katharine Elizabeth. *The Early Herdsmen*. Chicago: Rand McNally, 1923.
Du Bois, Shirley Graham. *The Story of Phillis Wheatley*. Illustrated by Robert Burns. New York: Messner, 1949.
Edel, May. *The Story of People: Anthropology for Young People*. Boston: Little, Brown, 1953.
Edelstadt, Vera. *A Steam Shovel for Me!* Illustrated by Romano. New York: Stokes, 1933.
Efron, Benjamin. *The Story of Passover*. Illustrated by Herbert Kruckman. New York: Committee for Progressive Jewish Education, 1952.
———. *The Story of Purim*. Illustrated by Herbert Kruckman. New York: Jewish People's Fraternal Order, n.d.

Elting, Mary. *The Lollipop Factory and Lots of Others*. Illustrated by Jeanne Bendick. Garden City, N.Y.: Doubleday, 1946.

———. *We Are the Government*. Illustrated by Jeanne Bendick. Garden City, N.Y.: Doubleday, Doran, 1946.

———. *The Answer Book*. New York: Grosset and Dunlop, 1959.

Elting, Mary, and Robert T. Weaver. *Soldiers, Sailors, Fliers and Marines*. Illustrated by Jeanne Bendick. Garden City, N.Y.: Doubleday Doran, 1943.

———. *Battles: How They Are Won*. Illustrated by Jeanne Bendick. Garden City, N.Y.: Doubleday, Doran, 1944.

Epstein, Beryl Williams, and Sam Epstein. *Francis Marion: Swamp Fox of the Revolution*. New York: Messner, 1956.

———. *The Rocket Pioneers on the Road to Space*. New York: Messner, 1958.

———. *George Washington Carver: Negro Scientist*. Illustrated by William Moyers. New York: Garrard, 1960.

Evans, Eva Knox. *All about Us*. Illustrated by Vana Earle. New York: Capitol/Golden Press, 1947.

———. *People Are Important*. Illustrated by Vana Earle. Irvington-on-Hudson, N.Y.: Capitol, 1951.

Fast, Howard. *Haym Solomon: Son of Liberty*. Illustrated by Eric N. Simon. New York: Messner, 1941.

———. *Tony and the Wonderful Door*. Illustrated by William Vigoda. New York: Blue Heron, 1952.

Felsen, Henry Gregor. *Navy Diver*. New York: Dutton, 1942.

———. *Struggle Is Our Brother*. Illustrated by Woodi Ishmael. New York: Dutton, 1943.

———. *Submarine Sailor*. New York: Dutton, 1943.

Folsom, Franklin. *Science and the Secret of Man's Past*. Irvington-on-Hudson: Harvey House, 1966.

———. *Red Power on the Rio Grande: The Native American Revolution of 1680*. Billings, Mont.: Council for Indian Education, 1973.

Forbes, Esther. *Johnny Tremain: A Novel for Old & Young*. Illustrated by Lynd Ward. Boston: Houghton Mifflin, 1943.

Freeman, Don. *Corduroy*. New York: Viking, 1968.

Gág, Wanda. *Millions of Cats*. New York: Coward McCann, 1928.

Gates, Doris. *Blue Willow*. New York: Viking, 1940.

Gibson, Lydia. *The Teacup Whale*. New York: Farrar and Rinehart, 1934.

Gold, Michael. *Charlie Chaplin's Parade*. Illustrated by Otto Soglow. New York: Harcourt Brace, 1930.

Gollomb, Joseph, and Alice Taylor. *Young Heroes of the War*. Illustrated by Nedda Walker. New York: Vanguard, 1943.

Gorham, Michael [Franklin Folsom]. *The Real Book about Abraham Lincoln: Behind-the-Scenes Incidents and Lively Anecdotes in the Story of a Great American*. Illustrated by Elinore Blaisdell. Garden City, N.Y.: Garden City Books, in arrangement with Franklin Watts, 1951.

———. *The Real Book about Indians*. Illustrated by Fred Collins. Garden City, N.Y.: Garden City Books, in arrangement with Franklin Watts, 1953.

———. *Real Book of Great American Journeys*. Illustrated by Deane Cate. Garden City, N.Y.: Garden City Books, in arrangement with Franklin Watts, 1953.

Graham, Lorenz B. *South Town.* Chicago: Follett, 1958.

Graham, Shirley. *Paul Robeson: Citizen of the World.* New York: Messner, 1946.

———. *There Was Once a Slave: The Heroic Story of Frederick Douglass.* New York: Messner, 1947.

———. *Your Most Humble Servant.* New York: Messner, 1949.

———. *Jean Baptiste Pointe Du Sable, Founder of Chicago.* New York: Messner, 1953.

———. *The Story of Pocahontas.* Illustrated by Mario Cooper. Edited by Enid Lamonte Meadowcraft. New York: Grosset and Dunlop, 1953.

———. *Booker T. Washington: Educator of Hand, Head, and Heart.* New York: Messner, 1955.

———. *Julius K. Nyerere: Teacher of Africa.* New York: Messner, 1975.

Graham, Shirley Dredge, and George D. Lipscomb. *Dr. George Washington Carver, Scientist.* Illustrated by Elton C. Fax. New York: Messner, 1944.

Granick, Harry. *Run, Run! An Adventure in New York.* Illustrated by Gregor Duncan. New York: Simon and Schuster, 1941.

———. *Underneath New York.* Illustrated by Philip Westerfield May. New York: Rinehart, 1947.

Gropper, William. *The Little Tailor.* New York: Dodd, Mead, 1955.

Guy, Rosa. *Ruby: A Novel.* New York: Viking, 1976.

Hoff, Syd. *Danny and the Dinosaur.* New York: Harper, 1958.

———. *Sammy the Seal.* New York: Harper, 1959.

Hollos, Clara. *The Story of Your Coat.* Illustrated by Herbert Kruckman. New York: International, 1946.

Huberman, Leo. *We, the People.* Illustrated by Thomas Hart Benton. New York: Harper and Brothers, 1932, 1947, 1952.

———. *Man's Worldly Goods: The Story of the Wealth of Nations.* New York: Harper and Brothers, 1936.

Hughes, Langston. *The First Book of Negroes.* Illustrated by Ursula Koering. New York: Franklin Watts, 1952.

———. *Famous American Negroes.* New York: Dodd, Mead, 1954.

———. *The First Book of the West Indies.* New York: Franklin Watts, 1956.

———. *The First Book of Africa.* New York: Franklin Watts, 1960.

Il'in, M. *New Russia's Primer.* Translated by George S. Counts and Nucia P. Lodge. Cambridge, Mass.: Riverside, 1931.

———. *Black on White: The Story of Books.* Translated by Beatrice Kincead. Philadelphia: Lippincott, 1932.

———. *What Time Is It? The Story of Clocks.* Translated by Beatrice Kincead. Philadelphia: Lippincott, 1932.

———. *How the Automobile Learned to Run.* Illustrated by Herbert Kruckman. New York: International, 1945.

Il'in, M., and E. A. Segal. *How Man Became a Giant.* Translated by Beatrice Kincead. Illustrated by A. Komarov and E. A. Furman. Philadelphia: Lippincott, 1942.

James, Josephine [Emma Gelders Sterne et al.]. *Search for an Island.* New York: Golden, 1963.

Johnson, Crockett. *Harold and the Purple Crayon.* New York: Harper and Row, 1955.

Jones, Wilfred. *How the Derrick Works.* New York: Macmillan, 1930.

Karsavina, Jean. *Reunion in Poland.* Illustrated by Lynd Ward. Edited by Lynd Ward. New York: International, 1945.

———. *Tree by the Waters*. New York: International, 1948.

Kay, Helen. *Battle in the Barnyard: Stories and Pictures for Workers' Children*. Illustrated by J. Preval. New York: Workers Library, 1932.

———. *Apple Pie for Lewis*. New York: Aladdin, 1951.

———. *Lincoln: A Big Man*. New York: Hastings, 1957.

———. *Abe Lincoln's Hobby*. Chicago: Reilly and Lee, 1961.

Kennell, Ruth Epperson, and Russian War Relief, Inc. *That Boy Nikolka and Other Tales of Soviet Children*. New York: Russian War Relief, 1945.

Klein, Nicholas. *The Socialist Primer: A Book of First Lessons for the Little Ones in Words of One Syllable*. Girard, Kans.: Appeal to Reason, 1908.

Komroff, Manuel. *Thomas Jefferson*. New York: Messner, 1961.

Krauss, Ruth. *A Very Special House*. Illustrated by Maurice Sendak. New York: Harper, 1953.

Kreymborg, Alfred. *Funnybone Alley*. Illustrated by Boris Artzybasheff. New York: Macaulay, 1927.

Kruckman, Herbert. *Joey Meets His People*. New York: Hebrew Publishing, 1940.

Lent, Henry Bolles. *Diggers and Builders*. New York: Macmillan, 1931.

Lester, Julius, comp. *To Be a Slave*. Illustrated by Tom Feelings. New York: Dial Press, 1968.

Le Sueur, Meridel. *Little Brother of the Wilderness: The Story of Johnny Appleseed*. Illustrated by Betty Alden. New York: Knopf, 1947; repr., Duluth: Holy Cow!, 1995.

———. *Nancy Hanks of Wilderness Road: A Story of Abraham Lincoln's Mother*. Illustrated by Betty Alden. New York: Knopf, 1949; repr., Duluth: Holy Cow!, 1997.

———. *Sparrow Hawk*. Illustrated by William Moyers. New York: Knopf, 1950; repr., Duluth: Holy Cow!, 1987.

———. *Chanticleer of Wilderness Road: A Story of Davy Crockett*. Illustrated by Aldren Auld Watson. New York: Knopf, 1951; repr., Duluth: Holy Cow! 1989.

———. *River Road: A Story of Abraham Lincoln*. Illustrated by Aldren A. Watson. New York: Knopf, 1954; repr., Duluth, Holy Cow!, 1998.

Linton, Ralph, and Adelin Linton. *Man's Way from Cave to Skyscraper*. Illustrated by Raine Renshaw. New York: Harper and Brothers, 1947.

Lionni, Leo. *Swimmy*. New York: Pantheon, 1963.

London, Jack. *The Call of the Wild*. Illustrated by Philip R. Goodwin and Charles Livingston Bull. New York: Macmillan, 1903.

———. *Before Adam*. Illustrated by Charles Livingston Bull. New York: Macmillan, 1907.

Lucas, Eric. *Corky*. New York: International, 1938.

———. *Swamp Fox Brigade: Adventures with General Francis Marion's Guerillas*. New York: International, 1945.

———. *Voyage Thirteen*. Illustrated by Eric Wells. New York: International, 1946.

Marcy, Mary Edna. *Stories of the Cave People*. Chicago: Kerr, 1917.

McClintock, Marshall. *Here Is a Book*. New York: Vanguard, 1939.

McGovern, Ann. *If You Grew Up with Abraham Lincoln*. Illustrated by Brinton Turkle. New York: Four Winds, 1966.

McNeer, May Yonge. *America's Abraham Lincoln*. Illustrated by Lynd Ward. Boston: Houghton Mifflin, 1957.

Means, Florence Crannell. *The Moved Outers*. Boston: Houghton Mifflin, 1945.

Merriam, Eve. *The Real Book about Franklin D. Roosevelt*. Illustrated by Bette J. Davis. New York: Franklin Watts, 1952.

———. *The Voice of Liberty: The Story of Emma Lazarus*. Illustrated by Charles W. Walker. New York: Farrar, Straus and Cudahy, 1959.

———. *Mommies at Work*. Illustrated by Beni Montressor. New York: Knopf, 1961.

———. *Independent Voices*. New York: Antheneum, 1968.

———. *The Inner City Mother Goose*. Pictures by Lawrence Ratzskin. New York: Simon and Schuster, 1969.

———. *Project 1-2-3*. Illustrated by Harriet Sherman. New York: McGraw-Hill, 1971.

———. *Boys and Girls, Girls and Boys*. Illustrated by Harriet Sherman. New York: Holt, Rinehart, and Winston, 1972.

Mitchell, Lucy Sprague. *Here and Now Story Book: Two- to Seven-Year-Olds*. New York: Dutton, 1921.

———. *The Here and Now Primer: Home from the Country*. New York: Dutton, 1924.

———. *Another Here and Now Story Book*. Illustrated by Rosalie Slocum. New York: Dutton, 1937.

Moore, Lilian. *Little Raccoon and the Thing in the Pool*. New York: McGraw-Hill, 1963.

Morrow, Betty, with the editorial cooperation of Millicent E. Selsam. *See Up the Mountain*. Illustrated by Winifred Lubell. New York: Harper and Row, 1958.

Nelson, Caroline. *Nature Talks on Economics*. Chicago: Kerr, 1912.

Nesbit, Troy [Franklin Folsom]. *Sand Dune Pony*. Illustrated by Jules Gotlieb. Racine, Wis.: Whitman, 1952.

Novikoff, Alex. *Climbing Our Family Tree*. Illustrated by John English. New York: International, 1945.

———. *From Head to Foot: Our Bodies and How They Grow*. Illustrated by Seymour Nydorf. New York: International, 1946.

Olds, Elizabeth. *The Big Fire*. Boston: Houghton Mifflin, 1945.

Ovington, Mary White. *Hazel*. Illustrated by Harry Roseland. New York: Crisis, 1913.

———. *Zeke*. New York: Harcourt, Brace, 1931.

Petry, Ann Lane. *Harriet Tubman: Conductor on the Underground Railroad*. New York: Crowell, 1955.

———. *Tituba of Salem Village*. New York: Crowell, 1964.

Pomerantz, Charlotte. *The Day They Parachuted Cats on Borneo: A Drama of Ecology*. Reading, Mass.: Young Scott Books, 1971.

Red Corner Book for Children. New York: International, 1932.

Redfield, A. *Mr. His*. New York: New Masses, 1939.

Rey, Margret, and H. A. Rey. *Spotty*. New York: Harper and Brothers, 1945.

Riedman, Sarah. *How Man Discovered His Body*. Illustrated by Frances Wells. New York: International, 1947.

———. *Food for People*. Illustrated by Helen Ludwig. New York: Abelard-Schuman, 1954.

———. *Antoine Lavoisier: Scientist and Citizen*. New York: Abelard-Schuman, 1957.

Riedman, Sarah Regal, and Clarence Corleon Green. *Benjamin Rush: Physician, Patriot, Founding Father*. New York: Abelard-Schuman, 1964.

Ruchlis, Hyman, and Alice Hirsh. *Orbit: A Picture Story of Force and Motion*. Illustrated by Alice Hirsh. New York: Harper, 1958.

Sandburg, Carl. *Rootabaga Stories*. Illustrated by Maud Fuller Petersham and Miska Petersham. New York: Harcourt Brace, 1922.

———. *Rootabaga Pigeons*. Illustrated by Maude Petersham and Miska Petersham. New York: Harcourt Brace and World, 1923.

———. *Abe Lincoln Grows Up.* Illustrated by James Daugherty. New York: Harcourt Brace, 1954.

Schneider, Herman. *Everyday Weather and How It Works.* Illustrated by Jeanne Bendick. New York: Whittlesey House, 1951.

Schneider, Herman, and Nina Schneider. *How Big Is Big: From Stars to Atoms.* Illustrated by Symeon Shimin. New York: Scott, 1946.

———. *Let's Find Out.* Illustrated by Jeanne Bendick. New York: Scott, 1946.

———. *How Your Body Works.* Illustrated by Barbara Ivins. New York: Scott, 1949.

———. *Let's Look under the City: Water, Gas, Waste, Electricity, Telephone.* New York: Scott, 1950.

———. *You among the Stars.* Illustrated by Symeon Shimin. New York: Scott, 1951.

Schneider, Nina, and Herman Schneider. *Let's Find Out: A Picture Science Book.* Illustrated by Jeanne Bendick. New York: Scott, 1946.

Segal, Edith. *Be My Friend and Other Poems for Boys and Girls.* Illustrated by Herbert Kruckman. New York: Citadel, 1964.

Selsam, Millicent. *Egg to Chick.* Illustrated by Frances Wells. New York: International, 1946.

———. *Hidden Animals.* Illustrated by David Shapiro. New York: International, 1947.

———. *See through the Forest.* Illustrated by Winifred Lubell. New York: Harper and Brothers, 1956.

———. *Nature Detective.* Illustrated by Theresa Sherman. New York: Scott, 1958.

———. *Greg's Microscope.* Illustrated by Arnold Lobel. New York: Harper and Row, 1963.

Selsam, Millicent, and Betty Morrow. *See Through the Sea.* Illustrated by Winifred Lubell. New York: Harper and Brothers, 1955.

Shapiro, Irwin. *Yankee Thunder: The Legendary Life of Davy Crockett.* Illustrated by James Daugherty. New York: Messner, 1944.

———. *John Henry and the Double-Jointed Steam Drill.* Illustrated by James Daugherty. New York: Messner, 1945.

———. *Joe Magarac and His USA Citizen Papers.* Illustrated by James Daugherty. New York: Messner, 1949.

Shaw, Ruth, and Harry Alan Potamkin. *Our Lenin.* Illustrated by William Siegel. New York: International, 1934.

Siegmeister, Elie. *Work and Sing: A Collection of the Songs That Built America.* Illustrated by Julian Brazelton. New York: Scott, 1944.

Steig, William. *Sylvester and the Magic Pebble.* New York: Windmill, 1969.

Sterling, Dorothy. *Freedom Train: The Story of Harriet Tubman.* Illustrated by Ernest Crichlow. Garden City, N.Y.: Doubleday, 1954.

———. *Insects and the Homes They Build.* Edited by Myron Ehrenberg. Garden City, N.Y.: Doubleday, 1954.

———. *The Story of Mosses, Ferns and Mushrooms.* Illustrated by Myron Ehrenberg. Garden City, N.Y.: Doubleday, 1955.

———. *Captain of the Planter: The Story of Robert Smalls.* Illustrated by Ernest Crichlow. Garden City, N.Y.: Doubleday, 1958.

———. *Mary Jane.* Illustrated by Ernest Crichlow. Garden City, N.Y.: Doubleday, 1959.

———. *Caterpillars.* Illustrated by Winifred Lubell. Garden City, N.Y.: Doubleday, 1961.

———. *Forever Free: The Story of the Emancipation Proclamation.* Garden City, N.Y.: Doubleday, 1963.

———. *Lucretia Mott: Gentle Warrior.* Garden City, N.Y.: Doubleday, 1964.

———. *Tear Down the Walls! A History of the American Civil Rights Movement.* New York: Doubleday, 1968.

Sterling, Dorothy, and Donald Gross. *Tender Warriors.* New York: Hill and Wang, 1959.

Sterne, Emma Gelders. *Incident in Yorkville.* New York: Farrar and Rinehart, 1943.

———. *Printer's Devil.* Illustrated by Peter Burchard. New York: Aladdin, 1952.

———. *The Long Black Schooner: The Voyage of the Amistad.* Illustrated by Earl H. Pringle. New York: Aladdin, 1953.

———. *Mary McLeod Bethune.* New York: Knopf, 1957.

———. *Blood Brothers: Four Men of Science.* Illustrated by Oscar Liebman. New York: Knopf, 1959.

———. *I Have a Dream.* New York: Knopf, 1965.

———. *They Took Their Stand.* New York: Crowell-Collier, 1968.

———. *His Was the Voice: The Life of W. E. B. Du Bois.* New York: Crowell-Collier, 1971.

Swift, Hildegarde Hoyt. *The Railroad to Freedom: A Story of the Civil War.* Illustrated by James Daugherty. New York: Harcourt Brace and World, 1932.

———. *North Star Shining: A Pictorial History of the American Negro.* Illustrated by Lynd Ward. New York: Morrow, 1947.

Tetzner, Lisa. *Hans Sees the World.* New York: Covici, Friede, 1934.

Trease, Geoffrey. *Bows Against the Barons.* New York: International, 1934.

———. *Comrades for the Charter.* New York: International, 1934.

Tunis, John Roberts. *Keystone Kids.* New York: Harcourt Brace, 1943.

Vicar, Henry [Henry Felsen]. *The Company Owns the Tools.* Philadelphia: Westminster, 1942.

Ward, Lynd. *The Biggest Bear.* Boston: Houghton Mifflin, 1952.

Wedding, Alex. *Eddie and the Gipsey.* Translated by Charles Ashley. New York: International, 1935.

West, Wallace. *Betty Boop in Miss Gulliver's Travels.* Racine, Wis.: Whitman, 1935.

White, Anne Terry. *Lost Worlds: Adventures in Archaeology.* New York: Random House, 1941.

———. *George Washington Carver: The Story of a Great American.* Illustrated by Douglas Gorsline. New York: Random House, 1953.

———. *All about our Changing Rocks.* New York: Random House, 1955.

———. *The False Treaty: The Removal of the Cherokees from Georgia.* New York: Scholastic, 1970.

———. *North to Liberty: The Story of the Underground Railroad: Toward Freedom.* Champaign, Ill.: Garrard, 1972.

———. *Eugene Debs: American Socialist.* New York: Hill, 1974.

White, William Chapman. *Made in the USSR.* New York: Knopf, 1944.

Whitman, Walt. *I Hear the People Singing: Selected Poems of Walt Whitman.* Illustrated by Alexander Dobkin. Introduction by Langston Hughes. New York: International, 1946.

Williams, Jay. *The Sword and the Scythe.* New York: Oxford University Press, 1946.

———. *Philbert the Fearful.* Illustrated by Ib Ohlsson. New York: Norton, 1966.

———. *The Practical Princess.* Illustrated by Frisco Henstra. New York: Parents Magazine Press, 1969.

Williams, Jay, and Raymond Abrashkin. *Danny Dunn and the Anti-Gravity Paint.* Illustrated by Ezra Jack Keats. New York: Whittlesey House, McGraw-Hill, 1956.

——. *Danny Dunn and the Homework Machine.* New York: Whittlesey House, 1958.

Wyler, Rose. *First Book of Science Experiments.* Illustrated by Ida Scheib. New York: Franklin Watts, 1952.

——. *The First Book of Weather.* Illustrated by Bernice Myers. New York: Franklin Watts, 1956.

——. *Exploring Space.* New York: Simon and Schuster, 1958.

——. *Golden Picture Book of Science: Animals, Plants, Rocks, Gravity, Day and Night, Rain and Snow, the Sky and the Ocean; with 45 Experiments and Activities.* Illustrated by Marjorie Hartwell and Valerie Swenson. New York: Simon and Schuster, 1957.

Wyler, Rose, and Gerald Ames. *Life on Earth.* Illustrated by Gerald Ames. New York: Schuman, 1953.

——. *The Golden Book of Astronomy.* Illustrated by John Polgreen. New York: Simon and Schuster, 1955.

——. *The First People in the World.* Illustrated by Leonard Weisgard. New York: Harper and Brothers, 1958.

——. *Prove It!* Illustrated by Talivaldis Stubis. New York: Random House, 1963.

——. *What Makes It Go?* Illustrated by Bernice Myers. New York: Whittlesey House, 1958.

Zur Mühlen, Hermynia. *Fairy Tales for Workers' Children.* Translated by Ida Dailes. Chicago, Ill.: Daily Worker, 1925.

INDEX

Italicized page numbers refer to illustrations and their captions.

Printed in Great Britain
by Amazon.co.uk, Ltd.,
Marston Gate.